413

ADAPTING A SCENE FOR YOUR NEEDS

The majority of the scenes and monologues in the following pages have never before been available in print. Most of the suggestions for adaptation deal with considerations such as how best to bring a scene "in-doors," or how best to allow a two-person scene to play with just two characters when peripheral characters written into the scene will not be present in class or audition.

This material is being used for scene and monologue study for the first time, and no matter how elegant the solutions may appear in the notes, only the laboratory of rehearsal will confirm which choices work best for which actors. I hope you find here voices through which to speak your own—both those you've known were in you but which no one has yet heard, and those which you will discover within you, but which even you have not yet heard.

—JOSHUA KARTON

FILM SCENES
FOR
ACTORS
Volume II

Edited by Joshua Karton

BANTAM BOOKS
NEW YORK · TORONTO · LONDON · SYDNEY · AUCKLAND

FILM SCENES FOR ACTORS, VOLUME II

A Bantam Book / October 1987

Bantam Books are published by Bantam Books, Inc. Its trademark, consisting of the words ''Bantam Books'' and the portrayal of a rooster, is Registered in U.S. Patent and Trademark Office and in other countries. Marca Registrada. Bantam Books, Inc., 666 Fifth Avenue, New York, New York 10103.

PRINTED IN THE UNITED STATES OF AMERICA

O   0 9 8 7 6 5 4 3 2

Contents

Introduction

Forty-five monologues and forty scenes from the movies are gathered here to serve the actor who studies and auditions. This anthology is designed as a companion volume to *Film Scenes for Actors* published in 1983. The collection is now expanded to include monologues, as well as a far more comprehensive catalogue of those roles which have entered our psychic bloodstreams through the screen.

The excerpts come from original screenplays or from screen adaptations of novels, memoirs, short stories, magazine articles, case histories, conversations, dreams—everything. Everything, that is, *except* direct adaptations of stageplays, since play scripts are already widely published. Screenplays are rarely published, and when published, are quickly out of print.* The majority of the scenes and monologues in the following pages have never before been available in print, beyond the assorted copies circulated while the project was being written and produced. Afterwards, most of the scripts go into files, film libraries, private collections, or wastebaskets. Many of the characters, however, pass free of any archive, or even medium. They settle in the land of our collective unconscious and come to rule over truly vast dominions, wherein we impersonate, invoke, adore, blame, desire, and sometimes even try to become them.

Several of the scenes and monologues in this volume will require some degree of adaptation in order to be fully playable "indoors." Most of the suggestions for adaptation offered in the notes deal with considerations such as how best to adapt a continuous conversation that has been written to move through several locations so it can play without distortion in a single location; or how best to allow a monologue or two-person scene to play with

---

*See Source Appendix

just the speakers if peripheral characters written into the scene will not be present when the scene is brought into class or audition. In all of these cases, brackets [   ] are used to enclose those portions of text which would not be played. All dialogue spoken in a scene or monologue is preceded by the character's name in bold-face. The adaptation notes offer suggested solutions and alternate possibilities—places to start. These should not be misconstrued as instructions or directions. This material is being used for scene and monologue study for the first time, and no matter how elegant the solutions may appear on paper, only the laboratory of rehearsal will confirm which choices work best for which actors. The better the writing in a script and the more densely interwoven the dramatic construction, the more precarious it is to intervene: un-stitching the writing *anywhere* can lead to unravelings everywhere else. All of the adaptation notes in this collection work on the premise that you may need to alter the props or locations, but whatever lines are spoken come verbatim from the script.

When it appears that the personal truth of the speaker or the reality of the situation would be twisted by adaptation, the notes advise against it—for example, when a monologue will only function properly with the listener present; or when a basically two-character scene will only play properly with the other peripheral characters, as written, present in the scene.

I hope you find here voices through which to speak your own—both those you've known were in you but which no one has yet heard, and those which you will discover within you, but which even you have not yet heard.

—JOSHUA KARTON
Santa Monica, California
April 1987

FILM SCENES
FOR
ACTORS
Volume II

NINOTCHKA

A Metro-Goldwyn-Mayer Production. Producer & Director, Ernst Lubitsch. Screenplay by Charles Brackett, Billy Wilder, and Walter Reisch. Based on the original story by Melchior Lengyel. Director of Photography, William Daniels. Film Editor, Gene Ruggiero. Art Director, Cedric Gibbons. Set Decorator, Edwin B. Willis. Music, Werner R. Heyman. Running time, 110 minutes. 1939.

CAST

NINOTCHKA (NINA YAKUSHOVA)	Greta Garbo
COUNT LEON D'ALGOUT	Melvyn Douglas
GRAND DUCHESS SWANA	Ina Claire
IRANOFF	Sig Rumann
BULJANOFF	Felix Bressart
KOPALSKI	Alexander Granach
COMMISSAR RAZININ	Bela Lugosi
COUNT ALEXIS RAKONIN	Gregory Gaye
GASTON	Richard Carle

A half-century has dimmed not a glint of the sparkle in the wit of *Ninotchka*. What is no more is the particular world of the story's setting—Paris before the Second World War, the world's capital of love and lights. Here, champagne and a kiss can change the course of one's life, as they do for Ninotchka, entirely. Although the script makes an isolated, passing reference to two people greeting each other with a "Heil Hitler" salute in a train station, the Paris of *Ninotchka* has never been occupied by Nazis, by *anything* actually, other than the urgent and delicate possibilities of Romance.

At the time of this story, the Soviet Union is a political experiment but twenty years old, so Paris is also the city serving as home to the Russian aristocrats who have fled the Bolshevik Revolution. Some, like the Grand Duchess Swana, have somehow managed to escape with enough of their wealth to remain extravagantly haughty, elegant, and angry at their ousters. Others, like Count Alexis Rakonin, can't afford to be angry: they work as waiters. While delivering room service one morning to the Royal Suite of the Hotel Clarence, Rakonin realizes that the three unlikely guests in the shapeless winter coats are Soviet envoys, newly arrived in Paris to sell the court jewels confiscated during the Revolution from the estate of Swana. Rakonin races to Swana, who immediately telephones her attorney, demanding he slap an injunction on the sale of the jewels. Since France now recognizes the Soviet Union, whose government "legally confiscated" the jewels, Swana's attorney advises her that such a suit will be lengthy and very costly, if at all successful.

Swana's extremely charming and extremely personal "representative," Count Leon d'Algout, promptly offers to handle the matter for her. It will certainly be an improvement over his present occupation, which is urging Swana to sell her memoirs to a tabloid currently offering to pay any price. The unthinkable alternative, he has warned her, is that *he* will have to go to work.

The three Soviet envoys, Iranoff, Buljanoff, and Kopalski, have decided to stay in the Royal Suite, despite the enormous cost, because it has the necessary safe for storing the jewels. Actually, their decision is based on their thrill at all the capitalist splendor. They confess amongst themselves that if Lenin were alive and with them, they *know* he'd tell them, "For once in your life you're in Paris. Don't be fools." They melt under Leon's suave and gracious charm. With drunken gratitude, they toast him as he composes and cables their report to their superior for them—a fifty-fifty split with the Duchess would be the best possible solution. Soon, their most taxing decision of the day is whether to wear black tie or white tie to dinner. In the midst of their newfound enjoyments, they receive a telegram relieving them of their command and announcing the arrival of an "Envoy Extraordinaire" who will have full power to oversee the sale of the jewels. When they are surprised that this envoy turns out to be a female, Nina Yakushova raps their socialist knuckles: "Don't make an issue of my womanhood. We are here for work . . . all of us. Let's not waste time."

Comrade Nina Yakushova admonishes them with the gravity of their mission. The Soviets are selling their national treasures, won at such tragic cost from the czars, because without foreign currency there will not be enough tractors to harvest enough wheat. In the face of such a crisis, the mass starvation of her people, Ninotchka finds the frivolity of this or that year's hat styles distasteful. In the time it will take to gather attorneys and documents to validate the Soviet ownership and sale of the jewels, Ninotchka will not go shopping. Instead, she says, "I want to use my spare time to inspect the public utilities and make a study of all outstanding technical achievements in the city."

Outside the hotel, she asks directions of a passerby, who just happens to be Leon. They are mutually fascinated, but from opposite perspectives. "Must you flirt?" this stern ideologue asks Leon, who answers, "I don't have to, but I find it natural." She appears impervious; he's challenged. He follows her to the Eiffel Tower. High atop Paris, she looks him up and down and reassures him: "Do not misunderstand me. I do not hold your frivolity against you. As basic material you might not be bad, but you are the unfortunate product of a doomed culture." Having no idea of who this severe but lovely Russian actually is, Leon invites her up to his apartment. She surprises him by accepting, expecting that he will prove "an interesting subject of study." He promises he'll do his best, and does, in the scene below.

(*Note*: Double brackets indicate those parts of the original script that were not filmed; footnotes show additions in the completed film. For the purposes of scene study, single brackets are used throughout the collection to indicate dialogue or action or characters which are additional to the two-character scene.)

SCENE 1

DISSOLVE TO:
INTERIOR, ENTRANCE HALL—LEON'S APARTMENT

[[In the foreground stands a console on which is a telephone. GASTON, LEON'S elderly, dignified butler, is answering the phone.

GASTON: (*into phone*) No . . . Count d'Algout is still out. Yes, as soon as he returns I'll tell him. Yes . . . I'll tell him Monsieur Buljanoff.

He puts down the receiver as LEON opens the door with his key.]] NINOTCHKA and LEON *enter*. NINOTCHKA, during the following scene, is studying every detail of the apartment with the eye of a technical expert.

[LEON: Good evening, Gaston.

GASTON: Good evening, Monsieur.

NINOTCHKA: Is this what you call the "butler"?

LEON: Yes.

NINOTCHKA: (*takes* GASTON'*s hand*) Good evening, comrade. (*to* LEON) This man is horribly old. You should not make him work.

LEON: He takes good care of that.

NINOTCHKA: He looks sad. Do you whip him?

LEON: No, though the mere thought makes my mouth water.

NINOTCHKA: (*to the completely flabbergasted* GASTON) The day will come when you will be free. Go to bed, little father. We want to be alone.

LEON opens the door to the living room. NINOTCHKA enters. Just as he is about to follow her, GASTON addresses him.

GASTON: (*in a low voice*) Count d'Algout, there have been several telephone . . .

LEON: Go to bed.[1]

INTERIOR, LIVING ROOM—LEON'S APARTMENT

LEON enters the room. Closes the door. NINOTCHKA is examining the room.[2]]

---

[1]In the film, LEON calls him "little father," too.
[2]In the film, LEON helps her off with her coat and hat and puts them down.

LEON: Well, may I offer you a drink, or how about something to eat?

NINOTCHKA: Thank you. I've had all the calories necessary for today.

LEON feels a little uncertain as to how to approach this creature.

NINOTCHKA: What do we do now?

LEON: [[We take off our hat and coat. (*he takes her things*) We sit down—we make ourselves comfortable. We adjust ourselves to the prospect of a most enjoyable evening. We look at each other. We smile. (NINOTCHKA *doesn't respond*) Well ... we don't smile]] How about some music?

NINOTCHKA: Is that customary?

LEON: It helps. It has ever since King David wooed Bathsheba with the harp. As I am not so fortunate as to have my harp at hand, I shall turn on the radio.

[[**NINOTCHKA:** (*the observer*) I should say this room is eighteen by twenty-five.

LEON: Not too big and not too small. What I'd call the typical room of an average man. Or shall we say a little above average.]] Now if there are any special aspects you wish to study I have nothing to conceal. Just look around. That's my desk. Those are my books, and here am I. Where shall we begin?

NINOTCHKA: I will start with you.

LEON: That's great. I'm thirty-five years old. Just over six feet tall. I weigh a hundred and eighty-two pounds stripped.

NINOTCHKA: And what is your profession?

LEON: Keeping my body fit, keeping my mind alert, keeping my landlord appeased. That's a full-time job.

NINOTCHKA: And what do you do for mankind?

LEON: For mankind not a thing—for womankind the record is not quite so bleak.

NINOTCHKA: You are something we do not have in Russia.

LEON: Thank you. Thank you.

NINOTCHKA: That is why I believe in the future of my country.

LEON: I begin to believe in it myself since I've met you. I still don't know what to make of it. It confuses me, it frightens me a little, but it fascinates me, Ninotchka.

[[**NINOTCHKA:** You pronounce it incorrectly. Ni-notchka.

LEON: Ni-notchka.

NINOTCHKA: That is correct.]]

LEON: Ninotchka, do you like me just a little bit?

NINOTCHKA: Your general appearance is not distasteful.

LEON: Thank you.

NINOTCHKA: Look at me. The whites of your eyes are clear. Your cornea is excellent.

LEON: Your cornea is terrific. Tell me—you're so expert on things—can it be that I'm falling in love with you?

NINOTCHKA: You are bringing in wrong values. Love is a romantic designation for a most ordinary biological, or shall we say chemical, process. A lot of nonsense is talked and written about it.

LEON: Oh, I see. What do you use instead?

NINOTCHKA: I acknowledge the existence of a natural impulse common to all.

LEON: What can I possibly do to encourage such an impulse in you?

NINOTCHKA: You don't have to do a thing. Chemically we are already quite sympathetic.

LEON: (*bewildered, and yet completely intrigued*) You're the most improbable creature I've ever met in my life, Ninotchka, Ninotchka . . .

NINOTCHKA: You repeat yourself.

LEON: I'd like to say it a thousand times.

[[NINOTCHKA: Don't do it, please.]]

LEON: I'm at a loss, Ninotchka. You must forgive me if I appear a little old-fashioned. After all, I'm just a poor bourgeois.

NINOTCHKA: It's never too late to change. I used to belong to the petty bourgeoisie myself. My father and mother wanted me to stay and work on the farm, but I preferred the bayonet.

LEON: (*bewildered*) The bayonet? Did you really?

NINOTCHKA: I was wounded before Warsaw.

LEON: Wounded? How?

NINOTCHKA: I was a sergeant in the Third Cavalry Brigade. Would you like to see my wound?

LEON: (*dumfounded*) I'd love to. (*She pulls the blouse off her shoulder and shows him her scar*)

LEON: Tsk, tsk, tsk.

NINOTCHKA: A Polish lancer. I was sixteen.

LEON: Poor Ninotchka. Poor, poor Ninotchka.

NINOTCHKA: (*readjusting her blouse*) Don't pity me. Pity the Polish lancer. After all, I'm alive.

More and more puzzled and fascinated, LEON sits down close to her.

LEON: What kind of a girl are you, anyway?

NINOTCHKA: Just what you see. A tiny cog in the great wheel of evolution.

LEON: You're the most adorable cog I ever saw in my life. Ninotchka, [[Cogitska,]] let me confess something. Never did I dream I could feel like this toward a sergeant.

A clock strikes.

LEON: Do you hear that?

NINOTCHKA: It's twelve o'clock.

LEON: It's midnight. One half of Paris is making love to the other half. Look at the clock. One hand has met the other hand. They kiss. Isn't that wonderful?

NINOTCHKA: That's the way a clock works. There's nothing wonderful about it. You merely feel you must put yourself in a romantic mood to add to your exhilaration.

LEON: I can't possibly think of a better reason.

NINOTCHKA: It's false sentimentality.

LEON: (*trying desperately to make her mood more romantic*) You analyze everything out of existence. You analyze *me* out of existence. I won't let you. Love is not so simple. Ninotchka, Ninotchka, why do doves bill and coo? Why do snails, coldest of all creatures, circle interminably around each other? Why do moths fly hundreds of miles to find their mates? Why do flowers open their petals? Oh, Ninotchka, Ninotchka, surely you feel some slight symptom of the divine passion . . . a general warmth in the palms of your hands . . . a strange heaviness in your limbs . . . a burning of the lips that is not thirst but a thousand times more tantalizing, more exalting, than thirst?

He pauses, waiting for the results of his speech.

NINOTCHKA: You are very talkative.

That is too much for LEON. He takes her into his arms and kisses her.

LEON: Was that talkative?

NINOTCHKA: No, that was restful. Again.

LEON kisses her again.

NINOTCHKA: Thank you.

LEON: Oh, my barbaric Ninotchka. My impossible, unromantic, statistical . . .

The telephone rings.

LEON: (*continuing*) Glorious, analytical . . .

NINOTCHKA: The telephone is ringing.

LEON: Oh, let it ring.

NINOTCHKA: But one of your friends may be in need of you. You must answer.

LEON exits out of shot to answer telephone.

CLOSE SHOT—AT DESK

LEON enters, sits down, takes the telephone.

LEON: (*into phone*) Hello? . . . Yes . . . I'm sorry but I couldn't make it. I ran into a friend from the army. . . . What? . . . The deal is off! Are you crazy, Buljanoff? . . .

CLOSE-UP—NINOTCHKA

She is startled by the name.

LEON—AT TELEPHONE

LEON: . . . A special envoy arrived. . . . What? . . . That sounds better. I'll be glad to see her any time she wants. . . . Oh, she doesn't want to see me? What do you know about that? Why? . . . Well, I'll get in touch with her myself. What's her name? . . . (*He takes a pencil and a piece of paper.*) . . . What? . . . Yaku . . . How do you spell it? . . . Heavens! those Russian names! (*He starts to write it down.*) . . . I . . . Oh, Y . . .

CAMERA PULLS BACK and NINOTCHKA enters the shot. She takes pencil from LEON's hand, writes out the name, and leaves again. At first LEON is not aware of the full significance of her action. Then it dawns on him.

LEON: (*continuing*) Yakushova . . . Ninotch . . .

At last the situation is entirely clear to him.

LEON: (*into phone*) All right. Thank you.

He hangs up and stares at NINOTCHKA. She is putting on her jacket.

LEON: (CAMERA PANNING *with him as he walks over to her*): Ninotchka . . .

He takes her arm.

NINOTCHKA: I must go.

LEON: Ninotchka, or shall I say Special Envoy Yakushova...

NINOTCHKA: Let's forget that we ever met.

LEON: I have a better suggestion. Let's forget that the telephone ever rang. I never heard that you are Yakushova... you are Ninotchka... my Ninotchka...

NINOTCHKA: (*firmly*) I was sent here by my country to fight you.

LEON: All right, fight me, fight me as much as you want, but fight me tomorrow morning! There's nothing sweeter than sharing a secret with a bitter enemy.

[[**NINOTCHKA:**   (*uncompromisingly*) As a representative of Moscow...

LEON: Tonight let's not represent anybody but ourselves.]][3]

NINOTCHKA: It is out of the question. If you wish to approach me...

LEON: You know I want to...

NINOTCHKA: Then do it through my lawyer!

LEON: (*desperate*) Ninotchka, you can't walk out like this... I'm crazy about you, and I thought I'd made an impression on you. You liked the white of my eye.

NINOTCHKA looks at him for a second, then pulls herself together.

NINOTCHKA: I must go.

She starts for the door.

LEON: But, Ninotchka, I held you in my arms. You kissed me!

NINOTCHKA: I kissed the Polish lancer too... before he died.

As she goes out, we

FADE OUT.

---

[3]In the film, instead:
NINOTCHKA: You represent White Russia and I represent Red Russia.
LEON: No, no. Tonight let's not represent anybody but ourselves.

SCENE 2

Ninotchka, upon learning that Leon is Swana's representative, severs contact with him completely, holing herself up with lawyers and law books, unavailable even to Iranoff, Buljanoff, and Kopalski. Leon follows her when she leaves the hotel to go to lunch at a workingman's restaurant. (She leaves the hotel only because he's disguised his voice and answered her room service call by telling her the kitchen is on strike.) He sits himself down next to Ninotchka, tries every joke in the book, but she only cracks when he accidentally spills his lunch all over himself. They fall very much in love. In the middle of serious meetings, Ninotchka bursts out laughing at the memory of Leon's bad jokes. Her mind wanders to the songs of birds outside the window. She grows indulgently fond of Iranoff, Buljanoff, and Kopalski. She finally buys one of those charming, silly hats. Leon takes her to a nightclub, where Ninotchka has her first champagne. Swana appears, sees what this "proletariat" looks like, sees how Leon is behaving, and realizes that Ninotchka is her rival for more than the jewels:

SWANA: I must compliment you on your gown . . . Is that what they're wearing in Moscow this year?

NINOTCHKA: No, last year, madame . . .

SWANA: Isn't it amazing! One gets a wrong impression of the new Russia . . . It must be charming. I'm glad conditions are so improved. I assume this is what the factory workers wear at their dances?

NINOTCHKA: Exactly. You see, it would have been embarrassing for people of my sort to wear low-cut gowns in the old Russia. The lashes of the Cossacks across our backs were not very becoming, and you know how vain women are.

SWANA: You're absolutely right about the Cossacks. We made an unpardonable mistake when we let them use their knouts*. They had such reliable guns.

---

*"knout: an instrument of punishment used in Russia consisting of a handle two feet long, leather thong four feet, with a metal ring at the end to which the striking part, a flat tongue of hardened hide two feet long is attached."—*Webster's Columbia Concise Dictionary.*

Ninotchka, tanked-up for the first time in her life on love and champagne, will not be daunted by insults. She tries to picket the nightclub's powder room. Once Leon manages to escort her back to the Royal Suite, Ninotchka's mood curves in a manner most Russian—she becomes sad in her gaiety, simultaneously wistful and joyful. The jewels come out of the safe. Leon starts to put them on her playfully, but she protests that they belong to the people. So, Leon returns them to the people as he crowns her "Ninotchka the Great . . . Duchess of the People!" She falls asleep, bejewelled, in Leon's arms. He puts her to bed and leaves. Not having moved, Ninotchka is awakened the following day by Swana, who arrives in the second scene below, to point out that Ninotchka is no longer wearing the jewels.

FADE IN ON:
AN ESTABLISHING SHOT OF PARIS—DAY

In the foreground a clock shows that it is a quarter to twelve.

                                    DISSOLVE TO:
LONG SHOT—LIVING ROOM OF THE ROYAL SUITE

It is taken from an ANGLE which includes the door. The lights are still on, the curtains drawn, the empty champagne bottle and glasses litter the room. We hear the buzzer of the corridor door ring several times without an answer.

CAMERA MOVES through the door into the bedroom, never disclosing the bed. The lights in the bedroom are still lighted also and the curtains drawn. CAMERA STOPS on the door from the bedroom to the corridor. The buzzer rings. Apparently the caller has moved from the living-room door to the bedroom door.

CLOSE SHOT OF THE BED

NINOTCHKA is lying on the bed, still in her evening dress. The diadem is no longer on her head, but no special emphasis is laid on that detail in the camera angle. We hear the sound of the buzzer ringing again and again. NINOTCHKA half wakens and calls out something which sounds like "come in" without being fully aware of what she is doing.

BEDROOM—AT THE DOOR

The door is opened from the outside by a maid, who lets in the DUCHESS SWANA, dressed in a smart morning outfit. SWANA looks around, surprised and amused at the state of the room. She walks over to the bed where lies NINOTCHKA, still not enough awake to face reality. SWANA is delighted to have surprised NINOTCHKA in this condition.

SWANA: (*ironically*) Good morning.

NINOTCHKA: (*awakening gradually*) What?

SWANA: It is tomorrow morning . . . tomorrow noon, to be exact. I hope you will forgive me. I know it's extremely cruel to waken anyone at such an hour. Don't you recognize me? I am the Duchess Swana.

By now NINOTCHKA is awake. She gets up and realizes to her acute embarrassment the condition in which SWANA has found her.

SWANA: I know how you feel, my dear. The morning after always does look grim if you happen to be wearing last night's dress. Don't be embarrassed by my presence, though. You couldn't have found anybody more sympathetic to your condition. [[I remember once in Petrograd when I felt exactly as you do. I had to bow from a balcony to the crowd. My dear, the masses have no understanding of the feelings of a lady before noon. Don't you find that true?]]

During SWANA's speech NINOTCHKA has found herself completely.

NINOTCHKA: I think we can cut your visit short. Leon is not here.

SWANA: Of course not, my dear! I didn't come here with any such suspicion. How ridiculous! (*With a glance toward the living room*) Nor did I come here to pick up his hat.

CLOSE SHOT—LEON'S HAT, shot through the bedroom door into the living room where it lies on the table.

LONG SHOT—LIVING ROOM—TOWARD BEDROOM DOOR

By the bed stand NINOTCHKA and SWANA. SWANA starts toward the living room, NINOTCHKA following her.

[[SWANA: (*as she reaches the threshold*) How stale last night's gaiety looks! It has the taste of a dead cigarette.

NINOTCHKA: If you were encouraged to come here by our meeting last night I am afraid you misunderstood my attitude.

SWANA: Don't worry, you were quite rude enough. (*During the following speech, she draws the curtains and opens the windows.*) Do you mind if I let in a little fresh air and sunshine? I'm sure it will make you feel better and I want you to be at your very best. In full possession of your faculties, at least.

NINOTCHKA: (*regaining her usual firmness*) Please come to the point. What is it you want?

SWANA: I just dropped in to have a little heart-to-heart talk with you.

NINOTCHKA: We have nothing to discuss.

SWANA: Now there you are completely wrong. If we sit down for a little chat, I'm sure we won't run out of conversation and what's more it won't be dull.]]

NINOTCHKA: Madame, what is it you people always say, regardless of what you mean . . . "I am delighted to have you here"? I have not reached that stage of civilization.

[[SWANA: That's all right . . . I grow on people.]]

NINOTCHKA: I must ask you to leave.

SWANA: Leave? That's exactly what I came here to ask *you* to do. Leave! I don't mean this hotel and I don't mean Paris . . . I mean France. There's a plane for Moscow at five-forty.

[[NINOTCHKA: (*puzzled*) Madame, if you . . .

SWANA: Don't worry. I have already made reservations. It's perfect flying weather. They assure me there's a fine tail wind which will sweep you back to Moscow in no time.

NINOTCHKA: (*still not understanding*) If this is meant to be a joke it is not funny. Or]] do you still think you're issuing orders from your palace in Petrograd?

NINOTCHKA's words for the first time sting SWANA out of her apparently superficial attitude.

SWANA: (*bitterly*) My palace in Petrograd . . . yes, you took that away from me. You took away my czar, my country, my people, everything I had . . . (*with emphasis*) but nothing more—I warn you.

NINOTCHKA: (*simply*) People cannot be taken away, madame, neither a hundred and sixty million nor one. Not if you have their love. You hadn't. That's why you're not in Russia any longer, and that's why you came here this morning.

[[SWANA: Very interesting, my dear, but couldn't you write all that from Moscow? A dissertation on love on Soviet stationery—would be an amusing paradox.

NINOTCHKA: It is not enough to be witty, madame. People grow tired of being entertained. You made that mistake before.]] Problems were never solved by bowing from a balcony.

SWANA: My dear, you don't know how impressive I could be. Did you ever see me in my regalia with my diadem and all my jewels?

The word diadem startles NINOTCHKA. She starts to remember the night before, and she looks toward the safe.

INSERT OF THE DOOR OF THE SAFE, which is closed by now.

[[CLOSE SHOT—NINOTCHKA AND SWANA
NINOTCHIKA stares in the direction of the safe as SWANA chatters on.

SWANA: You can't deny we gave the people their money's worth—almost—eight tumbling Romanoffs—eight!

NINOTCHKA: (*desperately*) I must insist that you leave.

SWANA: Not before you agree to use those reservations to Moscow.

NINOTCHKA: In that case I can only say good-by.

Abruptly she walks toward the bedroom.]]

TRAVELING SHOT OF NINOTCHKA

She enters the small room connecting the living room and bedroom and closes the door to the living room. She walks into the bedroom toward the bed and glances at it. The diadem is not there. After going back into the anteroom, she opens the outer door of the safe and pulls on the inner door. It has not been properly closed and opens at once. The safe is empty. NINOTCHKA stands staring in frozen horror for a moment, then rushes to the telephone by the bed.

NINOTCHKA: (*into the telephone*) Élysée 2763.

LONG SHOT—NINOTCHKA AT THE TELEPHONE, waiting for her connection. In the background the door to the living room is opened by SWANA.

[[SWANA: (*standing in the door*) I wouldn't waken Leon. After last night I would say not before three o'clock at the earliest.

NINOTCHKA: I told you to go, madame.]]

SWANA: Believe me, Leon can't help you. He doesn't know anything about the jewels...I give you my word...I swear it.

NINOTCHKA hangs up the receiver and stares at SWANA. She walks toward her.

LIVING ROOM, shooting into the bedroom. In the foreground SWANA, in the background NINOTCHKA, who is hurrying toward her.

NINOTCHKA: Where are they?

SWANA: You were very careless with our precious jewels, my dear. They're too expensive a toy for two children to play with.

NINOTCHKA: Where are they?

SWANA: Don't worry. Fortunately last night a very trustworthy friend kept his eyes open. Perhaps he overstepped his function as a waiter but he fulfilled his duty as a Russian. (*She draws back the fur scarf she is wearing, revealing a diamond star, one of the jewels we have seen.*) I just put this on for sentiment. The rest are absolutely safe. I assure you. But if you feel like notifying the police . . .

NINOTCHKA: You leave me no choice.

SWANA: Won't it be rather embarrassing for a Soviet Envoy to disclose the circumstances under which she lost them?

NINOTCHKA: I will have to face the consequences, but so will you. Don't forget they will ask how you got them.

SWANA: That's very simple to answer. They were given to me by my mother. They were given to her by her mother, in fact they're mine, you cannot steal what belongs to you!

She proceeds into the living room, followed by NINOTCHKA.

NINOTCHKA: They always belonged to the Russian people. They were paid for with their sweat, their blood, their lives and you will give them back!

SWANA: (*triumphantly*) I told you we had plenty to talk about. Shall we sit down?

They both sit.

SWANA: (*very matter-of-fact*) Now, let's free ourselves from emotionalism and try to solve the problem in a practical way. Our situation has changed considerably. Before I had only a claim to the jewels. Now I have the jewels.

NINOTCHKA: In other words moral ideas have no weight with you . . . all right, then let's deal with legal facts. You know that France has recognized the Soviet.

SWANA: Unfortunately.

NINOTCHKA: Under Soviet law the jewels belong to the State. France is going to uphold that ownership.

SWANA: My lawyer agrees with you. He says France will uphold it in every court, but I will drag you through every court, don't forget that. And when I say it will take two years I am, as always, conservative.

NINOTCHKA: Won't those two years in court be expensive for you? I know that money was no object as long as you could squeeze it from the pockets of the people, but now...

SWANA: I may run out of money, but you have already run out of bread. Two years is a long time for your comrades to wait.

NINOTCHKA: I see. You have calculated in terms of hunger.

SWANA: No, I just wanted to be absolutely impartial. Both of us are faced with two rather uncomfortable years. We can condense these two years to two minutes if you want to accept my proposition.

NINOTCHKA now realizes what she is after.

NINOTCHKA: Go on.

SWANA: I am willing to hand over the jewels and sign the necessary papers if you take that five-forty plane to Moscow.

NINOTCHKA: (*quietly*) That's not the way to win him back . . . not Leon.

SWANA: I think I know Leon quite as well as you . . . possibly a little better. Leave that worry to me. Five-forty leaves you time enough to close the deal with Monsieur Mercier, but naturally you'll be too busy for any farewells. I'll see to it that everything is done in the most expeditious manner and I will also see you to the airport. That's my proposition, Comrade Yakushova.

NINOTCHKA knows herself to be faced with an inevitable decision. For a moment she cannot answer. The telephone rings. NINOTCHKA takes the receiver.

NINOTCHKA: (*into telephone*) Yes . . . (*It is* LEON.) Oh hello . . .

Much as she wants to talk to him she hesitates in the presence of

SWANA. SWANA realizes the situation, gets up, and walks over to the window, where she stands looking out.

CLOSE-UP—NINOTCHKA AT TELEPHONE

NINOTCHKA: Good morning, Leon . . . (*forcing herself to be gay so that he will not suspect anything*) . . . no, you didn't waken me . . . I am fine, thank you. . . . Yes, it was . . . marvelous. . . . What? . . . for luncheon? I'm afraid I can't. I am going to be very busy . . . (*looking for excuses*) well, I have a lot of things to attend to today. . . . What? . . . Well to tell you the truth I am a little tired and I would like to rest . . . (*She forces herself to laugh.*) you may be right . . . perhaps it is the champagne. . . . For dinner? . . . Of course . . . seven o'clock here? . . . (*realizing that she will be gone by then*) seven o'clock is all right. . . . Where? . . . That will be lovely. . . . Yes . . . (*There is a knock on the door.*) Come in. (*into the telephone*) Yes? . . . (*Looking toward the door she sees something which makes her stop the conversation.*) Just a moment. . . . (*She puts the receiver on the table and walks toward the door.*)

ANTEROOM BETWEEN LIVING ROOM AND CORRIDOR, shooting toward the living room. In the background we see SWANA standing at the window. NINOTCHKA comes into the anteroom, closes the door in order to shut off SWANA's view. CAMERA PANS with NINOTCHKA as she walks toward the hall door where the bellboy is putting down a big flower basket.

NINOTCHKA: (*to bellboy*) You can leave it here.

The bellboy exits. NINOTCHKA looks at the basket of flowers for a moment, then takes the envelope which is attached to the handle. She opens it and reads the enclosed letter. It must be a love note, for her eyes grow wet. She turns to the last page.

INSERT

"*. . . and sweetheart, I have kept my first promise. I sent poor old Gaston to the market this morning and if you will look deep into the flowers you will see what I got for him. . . .*"

CLOSE SHOT—NINOTCHKA

She puts her hand in the basket and takes out a bottle of milk.

INSERT OF THE BOTTLE

On the label we see a picture of a goat.

NINOTCHKA

She smiles sadly and goes to the telephone, which is on the console in the anteroom.

NINOTCHKA: (*into telephone*) Operator, will you switch the call please?...Hello?...Darling, your present just arrived....It's very silly and very wonderful...thank you....No, I won't forget...seven o'clock....(*With great tenderness*) Good-by, my darling....What?...Oh...(*softly*) salute!

She puts down the receiver. CAMERA PANS with her as she goes to the door of the living room. She opens the door and goes in. SWANA turns from the window.

NINOTCHKA: I am sorry to have kept you waiting, madame.

(*Note*: We see Ninotchka some time later in a May Day Parade in Red Square. She is marching to her highest ideals, but her face once again wears the grim, humorless cast as when we first met her. In a nostalgic reunion, she and Iranoff, Buljanoff, and Kopalski all pool their ration eggs into a single omelet, sharing it along with their tender Paris memories. Meanwhile, Leon has long since broken off with Swana, and has been trying, unsuccessfully, to get a visa into the Soviet Union. Even when his letters to Ninotchka reach her, they are completely blacked out by the censors. Eventually, the three envoys are sent on a mission to Constantinople, primarily due to the wonderful write-up Ninotchka had given them in her final Paris report. In no time at all, they are trying to fly carpets out their hotel window. Ninotchka is sent to retrieve them, and Soviet prestige. But it's all been a plan—Leon is waiting for her. If she tries to return again to Russia where he cannot follow, he vows to travel the world corrupting Russian commissions everywhere so she'll be sent back out to him. He tells Ninotchka that it is her choice—return home, or stay with him and save her country. She knows what she must do: "Well, when it is a choice between my personal interest and the good of my country, how can I waver? No one shall say Ninotchka was a bad Russian." Kiss. Final fade.)

SULLIVAN'S TRAVELS

A Paramount Pictures, Inc. Production. Director, Preston Sturges.
Screenplay by Preston Sturges. Associate Producer, Paul Jones.
Photography, John F. Seitz. Process Photography, Farciot Edouart.
Editor, Stuart Gilmore. Art Directors, Hans Dreier, Earl Hedrick.
Musical Director, Sigmund Krumgold. Music Score, Leo Shuken
and Charles Bradshaw. Running time, 90 minutes. 1941.

CAST

JOHN L. SULLIVAN	Joel McCrea
THE GIRL	Veronica Lake
MR. LEBRAND	Raymond Walburn
MR. JONES	William Demarest
MR. CASALSIS	Franklin Pangborn
MR. HADRIAN	Porter Hall
MR. VALDELLE	Byron Foulger
SULLIVAN'S BUTLER	Robert Greig
SULLIVAN'S VALET	Eric Blore
MIZ ZEFFIE	Esther Howard

The character of John Sullivan, like his creator Preston
Sturges, is a writer/director of successful comedy films in Hollywood
in the late 1930's and early 1940's. Unlike Sturges, however,
Sullivan reserves his greatest respect for the highbrow film with
a "message." Sullivan contemptuously dismisses his own hits

(*Hey, Hey in the Hayloft, Ants in Your Plants,* etc.) as he looks about at what he calls a "world committing suicide." He informs his studio bosses that he wants to make a movie entitled *Oh Brother, Where Art Thou?*, which will be "a true canvas of the suffering of humanity." Certain that such a venture will be a financial flop, Sullivan's producers argue that his life has simply been too affluent and protected for him to create such a movie. He finds himself agreeing, but his solution is not to drop the project. Sullivan borrows old clothes and shoes from wardrobe, puts one dime in his pocket, and sets out as a tramp, seeking to learn what real trouble is.

Sullivan's butler, who's made quite an unwilling study of poverty in his time, takes a very dim view of his employer's quest:

> You see, sir, rich people and theorists, who are usually rich people, think of poverty in the negative . . . as the lack of riches . . . but it isn't, sir. Poverty is not the lack of anything, but a positive plague . . . contagious as cholera, with filth, criminals, vice and despair as only a few of its symptoms . . .

At first, Sullivan remains immune to any real suffering, since as he tramps along the open highway he's followed at a discreet distance by a fully equipped luxury land yacht which the studio insists must trail him. It's stocked with a chef, physician, and studio P.R. people churning out noble-sounding copy for the newspapers. The inhabitants of the trailer are not prepared for the kind of wild chase that ensues when Sullivan tries to ditch them. He strikes a bargain with them—give him two weeks free, and he'll meet them in Las Vegas for enough pictures and stories to keep them safely in their jobs.

He thumbs a ride from a friendly enough man, on whom Sullivan tries out some sample lines about how hard it is to find work nowadays. The driver turns out to be the local sheriff. He offers Sullivan the alternative of working as a handyman for a pair of spinster sisters, or going to jail for vagrancy. One of the sisters, Miz Zeffie, is looking for quite a bit more than household repairs. She ogles Sullivan's body while he's working and locks him into his bedroom at bedtime. He escapes at night down a rope of knotted bed sheets, gets picked up by a truck driver, falls asleep, and when he awakens the driver informs him that he has just arrived right back in Hollywood! Disgusted that he can't even seem to get out of town effectively, Sullivan stops in at the Owl Wagon diner. Here, in the first scene below, he meets a young actress who is giving up on her career and returning home. "The Girl," as she is called in the script, is proud, funny, ironic and generous, offering to buy breakfast for this bum. She presents quite a contrast to Sullivan's greedy, shrewish wife. Sullivan is so used to being the famous director that he behaves protectively towards the girl, not even realizing how pathetic *he* appears in his tattered clothes, as he offers to introduce her to the "right people" to help her career. He fetches his car to give her a lift, is stopped for speeding, and then arrested for driving without a license, presumably a stolen vehicle. His butler and valet bail him out and take Sullivan and the Girl back to Sullivan's mansion. She's sore at him for having elicited her sympathy, when he is really living the life of exactly the kind of rich, lying Hollywood creeps she is fleeing. The sight of his swimming pool is just too much for her wounded pride, and she shoves him into it.

He pulls her right in after him. Drying off over a poolside breakfast, in the second scene below, the Girl demands that Sullivan take her with him on his adventure. She can see that without her keeping an eye on him, he is so naive that he'll get himself hurt. Sullivan is alternately touched and offended by her concern. He's flattered when she praises his movies, but bristles when he realizes that what she likes the best is just the kind of slapstick humor he wants to reach beyond. He is definitely attracted to her, but she's just too honest and ornery to be taken casually. Nonetheless, when she threatens to follow him and blow his cover, he has little choice but to accept her as a companion hobo.

Sullivan and the Girl hop a freight train and begin to get their first real taste of the life of the homeless. Together, they pass through the world of soup kitchens, shelters, and midnight missions. When his "research" ends, Sullivan returns alone to these locales to leave money. He is observed carrying cash by a bum who knocks him out, robs him, and then drags his unconscious body onto a departing freight car. The bum is caught between trains on the tracks and killed, and his body is believed to be Sullivan's corpse. When Sullivan awakens, unable to even remember his name, he finds himself in a strange freight yard. A vicious yard boss treats him like the scum he appears to be. Sullivan slugs back. Too woozy to even know what's happening, Sullivan is sentenced to six years of hard labor for trespass and aggravated assault. He is starting to discover what real trouble is.

In prison, Sullivan begins to piece together who he is and how he must have got there. He demands to see his lawyer and to make telephone calls. To the warden, however, he is just an arrogant, lying lunatic who needs to be broken, and the warden is only too happy to do it. One day, Sullivan spots a newspaper with headlines about the strange death of the famous Hollywood film director, John Sullivan. Even his only friend in the prison doesn't believe him when Sullivan insists that's *him*. "Don't I *look* like a picture director?" Sullivan asks. The friend replies, " 'Course I never seen one... to me you look more like a soda jerk... or maybe a plasterer." Sullivan worries, "If ever a plot needed a twist, this one does." Then he realizes that he needs to get his picture in the paper if the people who can help him are to know that he's even alive. Suddenly, he begins calling to see the warden so that he can make a full confession to having been the murderer of John Sullivan...

Sullivan comes out of prison with a new understanding of the purpose and value of comedy. The only time during his imprisonment when he saw others laugh freely and openly, when he himself was released into the cleansing relief of joyful laughter, was when a local black church invited the convicts to join them for the screening of a comedy film. Sullivan returns to Hollywood wanting to make a picture that will make people laugh. As he tells his bewildered producers, "There's a lot to be said for making people laugh... did you know that's all some people have? It isn't much... but it's better than nothing in this cockeyed caravan..."

Scene 1

INT. THE OWL WAGON

SULLIVAN comes in and rubs his hands.

SULLIVAN: Give me a cup of coffee and a... doughnut, if that's enough for it. (*He puts his dime on the counter.*)

THE COUNTER MAN: You want it plain or with powdered sugar.

SULLIVAN: With a little cream.

THE COUNTER MAN: The sinker.

SULLIVAN: Oh, just any kind . . . or some rolls, I don't care.

He shivers, rubs his hands again and climbs on the stool. The CAMERA PANS WITH him and brings the GIRL into view. She is getting some cigarettes from a slot machine. She is young, dressed in evening dress with a coat over it. Now she turns, starts taking the cellophane off her cigarettes and looks at SULLIVAN pitifully.

THE GIRL: Give him some ham and eggs.

She takes thirty-five cents from her bag, walks next to SULLIVAN and puts the money on the counter.

SULLIVAN: (*embarrassed*) That's very kind of you, sister, but I'm not hungry . . . a cup of coffee and a . . . sinker will fix me fine.

THE GIRL: Don't be a sucker . . . give him some ham and eggs. (*then to Sullivan*) The way I'm fixed, thirty-five cents isn't going to make any difference . . . here.

She offers him a cigarette.

SULLIVAN: Thanks.

He lights her cigarette and then his own.

SULLIVAN: Thanks . . . things a little tough, huh?

THE GIRL: I'm not sitting in an owl wagon for local color . . . they locked me out of my room.

SULLIVAN: Oh, that's too bad. . . . Things are tough every place . . . The war in Europe . . . the strikes over here . . . There's no work . . . there's no food . . .

THE GIRL: Drink your coffee while it's hot.

SULLIVAN: Thanks. (*then after a sip*) What did they lock you out of your room for?

THE GIRL: Did I ask *you* any questions?

SULLIVAN: I'm sorry.

THE GIRL: (*relenting*) That's all right.

SULLIVAN: You been in Hollywood long?

THE GIRL: Long enough.

SULLIVAN: Trying to crash the movies or something?

THE GIRL: Something like that.

SULLIVAN: I guess that must be pretty hard to do, hunh?

THE GIRL: I guess so . . . I never got close enough to find out.

SULLIVAN: I'm sorry.

THE GIRL: Say, who's being sorry for who? Are you buying *me* the eggs or am I buying them for *you*?

SULLIVAN: I'd like to repay you for them.

THE GIRL: All right, give me a letter of introduction to Lubitsch.

SULLIVAN: I might be able to do that too . . . Who is Lubitsch?

THE GIRL: Eat your eggs.

SULLIVAN (*his mouth full*) Can you act?

THE GIRL: What did you say?

SULLIVAN: (*swallowing*) I said, can you act?

THE GIRL: Sure I can act . . . Would you like me to give you a recitation?

SULLIVAN: Go ahead.

THE GIRL: (*not expecting to be taken seriously*) Skip it. My next act will be an impersonation of a young lady going home . . . on the thumb.

SULLIVAN: In that outfit?

THE GIRL: How about your own outfit?

SULLIVAN: (*after a moment*) Haven't you got a car?

THE GIRL: No, have you?

SULLIVAN: Well . . . no . . . but . . .

THE GIRL: Then don't get ritzy. And I'll tell you some other things I haven't got: I haven't got a yacht, or a pearl necklace, or a fur coat, or a country seat or even a winter seat . . . and I could use a new girdle too.

SULLIVAN: I wish I could give you . . . a few of the things you need.

THE GIRL: You're not trying to to lead me astray, are you? You big bad wolf!

SULLIVAN laughs sheepishly.

THE GIRL: You know the nice thing about buying food for a man is you don't have to laugh at his jokes . . . Just think, if you were some big shot like a casting director or something, I'd be staring into your bridgework . . . (*She rests her chin on her hand.*) . . . saying: "Yes, Mr. Smearkase . . . not really, Mr. Smearkase. . . . Now there's a funny one, Mr. Smearkase, ha, ha, ha! How you carry on, Mr. Smearkase. Stop it, that's my knee! (*She laughs archly, then speaks to the counter man.*) Give Mr. Smearkase another cup of coffee . . . make that two. (*then to* SULLIVAN) You want a piece of pie?

SULLIVAN: No, thanks, kid.

THE GIRL: Why, Mr. Smearkase, aren't you getting a little familiar on such short acquaintance?

SULLIVAN: (*seriously*) Look: If you wanted to stay in Hollywood a little longer . . .

THE GIRL: (*bitterly*) Well, I don't want to stay in Hollywood a little longer! I've used up all my money and all my going home money and my date got fresh . . . and they locked me out of my room and . . .

SULLIVAN: (*interrupting*) I was going to say I've got a friend who's out of town and you could use his place for a couple of weeks and maybe by then things would break a little better or he might even be able to help you a little.

THE GIRL: No thanks.

SULLIVAN: (*quietly*) They're no strings to this, kid. You don't know who I am but I used to know... a few people around here and this guy is really out of town...

THE GIRL: ... and you know the way in through a window or something. No thanks. The guy always comes back unexpectedly... or his wife drops in... or they take away the furniture or something.

SULLIVAN: I'm pretty sure that in this case...

THE GIRL: I'm going home, big boy. I'll get a ride out of here in the morning.

SULLIVAN: (*after a pause*) I don't like to think of your asking a bunch of thugs for lifts along the highway.

THE GIRL: Then, don't think about it.

SULLIVAN: You just get in any car that comes along?

THE GIRL: Anything but a Stanley Steamer... my uncle blew up in one.

SULLIVAN: But, that's terrible. You can't tell *what* kind of a heel is apt to be... behind the wheel.

THE GIRL: All heels are pretty much the same.

SULLIVAN: Say, look—

THE GIRL: (*archly*) Yes, Mr. Smearkase.

SULLIVAN: This friend of mine... this guy who's out of town... I don't think he'd mind if I borrowed his car.

THE GIRL: What is it, a street car?

SULLIVAN: (*rising*) It's a car. You wait here.

THE GIRL: (*anxiously*) You're just going to get yourself in trouble.

SULLIVAN: I'm not going to get myself in trouble and I want to repay you for that ham and eggs.

THE GIRL: (*touched*) That isn't necessary, big boy... Some day, when your ship comes in, buy somebody who's hungry some ham and eggs... and we'll be all square.

SULLIVAN: (*putting his hand on her shoulder*) You wait here...I'll be back here before you can say... what's that big director's name?

THE GIRL: Lubitsch.

SULLIVAN: (*raising a finger*) Lubitsch.

SCENE 2

THE GIRL and SULLIVAN—AT A GLEAMING BREAKFAST TABLE NEXT TO THE POOL

They each wear voluminous white terry-cloth bathrobes. They have already eaten the eggs. SULLIVAN pours THE GIRL some more coffee. She crosses her legs which are sensational and picks up a cigarette. SULLIVAN lights it for her.

THE GIRL: You might have shaved.

SULLIVAN: I need these whiskers... for my experiment.

THE GIRL: Oh, yes... the noble experiment.

SULLIVAN: You don't have to make any cracks. I don't starve and suffer because I like it, you know.

THE GIRL: Neither does anybody else. (*contrite*)... I'm sorry.

SULLIVAN: S'all right.

THE GIRL: I'm sorry I pushed you in the water, too.

SULLIVAN: I probably needed it.

THE GIRL: You certainly did.

SULLIVAN: (worried) Did I?

THE GIRL: I didn't mind you . . . as a matter of fact, I had kind of
a yen for you . . .

SULLIVAN: (surprised) You have?

THE GIRL: (pointing to his kimono) Not in that thing . . . I liked
you better as a bo.

SULLIVAN: Well, I can't help what kind of people you like.

THE GIRL: Maybe I'm vicious . . . it's funny . . . I suppose I ought
to be very happy for you, as if you'd just struck oil or
something . . . instead of that, I'm sore.

SULLIVAN: Don't frown, it'll make lines in your face.

THE GIRL: You've taken all the joy out of life . . . I was all
through with this kind of stuff . . . (She indicates around.) I
mean I knew I'd never have it . . . there was no envy in my
heart . . . I'd found a friend who'd swiped a car to take me
home . . . and now I'm right back where I started.

SULLIVAN: (crossly) So am I.

THE GIRL: Just an extra girl having breakfast with a director . . . only
I didn't use to have breakfast with them . . . maybe that was
my trouble.

SULLIVAN: Did they ever ask you to?

THE GIRL: No.

SULLIVAN: Then don't pat yourself on the back.

THE BUTLER comes into THE SHOT and takes the coffee pot to a
side table to refill it.

THE GIRL: Take me with you.

SULLIVAN: (indignantly) What? . . .

THE GIRL: I don't want to be sent home on the rattler.

SULLIVAN: (after a pause) Don't be childish. I'll tell you what

I'll do. You can stay here for a couple of weeks like I told you in the owl wagon... and when I come back I'll see what I can do for you... or I'll write you a couple of notes before I go.

THE GIRL: I don't want you to write me any notes... I don't want to start all that stuff again... take me with you and when you get as far as you're going we'll say goodbye and I'll go the rest of the way alone... it'll make a nice ending... and we'll finish what we started this morning.

SULLIVAN: That is absolutely out of the question.

THE GIRL crosses and sits on the arm of his chair.

THE GIRL: Please. You don't know anything about... anything. You don't know how to get a meal; you don't know how to keep a secret... you can't even stay out of town.

SULLIVAN: Thanks.

THE GIRL: I know fifty times as much about trouble as you ever will... and besides, you owe it to me, you sort of belong to *me*... when you're a bum... I found you.

SULLIVAN: Piffle!

THE GIRL: (*leaning closer*) Please.

SULLIVAN: I tell you it's absolutely out of the...

THE GIRL: (*leaning still closer*) I'll throw you in the water.

SULLIVAN: You'd take my mind off my work.

THE GIRL: (*mockingly*) Ho, ho, the big director... who has all the girls panting for him...

SULLIVAN: (*wearily*) I tell you...

THE GIRL: (*inspired*) I'll follow you and tell everybody who you are... like a kid sister.

SULLIVAN: (*tauntingly*) You'll follow me!

THE GIRL: Yes I'll follow you, and I'll holler: this guy is a

phoney, ladies and gentlemen . . . this is Sullivan, the big
director from Hollywood, a phonus balonus, a faker, a heel
who's just trying to . . .[1]

THE BUTLER: (*coming into* THE SHOT *with a pot of fresh coffee*)
If I may join in the controversy, sir, I believe the young
lady's suggestion is an excellent one for the reason . . .

SULLIVAN: (*severely, looking around* THE GIRL) Yes, well you
may *not* join in the controversy, Mr. Burrows.

THE GIRL: (*bouncing up and down on* SULLIVAN'*s lap*) I will, I
will, I will! I'm going with you.

SULLIVAN: Well, you're not going to do anything of the kind.
Burrows, you go down to the station and. . . .

THE GIRL puts her hand over his mouth and SULLIVAN starts to
yammer.

THE GIRL: Will you get me some tramp clothes, Mr. Burrows?

THE BUTLER: Certainly, Miss.

SULLIVAN: (*getting up with the struggling* GIRL *in his arms*) You
go down to the station and get me a ticket to . . . (*then to*
THE GIRL) Where do you live?

THE GIRL: I won't tell you. I won't be sent home, I'll . . .

She grabs SULLIVAN's ears and starts to kick her feet up and down.

SULLIVAN: Stop that! . . . grab her feet, Burrows!

THE BUTLER: Yes, sir . . . now, Miss . . .

THE GIRL: I won't be sent home. You leave me alone. Let go my
feet.

THE BUTLER: Now, Miss.

THE GIRL: Oh, you will, will you!

She straightens out her legs and THE BUTLER starts teetering
backwards.

---

[1]From this point on, unless your acting studio set is equipped with a swimming pool, an
alternate ending for this scene from another draft of the screenplay is necessary.

SULLIVAN: Stop that!

THE GIRL gets a death-grip around SULLIVAN's neck and THE BUTLER gets a death-grip on the girl's legs. The result is inevitable and the three of them swan-dive into the pool. At the splash—

THE DOOR OF THE HOUSE

THE VALET comes hurrying out and stops in dismay.

THE VALET: (*under his breath*) Good God!

He hurries to the edge of the pool where SULLIVAN and THE GIRL are occupied in dunking each other.

THE VALET: (*seizing* THE BUTLER's *hand*) My dear Burrows . . . here now, one, two, three, PULL HARD!

With a tremendous effort on THE BUTLER's part THE VALET flies into the pool.

FADE OUT

SULLIVAN: (*sourly*) You'll follow me.

THE GIRL: (*threateningly*) You just try and shake me.

THE BUTLER: (*coming into* THE SHOT *with a pot of fresh coffee*) If I may join in the controversy, sir, I believe the young lady's suggestion to be an excellent one.

SULLIVAN: (*severely, looking around* THE GIRL) Yes, well you may *not* join in it, Mr. Burrows.

THE GIRL: (*putting her hand on* SULLIVAN's *mouth and turning around*) Could you get me some tramp clothes, Mr. Burrows?

THE BUTLER: With ease, Miss.

SULLIVAN starts to yammer under her hand.

THE GIRL: (*gently*) Quiet . . . doesn't know what's good for him.

Suddenly, for some unexplained reason, she leaps to her feet.

THE GIRL: Ouch!

FADE OUT

LAURA

A Twentieth Century-Fox presentation. Producer and Director, Otto Preminger. Screenplay by Jay Dratler, Samuel Hoffenstein, and Betty Reinhardt. Adapted from the Novel *Laura* by Vera Caspary. Director of Photography, Joseph La Shelle. Film Editor, Louis Loeffler. Art Directors, Lyle Wheeler, Leland Fuller. Set Decorator, Thomas Little. Sound, E. Clayton Ward, Harry M. Leonard. Music, David Raskin. Song "Laura," lyrics by Johnny Mercer. Musical Director, Emil Newman. Special Effects, Fred Sersen. Running time, 87 minutes. 1944.

CAST

LAURA HUNT	Gene Tierney
MARK MCPHERSON	Dana Andrews
WALDO LYDECKER	Clifton Webb
SHELBY CARPENTER	Vincent Price
ANN TREADWELL	Judith Anderson
BESSIE CLARY	Dorothy Adams

Laura Hunt is murdered . . . only not really. Her devoted maid Bessie discovers a shot body dressed in Miss Hunt's robe, and is so unhinged that she identifies the corpse incorrectly. The actual Laura is quietly, seriously thinking over her future at her country place, with no radio or newspapers, so she has no idea that she's just been mysteriously murdered back in her own apartment in New York. The officer in charge of the investigation, Mark McPherson, is almost a parody of the tough-guy cop. Yeah, he knew one once, who wasn't just a broad or a dame, but she kept walking him by the parlor suites in the windows of furniture stores. He is contemptuous of all the suspects and their fancy lives, and indeed they all do have too many neuroses and motives and appetites to tell him the truth. In the course of his investigation, McPherson studies Laura's diaries and letters. He touches her clothes, smells her perfume. There's even a portrait of her hanging over the mantel that he's tried to buy from the art dealer who'll auction off the deceased's collections. There's something about her... The most perceptive and nasty of the suspects warns McPherson that he has become infatuated with the dead victim, and that if he's not careful, he's going to end up in a psychiatric ward. In the scene below, McPherson is alone in Laura's apartment in the middle of the night. He's starting to get a little drunk, holding a vigil for a memory he's never even had, transfixed by the beautiful young woman in the portrait. "That's Laura," the haunting title song tempts, "but she's only a dream." And then the door opens, and in walks Laura Hunt, very much alive.

So, who was the victim? She was Diane Redfern, a model who'd been staying in Laura's apartment. Diane had caught the interest of Laura's fiancé (and employee) Shelby Carpenter, an impoverished but professionally charming Southern gentleman, a ladies' man. He'd come to the apartment the night of the murder, knowing that Laura was away, to break off with Diane, now that he'd proposed to Laura. It was in order to think over Shelby's proposal that Laura had gone away for the few days. According to Shelby, he and Diane had talked for three hours, the bell rang, she answered the door, shots were fired into the body of the woman wearing Laura's robe, and by the time Shelby got to the door the murderer had fled. Shelby confesses all this, finally admitting that he didn't report the event to the police because he was afraid it was Laura who had committed the murder out of jealousy. He certainly could be lying, and always sounds as if he were. As Shelby readily remarks, "I've spent very little time in observing my own character."

The other prime suspects are Laura's two other closest associates—literally, her kith and her kin. The kin is Ann Treadwell, Laura's aunt, who is in love with Shelby; Ann tells her niece:

I can afford him, and I understand him. He's no good,

but he's what I want. I'm not a nice person, Laura, and
neither is he. He knows I know just what he is. He also
knows that I don't care. We belong together because
we're both weak and can't seem to help it. That's why
I know he's capable of murder. He's like me...No
dear, I didn't. But I've thought of it.

The kith is Laura's mentor, and, it turns out, the murderer:
Waldo Lydecker. Waldo is one of those arbiters of social taste
who through a column or a regular spot on the air wield
enormous power; but it's a bitchy authority based finally on little
more than its own superciliousness and irritable clubbiness.
Years earlier, while lunching at his regular table in the Algonquin
Hotel, Lydecker had been interrupted by a shy-brash, ingenuously
eager Laura. She wanted the supremely witty and famous Mr.
Lydecker to endorse a certain pen which had just been assigned
to her as an account in the ad agency in which she was working.
He was haughtily offended: "I don't use a pen. I write with a
goose quill dipped in venom." But he was also seriously charmed
by her, gave the endorsement, and spent the next year watching
Laura's career climb, and helping to cultivate her personal
style. Lydecker's appetite is not sexual, but it demands complete control. When asked by McPherson whether he and
Laura were in love, Lydecker answers, "Laura considered me
the wisest, the wittiest, the most interesting man she'd ever
met. I was in complete accord with her on that point."
Laura's effort to get out from under Waldo's suffocating wing,
in addition to her consideration of Shelby's proposal, simply
pitches Waldo over the edge. But he has killed the wrong girl.
McPherson enters the picture, and now it becomes even more
important to Waldo to kill Laura. If he was not going to allow
Shelby to have her, he certainly has no intention of letting her
fall into the arms of uncultivated, unselfconscious male sexu-
ality. About to murder Laura (for the second time), Waldo
explains to her, "The best part of myself—that's what you
are. Do you think I'm going to leave it to the vulgar pawings
of a second-rate detective?" McPherson breaks down the door
in the nick of time, saves Laura, and that's *exactly* what
happens.

SCENE

SEMI CLOSE SHOT* MARK standing by liquor cabinet, as he tosses down another drink. CAMERA FOLLOWS as he crosses living room, bottle in hand, and HOLDS as he sits in chair placed in front of mantel over which hangs portrait of LAURA. He pours drink from bottle, places bottle on nearby table. He downs drink and finally turns his head in direction of picture. CAMERA MOVES TO CLOSER SHOT as he leans head back and falls to sleep. CAMERA HOLDS in SEMI CLOSEUP. CAMERA MOVES TO LONGER SHOT AND HOLDS IN SEMI CLOSE SHOT as door is heard opening, offscene.

SEMI LONG SHOT LAURA closing entrance door, week-end bag at her feet on floor. She hesitates momentarily when she sees MARK asleep in chair, offscene. CAMERA FOLLOWS as she crosses to corner of mantel, including MARK in chair in f.g. CAMERA HOLDS in MEDIUM SHOT as she stops by mantel and turns on lights. MARK awakens, rubs his eyes and sits forward in chair.

LAURA: What are you doing here?

MARK rises, back to camera. CAMERA MOVES TO CLOSER SHOT as he takes a step toward her.

MARK: You're alive.

SEMI CLOSEUP LAURA.

LAURA: If you don't get out at once, I'm going to call the police.

SEMI CLOSEUP MARK.

MARK: You are Laura Hunt, aren't you?

He steps forward.

MARK: Aren't you?

SEMI CLOSEUP LAURA.

---

*This scene is excerpted from the Dialogue Continuity of the completed film, not from the writers' screenplay. (Please see the Sample Scripts Appendix, Volume I, for a discussion of these terms.) The action is a transcription of what appeared on the screen, and the dialogue is a transcription of what was heard on the soundtrack.

LAURA: I'm going to call the police.

CAMERA FOLLOWS as she starts to go and HOLDS as she stops.

MARK'S VOICE: Well, I am the police.

SEMI CLOSE SHOT MARK standing back to camera, as he takes credentials from hip pocket. He holds them forth for LAURA, standing at end of divan, to see.

MARK: Mark McPherson.

MARK replaces credentials in hip pocket.

SEMI CLOSEUP LAURA

LAURA: What's this all about?

She steps forward.

CLOSE SHOT of two.

MARK: Don't you know? Don't you know what's happened?

LAURA: No.

MARK: Haven't you seen the papers? Where have you been?

SEMI CLOSEUP LAURA.

LAURA: Up in the country. I—I don't get a newspaper.

CLOSE SHOT of two.

MARK: Haven't you got a radio?

LAURA: It was broken.

He looks off to f.g.

LAURA: What—

CAMERA PULLS BACK in LONGER SHOT as MARK walks forward. LAURA follows as he stops and picks up paper. CAMERA HOLDS as she stops beside him. He unfolds paper and hands it to her. She looks at headlines. CAMERA FOLLOWS as she sinks on arm of divan. CAMERA MOVES TO CLOSE SHOT as she reads. She looks up dazed.

MARK: Somebody was murdered in this room. Do you have
any idea who it was?

LAURA: No.

MARK: Who had a key to your apartment?

LAURA: Nobody.

MARK: You sure?

LAURA: When did it happen?

MARK: Friday night.

She looks at him questioningly.

LAURA: What are you going to do now?

MARK: Find out who was murdered and then find the murderer.

She drops her eyes and looks down.

MARK: You'd better take off those wet clothes—you might
catch cold.

She looks at him—then looks down.

LAURA: Yeah.

LAURA exits f.g. CAMERA MOVES TO SEMI CLOSEUP of MARK as
he looks off in LAURA's direction, offscene.

DISSOLVE TO:

SEMI CLOSE SHOT as LAURA bursts through bedroom door into
living room carrying dress on hanger and magazine. CAMERA
FOLLOWS as she crosses room.

LAURA: I found this in my closet.

CAMERA HOLDS as MARK enters to her and they stop. She holds
dress up.

LAURA: It's Diane Redfern's. It wasn't here when I left.

He takes dress from her.

LAURA: She's one of our models—just about my size.

She holds up magazine for him to see.

CLOSEUP of open magazine held in LAURA's hands showing picture of girl.

MARK'S VOICE: Beautiful, wasn't she?

CLOSE SHOT of two as they look at magazine.

LAURA: Do you suppose—

He takes magazine from LAURA's hands. CAMERA FOLLOWS IN LONGER SHOT, excluding LAURA, as he goes to b.g.

MARK: Sit down, please.

CAMERA MOVES TO CLOSER SHOT as she enters f.g. and sits at side of desk.

He starts to put on coat.

MARK: This is Monday night. You left on Friday.

CAMERA HOLDS IN SEMI CLOSE SHOT.

MARK: Rather a long weekend, isn't it?

LAURA: Yes.

MARK: What train did you take?

LAURA: The seven twenty-six.

MARK: See anybody you knew on the train?

He pulls his tie into place.

LAURA: No.

MARK: Then what?

He takes notebook out of coat pocket.

LAURA: Then I got off the train at Norwalk.

He drops book on table, opens it.

MARK: Saw nobody you knew at the station either?

LAURA: No.

MARK: Go on.

He starts making notes in book.

SEMI CLOSEUP LAURA.

LAURA: Then I went to the garage where I keep my car. It's a private garage. Nobody saw me there, either. Then I drove to my house.

SEMI CLOSEUP MARK as he looks down making notations in book.

MARK: You were there three days. What did you do?

LAURA: Worked in my garden.

MARK: You didn't go out in all that time?

SEMI CLOSEUP LAURA.

LAURA: No—I had everything I needed in the house.

MARK'S VOICE: Nobody came to see you?

LAURA: Nobody. I went there to be alone.

SEMI CLOSEUP MARK.

MARK: The police were there on Saturday and there was no one in the house.

SEMI CLOSEUP LAURA.

LAURA: Oh, yes—Saturday, I took a long walk. I walked for hours—in the woods.

SEMI CLOSEUP MARK.

MARK: Uh-huh—

CAMERA FOLLOWS IN LONGER SHOT as he walks to b.g.

MARK: —you were going to marry Shelby Carpenter this week— Thursday, if I'm not mistaken.

CAMERA HOLDS as he stops at mantel and turns to f.g.

SEMI CLOSEUP of LAURA. She drops her eyes.

LAURA: Yes.

CAMERA PULLS BACK IN SEMI CLOSE SHOT as MARK strolls forward.

MARK: Yet you went away just before your wedding, for a long weekend—to be alone.

CAMERA HOLDS as he enters to her.

LAURA: I was tired—I'd been working hard.

MARK: You know Shelby Carpenter has a key to this apartment. Why didn't you tell me?

LAURA: I know nothing of the sort!

CAMERA MOVES TO SEMI CLOSEUP as she rises defiantly.

LAURA: He hasn't!

MARK: How else did the girl get into the apartment? You know she was in love with Carpenter—

SEMI CLOSEUP of LAURA. MARK in f.g., back to camera.

MARK: —that he'd given her your cigarette case. You know all that, don't you?

LAURA: I knew that she was in love with him. She told me so herself.

MARK: When did she tell you?

LAURA: At lunch—last Friday. I also—

She turns away from him. CAMERA FOLLOWS as she goes to b.g.

LAURA: —know that she meant—

CAMERA FOLLOWS LAURA, excluding MARK.

LAURA: —nothing to Shelby.

CAMERA FOLLOWS LAURA, including MARK in f.g., as she stops at desk in b.g.

LAURA: I understand him better than you do.

CAMERA FOLLOWS as MARK goes to b.g.

MARK: She was found in your dressing gown and slippers.

CAMERA HOLDS IN SEMI CLOSE SHOT as MARK stops on opposite side of desk.

MARK: That's hardly the regulation costume for an impersonal chat between a man and woman who mean nothing to each other. Did you know—or did you suspect that he was going to bring her here Friday night, Miss Hunt?

LAURA: How could I? I don't know that he brought her here— and neither do you. You merely assume it.

MARK: What other assumption is possible? Do you love this fellow Carpenter so much, you'd risk your own safety to protect him?

LAURA: My own safety? You suspect me?

MARK: I suspect nobody and everybody.

He picks his pencil up from desk.

MARK: I'm merely trying to get at the truth.

He puts pencil in his coat pocket.

SEMI CLOSEUP of LAURA as she looks at her diary. MARK in f.g., back to camera.

LAURA: I see you have been trying to get at the truth. You've read things that I never meant anyone else to look at.

SEMI CLOSEUP of MARK as he places his notebook in his inside breast pocket. LAURA in f.g., back to camera.

MARK: Strictly routine. I'm sorry, really.

SEMI CLOSEUP of LAURA as she looks at MARK in f.g., back to camera—She looks down at diary, which she holds in her hands.

SEMI CLOSEUP of MARK. LAURA in f.g., back to camera.

MARK: I'd better be going. I'll see you in the morning, Miss Hunt.

SEMI CLOSE SHOT of two as MARK starts to f.g. from desk, carrying Diane Redfern's dress in his hand.

He stops momentarily.

MARK: Oh—I must ask you not to leave the house or use the phone.

MARK exits. CAMERA FOLLOWS as LAURA races across room after him.

LAURA: But—but I've got to let my friends know I'm alive.

MARK'S VOICE: Sorry, Miss Hunt, but I must insist you do as I say.

CAMERA HOLDS as she stops beside him.

MARK starts to put on his raincoat.

LAURA: Am I under arrest?

MARK: No, but if anything should happen to you this time, I wouldn't like it.

He draws his coat about him.

LAURA: All right, I promise.

He leans down and picks up his hat.

MARK: There's one more thing. You may as well know what I know—some of it, at any rate. It'll save time and a lot of unnecessary fencing. I know that you went away to make up your mind—

He goes to b.g., picks up packet of letters from chair. CAMERA MOVES to CLOSER SHOT as he walks forward to her. CAMERA HOLDS in SEMI CLOSEUP as he stops beside her.

MARK: —whether you'd marry Shelby Carpenter or—or not. What did you decide?

She lowers her eyes.

MARK: I want the truth.

She raises her eyes to his.

LAURA: I decided not to marry him.

He smiles faintly.

MARK: I'll see you in the morning. Good-night.

LAURA: Good-night.

He exits. She stands looking after him. (DOOR HEARD CLOSING)

CAMERA FOLLOWS IN LONGER SHOT as she goes to phone on table in b.g. She places hand on receiver, takes it off, looks at phone, puts hand on phone again, defiantly.

BRIEF ENCOUNTER

An Eagle-Lion release of a Cineguild Production. In Charge of Production, Anthony Havelock-Allan, Ronald Neame. Producer, Noël Coward. Director, David Lean. Screenplay by Noël Coward. Adapted from Noël Coward's *Still Life* from *Tonight at 8:30*. Director of Photography, Robert Krasker. Editor, Jack Harris. Sound Editor, Harry Miller. Art Director, L.P. Williams. Production Manager, E. Holding. Assistant Director, George Pollock. Running time, 86 minutes. 1945.

CAST

LAURA JESSON	Celia Johnson
ALEC HARVEY	Trevor Howard
FRED JESSON	Cyril Raymond
ALBERT GODBY	Stanley Holloway
MYRTLE BAGOT	Joyce Carey
BERYL WATERS	Margaret Barton
DOLLY MESSITER	Everley Gregg
MARGARET	Henrietta Vincent
BOBBIE	Richard Thomas

Fred is a "pleasant looking man in his forties." His wife, Laura, loves and respects him, their pleasant marriage, and their two pleasant children, Margaret and Bobbie. Existence is very

Brief Encounter © 1945 by the Noël Coward Estate. Published in *Masterworks of the British Cinema* © 1974 by Lorrimer Publishing Limited. Reprinted by permission of Lorrimer Publishing Limited.

pleasant for Laura in her suburban life outside of London in the winter of 1938–1939. But what is "pleasant" worth in the face of the overwhelming convulsion of romantic passion that completely overturns Laura's inner life when she meets Alec? It couldn't have begun less remarkably. Alec happened by the Milford Junction train station refreshment room just as Laura was trying to remove a piece of grit caught in her eye. "Please let me look. I happen to be a doctor." And one thing surged on into another, a kind of freak accident of grand passion. But Alec's outer life is just as enmeshed as Laura's in a middle-class, early middle-aged, happily married, tidy-as-a-cup-of-tea home life. For dutiful, decent people of this sort, living in the world in which they live, there really is no choice: you do not throw over the outer life to accommodate the inner one. You part forever. Alec decides to leave with his family for work in Africa. Laura, after seriously considering suicide, returns to Fred and her children. Had Fred any idea? Laura had once tried to casually mention to him that she'd had lunch with a rather nice doctor, and Fred suggested both couples have dinner. But it is just possible, from the way Fred thanks Laura in the last line of the film, that he was indeed aware of just how close he'd come to losing her.

Laura is the narrator of the film, telling the whole story in flashbacks linked by her present tense, voice-over inner monologue, addressed to Fred. She has just returned home from her final parting with Alec, and she sits in her living room watching Fred—cheerful, dependable Fred—working on his crossword puzzle. Laura's thoughts reconstruct moments from her affair with Alec—an affair they never consumated. The intensity of the emotions that Laura experiences are always operating in counterpoint to the contented ordinariness of her world, and to the reins of British reserve that her feelings for Alec strain to their limit. Her inner life (monologue, flashbacks) and outer life (Fred across the room) finally converge at the end of the film when Laura moves out of memory, having just recalled her reasons for rejecting suicide and returning to Fred. When Fred speaks to her and she doesn't seem to hear him, he comes to her and kneels beside her. He asks if she's been a long way off:

> FRED moves a little closer to her and quietly rests his face against her hand. FRED with a catch in his voice: "Thank you for coming back to me." FADE OUT.

MONOLOGUE 1

LAURA'S VOICE: Fred—Fred—dear Fred. There's so much that I
want to say to you. You are the only one in the world with
enough wisdom and gentleness to understand—if only it
were somebody else's story and not mine. As it is you are
the only one in the world that I can never tell—never—
never—because even if I waited until we were old, old
people, and told you then, you would be bound to look back
over the years . . . and be hurt and oh, my dear, I don't want
you to be hurt. You see, we are a happily married couple,
and must never forget that. This is my home. . . .

A shot of FRED over LAURA's shoulder. He is engrossed in his
crossword puzzle.

LAURA'S VOICE: . . . you are my husband—and my children
are upstairs in bed. I am a happily married woman—or
rather, I was, until a few weeks ago. This is my whole
world and it is enough—or rather, it was, until a few weeks
ago.

Close shot of LAURA.

LAURA'S VOICE: . . . But, oh, Fred, I've been so foolish. I've
fallen in love! I'm an ordinary woman—I didn't think such
violent things could happen to ordinary people.

Again a shot of FRED over LAURA's shoulder.

LAURA'S VOICE: It all started on an ordinary day, in the most
ordinary place in the world.

The scene, with the exception of LAURA, slowly starts to dim
out. LAURA remains a solid figure in the foreground. As the
room fades away, the station refreshment room takes its place.
LAURA, as well as being in the foreground of the picture, is also
seated at one of the tables in the refreshment room, thus giving
the impression that she is watching herself. Dissolve.

It is now night time, about 5:30 p.m. The scene takes place in
the refreshment room at the Milford Junction Station. There are
only two or three other people in the room. MYRTLE and BERYL

are behind the counter, against which ALBERT is lolling, sipping a cup of tea.

LAURA'S VOICE: . . . the refreshment room at Milford Junction. I was having a cup of tea and reading a book that I'd got that morning from Boots—my train wasn't due for ten minutes. . . . I looked up and saw a man come in from the platform. He had on an ordinary mac with a belt. His hat was turned down, and I didn't even see his face. He got his tea at the counter and turned—then I did see his face. It was rather a nice face. He passed my table on the way to his.

● ● ● ● ●

LAURA'S VOICE: I completely forgot the whole incident—it didn't mean anything to me at all, at least I didn't think it did.

There is the sound of a guard's whistle and the train starts to move off.

Fade out.

As the screen goes black, we hear LAURA'S voice.

LAURA'S VOICE: The next Thursday I went into Milford again as usual. . . .

Fade in on Milford High Street where LAURA walks along, carrying a shopping basket. She checks the contents of the basket with a shopping list and, having decided on her next port of call, she quickens her step. Dissolve.

We are inside Boots Chemist. LAURA is walking away from the library section and goes over to a counter with soaps, toothbrushes, etc.

LAURA'S VOICE: I changed my books at Boots—Miss Lewis had at last managed to get the new Kate O'Brien for me—I believe she'd kept it hidden under the counter for two days! On the way out I bought two new toothbrushes for the children—I like the smell of a chemist's better than any other shop—it's such a mixture of nice things—herbs and scent and soap. . . .

Close shot of MRS. LEFTWICH at the end of the counter.

LAURA'S VOICE: . . . that awful Mrs. Leftwich was at the other
end of the counter, wearing one of the silliest hats I've ever
seen.

Cut to LAURA placing the toothbrushes in her shopping bag and
leaving the counter.

LAURA'S VOICE: . . . fortunately she didn't look up, so I got out
without her buttonholing me. Just as I stepped out on to the
pavement. . . .

Dissolve to LAURA as she comes out of Boots. ALEC comes by
walking rather quickly. He is wearing a turned-down hat. He
recognizes her, stops, and raises his hat.

[ALEC: Good morning.]

LAURA: (jumping slightly) Oh—good morning.

[ALEC: How's the eye? (Still)

LAURA: Perfectly all right. How kind it was of you to take so
much trouble.

ALEC: It was no trouble at all.

After a slight pause.

ALEC: It's clearing up, I think.

LAURA: Yes—the sky looks much lighter, doesn't it?

ALEC: Well, I must be getting along to the hospital.

LAURA: And I must be getting along to the grocer's.

ALEC: (with a smile) What exciting lives we lead, don't we?
Good-bye.

Dissolve to the interior of the subway. It is night time. LAURA is
walking along, a little out of breath.]

LAURA'S VOICE: That afternoon I had been to the Palladium as
usual, but it was a terribly long film, and when I came out I
had had to run nearly all the way to the station.

LAURA starts to go up the steps leading to Number 3 platform. She comes up the subway on to the platform.

LAURA'S VOICE: As I came up on to the platform the Churley train was just puffing out.

Cut to the train leaving Number 4 platform.

Close shot of LAURA, watching the Churley train.

LAURA'S VOICE: I looked up idly as the windows of the carriages went by, wondering if he was there.... I remember this crossing my mind but it was quite unimportant—I was really thinking of other things—the present for your birthday was worrying me rather. It was terribly expensive, but I knew you wanted it, and I'd sort of half taken the plunge and left a deposit on it at Spink and Robson's until the next Thursday. The next Thursday....

Dissolve to the interior of Spink and Robson. Close-up of a travelling clock with a barometer and dates, all in one. It is standing on a glass show case.

LAURA is looking down at it admiringly.

LAURA'S VOICE: ... Well—I squared my conscience by thinking how pleased you would be, and bought it—it was wildly extravagant, I know, but having committed the crime, I suddenly felt reckless and gay....

Dissolve to Milford High Street. LAURA walks along the street, carrying a small parcel in her hand. It is a sunny day and she is smiling. A barrel organ is playing.

LAURA'S VOICE: The sun was out and everybody in the street looked more cheerful than usual—and there was a barrel organ at the corner by Harris's, and you know how I love barrel organs—it was playing 'Let the Great Big World Keep Turning', and I gave the man sixpence and went to the Kardomah for lunch.

Dissolve to inside of the Kardomah Café. LAURA is sitting at an alcove table. A waitress is just finishing taking her order.

LAURA'S VOICE: It was very full, but two people had got up from the table just as I had come in—that was a bit of luck, wasn't it? Or was it? Just after I had given my order, I saw him come in. He looked a little tired, I thought, and there was nowhere for him to sit, so I smiled and said . . .

LAURA: Good morning.

[Close-up of ALEC.

ALEC: Good morning. Are you alone?

Resume on LAURA and ALEC.

LAURA: Yes, I am.

ALEC: Would you mind very much if I shared your table—it's very full and there doesn't seem to be anywhere else?

LAURA: (*moving a couple of parcels and her bag*) Of course not.

ALEC hangs up his hat and mackintosh and sits down next to her.

ALEC: I'm afraid we haven't been properly introduced—my name's Alec Harvey.

LAURA: (*shaking hands*) How do you do—mine's Laura Jesson.

ALEC: Mrs. or Miss?

LAURA: Mrs. You're a doctor, aren't you? I remember you said you were that day in the refreshment room.

ALEC: Yes—not a very interesting doctor—just an ordinary G.P. My practice is in Churley.

A waitress comes to the table. . . .]

MONOLOGUE 2

LAURA'S VOICE: I stood there and watched his train draw out of the station. I stared after it until its little red tail light had vanished into the darkness. I imagined him arriving at

Churley and giving up his ticket and walking through the streets, and letting himself into his house with his latchkey. Madeleine, his wife, would probably be in the hall to meet him—or perhaps upstairs in her room—not feeling very well—small, dark and rather delicate—I wondered if he'd say 'I met such a nice woman in the Kardomah—we had lunch and went to the pictures'—then suddenly I knew that he wouldn't—I knew beyond a shadow of doubt that he wouldn't say a word, and at that moment the first awful feeling of danger swept over me.

A cloud of steam from an incoming engine blows across the screen, almost obscuring LAURA. The grinding of brakes and hiss of steam as her train draws to a standstill, interrupts her thoughts. She walks out of view towards the train.

Through the clearing steam we see her enter a third-class compartment, crowded with people.

She sits down between two other passengers, and glances around the carriage.

LAURA'S VOICE: I looked hurriedly around the carriage to see if anyone was looking at me.

The camera pans along the passengers seated on the opposite side of the carriage.

LAURA'S VOICE: . . . as though they could read my secret thoughts. Nobody was looking at me except a clergyman in the opposite corner.

The clergyman catches her eye and turns his head away.

Close-up of LAURA as she opens her library book.

LAURA'S VOICE: I felt myself blushing and opened my library book and pretended to read.

The train gives a jerk as it starts to move off.

Dissolve to Ketchworth Station, where LAURA walks along the platform towards the barrier. There are several other passengers around her.

LAURA'S VOICE: By the time we got to Ketchworth, I had made up my mind definitely that I wouldn't see Alec.

[A WOMAN'S VOICE: Good evening, Mrs. Jesson.

LAURA does not hear.]

LAURA'S VOICE: It was silly and undignified flirting like that with a complete stranger.

[She walks on a pace or two, then turns.

LAURA: Oh—oh—good evening.]

Dissolve to LAURA's house. She walks up the path to the front door.

LAURA'S VOICE: I walked up to the house quite briskly and cheerfully. I had been behaving like an idiot admittedly, but after all no harm had been done.

LAURA opens the front door.

She enters the hall, and looks up towards the stairs.

LAURA'S VOICE: You met me in the hall. Your face was strained and worried and my heart sank.

MONOLOGUE 3

[Dissolve to a shot over LAURA's shoulder. The subway has suddenly disappeared, and FRED and the library have taken its place.

LAURA: (*jumping*) Yes, dear?

FRED: You were miles away.

LAURA: Was I? I suppose I was.

FRED: (*rising*) Do you mind if I turn it down a little—it really is deafening. . . .

He goes towards the radio.

LAURA: (*with an effort*) Of course not.

She bends down and starts sewing. FRED turns down the radio, and returns to his place.

FRED: I shan't be long over this, and then we'll go up to bed. You look a bit tired, you know. . . .]

LAURA: Don't hurry—I'm perfectly happy.

She continues her sewing for a moment or two, then she looks up again. FRED's head is down, concentrating on the paper.

LAURA passes her hand across her forehead wearily.

LAURA'S VOICE: How can I possibly say that? 'Don't hurry, I'm perfectly happy.' If only it were true. Not, I suppose, that anybody is perfectly happy really, but just to be ordinarily contented—to be at peace. It's such a little while ago really, but it seems an eternity since that train went out of the station—taking him away into the darkness.

Dissolve to LAURA walking in the subway. The sound of her train is heard pulling in overhead.

LAURA'S VOICE: I went over to the other platform and got into my train as usual.

Close shot of LAURA in the railway compartment. She is seated in a corner.

LAURA'S VOICE: This time I didn't attempt to read—even to pretend to read—I didn't care whether people were looking at me or not. I had to think. I should have been utterly wretched and ashamed—I know I should but I wasn't—I felt suddenly quite wildly happy—like a romantic school-girl, like a romantic fool! You see he had said he loved me, and I had said I loved him, and it was true—it was true! I imagined him holding me in his arms—I imagined being with him in all sorts of glamorous circumstances. It was one of those absurd fantasies—just like one has when one is a girl—being wooed and married by the ideal of one's dreams—generally a rich and handsome Duke.

As LAURA turns to look out of the window, the camera tracks and pans slowly forward until the darkened countryside fills the screen.

LAURA'S VOICE: I stared out of the railway carriage window into the dark and watched the dim trees and the telegraph posts slipping by, and through them I saw Alec and me.

The countryside fades away and ALEC and LAURA are seen, dancing a gay waltz. The noise of the train recedes, and is replaced by music.

LAURA'S VOICE: Alec and me—perhaps a little younger than we are now, but just as much in love, and with nothing in the way.

The sound of the train returns for a moment and the dancing figures fade away. The train noise dies away again, and is replaced by the sound of an orchestra tuning up, as the passing countryside changes to a picture of ALEC and LAURA in a theatre box. ALEC gently takes a beautiful evening cloak from her shoulders and hands her a programme and opera glasses.

LAURA'S VOICE: I saw us in Paris, in a box at the Opera. The orchestra was tuning up. Then we were in Venice—drifting along the Grand Canal in a gondola.

LAURA and ALEC are reclining in a gondola. There is the sound of lovely tenor voices and mandolins coming over the water. The scene changes to one of ALEC and LAURA in a car. They are driving through beautiful countryside, and the wind blowing LAURA's hair accentuates the feeling of speed.

LAURA'S VOICE: I saw us travelling far away together; all the places I have always longed to go.

We now see the rushing wake of a ship; then a ship's rail.

LAURA'S VOICE: I saw us leaning on the rail of a ship looking at the sea and the stars—standing on some tropical beach in the moonlight with the palm trees sighing above us. Then the palm trees changed into those pollarded willows by the canal just before the level crossing. . . .

The camera pulls back from the window of the railway compartment and pans to include LAURA.

LAURA'S VOICE: . . . and all the silly dreams disappeared, and I got out at Ketchworth and gave up my ticket. . . .

Dissolve to the booking hall and station yard of Ketchworth Station. LAURA gives up her ticket and walks away across the station yard.

LAURA'S VOICE: . . . and walked home as usual—quite soberly
and without any wings at all.

Dissolve to the interior of LAURA's bedroom. It is night time.
LAURA is seated at her dressing table. The camera shoots on to
the mirror of the dressing table.

LAURA'S VOICE: When I had changed for dinner and was doing
my face a bit—do you remember? I don't suppose you do,
but I do—you see you don't know that that was the first
time in our life together that I had ever lied to you—it
started then, the shame of the whole thing, the guiltiness,
the fear. . . .

[The reflection of FRED can be seen coming into the bedroom.
He comes forward and kisses LAURA lightly.

FRED: Good evening, Mrs. Jesson.

LAURA: Hullo, dear.

FRED: Had a good day?

LAURA: Yes, lovely.

FRED: What did you do?

LAURA: Well—I shopped—and had lunch—and went to the
pictures.

FRED: (*moving away*) All by yourself?

LAURA: (*in sudden panic*) Yes—no—that is, not exactly.]

● ● ● ● ●

CHILDREN OF PARADISE

A Tri-Colore Films-Korda Release of a Pathé Cinema Production. Director, Marcel Carné. Screenplay by Jacques Prévert. Music by Maurice Thiriet, in collaboration with Joseph Kosma; pantomime music, Georges Mouqué. Director of Photography, Roger Hubert. Cameraman, Marc Fossard. Sound, Robert Tesseire, Jacques Carrère. Art Director, Alexandre Trauner. Décor, Lucien Barsacq, Raymond Gabutti. Editors, Henri Rust, Madeleine Bonin. Production Manager, Fred Orain. Executive Producer, Raymond Borderie. 195 minutes. 1945.

CAST

GARANCE	Arletty
BAPTISTE DEBUREAU	Jean-Louis Barrault
FREDERICK LEMAÎTRE	Pierre Brasseur
PIERRE-FRANCOIS LACENAIRE	Marcel Herrand
JERICHO	Pierre Renoir
NATALIE	Maria Casares
ANSELME DEBUREAU	Etienne Decroux
AVRIL	Fabian Loris
MADAME HERMINE	Jeanne Marken
FIL DE SOIE, THE BLIND BEGGAR	Gaston Modot
COUNT EDWARD DE MONTERAY	Louis Salou
DEBT COLLECTOR	Guy Favière
THE POLICEMAN	Louis Florencie
THE TICKET SELLER	Lucien Walter
LITTLE BAPTISTE	Jean-Pierre Delmon

Children of Paradise, A Film by Marcel Carné, published screenplay by Jacques Prévert in the Classic Film Series by Simon & Schuster, translated from the French by Dinah Brooke, © 1968 Lorrimer Publishing Limited. Reprinted by permission of Lorrimer Publishing Limited.

58

"Les Enfants du Paradis," said its director, Marcel Carné, "is a tribute to the theatre; nowadays it would be known as the children of the gods; they are the actors, the beloved heroes of the public." The "gods" in the French theater of 1840 were the high, cheap balcony seats where the working class came to cheer, jeer, laugh, drink, and weep. Those up in the gods were the real lords of the house; their relationship to those down on the stage was a boisterous, intimate, and exacting one. Tumultuous crowds roamed the Boulevard du Temple each night, debating which attraction would be worth the cost of skipping their dinners. This street, home to theaters, jugglers, barkers, orchestras, and fire-eaters, was also known as the Boulevard du Crime. Murder was not unknown. Melodramas inside, intrigue outside. The stars weren't just loved in the streets; they came from—and in some cases still lived in—those streets.

The great silent poetry of movement was the province of the beloved mime Baptiste Debureau. The booming heroes of myth and legend were the swashbuckling vehicles for the antics of the adored actor, Frederick Lemaître. Behind corners, in the alleys, if a murder *was* in progress, it might well have been under the direction, and often the hand, of Pierre Lacenaire, a well-known criminal dandy of the Boulevard. All three men actually lived. *Children of Paradise* brings them together in a fictitious story that revolves around Garance, a woman who inspires the love of each of them. The word "Garance" is the name of a flower. With her ambiguous smile and seen-it-all eyes, seeming to beckon and renounce simultaneously, Garance is a centrifugal force of such ultimate mystery and beauty that her theatrical appearances require only that she silently pose, and whole stories and audiences gather themselves around her. The tone and atmosphere is rich and dense, as in Dickens or Hugo. The characters are also in the manner of the nineteenth-century novels—full-blooded archetypes (and here, *theatrical* ones: the Muse, the Pierrot, the Matinee Idol, the Fastidious Villain), playing out a vast story of passionate, sentimental, funny, crammed-with-detail, dangerous, romantic intensity. And above all, these characters are *performers* in the grand tradition in which their art roles and life roles transfuse. Their onstage selves bounce and reflect against their offstage selves, back and forth, until the vibration between them gels into the single, self-created, living poem each one performs as an individual destiny. The screenwriter of *Children of Paradise* was widely quoted as saying that "cinema and poetry are about the same thing."

The apex of artistry is embodied in Baptiste, the mime. When we first see him, he's the outcast of his father's troupe, dressed like an idiot, seated outside the Funambules (the mime theater). He's left there to amuse whoever cannot afford the price of admission. Garance is on a stroll. She stops to listen to Baptiste's father pitch the upcoming show inside. Accompanying her is Lacenaire, who, as always, wears his trademark—a beautifully elaborate, immaculately white shirtfront behind which crouches a heart of chilly, mercenary evil. He confides to Garance, "When my heart beats I delight in being the only one to hear it." Lacenaire runs a public letter-writing shop, where the illiterate pay him to put their official or passionate needs into written language. Of course the shop also serves as a front for stolen goods. The script notes of Lacenaire, "He expresses himself carefully, his bearing is distinguished, even elegant, but in his eyes are fleeting glimpses of a disturbing cruelty." While standing with Garance in front of the Funambules, Lacenaire picks a fat burgermeister-type's pocket and ambles off. The victim accuses Garance, who is left standing next to him. The policeman is all too ready to lock her up. But Baptiste has seen everything, and with a humor and grace that prefigures the great success he will someday enjoy, he silently acts out for the crowd the whole story, playing all the parts, of how the theft actually occurred. The crowd and Garance are enchanted. She asks the policeman if now she is free to go; when he reluctantly agrees, she says, "Good—because the only thing I really love is my freedom." She throws Baptiste her rose and disappears.

When Lacenaire learns that Garance never mentioned his name to the policeman, he is disappointed: "I'd have been so happy if you'd betrayed me a little, just a little." He promises her if necessary, he'll even help her to betray him: "It's a pity. We could have done remarkable things together. I would have caused oceans of blood to flow for you! . . . and rivers of diamonds!"

Baptiste takes nighttime walks, just "to see." He is befriended by a blind beggar who isn't really blind at all, and who conducts him to a low-down cafe where he finds Lacenaire and Garance.

When he overhears Garance, who is exhausted by Lacenaire's bitter tauntings, wishing she could dance, he offers himself to her as a partner. Lacenaire's henchman, a rather innocent thug named Avril, hurls Baptiste out through the window. With Little Tramp aplomb, Baptiste amazes everyone when he returns to retrieve Garance's rose which he had lost in the fray, and then he flattens Avril. In the first scene below, Baptiste escorts Garance home in the moonlight to the Grand Relais, the inn where he lives. He is too shy to spend the night with her, too in awe of what she inspires in him. It will be years before he has another chance, before he understands what she means when she tells him, "You mustn't be angry with me but I'm not... well, not how you dream of me. You must understand me—I'm simple— very simple..." Garance's real name is Claire, and that's precisely what she is—*clear*, to be believed for just what she appears to be, not for the projections she can inadvertently reflect. Garance is, in so many senses of the word, *unaffected*.

The room adjacent to Garance is occupied by Frederick Lemaître. He is at the beginning of his career, still unknown, "a handsome young man with a bright, malicious glance, who, although he is dressed in sober, even poor clothes, is extremely attractive and has a natural elegance." Frederick had earlier tried, unsuccessfully, to pick up Garance in the street, but she had checked his come-on by ironically reassuring him that he wasn't losing her forever: "For those who love each other with such a grand passion, Paris is very small!" Indeed, they remeet, and live together. Through Baptiste's growing influence at the Funambules, both Garance and Frederick are soon working with him in a pantomime, which not until he is actually performing it, does Baptiste realize is the staged parallel of their real-life situation. When we first saw Garance, she was playing "The Naked Truth" in a peep show, submerged to just below her shoulders in a rotating tub of water, absorbed in her own reflection in a hand mirror. Now, Baptiste has cast her as a statue of Phoebe, Goddess of the Moon, wearing a jeweled crescent in her hair. His character adores her, but she is a frozen dream, coolly reflecting back the light of his worshipping love. But when Frederick enters as Harlequin, the statue comes alive and he carries her off. The offstage relationship between Garance and Frederick, however, is collapsing. Frederick's entertainer's ego, however magnanimous and robust, is relentless. He is so extroverted he seems more a smörgasbord than a person. He heard

Garance in her sleep murmuring Baptiste's name. And he's restless and frustrated at the Funambules; he considers imposing the silence of mime on a talent such as his to be a desecration. He symbolically lifts his fingers from the jeweled crescent, and leaves Garance alone in her dressing room.

Enter Count Edward de Monteray, a wealthy, juiceless aristocrat, who presents himself to Garance in the second scene below. He is described as "about forty, very phlegmatic, and without a doubt accustomed to being heard and obeyed." Garance laughs him off, but soon she needs him. Lacenaire has moved into the Grand Relais under an alias, using her name as a reference. He invites to his room a debt collector under the pretext of squaring an overdue account and then tries to rob and murder the man. Lacenaire escapes. The landlady tells the police that Garance knows this "Mr. Forestier." Though Garance is ignorant of the entire affair, and protests so, the policeman is the same one from that day in front of the Funambules, and this is his chance to finally nail her. He is astonished when she hands him the card of Count Edward de Monteray and claims herself his special friend.

The story jumps ahead several years. Garance has returned with the Count from Scotland, where they have been living while he has been hunting. She found Scotland beautiful, but it was not Paris. Every night now she rents a private box at the Funambules and sits alone, veiled, watching Baptiste hypnotize *tout Paris* in *The Rag and Bone Man*, a pantomime which has catapulted him into the ranks of celebrity and genius. He is married to Natalie, who has loved him deeply from the start, and they have a little boy. But Baptiste's sorrow for the lost Garance transfigures his every movement; much of what illumines his presence on stage is this aura of the most exquisitely broken of hearts.

Frederick is now Paris's favorite personality star. He's contractually obligated to open in a turkey, which he saves on opening night by ad-libbing and hamming it up so wildly (leaping offstage into the authors' box and declaring them the real villains of the play), that he outrages the playwrights smack into a duel. He returns to his dressing room after the challenge has been issued to find Lacenaire waiting to meet him, in the third scene below. Time has only ripened Lacenaire's unbound insolence. He is enraged that Garance has returned, and that she is using her freedom as a gilded cage. She is no less amused by him, not any more disapproving of him, but not any more needing of him either, and he cannot stand it: "I would have been so much happier to see you spoiled, cheapened, disappointed, turned into an idiot by money! Like that I could have gone on living, with a good conscience, with my idea of what people are like."

Frederick is wounded in the duel. With his play euphemistically "in rehearsal" and his arm in a sling, he has an unexpected night off. He goes to see *The Rag and Bone Man,* to see what it is his old friend is doing that is occasioning such acclaim. The theater is completely sold out, but the ticket seller recognizes Frederick, and in honor of the good old days, begs pardon of a veiled lady, but wonders would it be alright, if just this once, a wounded gallant were to occupy the rear of her box. Thus Garance and Frederick are reunited for the first time in many years in the fourth scene below. She explains to him the secret of Baptiste's success: he is not acting, he is inventing dreams. Frederick knows he can't compete with that; it's devastating, certainly—but wait: isn't this jealousy just what he has been needing for Othello? To crown his career with this tragic hero, who has until now eluded him, isn't this the very feeling he has needed?!

Frederick triumphs in *Othello.* All Paris is there . . . climactically so. The Count, who has recently been apprised of Garance's true feelings just after Lacenaire insulted him in his own house, is visiting backstage at *Othello.* Lacenaire literally pulls open a curtain to reveal Garance and Baptiste, finally reunited, standing together in each others' arms. Baptiste and Garance have their one night together, but no more than that. Natalie pleads for her home and family, and Garance runs out into the teeming throngs of the Boulevard du Temple. Where to? No longer to Edward, who has been murdered by Lacenaire in the Turkish Baths. Who knows? Baptiste runs after, losing her in the crowded street.

SCENE 1

Outside it is night. The wall of Ménilmontant—empty and deserted in the darkness. A couple are walking slowly along in the background, following the wall where the BLIND BEGGAR had been sitting earlier. Long shot, then medium shot, with the camera tracking sideways and backwards in front of them.

GARANCE: (*looking at* BAPTISTE *and smiling*) All the same, looking at you one would never think you were so strong.

BAPTISTE: I'm not strong.

GARANCE: But—just now you knocked down that great bully!

BAPTISTE: I had a tough childhood. I had to learn to defend myself.

GARANCE stops to reply to BAPTISTE, and so does the camera.

GARANCE: You were unhappy.

BAPTISTE: (*medium close-up, full face*) When I was unhappy I slept. I dreamed...but people don't like it if you dream. (*Smiling.*) So they knock you about, as they say 'to wake you up a bit.' (*eyes bright, teeth clenched*) Luckily my sleep was tough, tougher than their blows, and I escaped them by dreaming. I dreamed...I hoped...I waited...

He turns towards GARANCE. Pan to a shot of both of them from the front. He takes her hand.

BAPTISTE: Perhaps it was for you that I was waiting.

GARANCE pulls away her hand gently and goes over to lean against the wall on the right, the camera panning to follow her.

GARANCE: (*ironic*) Already!

BAPTISTE has followed her. He is on her right, leaning only his hand on the wall. Close-up of BAPTISTE three-quarters view and GARANCE in profile half out of shot. Then a series of reverse shots favouring the one who is speaking.

BAPTISTE: (*very serious*) Why not? Perhaps I saw you in my dreams...don't smile at me. Today, when you threw me that flower, perhaps you woke me up for ever!

GARANCE: (*surprised and touched*) What a strange boy you are!

BAPTISTE: (gazing at her, enraptured) How beautiful you are!

GARANCE: (*shrugging her shoulders*) I'm not beautiful. I'm alive, that's all.

BAPTISTE: (*leaning his face close to hers, his voice trembling with emotion*) You are the most alive of all. I will never forget tonight, and the light of your eyes.

GARANCE: Oh, the light of my eyes! (*She smiles.*) Just a little flicker like everyone else! (*She takes him by the arm and makes a gesture of the head to indicate something in the distance.*) Look at all those little points of light. The lights of Ménilmontant. (*Cut to a long shot of Ménilmontant by night, with a few windows still alight; she continues off.*) People go to sleep, and wake up. Each one has a lamp that lights up and is put out. (*Cut back to her in close-up, full face, he is backview, half out of shot.*) When I think . . . (*Very melancholy*) . . . that I can't even recognise the room where I lived with my mother when I was little.

Series of reverse shots in medium close-up, favouring the one who is speaking.

BAPTISTE: You used to live in Ménilmontant?

GARANCE: I was born here, and I lived here happily for a long time. Very happily, . . . and yet my mother was poor, and my father had left her. She worked in other people's houses, as a laundress. (*Quick cut to him, and medium shot of them both. She takes a few steps; he follows her.*) She loved me and I loved her. She was beautiful, she was gay, . . . she taught me to laugh, and to sing. . . . (*Abruptly*) . . . Then she died, and everything changed.

BAPTISTE: (*camera on him*) So you were all alone?

GARANCE: (camera on her) At fifteen! (*She gestures towards Ménilmontant.*) Round here a girl who has grown up too fast doesn't stay alone very long.

Medium close-up of them both: BAPTISTE turns to face GARANCE, resting his right arm against the wall.

BAPTISTE: (*moved*) I beg you, don't be sad. It wrings my heart.

GARANCE: Sad, me? But I'm as gay as a lark. (*She bursts out laughing.*)

BAPTISTE: I love your laugh.

GARANCE: So do I . . . (*laughing*) . . . What would I do without it?

BAPTISTE: (*seriously*) And what would I do without you? (*She looks at him, astonished.*) Tell me your name?

GARANCE: Garance.

BAPTISTE: (*dreamily*) Garance!

GARANCE: (*staring at him*) But you're trembling. Are you cold?

Close-up of BAPTISTE full face, GARANCE half out of shot.

BAPTISTE: I'm trembling because I'm happy . . . and I'm happy because you are there . . . close to me . . . I love you . . . and you, Garance . . . do you love me?

Reverse shot. GARANCE puts her hand on BAPTISTE'S shoulder.

GARANCE: (*disturbed*) You talk like a child . . .

She caresses his hair, as he had caressed NATALIE'S.

GARANCE: In books people love like that, and in dreams—but in life! . . .

BAPTISTE, full face, in medium close-up, and GARANCE back view, half out of shot.

BAPTISTE: (*interrupting her abruptly*) Dreams and life are the same—or else it's not worth living. And then . . . what do you think I care about life? It's not life I love, it's you!

GARANCE: (*more and more disturbed, close-up*) You are the sweetest boy I've ever met. (*Leaning her face close to his.*) I won't forget tonight, either. (*Lowering her voice.*) I like you very much.

BAPTISTE: I love you.

They kiss. Then close-up of BAPTISTE. The two faces separate.

BAPTISTE: (*enraptured*) Garance!

GARANCE: (*camera on her, who, sure of herself, pulls him towards her again*) Love is so simple!

They kiss again.

Medium long shot of them against the wall, their silhouettes mingling. Suddenly, a flash of lightning lights up the sky, ... followed by a violent clap of thunder. GARANCE and BAPTISTE separate suddenly.

GARANCE: Heavens, a thunderstorm.

BAPTISTE, shocked out of his trance of love, looks at the sky, then ...

BAPTISTE: If it rains you'll get soaked, Garance!

GARANCE: What does that matter?

BAPTISTE: Your clothes are so thin ... Come on, come on, I'll take you back.

GARANCE: Where to?

BAPTISTE: To your home.

GARANCE: Home! (*She bursts out laughing.*) I haven't got a home!

BAPTISTE: (*medium close-up, full face*) Ah! ...

GARANCE full face, BAPTISTE half out of shot. Then series of reverse angle shots.

GARANCE: (*still smiling*) Yes ... I left my job, and the job and the room ... they went together. So!

BAPTISTE: If you like ... where I live ... I could find you a room ...

GARANCE: (*looking at him with a tender smile*) A room?

BAPTISTE: (*not understanding*) Yes ... Please, come on.

SCENE 2

STAGE MANAGER: Mademoiselle Garance, there's someone here who absolutely insists on seeing you!

Medium shot of the door, FREDERICK is about to go out, but is prevented by a huge bouquet of flowers which fills the whole doorway as it comes in. Cut back to medium shot of GARANCE, she seems very surprised, and stares up at the STAGE MANAGER.

GARANCE: What on earth are all these flowers? I don't believe it. Someone must be dead. (*She gets up slowly as she speaks.*)

Long shot of the dressing room shot slightly from above. The bouquet of flowers, carried by two little pages, is put down in the centre of the room in front of GARANCE who has taken a few steps forward. The two pages leave, followed by the STAGE MANAGER, and then FREDERICK. The camera pauses for a second on the empty doorway which is immediately filled by the figure of COUNT EDWARD, who comes forward, hiding his embarrassment and emotion beneath an impressive calm. He comes down the steps stiffly, playing with his cane in one hand as he speaks.

THE COUNT: Yes, Mademoiselle, someone is dead. A man who thought he was secure, who thought he understood himself. That man is dead, and you have killed him!

Close-up as he comes to the floral display and stops. GARANCE is standing on the opposite side of the flowers.

GARANCE: (*amused, but also a bit irritated*) Please, you're frightening me.

THE COUNT: (*facing the camera*) Don't be afraid; because of you, thanks to you . . . another man is born . . . a new man, who places his life in your hands.

Close-up of GARANCE, alone, as she sits down again, near the flowers. She smiles.

GARANCE: What do you expect me to do with it?

THE COUNT: Whatever you like.

He approaches her, as she sits with her back to the dressing table. Close-up of the two of them. He remains standing.

THE COUNT: I make myself your prisoner. Yes, you can do what you like with me. (*Becoming rather affected as he emphasises his words.*) All that I possess, and I possess much, all that belongs to me, I lay at your feet.

He leans down, takes her hand and kisses it. The camera moves in to a close-up of GARANCE, shot slightly from above. The COUNT is three-quarters back view, half out of the picture. She looks automatically at THE COUNT, then at her hand. As he begins to speak he is partly out of shot.

THE COUNT: Forgive me, Mademoiselle, but I have never been so moved, so overcome as I am at this moment. (*Low angle shot from her point of view of the* COUNT *facing the camera.*) I am expressing myself badly, I know. I repeat platitudes, trivialities. (*Tilt down on her.*) Anyway, what I say is of no importance! (*Cut back to him, feverish and excited.*) What is important, is what you are going to reply to me. One word, Mademoiselle, and your life can change completely. (*Cut back to her.*) Tomorrow, if you wish, the most beautiful women, the toasts of Paris . . . (*Cut back to him.*) . . . will bite their lips till they run with blood, just to hear your name mentioned. Beside yours, their rarest jewels will be as dull as coal. You will have the most splendid carriage—

GARANCE: (*camera on her*) I'm frightened of horses.

THE COUNT: (*camera on him—abashed*) Oh, please, don't say no.

GARANCE: (*camera on her*) But why do you want me to say yes if it gives me no pleasure?

THE COUNT: (*camera on him*) Say nothing then . . . let me hope!

Close-up of the two of them; as GARANCE speaks, she gets up and goes over to her screen; the camera pans to follow her, always keeping him in shot.

GARANCE: That's it; I'll be quiet, and you can talk away to yourself. And because you're moved, 'overcome', you'll go on talking 'platitudes' as you put it: diamonds, horses, bridles, hay and then the harness . . . you know, the grand life! (*She shrugs her shoulders.*)

Close-up of THE COUNT facing the camera. More and more taken aback and upset, he walks a few steps without replying. The camera comes back to GARANCE, in close-up, as she goes behind her screen. Her face can hardly be seen. She undresses as she

speaks, and hangs her costume over the edge of the screen. Cut
back to THE COUNT who sits down in a corner of the room on a
basket, facing the screen as seen by her.

GARANCE: Oh, if all that just fell from the skies and landed in
my lap perhaps I wouldn't say no. But, all the same, that
way of talking: 'One word and your whole life can
change' . . . I suppose that means that my life is nothing . . .
you're trying to say that my life is nothing at all! (*He does
not say a word, but seems to take in what she is saying,
though he does not show it; she becomes more agressive.*)
And what if I like my life, my own little life? I'm a big girl,
after all; I know what I'm saying and I know what I'm
doing. Whereas you, to look at you . . . (*Cut back to her as
she examines him coldly.*) . . . you may have a 'grand life',
but really, when one takes a good look at you, perhaps you
are only a little man; a very little man.

Close-up of THE COUNT, sitting, unperturbed, but slightly hurt all
the same.

THE COUNT: Never . . . you understand, never, has anybody ever
spoken to me like that!

GARANCE: (*shot of her behind the screen, putting on a dress*)
Nor to me, neither! . . . You mustn't be cross, but all the
same, you turn up, you decide what's going to be done with
me, you make your inventory . . . you find me attractive . . .
fine, everything's understood. (*She stops for a moment and
becomes dreamy.*) But what if somebody loves me?

THE COUNT: (*airy and sure of himself*) There's no question of it.
You are far too beautiful for anyone really to love you!
Beauty is an exception, an insult to the world . . . which is
ugly! It is exceedingly rare for a man to love beauty. They
simply buy it so that they won't have to hear about it any
more—to wipe it out and forget it.

GARANCE: (*off, she is hidden behind the screen*) Perhaps you're
a hunter?

THE COUNT: Don't make a mistake, Mademoiselle. I meant
every word that I said. I offered you a refuge, that is all!

Close-up of GARANCE, facing the camera as she comes round the edge of the screen buttoning the bodice of her dress.

GARANCE: A refuge?

Medium shot of THE COUNT playing with a cardboard roast chicken, one of the theatre props, which he has picked up. He is still sitting in his corner.

THE COUNT: Yes. (*feverish and a bit pathetic*) I've changed. I regret it, there's no doubt about that, but there's nothing I can do about it. Since I first saw you, I find myself indulging in absurd, childish daydreams! (*He gets up and paces up and down with a derisory little laugh.*) Perhaps I've got older—or perhaps it's what's called a 'coup de foudre'. (*shaking his head in medium close-up*) I don't exist any longer. I'm reduced to nothing, bound hand and foot; I have no will of my own; I'm no more than air and cardboard— like this chicken.

He looks at the chicken, and laughs again, more bitterly. Medium shot, facing the camera.

THE COUNT: A coup de foudre!... Yes! That's just what it is!

Suddenly and violently, he hurls the chicken towards the end of the room, with all his strength. The camera pans swiftly to follow the flight of the chicken in close-up as it hits the thunder sheet. There is a violent and prolonged clap of thunder. Medium long shot of GARANCE in her street clothes, facing the camera; long shot of the dressing room: they are facing each other, two or three yards apart.

GARANCE: And that's a clap of thunder. Three francs fine. (*She smiles.*)

THE COUNT comes closer.

THE COUNT: Forgive me, Mademoiselle. I realise that I've been indiscreet, importunate ...

In the background the STAGE MANAGER comes running in, mad with rage and stuttering threats.

STAGE MANAGER: But . . . but . . . who made that thunder? The old man is furious!

High angle long shot of the room as seen by the STAGE MANAGER; he is half out of shot in the foreground.

GARANCE: (*calm*) I did.

Medium shot of the STAGE MANAGER on the threshold.

STAGE MANAGER: (*grumbling as he tries to calm down*) All right, all right . . . You know the tariff. That's three francs! (*He goes out quickly.*)

Close-up of THE COUNT and GARANCE.

GARANCE: (*ironic*) You owe me three francs!

THE COUNT looks at her, speechless. She comes closer to him as she speaks. Pan in a slight curve to frame them again in medium close-up, one beside the other.

GARANCE: But there's no hurry, I'm working at the moment, and I've got enough to live on!

THE COUNT: (*more and more disturbed*) Enough to live on! I hope you're telling the truth, Mademoiselle. But let me withdraw, and if I have seemed ridiculous to you, you mustn't judge me too harshly. Your beauty alone is the cause of my confusion. (*with a sigh*) And I haven't even introduced myself yet!

Out of his waistcoat pocket he takes a card which he holds out to GARANCE.

THE COUNT: It's incredible! (*He bows and straightens himself as he declaims his identity.*) Count Edward de Monteray. Please, Mademoiselle, keep my card. You never know. Misfortune doesn't always choose which door it knocks at, and one day you may need help, protection. In that case, and whatever happens, do not forget that I am your devoted slave, body and soul, and that you can have the most absolute confidence in me.

He bows again, one last time, and cold and phlegmatic, walks towards the door. The camera follows him: he climbs the stairs, and the camera reveals BAPTISTE who comes in and stares after this unusual visitor. THE COUNT, ignoring him completely, goes out.

(*Note:* The thunder effect, if not possible in the acting studio, can be replaced by some other disturbance—a fired prop pistol, a prop chicken flung against a gong—as long as it's loud enough.)

SCENE 3

Medium shot of the door of FREDERICK's dressing room: FREDERICK, happy to be alone, shuts the door and locks it, and heaves a sigh of relief . . . But he is immediately on the alert again.

LACENAIRE: (*off*) Wise precaution!

Stupefied, FREDERICK turns towards the voice. The camera pans to follow his look to frame LACENAIRE, in medium shot, sitting at a table laid for supper for several people. He plays, negligently, with his cane; his linen is, as always, dazzlingly white (special lighting effect) but his clothes are smarter and newer than they used to be. His features are drawn, and his face has aged far too rapidly.

Cut back to FREDERICK absolutely dumbfounded to find this man here, comfortably installed as if he was in his own home, examining him with curiosity and a tight smile.

FREDERICK: How did you get in?

The camera pans rapidly towards what LACENAIRE is holding in his hands—Phoebe's crescent. Pan back again to FREDERICK who leaps forwards; close medium shot of the two of them, FREDERICK standing, LACENAIRE sitting, very relaxed.

FREDERICK: Leave that alone! . . . (*He seizes it.*) . . . It's a souvenir.

LACENAIRE: (*letting go of the object with affected indifference*) Perhaps it's also a souvenir for me . . . who knows?

FREDERICK: (*beside himself*) Impossible! You must be either drunk or mad. And first of all, what are you doing here? Who are you?

LACENAIRE: (*very calm*) My name wouldn't mean anything to you. And since you are famous enough for two, let's leave aside the introductions, and go straight to the object of my visit. Here it is in three words—I need money.

FREDERICK: (*put out of countenance*) So does everyone else, you know.

LACENAIRE: (*smiling*) More or less.

As he speaks, FREDERICK, followed by the camera in close shot, goes to put Phoebe's crescent back on the wall.

FREDERICK: Perhaps, but I must admit that I don't quite see why you come to me, when I don't know you at all.

LACENAIRE: (*playing with his cane*) That doesn't matter in the least since I know you. Since the whole of Paris knows you!

FREDERICK followed by the camera again comes back to the table and picks up a cold chicken; he tears it apart with his hands, and voraciously begins on a leg as he speaks.

FREDERICK: (*trying to be modest*) You're very polite, but I'm afraid you're exaggerating.

LACENAIRE: (*off*) You are already famous . . . and obviously rich . . . (*Shot of him*) . . . Isn't that a sufficient reason for a man who's down and out to come to you, quite simply, and ask for what he needs.

FREDERICK: (*standing up and eating*) Down and out?

LACENAIRE: (*icy and definite*) It's a question of life or death.

FREDERICK: (*sitting down at the table and pouring himself a drink*) Honestly?

LACENAIRE: Do I look as if I'm joking?

FREDERICK: (*looking at him, his mouth full*) No! (*He takes another swig of his drink.*) Listen, I'm far from rich! I can assure you! (*He gets up, rubs his hands and leans down towards his topcoat.*) But perhaps you've been sent by Fate.

(*He laughs.*) Because last week I had a win on the lottery, and I haven't spent it all yet. You're in luck!

He takes the money out of his pocket and approaches LACENAIRE, who is still sitting. Shot of the two of them, FREDERICK standing facing the camera, and LACENAIRE three-quarters back view.

FREDERICK: Of course, if you were my friend, my brother, I'd say here you are, take the lot . . . (*Showing a wad of money*) . . . it's yours. But since I have only had the honour of meeting you, I say to you, we'll share it.

He divides the money in two, holds out half to LACENAIRE, and puts the rest in his pocket.

FREDERICK: If this sum can be of any use to you . . . (*gently ironic*) . . . quite simply, accept it.

Close shot of LACENAIRE, facing the camera, with FREDERICK half out of the picture. LACENAIRE gets up and takes the money as if it was his by right.

LACENAIRE: Thank you. (*Then he looks at FREDERICK without being able to hide his surprise. Sitting down.*) You astonish me. Actors are reputed to be very mean, especially great actors.

FREDERICK: (*medium close-up, amused*) Well, that's splendid!

The camera pans to follow FREDERICK; he breaks off a piece of bread and goes on eating.

FREDERICK: There's still room for improvement!

LACENAIRE: (*close shot*) Your profession is a very strange one.

Close reverse angle shot of FREDERICK facing the camera; he takes a piece of meat off the table and begins to eat it.

FREDERICK: The most glorious of all!

LACENAIRE: (*dreamily*) Perhaps, but it's very surprising, this ability to make people's hearts beat faster at exactly the same time every evening!

FREDERICK sits down and goes on eating.

FREDERICK: (*becoming more and more lyrical*) You don't understand anything about it. That's exactly what is so beautiful, so intoxicating about it; to feel one's heart and the hearts of the audience beating together!

LACENAIRE: (*more and more distant*) What promiscuity. As for me, when occasionally my heart begins to beat, it beats so strongly that there is a quite particular sensuality in knowing that I am the only one to hear it.

FREDERICK: (*ironic, emptying his glass*) May one ask what the possessor of such a heart does in the world?

LACENAIRE: (*in profile*) If I told you, you would find it difficult to believe. In my spare time I write plays.

Medium close-up of FREDERICK eating: he has a reflex of disappointment, and replies, with a certain aggressiveness.

FREDERICK: Ah, you are an author! . . . and of course you're not well-known.

LACENAIRE: (*not in the least put out*) Yes, unknown. (*He gets up and comes over to* FREDERICK *who is eating and drinking.*) But it doesn't worry me in the least. I write light, delicate little pieces . . . (*He walks round* FREDERICK.) . . . and these days people prefer melodramas! (*He stops close to* FREDERICK *and smiles; close shot of both of them.*) But I have done one thing which I'm weak enough to be rather fond of. One simple little act full of gaiety and melancholy. Two young things who love each other, lose each other, find each other and lose each other again . . . Décor in delicate green, a garden, a fountain!

FREDERICK: (*in order to say something*) Well, how interesting. (*High angle shot of him looking at* LACENAIRE *who is three-quarters backview and half out of shot.*) But look, you can tell me now, since we know each other a little better. (*He picks his teeth with a fingernail.*) Just between us two, this business about the money, was it really a question of life or death?

Series of reverse angle shots: LACENAIRE low angle, FREDERICK high angle.

LACENAIRE: (*icy*) Yes. For you.

FREDERICK: (*surprised*) For me?

LACENAIRE: Yes—if you had had the imprudence to refuse. (*He half opens his topcoat and shows, sticking out of an interior pocket the handle of a dagger.*) . . . And I can promise you that the blade doesn't slide into the handle!

High angle shot of FREDERICK, LACENAIRE half out of shot, more and more dumbfounded: suddenly he bursts into laughter, bending right over, and hitting his chest.

FREDERICK: And you think that Frederick would have let you do whatever you wanted?

FREDERICK gets up; they are facing each other in close shot.

LACENAIRE: (*very calm*) Yes, because I did not come alone. (*He turns towards the back of the dressing room.*) Avril! . . .

Close shot of the curtain which is pushed aside. AVRIL comes towards the camera, with his flower in his mouth and his blissful smile.

Medium shot of all three, with the table between them.

FREDERICK: Well, I'll be . . . (*Nodding his head, suddenly delighted.*) Unbelievable! It's exactly the 'Brigands Inn'.

LACENAIRE: (*more and more serious, speaking to* AVRIL) Well, Avril, are you satisfied?

AVRIL: (*staring at* FREDERICK *with great round eyes*) Oh, yes, I'm satisfied!

LACENAIRE: (*to* FREDERICK) I must tell you that this great oaf has the deepest admiration for you. And the idea of . . . (*He makes a gesture signifying robbery and murder.*)

AVRIL: Yes, it made me feel sick!

FREDERICK: (*more and more delighted*) Really? I'm delighted to find that there are good fellows in every profession. (*To* AVRIL.) So what did you think of the show tonight, the 'brigands'—did you like it?

AVRIL: (*blushing*) Er . . .

LACENAIRE: Don't press him, he's a boy who is modest about his feelings.

FREDERICK: And you? Were you in the audience?

LACENAIRE: Yes.

FREDERICK: Well?

LACENAIRE: It's interesting . . . of course, I don't want to criti-
cise, but . . .

FREDERICK: (*interrupting him happily*) Please. It's not every day
that one can have the advice of a specialist . . . a connois-
seur. It's marvellous . . . unhoped for. You must both do me
the pleasure of dining with me. I had prepared a little dinner
for the authors, but now . . .

FREDERICK takes off his hat and invites them both to sit down.

AVRIL: (*embarrassed*) Oh! . . . Monsieur Frederick!

LACENAIRE: You're very kind, but we don't wish to force our
company on you. Perhaps you want to sleep?

FREDERICK: Sleep, no. But I'm as hungry as a wolf! . . . (*tapping
on* AVRIL'*s shoulder*) . . . Come on, sit down and no fuss.

LACENAIRE: If you insist.

Medium shot of the three of them sitting down. FREDERICK
immediately picks up a bottle of champagne and uncorks it.

FREDERICK: Anyway, I have to fight a duel in the morning, and I
must keep up my strength. (*They all shout with laughter as
the champagne spurts out in an arc, right across frame.*) It
must be disagreeable to die hungry.

LACENAIRE: You're fighting a duel? Who with?

Medium close-up of LACENAIRE interested, with FREDERICK half
out of the picture, drinking and replying.

FREDERICK: With an imbecile!

LACENAIRE: I hope you intend to kill him?

FREDERICK: Oh, if one could kill all the imbeciles!

LACENAIRE: (*dreaming*) Absolutely. (*With a deep sigh, he unfolds his serviette.*) And, after all, it would simplify an awful lot of things!

SCENE 4

[In a corridor of the '*Theatre des Funambules*', the camera tracks backwards in front of FREDERICK and the TICKET SELLER. Music sounds faintly in the background.

TICKET SELLER: (*continuing his story*) Exactly, a young society woman who comes every evening, alone, no one knowing who she is . . . (*he winks*) . . . to see Baptiste.

FREDERICK: Lucky Baptiste! (*Interested.*) Is she pretty?

TICKET SELLER: (*making a gesture in front of his face*) Can't tell. She wears a veil. She comes and she goes, without seeing anyone.

He stops in front of the door of the box. So does the camera. He knocks, and without waiting for a reply opens the door. Medium shot of the box, the TICKET SELLER, FREDERICK in the background. The TICKET SELLER speaks to someone out of shot.

TICKET SELLER: Do you mind, Madame? Just for once. A chair at the back for someone who is wounded.

Reverse angle shot: the box in medium shot as seen from the stage. The 'person', a young woman, dressed very elegantly, with a low décolletage, is recognisable in spite of her veil. It is GARANCE. She neither turns round nor replies. The TICKET SELLER, behind her, makes a sign to FREDERICK to sit down.

TICKET SELLER: (*in a low voice*) It's all right.

FREDERICK: (*also in a low voice*) Thanks.]

The camera moves backwards to show the box and a part of the auditorium. FREDERICK who has not recognized GARANCE, leans forward discreetly to get a better look at this mysterious creature. Suddenly, medium shot of both of them facing the camera. He jumps.

FREDERICK: Garance!

Medium close-up of GARANCE full face, with FREDERICK half out of the picture.

GARANCE: (*surprised*) Frederick? . . . What are you doing here?

Reverse angle shot: FREDERICK in medium close-up, full face; GARANCE half out of shot.

FREDERICK: (*smiling and debonair*) Paris is small for those who love each other as we do . . . (*Suddenly, he interrupts himself.*) But I don't believe it Garance—you treat me like a stranger—you call me "vous"?

Series of reverse angle shots according to the dialogue.

GARANCE: (*very sweet and a little wearily*) Don't be angry. It's a very long time since I said "tu" to anyone.

FREDERICK: (*coming closer to* GARANCE) Oh! Desdemona, perfidious creature, who left me, one fine day, in the middle of the street. 'See you this evening, Frederick.' And she disappears for years. (*Nodding his head.*) And when she decides to reappear she asks innocently, as if I was a stranger, 'What are you doing here?' But I am here because I never went away. I knew that you would come back, and I've waited here, sitting on this chair, for years!

GARANCE: (*smiling*) You haven't changed, Frederick.

FREDERICK: (*moving closer*) Nor have you, Garance. Or rather, yes. (*Leaning down towards her.*) You've changed. You are even more desirable than before. And I don't know, you're more, more . . .

GARANCE: (*with sudden tenderness in her voice*) More sophisticated, isn't that what you mean? (*without waiting for a reply*) But what's the matter with your arm? You're wounded?

FREDERICK: It's three times nothing and it's better already. (*Suddenly more serious and regarding* GARANCE *with severity.*) There are other wounds that take longer to heal. (*Close* *shot of both of them favouring* FREDERICK. GARANCE *is staring at him fixedly*.) Only wounds to one's self-respect, perhaps, but wounds all the same! (*abruptly*) It was with that man, Desdemona, that man with his arms laden with flowers, that you disappeared, wasn't it? And where did you go? Where did he take you, this Nabob? To India, perhaps?

Reverse angle shot favouring GARANCE; FREDERICK is three-quarters backview.

GARANCE: (*with the utmost naturalness*) It's true, I did go to India. But I didn't stay there very long. I lived for most of the time in England . . . in Scotland.

FREDERICK: (*bitterly*) I suppose it's beautiful, Scotland?

GARANCE: Yes, it's beautiful. But it's a long way away. And Paris is the only place I love.

Medium shot of both of them facing the camera.

FREDERICK: (*ironic, lowering his voice*) Paris and its memories! . . . Baptiste, for instance. Baptiste, whom you come here to see every evening.

She shrugs her shoulders without replying, and looks dreamily towards the stage.

FREDERICK: Are you asking me to believe you don't know Frederick Lemaître, too, is on stage every evening?

She looks at FREDERICK for a moment, and then turns back to the stage. General shot in the direction of the stage. The curtain has just risen, and the décor represents a little square. It is evening. On the right, a house with a flight of steps leading up to the entrance. On the first floor, in the frame of the windows which are very brightly lit, the clear-cut shadows of dancing couples are thrown, like in the Chinese puppet theatres. A carriage, drawn by an ingenious model horse, stops in front of the door: elegantly dressed guests get out.

Various general shots of the auditorium, full to bursting, the stall and boxes as well as the Gods.

Cut back to the stage, still in long shot, as seen from the stalls. Another carriage stops in front of the entrance to the house. The 'DUCHESS' (NATALIE), sumptuously dressed, gets out, while BAPTISTE, who is clinging on to the back of the carriage jumps down as well. The DUCHESS goes into the house. BAPTISTE, in transports of love, follows her in without hesitation—to come out again immediately, thrown plumb into the middle of the square by two FLUNKEYS in livery, who go back inside after having dusted off their hands, to express disgust. Medium long shot of the Gods: the audience shout with laughter. Close shot of GARANCE and FREDERICK facing the camera. GARANCE raises her shining eyes to the gallery and smiles nostalgically.

GARANCE: Listen to them up in the Gods, Frederick! (*gently shaking her head*) I used to laugh like that once. Yes, I used to burst out laughing, for no reason, without thinking of anything, just laughing. (*She sighs.*) And now!

FREDERICK: Are you sad?

GARANCE: (*turning towards* FREDERICK) No, but I'm not gay either. (*smiling a melancholy smile*) A little spring has broken in the music box. (*She turns round to the stage again.*) The melody is still the same, but the tone is different.

FREDERICK looks at GARANCE, and then turns towards the stage. Medium long shot of the stage: BAPTISTE gets up slowly. Not knowing what to do, he stares enviously at the beautifully dressed guests, who are going into the house. He compares their clothes to his own, and sinks into despair. A man passes, to put out the street lamps, and BAPTISTE is left alone, lit only by the lights from the ballroom where silhouettes representing the dancing guests twist round and round.

Quick cut, reverse angle shot, then medium shot of the Gods; the spectators are all silent and attentive.

Cut back to the stage: a call on the trumpet makes BAPTISTE jump.* BAPTISTE's face expresses joy and hope; he turns towards

---

*The script allowed for the cry of the Old Clothes Man, off—'Chand d'Habits, Chand d'Habits!' which was not really a heresy because this cry would have been the only words pronounced and those not even on stage, and it was intended by the author (Cot d'Ordan), but Carné and Barrault preferred to keep the mime as pure and silent as possible.

the trumpet call. The camera pans to frame the arrival of the OLD CLOTHES MAN (a role played by ANSELME DEBUREAU, dressed in a costume inspired by that of Jericho). BAPTISTE goes to meet him. The OLD CLOTHES MAN stops, happy to find a client so late. BAPTISTE chooses a marvellous apple green frock coat, and a superb pair of 'Cossack' breeches; but when it comes to paying he admits that he does not have a sou. Quick cuts to various parts of the audience, which is shrieking with laughter.

Close shot of GARANCE and FREDERICK; the latter leans over to GARANCE.

FREDERICK: He really is marvellous!

General shot of the stage: the OLD CLOTHES MAN is furious, and wants to go on his way, but BAPTISTE begs him for the clothes and, clinging to him, desperately pulls out of its scabbard an old National Guard sabre that the OLD CLOTHES MAN was carrying peaceably under his arm. The two men are face to face; the OLD CLOTHES MAN is terrified, and BAPTISTE carried away by what seems to be the intervention of fate, throws a glance towards the window of the ballroom to give himself courage. Quick cut to a general shot of the audience: they are holding their breath. Cut back to a medium long shot of the stage; the OLD CLOTHES MAN, terrified, staggers back before BAPTISTE who advances menacingly, his expression suddenly quite different, and very frightening. Close shot of FREDERICK and GARANCE.

GARANCE: It's funny, he is gentleness itself! How can he look so cruel?

Cut back to the stage. Suddenly BAPTISTE plunges the blade into the body of the OLD CLOTHES MAN, who collapses on the ground.* BAPTISTE stands immobile, his eyes wide, in front of the body of the OLD CLOTHES MAN.

FREDERICK: (*close-up*) What a technique!

GARANCE: (*close-up*) Baptiste has no technique; he's not acting; he's inventing dreams!

Close shot of both of them facing the camera.

---

*Translator's Note: At one point during the writing of the script, Carné and Barrault wanted to show Deburau so involved in this part that he ends by killing the real Jericho.

FREDERICK: (*slightly bitter, leaning over towards* GARANCE) You love him, don't you?

GARANCE: (*in a low voice full of tenderness*) Since the first day I left, not a single day has passed when I didn't think of him!

FREDERICK stares at GARANCE with a hostility which is quite new to him, then he turns away again to look at the show. The camera follows his look to frame the stage in long shot, as seen from the box. At last BAPTISTE decides to drag the body of the OLD CLOTHES MAN into the wings, like an animal dragging a victim into his lair. Very long shot of the stage seen from the back of the auditorium. Applause bursts out, some spectators stand up to clap more easily, while in the background the curtain falls. Bustle in the auditorium, and the atmosphere of the beginning of the interval.

[[Immediately, sellers of food and sweets, and waiters with their trays surge into the auditorium crying their wares.

SALESMEN: Fifteen minutes interval! Ask for the programme . . . Caramels, boiled sweets . . . beer, lemonade, white wine. Here are hot apple turnovers, still steaming.

(In fact, the sequence ends with a quick high angle shot of the auditorium, but the salesmen are not particularly visible. The cries, which were not filmed, had been dubbed into the original soundtrack.)]]

Fade out. Close shot of the box from the front: FREDERICK looks at GARANCE, shaking his head; then he questions her.

FREDERICK: And does he know that you come here to see him?

GARANCE: No. He has his life and I have mine . . . so what good would it be?

Medium close-up of FREDERICK; he looks at GARANCE, off screen, for a long time; then his face expresses the most profound astonishment.

FREDERICK: Oh! It's unbelievable, what's happening to me! It's enough to make you turn inside out . . . to burst!

GARANCE: (*quick close-up*) What's the matter?

FREDERICK: (*medium close-up of him, she half out of shot*) I think I'm jealous. No, I don't know . . . I've never felt anything like it. It's heavy, it's unpleasant. It gets hold of you by the heart . . . The head wants to defend itself . . . and . . . hop! it's gone, with the rest of them!

Reverse angle shot of GARANCE, who is staring blankly at FREDERICK, silent. Then close-up of the two of them: FREDERICK moves his face close to GARANCE; he talks almost into her ear, but never stops staring into her eyes.

FREDERICK: Do you hear, Garance . . . there, just a moment ago, I was jealous, because of Baptiste, because of you . . . yes, I was jealous! . . . So then, in one fell swoop, regrets flew in! That man, that traveller, who took you away, and I who let you go! And with it all, to make sense out of it all, Baptiste, who acts like a god! Oh, believe me, I didn't want him to act like a pig, but after all, do you understand, if he could have been . . .

GARANCE: (*interrupting*) Yes, I understand. Just a little bit bad.

FREDERICK: Bad, no! But, well . . . mediocre. That would have made me feel better. (*He smiles.*) Well, there's one piece of luck, when you talk it stops. (*He sighs.*)

GARANCE: You see—it's not so serious. Just a little spasm . . . you're cured already.

Medium shot: FREDERICK stands up. His face lights up again, he is inspired. The camera pans to follow him in close shot as he walks up and down the box, talking.

FREDERICK: Cured! Why do you want me to be cured so quickly? And what if it pleased me, if it was useful for me to be jealous . . . useful and even necessary? (*Suddenly feverish and exalted.*) Thank you, Garance. (*Close-up of her still sitting down, imperturbable. He continues, off.*) Thanks to you, thanks to all of you, I shall be able to play Othello! (*Cut back to him.*) I have been trying to find the character, but I didn't feel him. He was a stranger. (*He chuckles.*) There it is, now he's a friend, he's a brother. I know him...I have him in my grasp! (*He goes to the far end of the box and raises his arms to heaven.*) Othello!...(*Cut to* GARANCE, *and resume on him.*) The dream of my life...(*He comes back towards her and leans down; shot of the two of them.*) After you, Desdemona, of course, I shall clasp Baptiste to my heart, at least I owe him that, eh? Do you want me to tell him anything from you?

GARANCE: Really, Frederick!

FREDERICK: Oh, I'm speaking seriously. I'm jealous, it's true, but I understand how things are, and then he's married, he has a child, that consoles me! While the other...(*He stands upright again.*) Ah, the other!...the other!...(*A pause, then, smiling*)...Well, Garance?

GARANCE: (*close-up; after a hesitation*) Tell him something about me. And if you see that he seems interested, tell him that I am passing through Paris, that I'm leaving again soon, and that I would be happy, so happy, if he came to say hello.

Close shot of FREDERICK near the door of the box; he agrees, smiling, with a nod, and goes out.

THE BIG SLEEP

A Warner Bros. Production. Producer & Director, Howard Hawks. Screenplay by William Faulkner, Leigh Brackett, Jules Furthman. Based upon the novel *The Big Sleep* by Raymond Chandler. Photography, Sid Hickox. Film Editor, Christian Nyby. Art Director, Carl Jules Weyl. Set Decoration, Fred M. MacLean. Music, Max Steiner. Special Effects, E. Roy Davidson. Assistant Directors, Robert Vreeland, Chuck Hansen. Running time, 114 minutes. 1946.

CAST

PHILIP MARLOWE	Humphrey Bogart
VIVIAN RUTLEDGE	Lauren Bacall
CARMEN STERNWOOD	Martha Vickers
GENERAL STERNWOOD	Charles Waldron
NORRIS	Charles D. Brown
ARTHUR GEIGER	Theodore Von Eltz
JOE BRODY	Louis Jean Heydt
AGNES	Sonia Darrin
CAROL LUNDGREN	Thomas Rafferty
WILDE	Thomas Jackson
BERNIE OHLS	Regis Toomey
GIRL IN BOOKSTORE	Dorothy Malone
EDDIE MARS	John Ridgely
MONA MARS	Peggy Knudsen

Yeah, money talks, all right. It talks and its breath
smells of blood.

The line has it all—tough, pungent, slangy-poetic, the
imagery just a little too close for comfort, the temperature turned
up just a little too high. It's Raymond Chandler's vision of a
sinister, sleazy-baroque Los Angeles in the 1930's and 1940's, a
world of exotic greenhouses, kinky killers, and dangerous,
desirable women with expensively padded chips on their shoulders. Through its snares moves Philip Marlowe, a private detective. Though Marlowe knows the boys down at the D.A.'s office
and can work with them, he's basically a loner who works
through them or around them. Marlowe ends up in greatest
danger looking for answers to his own questions, long after his
satisfied client has paid and no longer wants *any* more questions
asked or answered. Marlowe is described in the script as "husky,
confident, well-dressed but not flashy, 38 years old—unmarried."
Marlowe is not unwilling to fall in love; sometimes, it can't be
helped. But his principal relationship is with his own decency,
and it becomes Marlowe's full-time job to corner the whole truth
in the labyrinth of curlicued evil. He must stay incorruptible and
not expect credit for it—a gentleman tough-guy.

The plot line of the film adaptation of *The Big Sleep* is so
serpentine that its director has been quoted as saying he thought
they made a fine film, but he certainly "never figured out what was
going on." It all begins when, through a referral from the District
Attorney's office, Philip Marlowe is asked up to the estate of the
oil-wealthy, wheelchair-bound General Sternwood. The General is a
proud, wrecked hulk of a man, obviously dying. His constitution is
by now so fragile that he receives Marlowe politely enough, with
spirits cart and butler, but inside his steaming orchid hothouse. He
insists his sweating guest enjoy a generous drink, although his own
health prohibits him from joining. Marlowe is touched by the
cracked valor propping itself up before him.

Sternwood is a widower with two daughters. Carmen, the
younger, has run up some illegal gambling debts. The General
shows Marlowe her promissory notes, mailed to him with the
card of an "Arthur Gwynne Geiger, Rare Books and de Luxe
Editions." Carmen is described in the script as about twenty
years old, with "something hot and sullen about her . . . always
biting the thumb." Before Marlowe had even entered the green-
house and met her father, Carmen had managed to corner Marlowe

and tried to sit in his lap. The elder sister, Mrs. Vivian Rutledge, is a more aloof, less impulsive type. She first has the butler show Marlowe up to her bedroom. She's all dressed up, insolently lounging. Then she tries to grill him; he insolently lounges right back at her, refusing to hand over a summary of his meeting with her father. Marlowe senses her genuine concern for her father and sister, even if both women seem to spend most of their time, and their father's money, breaking the old man's heart. Vivian is described in the script as "spoiled, exacting, smart, ruthless, with a habit for getting married. She is beautiful, giving the impression of strong will, and strong emotions, the dangerous, unpredictable type." (Elsewhere in the script, however, it's mentioned that she was just married once, but it didn't take.) The day after this initial meeting, Vivian arrives at Marlowe's office in the first scene below. She has just received photographs of Carmen for which someone is trying to blackmail the Sternwoods.

The sisters' scandals in the past were cleaned up for the General by a man named Shawn Regan, an ex-rum-runner and ex–Irish Republican Army brigade commander. According to Marlowe, who knew him slightly, Regan was a man good at whatever he did. It was said Shawn had been hired by Sternwood to do the old man's drinking for him once Sternwood could no longer do it himself. Whatever their roles—whoever was doing the drinking or the paying—the two men were friends, and when Regan disappeared, Sternwood was devastated. As the mess deepens around Marlowe's investigation of the Geiger blackmailing, it's suggested to Marlowe by several different people that the real reason Sternwood has hired him is to make sure that the missing Shawn Regan has nothing to do with it. Once it becomes clear that Regan is not involved, General Sternwood pays Marlowe and doesn't want to know any more. But Marlowe needs to know what happened to Regan, and a few people need to make sure Marlowe never finds out.

After meeting the General, Marlowe goes to Geiger's book store. It's a complete sham. A hostile, illiterate blonde named Agnes fronts at the reception desk. A back room is used to move hot and/or pornographic goods. Unless Marlowe is pretending to be a customer, there never is one. He observes Joe Brody, Agnes's boyfriend, darting in and out of the back room. He also catches a glimpse of Carol Lundgren, the punk pretty-boy "employed" by Geiger. The boss is described as "fattish, soft all over—a Charlie Chan moustache, his left eye is glass."

Marlowe tails Geiger to his home. Staked out at night in the rain (one of *film noir*'s favorite atmospheres), Marlowe waits and watches Geiger's house, when suddenly, "a hard white flash of light shoots out . . . like a flash of lightning. Close on its heels comes a woman's thin, half-pleasurable scream." Someone can be heard running away on the other side of the house. Inside, amid bad-taste pseudo-Orientalia, Marlowe finds Carmen stoned and Geiger dead. Some recently used photographic plates are missing from a camera pointing at Carmen, who appears to have a man's dressing gown hastily tossed over her naked body. He takes Carmen home, but when he returns to Geiger's house, the corpse is gone. The following day Vivian will receive the photographs of her sister, courtesy of Agnes and Joe. She brings the photos to Marlowe, but she will also try to pay off Brody herself. Brody already received $5,000 from the Sternwoods a year ago to leave Carmen alone. It was also last year that Carmen had run off with Owen Taylor, the Sternwood chauffeur who wanted to marry her, but then both of them had been returned to the estate in their original capacities. Now, Taylor and the car suddenly disappear. A few days later, car and chauffeur are dredged up out of the ocean just off the Lido pier. Then, with Marlowe right there, Joe Brody is killed by an unseen gun. Marlowe gives chase, captures Carol Lundgren, and turns him over to the authorities. The District Attorney, Wilde, verifies with Marlowe that all the pieces fit together as follows:

> So Taylor killed Geiger because he was in love with the Sternwood girl. And Brody followed Taylor, sapped him and took the photograph and pushed Taylor into the ocean. And the punk [Lundgren] killed Brody because the punk thought he should have inherited Geiger's business and Brody was throwing him out.

The second scene below concludes with the death of Carmen, and then the silent entrance and sudden death of Eddie Mars. Who is Eddie Mars? He is the operator of the Cypress Club out at Las Olindas where Vivian seems to regularly drop a lot of money gambling. When she does win, however, she is held up by Mars's gunmen in the parking lot. Marlowe is there to foil the "robbers," but he senses that it is all a charade for blackmail payments from Vivian to Mars, although not until the second scene below will he understand fully the ambiguities of Eddie and Vivian's connection. Marlowe knows that Vivian was drawn to Shawn, and also that Mars's wife Mona disappeared two days after Regan disappeared. But they did not, despite the gossip, run off together. On the contrary, Mona has been in hiding because such a rumor keeps at bay any suspicion that Eddie was responsible for Regan's disappearance. Mona is a very beautiful and loyal woman who will be forced to learn that she has been very naive about her husband's character. Mars's manner is iced over with an aggressive/defensive cordiality which barely conceals the man's strike capacity. Not that Eddie Mars ever dirties his own hands—he's got henchmen who've knocked Marlowe around on more than one occasion when Marlowe has moved in too close to the truth about Shawn Regan. Vivian knows just how dangerous Mars can be, and she wants Marlowe to leave off trying to find Regan. She even lies, saying that she accidentally killed Regan; and then another time, she says that Regan has been found alive in Mexico and that she is going there to meet him. But Marlowe knows better. He tells Vivian that even if it gets him killed, he will find out what happened to Shawn Regan, since by now even her father has admitted to Marlowe that he, too, wants to know. Vivian tells Marlowe that this may be the first moment she actually *likes* him, and then walks out the door. We then cut to the second scene below.

Vivian and Carmen have both been trying for Marlowe since the beginning of the story. Carmen's weird baby-doll come-ons have repulsed Marlowe. But he has definitely been sparked by Vivian's cool, sharp edge, and the loyalty beneath. Nonetheless, Marlowe suspects that if Mars kills him, it will probably be with Vivian's help. Or perhaps, if Vivian *did* kill Regan, she will try to kill Marlowe herself. Marlowe receives a call from Mars inviting him up to Geiger's house. Mars owns the house, and has returned to it everything which Brody had stolen from out of the bookstore's back room. Mars offers Marlowe the opportunity to have a look at the goods, which is just what Marlowe is doing at the top of the scene when Carmen enters. It turns out to be Carmen's last entrance. Then Eddie Mars enters, or actually *starts* to enter. He is killed before he even gets in the door, and his crumpled body joins Carmen's on the ground . . . Last entrance, last exit...it's all the same: one way or the other, sooner or later, everybody sleeps the big sleep.

SCENE 1

INTERIOR BUILDING—HALLWAY—AT MARLOWE'S OFFICE DOOR

MARLOWE opens the door, which has PHILIP MARLOWE in gilt letters on the upper glass.

INTERIOR MARLOWE'S OFFICE—THE WAITING ROOM

A small room, cheaply furnished, with a closed door in one wall. VIVIAN sits waiting for him, beautifully but simply dressed, quite at ease. She seems in a better humor this morning, smiling at the surprised MARLOWE.

VIVIAN: Well, you *do* exist, after all. I'd begun to think I dreamed you out of a bottle of bad gin. (*with underlying hint of seriousness*) I've been trying to get you on the phone all morning.

MARLOWE: You can insult me just as well face to face. I don't bite—much.

VIVIAN: (*apologetically*) I was rather rude.

MARLOWE: (*smiling*) An apology from a Sternwood? (*unlocking the connecting door, holding it for her*) Come into my boudoir.

INTERIOR MARLOWE'S OFFICE

Like the waiting room, it's shabby and not large. The usual desk, chairs, and filing cabinets.

VIVIAN: (*sitting*) You don't put on much of a front.

MARLOWE: You can't make much money at this trade, if you're honest. If you have a front, you're making money—or expect to.

VIVIAN: Oh—are you honest?

MARLOWE: Painfully.

VIVIAN: (*taking out a cigarette*) How did you get into this slimy business, then?

MARLOWE: (*giving her a look as he lights it for her*) Because people like you pay good money to have the slime cleaned up.

She looks away from him, angry but not able to say anything. MARLOWE sits down behind the desk.

MARLOWE: What did you want to see me about? Taylor?

VIVIAN: (*softly*) Poor Owen. So you know about that.

MARLOWE: A D.A.'s man took me down to Lido. Turned out he knew more about it than I did. He knew Owen Taylor wanted to marry your sister—once.

VIVIAN: (*quietly*) Perhaps it wouldn't have been a bad idea. He was in love with her. We don't find much of that in our circle.... (*changing her tone*) But I didn't come here to see you about Owen. Do you feel yet that you can tell me what my father wants you to do?

MARLOWE: Not without his permission.

VIVIAN: Was it about Carmen?

MARLOWE: I can't even say that.

VIVIAN watches him for a moment, then gives in. She takes a thick white envelope from her bag and tosses it on the desk.

VIVIAN: You'd better look at this anyway.

MARLOWE examines the envelope.

VIVIAN: A messenger brought it this morning.

MARLOWE: Eight-thirty-five it says—for you or your father.

He opens the envelope, takes out a medium-sized photograph. We do not see the subject of the picture, but MARLOWE'S reaction is significant. He whistles softly.

MARLOWE: So that's what Carmen looks like! (*to* VIVIAN) How much do they want for this?

VIVIAN: Five thousand—for the negative and the rest of the prints. The deal has to be closed tonight, or they give the picture to some scandal sheet.

MARLOWE: The demand came how?

VIVIAN: A woman telephoned me, shortly after this thing was delivered.

MARLOWE: There's nothing in the scandal sheet angle. Juries convict on that racket without leaving the box. What else is there?

VIVIAN: Does there have to be something else?

MARLOWE nods—his face is uncompromising.

VIVIAN: (*giving in again*) The woman said there was a police jam connected with it, and I'd better lay it on the line fast or I'd be talking to my little sister through a wire screen.

MARLOWE: (*deadpan, nodding*) What kind of a jam?

VIVIAN: I don't know.

MARLOWE: Where's Carmen now?

VIVIAN: She's at home—still in bed, I think. She was sick last night.

MARLOWE: She go out at all?

VIVIAN: The servants say she didn't. I was up at Las Olindas across the state line playing roulette at Eddie Mars's Cypress Club. I lost my shirt. (*taking another cigarette—laughing wryly*)

MARLOWE: (*getting up to hold the match for her*) So you like roulette. You would.

VIVIAN: Yes, the Sternwoods all like losing games. The Sternwoods can afford to. The Sternwoods have money. (*bitterly*) All it's bought them is a raincheck.

MARLOWE: What was Owen doing with your car last night?

VIVIAN: Nobody knows. He took it without permission. Do you think . . . ?

MARLOWE: He knew about this photo? (*shrugging*) I don't rule him out. . . . Can you get five thousand in cash right away?

VIVIAN: I can borrow it—probably from Eddie Mars. (*sardonically*) There's a bond between us, you see. Shawn Regan ran away with Eddie's blonde wife.

MARLOWE: (*turning away—leaving a pause*) You may need the money in a hurry.

VIVIAN: How about telling the police?

MARLOWE: You know better than that. The police might turn up something they couldn't sit on—and then where would the Sternwoods be? (*after a pause*) How was it left?

VIVIAN: The woman said she'd call me back with instructions at five.

MARLOWE: Okay—call me here as soon as you've heard from her.

VIVIAN: Can you do anything?

MARLOWE: I think so. But I can't tell you how—or why.

VIVIAN: I like you. You believe in miracles.

MARLOWE: (*laughing*) I believe in people believing they're smarter than they are—if that's a miracle. Have a drink?

He reaches down into the desk drawer.

VIVIAN: I'll have two drinks.

MARLOWE grins at her. He comes up with a bottle and two glasses, fills them, and takes one to her. They salute, start to drink and find that their eyes have met over the glass rims and refuse to come apart. VIVIAN breaks it, not because she is shy or coy, but because suddenly there is a sadness in her face. Her gaze drops briefly, then returns to MARLOWE, clear, steady, and sad.

VIVIAN: You're a lot like Shawn Regan.

MARLOWE looks at her, almost with tenderness and understanding.

MARLOWE: You want to tell me now or later?

VIVIAN: What?

MARLOWE: What you're so anxious to find out.

VIVIAN: It couldn't be—you.

MARLOWE: Let's do one thing at a time.

VIVIAN: (*rising*) I think we've done enough for one day....

MARLOWE: (*gently*) Want that other drink?

VIVIAN: (*going toward door*) No....

MARLOWE sets his glass down on the desk and picks up the envelope.

MARLOWE: You forgot this...

She turns by the door as he approaches, holding out her hand for the envelope. MARLOWE gives it to her, but doesn't let go of it.

They are not thinking about the envelope. Slowly he bends to her—she leans back against the wall, her lips parted, her eyes soft, misted with tears. MARLOWE'S mouth covers hers. Presently they break—VIVIAN puts her hand on MARLOWE'S cheek.

VIVIAN: (*softly*) Your face is like Shawn's too—clean and thin, with hard bones under it...

She turns, neither slowly nor fast, away from him, opens the door, and goes out.

SCENE 2

[EXTERIOR HOBART ARMS—AT FRONT ENTRANCE—NIGHT

as MARLOWE comes out, wearing a hat and trench-coat against the rain which has begun to fall. He gets into his car and drives off. As he does so, a second car, a dark convertible seen indistinctly in the shadowy street, swings around the corner behind him, slows, falters, then picks up speed, following MARLOWE.

EXTERIOR LAVERNE TERRACE—RAIN—NIGHT

as MARLOWE drives slowly, cautiously toward GEIGER'S house. The street is dark, deserted. MARLOWE drives without lights. He stops in the tree-shadows by the angle of GEIGER'S hedge and slides quietly out of the car, keeping close to the hedge. His gun gleams faintly in his hand.

EXTERIOR LAVERNE TERRACE—RAIN—NIGHT

A section of the road over which MARLOWE has just come. The dark convertible creeps along in the shadows, also without lights. It is still impossible to see who is driving.

EXTERIOR GEIGER'S PLACE—RAIN

as MARLOWE makes his way like a stalking cat through the garden, toward the front door. Nothing stirs. There is no sound but the rain. MARLOWE crosses the exposed bridge at a crouching run. Nothing happens. He pauses in the shadows by the front door, then tries the knob. Silently the door swings open. He waits, then darts swiftly inside.

EXTERIOR LAVERNE TERRACE

The dark convertible, still shrouded in the heavy shadows of the trees, parks quietly behind MARLOWE'S car across the road.]

INTERIOR GEIGER'S HOUSE—LIVING ROOM

MARLOWE stands beside the door, which he has closed, listening. He is only a shadow among shadows. The house is utterly still. MARLOWE, still cautious, crosses into the rear part of the house, then returns.

MARLOWE: (*laughing softly*) Okay, Eddie. I get it—on the way out.

He draws the heavy curtains quickly across the windows, turns on the lights and sheds his hat and coat. The packing box from GEIGER'S back room stands on the hearth-rug. MARLOWE bends over to look inside.

INSERT: THE PACKING BOX

filled with manila filing envelopes, ledgers, etc. On the top of the stack is a folder labelled "Sternwood". It has obviously been placed there on purpose.

INTERIOR GEIGER'S HOUSE—LIVING ROOM

MARLOWE picks up the folder—a KNOCK SOUNDS on the front door. MARLOWE reacts, dropping the folder, and raises his gun. He moves quickly to turn out the lights, then stands beside the door, flat against the wall.

MARLOWE: Yeah?

CARMEN'S VOICE: Phil—let me in.

MARLOWE: (*after a pause, unlocking the door*) Come in fast and shut the door behind you.

He retains his wary position while CARMEN obeys. When he is sure she's alone, he sighs, relocks the door and turns on the lights. His face is beaded with sweat, his hand shaking slightly. CARMEN is lightly clad, without hat or coat. Apparently she has left home in a hurry.

CARMEN: Did I scare you?

MARLOWE: (*drily*) No—I was expecting visitors. . . . I thought you were in Santa Barbara.

CARMEN: They had me locked in my room. They even had my clothes locked up. But I climbed down the drain pipe. I had to see you again.

MARLOWE: Why did you come here?

CARMEN: You were just driving away when I got to your place. I followed you.

She is obviously wrought up, in a highly emotional state.

MARLOWE: It must have been important.

CARMEN: It was. Phil, I—I'm sorry about the other night.

MARLOWE: Forget it.

CARMEN: I can't. Phil, you... I don't know quite how to say this... have you ever seen something, perhaps in a dream? Something perfect and beautiful, a long way off, and you try to reach it but there are too many things in your way?

MARLOWE: Yeah. I know what you mean.

CARMEN: Maybe if everything had been different—if I hadn't been born a Sternwood, if my mother had lived—if I'd known a man like you before.... Oh, Phil, is there ever any way back?

MARLOWE: That depends.

CARMEN: (*softly, intensely serious*) You could help me find the way.

He looks at her, saying nothing. She comes closer to him, childlike, pleading.

CARMEN: Phil, you've got to help me. I'm getting lost. I don't know where I'm going any more, and I'm scared.

MARLOWE: Why me, Carmen?

CARMEN: Because.... Just because you came into the house, and I saw you. Just a little thing like that. Don't you understand, Phil? You've got something I need, something I've got to have. Strength, maybe. I don't know. But I've got to have it, or—I don't know what's going to happen to me.

She puts her hands on his chest, looking up into his face. For once she's completely honest.

MARLOWE: (*quietly*) Was that what you wanted from Shawn Regan?

She draws away from him, very slowly, her eyes changing, hardening, becoming wary.

CARMEN: Perhaps... Phil...

MARLOWE: (*gently*) I'm sorry, Carmen. That's how it goes.

People have to find their own way—wherever they're going. You can, if you really want to.

He turns away, to let CARMEN have that moment to herself.

MARLOWE: (*after a pause*) Before you go . . . I have something that belongs to you.

CARMEN: (*dully*) What?

MARLOWE: Your gun. I've been carrying it around, thinking I'd see you.

He hands her the little gun, out of his coat pocket.

MARLOWE: Careful of it, now. It's cleaned and loaded in all five.

CARMEN: (*taking the gun*) Thanks.

MARLOWE moves past her, as though to open the door.

CARMEN: Turn around.

He does so—she has the gun levelled, and there's no doubt what she's going to do with it.

MARLOWE: Carmen!

CARMEN: It's Vivian, isn't it?

MARLOWE: That has nothing to do . . .

CARMEN: It was Vivian with Shawn, too. It's always Vivian.

She fires point blank as MARLOWE takes a step toward her, continues to fire, four shots in all. Then she waits until he has almost reached her and thrusts the pistol almost into his face. He catches her wrist just before she fires, pushes her hand aside as the shot goes off. She snatches her hand free, steps back, hurls the pistol at his chest. It falls to the ground. He stoops and picks it up.

MARLOWE: So that's the way it was with Shawn.

CARMEN: (*dazedly*) But he died . . . why didn't you?

MARLOWE: I blanked the shells.

CARMEN: (*still stunned, breathless*) You knew I—You knew—

MARLOWE: I sort of figured it that way. And I'd like it better if Shawn had taken it in the back after all, from Eddie Mars.—He was teaching you to shoot, wasn't he? That's what he thought he was doing. Only you didn't fire at the target.

CARMEN: (*with half-dreamy vindictiveness*) No—they put him in the sump—down where the old wells are.

MARLOWE: Couldn't you have found a cleaner place?

CARMEN: He didn't mind.

MARLOWE: No. I suppose oil and water are the same as wind and air when you're dead . . . So Vivian paid Eddie Mars, and covered up for you.

CARMEN: Yes. You'd like to do something about it, wouldn't you? But you can't. I'm always safe.

MARLOWE: How do you figure that?

CARMEN: Because Vivian won't let you. And you won't do it, anyhow. You like my father, just as Shawn did. You know what would happen if you took me into court. Pictures, and long columns in the newspapers, and the Sternwood name all over the headlines. You know what that would do to father.

A pause. She is looking at him like a wicked changeling.

CARMEN: (*continuing*) And Vivian's in on this, too. Way in. You wouldn't want to see her go to prison.

MARLOWE: No. I wouldn't want that. And the old man. I wouldn't want to kill him—for you.

His attitude is one of defeat. CARMEN is pleased, triumphant. MARLOWE turns away dejectedly, picks up his hat and coat.

MARLOWE: (*not looking at her*) Better take these, Carmen, it's raining.

CARMEN: Thanks.

She puts them on quickly, then stands looking at MARLOWE.

CARMEN: I think I'm glad I didn't kill you. This is going to eat
   you. You're going to lie awake nights, thinking about it.
   And every so often you'll see me somewhere, and I'll laugh
   at you. . . . Goodbye, Phil.

She turns quickly toward the door. MARLOWE steps quickly to the
light switch. As she opens the door and steps through it, he
snaps off the light. There is a brief pause—then gunfire.

EXTERIOR GEIGER'S HOUSE—AT FRONT DOOR

as CARMEN crumples silently onto the doorstep. There is silence.
The door swings open. Presently from the dark shrubbery EDDIE
MARS comes, walking slowly toward the silent shape. His gun is
in his hand. He crosses the footbridge and moves the dead head
with his foot.

MARLOWE snaps the switch inside the door; light floods suddenly
out over MARS. MARLOWE stands in the door, facing MARS across
CARMEN's body as MARS reacts.

MARLOWE: You were a little too quick on the trigger that time,
   too, Eddie.

His voice seems to break the spell. MARS goes for his gun, starts
to raise it, but MARLOWE fires first. MARS drops beside CARMEN.
As MARS falls, the SOUND of a man running away through the
garden comes OVER. MARLOWE whirls, snaps a shot toward the
running man, takes a few quick steps, but stops as the SOUND of
a car starting and roaring frantically away comes OVER. MARLOWE
turns toward the door.

INTERIOR HOUSE—CLOSE SHOT—MARLOWE

as he gathers up the Sternwood folder out of the box of
blackmail stuff, puts it in his pocket as he turns.

[INTERIOR TELEPHONE PAY STATION—CLOSE SHOT—MARLOWE

as he speaks into phone.

MARLOWE: Bernie? It's me, Marlowe. I've got a couple of dead
   people up here at Geiger's. . . . Yeah . . . Carmen Sternwood

and Eddie Mars. . . . No, I didn't shoot—but one of them . . . Yeah, I hear you. And you hear me, too. I'll be at Sternwood's. I can talk just as well there.

He starts to put the phone down. As he does, OHLS's angry voice comes OVER.

OHLS'S VOICE: Marlowe—!

MARLOWE puts the phone down, turns to leave the booth.]

ad...
Nor... fee...

THE GHOST AND MRS. MUIR

A Twentieth Century-Fox Film release. Producer, Fred Kohl-mar. Director, Joseph L. Mankiewicz. Screenplay by Philip Dunne. Based on the novel *The Ghost and Mrs. Muir* by R. A. Dick. Camera, Charles Lang. Film Editor, Dorothy Spencer. Music, Bernard Herrman. Art Directors, Richard Day, George W. Davis, Stuart A. Reiss. Assistant Director, Johnny Johnson. Running time, 104 minutes. 1947.

CAST

LUCY MUIR	Gene Tierney
THE GHOST OF DANIEL GREGG	Rex Harrison
MILES FAIRLEY	George Sanders
MARTHA	Edna Best
ANNA (grown)	Vanessa Brown
ANNA (as a child)	Natalie Wood
COOMBE	Robert Coote
ANGELICA	Isobel Elsom
EVA	Victoria Horne

Lucy Muir's story begins in London just after the turn of the century, so she is a young woman in skirts down to her ankles, with hair turned and rolled atop her head. But what she wants, though quite simple really, causes an upheaval (and continues to cause an upheaval for characters from Nora to Private Judy Benjamin): she is a woman who wants both a life of her own, and the feeling that she has done something with that life in addition to mating and reproducing. Widowed for a year, Lucy Muir has been living in the home of her domineering sister-in-law, Eva, and her mother-in-law, to whom she one day announces:

> Please don't think I'm not grateful! You've both been so very kind to me. But I'm not really a member of the family, except for marrying your son. And now he's gone and I have my own life to live, and you have yours, and they simply won't mix. I've never had a life of my own. It's been Edwin's life—and yours—and Eva's. Never my own.

Always having wanted to live by the sea, Mrs. Muir arrives in Whitecliff. She is accompanied by her daughter, Anna, by Martha (the housekeeper she has employed since before she was widowed and who is described as a "capable-looking Cockney general"), and by the dog, Rummy. She tries to rent a house from Mr. Coombe, Jr., of Itchen, Boles, and Coombe, House Agents. He presents her with several expensive prospects "suitable to a young lady in—ah—bereaved circumstances." When he insists that the cheapest one, which he has passed right over, is simply not appropriate, Lucy insists on seeing it. And that is how Mrs. Muir first comes to Gull Cottage (scene one below).

What Coombe does not want to say is that the house has never stayed rented because it is haunted. But Lucy is not by nature fearful, so she rents the cottage and is fully willing to stand up to the ghost of Captain Daniel Gregg. Both discover that the other one is just as stubborn, direct, quick-tempered and unsentimental. The ghost of the sea captain comes to admire not just the widow's spirit and form, but her evident love of the house, which he had designed along some lines of Keats: "Magic casements opening on the foam/ Of perilous seas in faerie lands forlorn." He agrees to let her remain at Gull Cottage (scene two below).

The house is open to the sea. A window closed against a high wind, a gas heater accidentally turned on, and Daniel's nap had ended in death. But it certainly wasn't suicide, as reported, any more than it would have been when Lucy accidentally does the same thing when she first moves in. But this time Daniel opens the window; she sees him in her sleep and stirs. It is their first contact, and it continues to be as unsettlingly intimate. Although he has no earthly body, at any moment he might be watching *hers*. He asks her why she married Edwin when it's clear she wasn't thrilled by him. She remembers, "I was only seventeen—I remember I'd just finished a novel in which the heroine was kissed in the rose garden and lived happily ever after. So when Edwin kissed me in the orchard—" Though he has made himself at home in many ports, Captain Gregg's spirit has not been touched by anyone quite like this since before he ran away to sea, an orphan at sixteen. When Lucy's sister-in-law triumphantly informs her that her income from Edwin's gold shares has run dry, Daniel decides that he will write his autobiography and Lucy will front it, and it will be a financial success, "the unvarnished life of a seaman." Lucy trusts him, but wonders how wise it is to entrust one's whole future to someone else, especially someone who isn't real. Calling her "Lucia," Daniel reassures her, "But I am real. I'm here because you believe I'm here. I exist in your mind and the mind of the God who made us all. . . . Keep on believing, and I'll always be real to you. And as long as you have need of me, I'll be here."

Working hard together, they produce *Blood and Swash* by Captain X. Daniel dedicates it "to all who follow the hard and honorable profession of the sea." Its royalties will support Gull Cottage as a home for seamen, after Lucy's death. Its publisher also handles another author, the terribly sophisticated Miles Fairley, who under "Uncle Neddy" writes successful children's books. He courts Lucy, and she lets herself begin to desire *human* warmth and companionship. When Daniel sees them kissing in the garden, his loneliness, disembodiment, and jealousy are all confirmed. Later, as Lucy sleeps, he bids her good-bye (in the monologue below). But then Lucy discovers that Miles already has a wife. Lucy never marries again.

Alone with Martha, Lucy lives on at Gull Cottage, long enough to see her namesake granddaughter engaged. Then Daniel comes for his Lucia. We see her die, but only just to leave her body, for he is already there, waiting to escort her, and they can now for the first time occupy the same dimension.

SCENE 1

EXTERIOR—A CHALKY CLIFF ROAD OVERLOOKING THE SEA

COOMBE's old-fashioned car appears, passes the last houses and heads out on to a little promontory. Set in a little garden behind a wall of white stone is a small grey cottage of weatherbeaten shingle, two stories high. There is nothing remarkable about the cottage except for a huge bow window on the second floor, facing out to sea, opening into a broad veranda with a white railing. But it is an altogether charming and inviting place. COOMBE stops his car with a backfire. He sits with arms folded, a disapproving expression on his face. But LUCY is enchanted.

LUCY: Oh!

She gets slowly out of the car, moves to the garden gate, CAMERA PANNING. COOMBE follows reluctantly, at a little distance. LUCY goes into the garden.

EXTERIOR GARDEN—GULL COTTAGE

LUCY comes slowly in, stops to look. In the center of the garden is a large and hideous monkey-puzzle tree (Araucarnia). Beyond the garden wall is ten yards of heath, then a low chalky cliff and the white-capped sea. The middle f.g. is swarming with gulls, tossed high on the wind, soaring, dipping, filling the air with their wild, lonely cries. LUCY stares, enchanted. (The music should now give us some help. The Ghost Theme should now come in and begin to develop, continuing through this sequence up to the point that the CAPTAIN's laugh is heard) COOMBE, clearing his throat, comes into scene.

LUCY: (coming out of her reverie) I like it very much, Mr. Coombe.

COOMBE: (fingering his collar nervously) Yes. No doubt. It's only a short drive to Laburnum Mount.

LUCY: But I want to see the inside.

COOMBE: The inside?

LUCY: Of course. What on earth's the matter?

COOMBE: Very well. If you insist. I am here to serve you, Mrs. Muir.

Muttering "waste of time," COOMBE leads the way to the door, opens it with a large iron key. They go in.

INTERIOR HALLWAY—GULL COTTAGE

A small hall done in white panelling, with a white Georgian staircase leading up. Nautical prints on the wall, a large sea-chest near the stairs. There is a round window like a porthole beside the door. Doors open into living room and, at the rear, the "offices." Dust is thick everywhere, and what furniture we see is shrouded in dust covers. The house has long been unoccupied. LUCY is staring, scarcely able to believe her good luck. COOMBE, though still disapproving, feels obliged to perform his function as an agent.

COOMBE: Offices back there. Living on the right. Dining off the living.

LUCY looks to the right. Through the half open door we can see into the room, dim because the curtains are drawn. We are looking directly at a portrait of a ship's captain in uniform. Through a trick of lighting and the narrow framing of the door it seems for a fleeting moment to be not a portrait but a live man. Music underlines the moment. LUCY is breathless for a moment, then smiles.

LUCY: Of course—it's a painting! I thought for a moment—

She breaks off. COOMBE gives her a peculiar look. She goes into the living room. He follows.

INTERIOR LIVING ROOM—DIM LIGHT

LUCY comes in, eyes on the portrait. COOMBE follows her, nervously. She stands silent for a moment, looking at it. It is, seen close to, a stiff conventional portrait.

LUCY: Who is it?

COOMBE: The former owner. (*he hesitates—lowers his voice*) A Captain Gregg.

LUCY: A sea captain! That explains the scheme of decoration, doesn't it?

COOMBE: Which is in frightful taste.

LUCY: Oh, I don't agree with you.

She goes to a window, pulls aside the curtain, letting in light.

LUCY: It's really a lovely room. And most of the furniture will do as it is, though I shall bring some of my own things from storage. I think I shall re-do the walls in sea blue—with organdy curtains.

COOMBE: Mrs. Muir! I must beg you not to be so precipitous. I assure you this house won't suit you at all.

LUCY: But it does! It suits me perfectly!

She turns again to the window. COOMBE in b.g.

LUCY: What a hideous tree!

COOMBE: Quite.

LUCY: What kind of a tree is it?

COOMBE: I believe it is called a monkey puzzle tree.

LUCY: Why?

COOMBE: Because the bark is so smooth it defies the efforts of monkeys who desire to climb it.

LUCY: (*laughs*) How sad for the monkeys! Well, it ruins the view. I'll have it chopped down.

She breaks off with a puzzled expression. The music hits a discordant note.

LUCY: Did you say something, Mr. Coombe?

COOMBE: (*with a gulp*) No. I did not.

He looks quickly from side to side. LUCY is silent for a moment, as if listening. She looks across at the portrait—almost as if her eyes were dragged in that direction. Then she shakes off the mood.

LUCY: I think I'd better see the rest of it.

COOMBE: Yes, Mrs. Muir.

He leads the way out into the hall.

PAN SHOT—HALLWAY

LUCY: It's terribly dusty.

COOMBE: The house has been empty for nearly four years.

They go into the kitchen.

INTERIOR KITCHEN

As they come in, LUCY looks approvingly around.

LUCY: Perfect.

Then she sees something on the table, stares.

LUCY: What on earth!

She is definitely startled.

COOMBE: What, Mrs. Muir?

LUCY: That table!

DETAIL SHOT—ON TABLE

A cut loaf of bread, somewhat stale; a frying pan full of uncooked sausages; a haunch of cheese; an unopened bottle of beer.

BACK TO SCENE

LUCY turns to COOMBE.

LUCY: I thought you said there'd been no one here.

COOMBE: I said nothing of the sort. I said the house had been empty. It has. A charwoman was here last week.

LUCY: (*looking at the food*) She must have left in a frightful hurry.

COOMBE: (*noncommittally*) She must have.

LUCY: Did she tell you why?

COOMBE: She told me nothing. She returned the key to the office whilst I was out.

LUCY looks at him. He hesitates a moment, then bursts out:

COOMBE: Mrs. Muir—

LUCY: I know. It won't suit me. But it does! I'd like to see the upstairs.

COOMBE: As you wish.

He holds the door for her. They go out.

INTERIOR HALLWAY

LUCY and COOMBE come through, cross to the stairs. As they pass the open door to the living room, LUCY looks over rather nervously at the portrait, which once more can be seen, amazingly lifelike. They go up the stairs.

INTERIOR UPPER HALLWAY

As they appear.

COOMBE: The master bedroom is on this side.

He crosses, opens a door for her. They go in.

INTERIOR BEDROOM

As they come in. This is the room with the big bow window, fronting out on the sea. There are some excellent maritime water-colors on the walls. On the mantel stands a ship's chronometer. In the bow stands a shining brass telescope. Near the fireplace, which is equipped with a gas heater, is a big, worn leather chair. LUCY looks about with appreciation. Then her eye is caught by the telescope. She is puzzled for a moment, then:

LUCY: Of course. He liked to watch the ships.

COOMBE gives a disapproving grunt. The puzzled look returns to her face.

LUCY: But what—

She breaks off, goes over to the telescope, CAMERA FOLLOWING, touches it with her finger, looks at the finger.

LUCY: That's what it is! You're clean!

COOMBE: (*with dignity—off scene*) I *beg* your pardon!

LUCY: (*laughing*) Not you, Mr. Coombe! The telescope!

The music comes up; suddenly the room is filled with another laugh: a deep, virile chuckle. Lucy stops.

LUCY: Did you laugh, Mr. Coombe?

She turns. COOMBE has vanished, but the laugh continues. Then LUCY, frightened, follows.

INTERIOR HALLWAY—ANGLE TOWARDS STAIRS

COOMBE comes whizzing down, shoots out through the door. LUCY comes after him, glancing back over her shoulder.

EXTERIOR FRONT DOOR

MR. COOMBE, with shaking fingers, gets the key from his pocket. As LUCY comes out, he shakily locks the door, hurries to his car. LUCY follows, her hand on her heart, looking back at the house.

LUCY: So that's it! The house is haunted!

COOMBE: (*chattering*) You would come! I didn't want to show it to you—but oh, no—you had to see it!

LUCY, still staring at the house, is beginning to recover her composure.

LUCY: Haunted. How perfectly fascinating!

COOMBE gets out the crank, begins to crank his car.

COOMBE: (*feverishly—as he cranks*) Fascinating? I suppose it's fascinating that this house is driving me to drink. To drink! Now I shall have to have a small beer to settle my nerves. Four times I've rented it. Four times the tenants have left after the very first night. The owner's in Australia—Captain Gregg's cousin. I've written him. I've called him, begging him to release me. And he cables back: "Rely on you." I don't want to be relied on! I never want to see the house again! I wish Captain Gregg had lived to be a hundred! I wish he'd never been born!

The car starts with a violent backfire.

LUCY: I'm terribly sorry, Mr. Coombe.

COOMBE: At least you know know why it won't suit you.

LUCY: (*sighs*) Yes, I suppose so.

She looks up at the house. Somewhere a shutter creaks in the wind.

LUCY: Why does he haunt? Was he murdered?

COOMBE: No. He committed suicide.

LUCY: (*shocked*) Oh! I wonder why?

COOMBE: To save someone the trouble of assassinating him, no doubt! (*holding door for her*) Come. We'll go to Laburnum Mount.

LUCY is conscious of the gulls, their lonely cries. The music comes in again, underlining the mood.

COOMBE: Mrs. Muir!

But LUCY doesn't get in. She stands silently, the wind in her face, listening to the gulls off scene—and as if she were listening for a voice.

COOMBE: (*impatiently*) Mrs. Muir—if you please—

LUCY: Mr. Coombe, you'll probably think it very silly of me, but I've decided to take Gull Cottage after all. (*as* COOMBE *opens his mouth to protest*) I mean—if everyone rushes off at the slightest sound, of course the house gets a bad name. It's too ridiculous, really, in the twentieth century, to believe in apparitions and all that medieval nonsense.

COOMBE: But you heard him laugh!

LUCY: I heard what *might* have been a laugh. Or it might have been the wind roaring down the chimney.

COOMBE: If I may say so, Mrs. Muir—fiddlesticks!

LUCY: (*stubbornly*) I want Gull Cottage. You should be very glad to have me take it off your hands.

COOMBE: If you will forgive my saying so, Mrs. Muir, you are the most obstinate woman I have ever met.

LUCY: (*triumphantly*) There! I'm making progress.

COOMBE: Progress, Mrs. Muir?

LUCY: I've always wanted to be considered obstinate. (*then seriously*) Please, Mr. Coombe, rent me Gull Cottage, or— (*firmly*)—I shall go to the other agent!

COOMBE: (*through tight lips*) On the understanding that I disclaim all responsibility for what may happen—very well, Mrs. Muir.

FADE OUT

(*Note*: Although the dialogue plays continuously, the action in this scene moves through several locations in and around the house. These will have to be condensed carefully if the flow of activity and dialogue—from garden to living room to kitchen to bedroom—is to make sense in a single playing area. Certain rooms and exteriors will be played offstage. Will the dialogue move with them? Or, can sections of dialogue be moved into a different room with no violation of literal or dramatic sense? For example, Mrs. Muir sees abandoned luncheon fixings in the kitchen, thereby establishing that a charwoman has been in the house, and has fled from it in a hurry. The establishing dialogue makes no specific reference to the food or the room, so the dialogue seems like it could be moved, but how about the luncheon fixings? Would a still-filled bucket with a mop left under a table, or a fresh rag left beside something obviously half-polished, work better if the room is other than the kitchen? Or, does it actually have to be *food* if it's to work quite right?)

SCENE 2

[INTERIOR LOWER HALLWAY

LUCY comes down with her candle, which affords the only light. The wind is howling fiercely and eerily. She thinks she hears a strange sound in the living room. Rather timidly, she enters, holding her candle high. It illuminates the painted visage of CAPTAIN GREGG. LUCY screws up her courage, laughs at herself, and makes for the kitchen.]

INTERIOR KITCHEN

As LUCY comes in. A gas lamp in a wall bracket is burning. The wind buffets the house, whining eerily in the window cracks.

Music comes in, keyed to the wail of the wind. PAN with LUCY to the table. She blows out her candle, gets the hot water bottle, takes it to the stove, where the kettle waits. As she reaches for a match, the gaslight, seen in b.g., suddenly dims and goes out. She turns, startled. Her face can be seen dimly in the light from the window. She hesitates for a moment, wondering, then decides there is a natural explanation and lights a match. It goes out. Simultaneously there is a grating screech o.s. and a rush of wind. LUCY whirls. The window has blown open. The curtains, ghost-like, are streaming into the room. LUCY, goes over, wrestles with the window, pushes it closed against the gale. She stands panting a little with her efforts. LUCY, gathering her courage, goes to the kitchen table and picks up her candle. Controlling her shaking fingers, she lights a match to ignite the candle. It goes out. She lights another; it goes out, too. She puts down the match-box, squares her shoulders, draws a deep breath and addresses the unknown.

LUCY: (*quietly*) I know you're there.

There is no answer except the whistle of the wind.

LUCY: (*louder*) I say I know you're there!

Again there is silence. LUCY clenches her fists.

LUCY: What's wrong? Are you afraid to speak up? Is that all you're good for—to frighten women? Well, *I'm* not afraid of you!

No answer. LUCY stamps her foot.

LUCY: Whoever heard of a cowardly ghost! (*gaining courage— severely*) Now, if the demonstration is over, I'll thank you not to interfere while I boil some water for my hot water bottle.

This time a quiet voice answers her:

DANIEL: Light the candle.

LUCY gasps, steps back. Now really startled, she is left without words.

DANIEL: Go ahead. Light it.

LUCY finds her voice.

LUCY: H-how can I when you keep blowing out the match?

DANIEL: Light it.

LUCY picks up the matchbox; fumbling, takes a match, strikes it. As the flame grows we see, revealed by its growing light, the tall figure of a man. She gasps and almost drops the match.

DANIEL: The candle.

With trembling fingers, she applies the match. The increased light reveals his face. (Throughout the film, it is the intention that DANIEL should never be revealed in a strong light. He should always appear vague, shadowy. The lighting should be planned always to give this effect.) He appears to be about forty, lean and fit, simply dressed in a dark suit, soft white shirt and dark tie.

DANIEL: Well?

LUCY: You'll f-forgive me if I take a moment to get accustomed to you.

She sinks down in a chair by the table, staring at him.

LUCY: You're—Captain Gregg?

Her voice goes up in a little squeak and she puts her hand to her mouth. He inclines his head. There is a short silence. LUCY stares nervously while DANIEL looks gravely down at her.

LUCY: I'm sorry I called you names. Coward—and so forth. I—I didn't really believe in you or I wouldn't have. It—it must have been embarrassing to you.

DANIEL: Why?

LUCY: Why—I mean—because of the way you died.

DANIEL: The way I died, Madam?

LUCY: I mean because you—(*breaks; her voice drops to a whisper*) committed suicide.

DANIEL: What makes you think I committed suicide?

LUCY: (*nervously*) Mr. Coombe said—

DANIEL: Coombe's a fool. Always has been and always will be. I went to sleep in front of that confounded gas heater in my bedroom, and I must have kicked the gas on with my foot in my sleep. It was a stormy night—like this—with a half gale from the sou'west blowing into my windows—so I shut them as any sensible man would. Wouldn't you?

He glares accusingly at her.

LUCY: I—I suppose so.

DANIEL snorts.

DANIEL: The Coroner's jury brought it in as suicide because my confounded charwoman testified I always slept with my window open. And how the devil should she know how I slept!

He turns and paces an angry step away.

LUCY: Oh, I'm so glad!

DANIEL: You have a strange sense of humor, Madam.

LUCY: Oh—I mean because you didn't commit suicide. (*puzzled*) But if you didn't, why do you haunt?

DANIEL: Because I have plans for my house which don't include a pack of strangers barging in and making themselves at home.

LUCY: Then you *were* trying to frighten me away?

DANIEL: Do you call that trying? I had barely started. (*with a sudden chuckle*) Though that was enough for all the others. They didn't want any of it, let me tell you! Didn't even stop to weigh anchor—just cut their cables and ran.

LUCY: I think it's very mean of you, frightening people. Childish, too.

DANIEL: In your case, I'm prepared to admit I chartered the course with regret. (*looks her over*) You're not a bad-looking woman, you know—especially when you're asleep.

LUCY: (*blushing*) So you *were* in my room this afternoon.

DANIEL: *My* room, Madam.

LUCY: (*ignoring this*) I thought I'd dreamed it. Did you open the window to frighten me?

DANIEL: I opened it because I didn't want another accident with the blasted gas. Women are such fools.

At this, LUCY can't help laughing.

LUCY: You, of all people, shouldn't bring that up.

DANIEL: I wouldn't call that remark the best of taste.

LUCY: Well, I'm sure it was very kind of you, but I'm quite capable of taking care of myself. Now—if you don't mind—

She rises, takes the match-box and lights the stove under the kettle. DANIEL, watching her, sits down at the table, in the shadow. LUCY in f.g., pauses for a moment, blinks as she suddenly realizes she has been talking to a ghost, then whirls suddenly on DANIEL.

DANIEL: Well—what's the matter now?

LUCY: I just wanted to see if you were really there.

DANIEL: Of course I'm really here. And I'll still be here when you've packed up and gone.

LUCY: But I'm not going. The house suits me perfectly.

DANIEL: My dear woman, it's not your house.

LUCY: It is as long as I pay rent.

DANIEL: Pay rent to my blasted cousin!

LUCY: He's the legal owner.

DANIEL: Legal owner be hanged! It's my house and I want it turned into a home for retired seamen.

LUCY: Then you should have said so in your will.

DANIEL: (*angrily*) I didn't leave a will!

LUCY: Why not?

DANIEL: (*shouting*) Because I didn't expect to kick the blasted gas on with my blasted foot!

LUCY: I won't be shouted at! Everyone shouts at me and orders me about and I'm sick of it. Do you hear! (*stamps her foot*) Blast! Blast! Blast!

DANIEL: (*chuckling*) Temper!

LUCY: (*now in a rage*) Or laughed at either! I won't leave this house. You can't make me leave it! I won't!

Overwrought, confused, frightened, she sinks down in her chair and begins to cry. He leaps to his feet, agitated.

DANIEL: Here! Belay that! Don't cry! Stop now, d'ye hear me? If there's one thing I can't stand it's a woman crying. Stop it, blast it all, Madam—

LUCY: (*controlling her tears*) I love this house. I felt I must stay here as soon as I saw it. I—I can't explain it—it was as if the house itself were welcoming me and asking me to rescue it from being so empty. (*tearfully belligerent*) You can't understand that, can you? I suppose you think I'm just a silly woman. But that's the way I feel.

DANIEL has been listening intently as she talks, softening somewhat, a faraway look in his eyes.

DANIEL: (*grudgingly*) Might be some truth in it at that. Felt that way about a ship once. My first command. Found her rusting in the Mersey. Gear all foul and a pigsty below. I always swore she sailed twice as sweetly for me as she would have for any other master—out of gratitude.

LUCY looks up at him silently, tears in her eyes. He paces up and down, then turns to her.

DANIEL: Very well. You love the house—that counts for you. And you've got spunk—you didn't frighten like the others. That counts for you, too. You may stay—on trial.

LUCY: (*jumps up gratefully*) Oh, thank you!

She moves forward to him. He backs off, alarmed.

DANIEL: Keep your distance, Madam!

LUCY: (*laughing*) I'm sorry! You've made me so happy.

DANIEL: I have no intention of making you happy. I simply want to do what's best for the house.

LUCY: Then we're agreed. And—and—you'll go right away and leave us alone?

DANIEL: No, I will not go right away. Why should I?

LUCY: Because of Anna, my little girl. I don't want her frightened into fits.

DANIEL: I never frighten little girls into fits.

LUCY: But think of the bad language she'd learn, and the morals.

DANIEL: Confound it, Madam, my language is most controlled. As for my morals, I've lived a man's life and I'm not ashamed of it, but I can assure you that no woman has ever been the worse for knowing me, and I'd like to know how many mealy-mouthed bluenoses can say the same.

LUCY: She's much too young to see ghosts.

DANIEL: Very well. I'll make a bargain with you. Leave my bedroom as it is and I'll promise never to go into any other room in the house, so your brat need never know anything about me.

LUCY: But if you keep the best bedroom, where should I sleep?

DANIEL: In the best bedroom.

LUCY gulps.

LUCY: But—

DANIEL: (*testily*) In heaven's name, why not? Bless my soul, Madam, I'm not a man. I'm a spirit! I have no body. I've had none for four years! Is that clear!

LUCY: But I can see you!

DANIEL: (*impatiently*) All you see is an illusion. Like a blasted lantern-slide.

LUCY: (*staring at him*) It's very convincing—but—I suppose it's all right.

DANIEL: Then it's settled. I'm probably making a mistake, but I always was a fool for a helpless woman, and—

LUCY: (*flaring up*) I'm not helpless!

DANIEL: (*imperturbably*) If you're so confoundedly competent, you'll notice that your kettle is about to boil over.

LUCY: (*glancing over*) Oh, so it is!

She rushes over to the stove.

CLOSE SHOT

LUCY at stove. She hastily removes the kettle, which is now singing, from the gas-ring.

DANIEL: (*offscene*) One thing more. I want my painting hung in the bedroom—the one that's in the living room.

LUCY: (*busy with the kettle*) Must I? It's a very poor painting.

DANIEL: (*offscene*) It's my painting and I didn't invite your criticism. I make it part of the bargain. I want you to put it up there now—tonight. Goodnight.

LUCY: Goodnight. I mean it doesn't do you justice and—

She turns as she says it, blinks.

REVERSE—FROM LUCY'S ANGLE

The room is empty. LUCY stares for a moment, shakes her head dazedly. Then she picks up the kettle, crosses back to the table, picks up the hot water bottle. It is hard to fill it in the dim candlelight.

LUCY: (*half to herself*) You might at least have turned the light back on before you left.

As suddenly as it went out, the gaslight goes on again. As LUCY stares

[DISSOLVE TO:

INTERIOR BEDROOM—GULL COTTAGE—NIGHT—CLOSE SHOT—LUCY

Wind and rain still thunders outside. With much effort, she is propping the portrait of CAPTAIN GREGG up against the gas heater. She stands back, looks at it with distaste. She turns, CAMERA PANNING, and standing before the mirror, begins to undo the buttons on the back of her dress. Suddenly, she stops, glances over at the portrait. She has an eerie feeling that the portrait is watching her. She thinks she hears a sound and whirls suddenly. There is, of course, nothing there. MUSIC builds up the eerie feeling. Finally she crosses resolutely to the mantel, picks up a throw and drapes it over the portrait. Satisfied, she gets out of her dress. On this—

DISSOLVE TO:

LUCY

Tying a dressing gown over her night dress. She crosses to the window, opens it slightly. The wind howls in the crack and the curtains move. Shuddering in the sudden cold, LUCY crosses back to her bed, picking up the hot water bottle as she passes. She shoves the bottle into the bed, slips out of her dressing gown and climbs under the covers. She reaches out to turn off the light, stops for a moment to look at the portrait. She smiles a little, laughing at herself, then turns the light down and out. We now see her dimly, in semi-darkness.

DANIEL: (*offscene*) My dear, never let anyone tell you to be ashamed of your figger.

With a gasp, she grabs the bedclothes up to her chin. On her startled face,

FADE OUT]

MONOLOGUE

INTERIOR BEDROOM—NIGHT

CAMERA is on c.s. chronometer, its hands, dimly seen, pointing to four o'clock. It chimes eight bells. CAMERA PANS SLOWLY to window. The curtains are blowing gently in a faint breeze. The sky is beginning to lighten for dawn. We see the telescope in silhouette, then AS PAN CONTINUES, we see DANIEL standing straight and silent by the bed. PAN CONTINUES to bed, stops on LUCY. She is asleep, breathing gently.

DANIEL: I thought you were one woman with sense. But you're like all the rest of 'em—a fool for any man who'll promise you the moon, and end by taking everything you have to give.

He paces for a moment, turns back. She stirs a little in her sleep.

DANIEL: Don't trouble yourself, me dear. It's not your fault. I should have known it was on the chart. If it wasn't him, it would be the next one—or the one after that. You've made your choice, the only choice you could make. You've chosen life—with all its sorrows, hurts and heartbreaks. And that's as it should be—whatever the reckoning.

He pauses again, stops close to the bed.

DANIEL: And that's why I'm going away, me dear. There's no longer a place for me in your life, and there can never be again. I can't help you now—I can only confuse you more and destroy whatever chance you have left for happiness. You must make your own life—among the living—and whether you meet fair winds or foul, find your own way to harbor at the end.

He sits at the side of her bed.

DANIEL: Lucia—listen to me.

She turns her head toward him, eyes closed, breathing quietly.

DANIEL: Tomorrow and in the years to come, there must be no confusion in your mind. Listen, me dear. You've been dreaming. Dreaming of a sea-captain who haunted this house—of talks you had with him—even a book you wrote together. But *you* wrote the book—you and no one else—a book about a man you imagined from his house, his picture

on the wall, his gear lying about in every room. It's been a
dream, Lucia. And when morning comes, you'll only remember it as a dream, and it will die—as all dreams must
die at waking.

He rises and goes slowly out of SCENE. HOLD ON HER. She turns
restlessly, then is quiet once more.

DANIEL: (*offscene*) Oh, me dear. How you would have loved the
North Cape and the fiords in the midnight sun—to sail
across the reef at Barbados where the blue water turns to
green—to the Falklands when a southerly gale whips the
whole sea white. What we've missed, Lucia—what we've
both missed.

Again LUCY turns slightly in her sleep. There is a pause, then
DANIEL'S whisper:

DANIEL: (*whispers offscene*) Goodbye, me darling.

CAMERA PANS SLOWLY BACK. The curtains are blowing in the dawn
breeze. There is nothing else there.

FADE OUT

THE TREASURE OF THE SIERRA MADRE

A Warner Bros. Production. Producer, Henry Blanke. Director, John Huston. Screenplay by John Huston. Based on the novel *Treasure of the Sierra Madre* by B. Traven. Director of Photography, Ted McCord. Film Editor, Owen Marks. Art Director, John Hughes. Set Decorator, Fred M. MacLean. Sound Recorder, Robert B. Lee. Assistant Director, Dick Mayberry. Technical Advisors, Ernesto A. Romero, Antonio Arriaga. Special Effects, William McGann, H. F. Koenekamp. Music, Max Steiner. Musical Director, Leo F. Forbstein. Orchestrations, Murray Cutter. Running time, 126 minutes. 1948.

CAST

DOBBS	Humphrey Bogart
HOWARD	Walter Huston
CURTIN	Tim Holt
CODY	Bruce Bennett
MCCORMICK	Barton MacLane
GOLD HAT	Alfonso Bedoya
MEXICAN BOY	Robert Blake
WHITE SUIT	John Huston

The treasure of the Sierra Madre is gold. Three down-and-out Americans—Howard, Dobbs, and Curtin—meet in a fifty-centavo-a-night flophouse in Tampico, Mexico, and set out on a prospecting expedition with nothing binding them together beyond the one common goal to strike it rich. The harsh, lonely landscape is killing. The vicious, amoral bandits are killing. The labor to build and work the mine, *in secret,* is killing. But their enterprise survives through the ten months it takes to find gold and take it out of the earth. How these three govern and protect themselves during this expedition, and when and whether they choose self-interest or collective survival, is what determines their fate. Dobbs, the voice of paranoic self-centeredness and a mistrust-monger, is ultimately killed by the consequences of his own refusal to appreciate that he cannot survive alone.

Just as the trio close the mine and are returning to civilization to be rich men, each with quite a different vision in his head, a group of Indians appear. They need help with a child who has almost drowned, is still alive, but remains unconscious. Howard goes off to their village and applies standard first aid for hypothermia—massaging extremities to get blood back into the heart, mouth-to-mouth resuscitation, and a teaspoonful of tequila. The child revives, and the Indians feel they've witnessed a miracle. Unless Howard remains among them for awhile to be feasted and worshipped, the Indians are convinced the Saints will damn them. They leave Howard no choice. But without his presence to balance the precarious triangle of temperaments, Dobbs's fearfulness corrodes into madness. He becomes convinced that Curtin, who'd saved his life in a mine cave-in, is now plotting to kill him and steal his gold (not to mention Howard's share, which they are temporarily carrying till Howard can get sprung from Paradise and regroup). Dobbs kills Curtin. Now Dobbs is alone, with all the gold to himself. But Curtin's body disappears from where he left it. Dobbs begins to unravel. This time when his path crosses the bandits, he is slaughtered. The bandits don't recognize the gold hidden in bags beneath the hides for what it actually is; they assume it is just sand to increase the weight of the hides at market in Durango. The bags are torn open, flung aside, and the gold dust is scattered in the wind back over the earth. Curtin has survived, dragged himself to aid, found Howard, and the two of them learn of the fate of Dobbs and their wealth. The script describes Howard's reaction as ''a roar of Homeric laughter.''

Laugh, Curtin, old boy, it's a great joke played on us by the Lord or fate or by nature—whichever you prefer, but whoever or whatever played it, certainly has a sense of humor. The gold has gone back to where we got it. Laugh, my boy, laugh...

Howard is not merely the oldest and the wisest of the three, he is also the only one with any prospecting experience. He's made and lost his fortune before. When Dobbs and Curtin first meet him, they don't even know what gold in the ground looks like. They've just returned from an oil derrick construction job where they've been stiffed by the boss, and without any money, they find themselves in the Tampico flophouse. There, in the first monologue below, they overhear this tough old bird talk about gold. Howard's speeches awaken them into the dream of striking it rich, and it's no more than ten days distance away. They follow Howard's map. He is the only one of them who speaks Spanish. It's Howard who knows that when the mine is exhausted it cannot merely be abandoned; it has to be broken down, closed, and the mountain repaired. There is nothing sentimental in Howard's lively, grizzled dignity. Rather, it stems from a deep and pleasurable acceptance of the actual proportions of things. For example, when it appears that all of them are about to die in a gunfight with the bandits, Dobbs says, "All we can do is sell our lives at the highest price possible. I mean to take as many of 'em as I can to hell with me." But Howard then reminds him, "Don't forget to save one bullet for yourself. God forbid any of us fall alive into the hands of those we have wounded. If you can't shoot yourself, try to stab yourself to death." Good common sense, under the circumstances. The Indians' exaltation of Howard into a semi-deity is the direct result of his practical know-how in first aid. The miracle or the divinity is in the eye of the beholder. But it's Howard's willingness to cooperate and to help that brought him to the village in the first place. In the end, he gives his share of the hides and burros to Curtin so that Curtin can buy a ticket back to the States.

Curtin will return to a woman he knows only by letter and who does not know him. She'd written a very loving letter to her husband, a prospector named Cody, who'd been trying to horn in on the three prospectors' claim. When Cody is killed in a bandit raid, the letter is discovered on his body. Curtin is touched by what he reads. The youngest of the three, Curtin is at first still unseasoned by either Dobbs's bitterness or Howard's ironic levelheadedness. During much of the story, Curtin is simply trying to learn from Howard the basic skills he needs to survive, and at the same time field Dobbs's wildly shifting suspicions. Curtin's dream is to someday return to the pastoral kibbutz atmosphere in which he'd once spent a summer working in a peach harvest in the San Joaquin Valley. "It sure was something. Hundreds of people—old and young—whole families working together. After the day's work, we used to build big bonfires and sit around 'em and sing to guitar music, till morning, sometimes. Everybody had a wonderful time."

Curtin is shot and left for dead by Dobbs in the first scene below, which is immediately followed by Dobbs's monologues when he returns the next morning and the body is gone. Dobbs is killed by bandits, but had he survived them, Curtin would have found him and taken his revenge. But with things as they are—Dobbs dead and Howard installed with the Indians as high priest/medicine man—Curtin says it's all the same to him now, wherever he goes. Howard suggests that Curtin should go to Dallas and tell Mrs. Cody in person what happened to her husband. After all, Howard reminds him, when Cody was killed it was Curtin who'd thought they should send the widow a share of their gold.

When Curtin survives the attack of Dobbs, it's his soul as well as his body which has somehow pulled through the assault of Dobbs's fearful meanness. Dobbs is the kind of man whose dearest dream of wealth is a vision of himself preening in snappy clothes and expensive cafes, mistreating the waiters, and then occupying himself with very available women. The first image we have of Fred C. Dobbs is of a man chasing someone's discarded cigarette butt into the street, only to have a boot-black urchin snatch it first. It is Dobbs who initiates the disastrous procedure of each man protecting his own share after the day's haul has been divided, rather than keeping all the gold a collective responsibility until such time as it is to be sold, and *then* dividing it. Just as Howard predicted, the early division and separate safekeeping leads to hiding places, all-night vigils over one's partners, and ceaseless mistrust. Dobbs is the one who always wants so much credit for doing so little, who is always proclaiming his innocent righteousness. His one generous act is offering Curtin a cigarette the day they meet on a bench in the Tampico's plaza. Even his paltry lottery winning, donated into the kitty to buy tools and supplies at the beginning of the expedition, will later be claimed by Dobbs as a reason why he should receive a greater share of the profits. He is so scared of not getting his own that he makes the worst for himself come true. Curtin, however, seems to have understood Dobbs's fate and taken a turn in the other direction, because he sounds quite like Howard when at the end of the story Curtin says, "The worst ain't so bad when it finally happens. Not nearly as bad as you figure it will be before it's happened . . . All I'm out is a couple hundred bucks, come right down to it. Not very much compared to what Dobbsie lost . . ."

MONOLOGUE 1

[INTERIOR OSO NEGRO—SLEEPING QUARTERS

CAMERA DOLLIES AHEAD of DOBBS and CURTIN as they move down the narrow aisle between two rows of cots on which men are sitting or lying. We OVERHEAR scraps of conversations.

FIRST MAN: I been in on half a dozen oil booms. It's always the same story. One day the price per barrel goes down two bits. Nobody knows why. It just does. And the next day it's down another two bits. And so on until, after a couple of weeks, jobs that were a dime a dozen ain't to be had, and the streets are full of guys pushing each other for a meal.

DOBBS and CURTIN have found their cots by this time and have begun to undress. Another conversation is taking place in the far corner of the room among three Americans. One, an elderly fellow whose hair is beginning to show white, is lying on his cot. The other two sit, half undressed, on their cots.]

HOWARD: (the old man) Gold in Mexico? Sure there is. Not ten days from here by rail and pack train, a mountain's waiting for the right guy to come along, discover her treasure, and then tickle her until she lets him have it. The question is, are you the right guy . . . ? Real bonanzas are few and far between and they take a lot of finding. Answer me this one, will you? Why's gold worth some twenty bucks per ounce?

[MAN: (after a pause) Because it's scarce . . .

DOBBS and CURTIN, undressing, listen to the old man.]

HOWARD: A thousand men, say, go searching for gold. After six months one of 'em is lucky—one out of the thousand. His find represents not only his own labor but that of the nine hundred ninety-nine others to boot. Six thousand months or fifty years of scrabbling over mountains, going hungry and thirsty. An ounce of gold, mister, is worth what it is because of the human labor that went into the finding and the getting of it.

[MAN: Never thought of it just like that . . .

HOWARD: There's no other explanation, mister.] In itself, gold ain't good for anything much except to make jewelry and gold teeth.

They are silent for a while thinking their thoughts. The old man rolls a cigarette and lights it. Then he resumes:

HOWARD: Gold's a devilish sort of thing anyway. (*He has a faraway look in his eye.*) When you go out you tell yourself, "I'll be satisfied with twenty-five thousand handsome smackers worth of it, so help me Lord and cross my heart." Fine resolution. After months of sweating yourself dizzy and growing short on provisions and finding nothing, you come down to twenty thousand and then fifteen, until finally you say, "Lord, let me find just five thousand dollars worth and I'll never ask anything more of you the rest of my life."

[FIRST MAN: Five thousand's a helluva lot.

HOWARD: Here in the Oso Negro it seems like a lot.] But I tell you, if you were to make a real find, you couldn't be dragged away.

[DOBBS and CURTIN have stopped undressing to listen to what the old man is saying.]

HOWARD: Not even the threat of miserable death would stop you from trying to add ten thousand more. And when you'd reach twenty-five, you'd want to make it fifty, and at fifty, a hundred—and so on. Like at roulette . . . just one more turn . . . always one more. You lose your sense of values and your character changes entirely. Your soul stops being the same as it was before.

[DOBBS: (*unable to restrain himself*) It wouldn't be like that with me. I swear it. I'd take only as much as I set out to get, even if there was still half a million bucks worth lying around howling to be picked up.

HOWARD looks at him, examining, it seems, every line in his face. The scrutiny goes on for some time; then he shifts his eyes away and continues as though he had not been interrupted.]

HOWARD: I've dug in Alaska, and in Canada and Colorado. I was in the crowd in British Honduras where I made my boat fare back home and almost enough over to cure me of a fever I'd caught. I've dug in California and Australia . . . all over this world practically, and I know what gold does to men's souls.

[SECOND MAN: You talk like you struck it rich some time or other. How about it, Pop, did you?

The faraway look comes back in HOWARD's eyes, and he nods.

SECOND MAN: Then how come you're sitting here in this joint—a down-and-outer?

HOWARD: Gold, my young man. That's what it makes of us.] Never knew a prospector that died rich. If he makes a fortune, he's sure to blow it in trying to find another. I ain't no exception to that rule. (*He shakes himself as though to throw off past memories.*) Sure, I'm an old gnawed bone now, but don't you kids think the spirit is gone. I'm all set to shoulder a pickax and shovel again any time somebody's willing to share expenses. I'd rather go all by myself. That's the best way . . . going it alone. Of course, you've got to have the stomach for loneliness. Lots of guys go nutty with it. On the other hand, going with a partner or two is dangerous. All the time murder's lurking about. Hardly a day passes without quarrels—the partners accusing each other of all sorts of crimes, and suspecting whatever you do or say. As long as there's no find, the noble brotherhood will last, but when the piles begin to grow, that's when the trouble starts.

[CURTIN: Me, now, I wouldn't mind a little of that kind of trouble.

FIRST MAN: Me neither, brother!

DOBBS: Think I'll go to sleep and dream about piles of gold getting bigger and bigger...

HOWARD reaches out, turns off the kerosene lamp.]

SCENE(S) INCLUDING MONOLOGUES 2 AND 3

EXTERIOR MOUNTAINS—A HIGH, STEEP PASS

DOBBS and CURTIN, their breath coming in agonizing gasps, struggle up the trail, beating the burros, pushing them on, shoulder to quarters. Every few yards they have to halt to give their pounding hearts a rest.

DOBBS: (*raises the water bottle to drink*) Isn't it always his burros that won't march in line and stray off and smash their packs against the trees and rocks. I wish they'd break off the trail and drop down a few thousand feet of gorge and crash their bones. What was in your head when you offered to carry his goods? As if he couldn't manage by himself. He knew what he was doing when he turned them over to us. Mighty cute of him, wasn't it?

CURTIN: What's the use of railing against the old man. It won't do any good. Save your breath for that next piece of trail.

DOBBS: I'm stopping here for the night. If you want to go on it's okay by me, only take the old man's burros with you. They ain't my responsibility.

CURTIN: (*looking at the sun*) It's still early. We might make four or five miles more before dark.

DOBBS: No one's ordered you to camp here. You can go twenty miles more for all I care.

CURTIN: (*losing his temper*) Ordered me? You? Who's ordering who to do anything? You talk like you were boss of this outfit.

DOBBS: Maybe you are. Let's hear you say it. (*He looks as though he were ready to spring upon* CURTIN.)

CURTIN: Okay, if this is as far as you can go.

DOBBS: Who says it is? (*He advances a step on* CURTIN*; his face is dark and wicked looking in his anger.*) Don't make me laugh. I can go four times as far as a mug like you. I don't want to go any further that's all. I could but I don't want to. See, mug!

CURTIN: What's the good of hollering. We're started on something. Like it or not, we got to finish it. All right, let's camp here.

DOBBS: That was my idea in the first place.

He begins to unload the burro standing next to him. CURTIN comes close and gives him a hand at the job.

DISSOLVE TO:

DOBBS AND CURTIN BY THE CAMPFIRE—NIGHT

CURTIN: I wonder what the old man's doing now?

DOBBS: Finishing a meal of roast turkey and a bottle of tequila most probably.

CURTIN: This is the first day we've had to handle everything without his help. Once we get the hang of it, it'll be lots easier.

DOBBS: How far from the railroad do you think we are?

CURTIN: Not so far as the crow flies.

DOBBS: But we ain't crows.

CURTIN: I figure we can make the high pass in two days more. Then it'll be three or four days before we get to the railroad. That's figuring no hard luck on the trail.

CURTIN puts more wood on the fire. DOBBS sits staring into space. All at once he laughs.

CURTIN: (*looks around at* DOBBS) What's the joke?

DOBBS laughs again, louder this time.

CURTIN: Won't you let me in on it, Dobbsie?

DOBBS: In on it? Sure I will. Sure. (*He keeps on laughing.*)

CURTIN: Well, go ahead. Spill it. What's so funny?

DOBBS: It just came to me what a bonehead play that old jackass made when he put his packs in our keeping.

CURTAIN: How do you mean?

DOBBS: Figured to let us do his sweating for him, did he? We'll show him! (*He laughs again.*)

CURTIN: What are you getting at?

DOBBS: Man, can't you see? It's all ours now. We don't go back to the port, savvy? Not at all.

CURTIN: (*unable to believe his ears*) I don't follow you, Dobbsie.

DOBBS: Don't be such a sap. Where'd you grow up? All right, to make it plain to a dumb-head like you—we take all the goods and go straight up north leaving the old jackass flat.

CURTIN: You aren't serious are you? You don't really mean what you're saying?

DOBBS: I never say anything I don't mean.

CURTIN puts another stick of wood on the fire, then he gazes up at the clear night sky.

CURTIN: (*finally*) As long as I can stand on my two legs you won't take a single grain from the old man's goods. You understand?

DOBBS: (*craftily*) Sure, babe. Sure I do. I see very plainly what you mean. You want to take it all for yourself and cut me out.

CURTIN: No, Dobbs. I'm on the level with the old man. Exactly as I'd be on the level with you if you weren't here.

DOBBS: (*takes up his pouch and starts filling his pipe*) Maybe I don't need you at all. I can take it alone. I don't need no outside help, buddy. (*He laughs.*)

CURTIN: (*looks him over from head to foot*) I signed that receipt.

DOBBS: So did I. What of it? I've signed many receipts in my life.

CURTIN: I guess I've signed things, too, which I forgot about before the ink was dry, but this case is different. The old man worked like a slave for what he got. It was harder on him old as he is than it was on us. I don't respect many things in life, but one thing I do respect—a man's right to what he's worked and slaved for honestly.

DOBBS: Get off your soapbox, will you. You only succeed in sounding funny out here in the wilderness... Anyway, I know you for what you are. I've always had my suspicions about you. Now I know I've been right.

CURTIN: What suspicions are you talking about?

DOBBS: You can't hide anything from me, brother. I see right through you. For some time you've had it in your mind to bump me off at the first good opportunity and bury me somewhere out here in the bush like a dog so's you could make off not only with the old man's goods but with mine in the bargain.

CURTIN shakes his head in a dazed way. His pipe drops from his fingers.

DOBBS: (*continuing*) When you reach the port safely you'll laugh like the devil, won't you, to think how dumb the old man and I were not to guess what was brewing. I'm wise to you, babe.

CURTIN looks into DOBBS's eyes, at once fascinated and terrified by the malignancy he sees. He tries to pull his eyes away from DOBBS—cannot. To cover his agitation he bends down to pick up his pipe. DOBBS, mistaking this for hostile, draws his gun.

DOBBS: Another move, brother, and I pull the trigger. Get your hands up. (*shouting*) Up, up!

CURTIN raises his hands.

DOBBS: Higher.

CURTIN obeys. DOBBS smiles, satisfied, nods his head.

DOBBS: Was I right or was I? You and your Sunday school talk protecting other people's goods. You. (*yells suddenly*) Stand up and take it like a man.

CURTIN rises slowly, his hands still in the air. DOBBS reaches for CURTIN'S gun. As he does so his own gun goes off. For a fraction of a second he is surprised. CURTIN, instinctively sensing his opportunity, lands DOBBS a hard blow on the jaw, knocking him to the ground. He throws himself upon DOBBS quickly and disarms him. Then he springs up and steps a few paces back.

CURTIN: (*two guns pointed at Dobbs*) The cards are dealt the other way now, Dobbsie.

DOBBS: So I see.

CURTIN: (*calmly*) Listen to me. You're all wrong. Not for a moment did I ever intend to rob you or do you any harm. Like I said, I'd fight for you and yours just as I'd fight for the old man.

DOBBS: If you really mean what you say then hand over my cannon.

CURTIN waves the gun in his hand, than breaks it open and empties the cartridges out. He throws it up in the air, catches it cowboy fashion, then holds it out toward DOBBS. DOBBS looks at it sneeringly.

DOBBS: My pal.

He spits, then retires to his former place by the fire. A long silence follows, broken only by CURTIN.

CURTIN: Wouldn't it be better, the way things stand, to separate tomorrow—or this very night?

DOBBS: That would suit you fine, wouldn't it.

CURTIN: (*perplexed*) Why me more than you?

DOBBS: So you could fall on me from behind, sneak up, and shoot me in the back.

CURTIN: I'll go ahead.

DOBBS: And wait for me on the trail and ambush me? My pal.

CURTIN: Why shouldn't I do it here and now if I meant to kill you?

DOBBS: I'll tell you why. You're yellow. You don't dare pull the trigger while I'm looking at you in the eye that's why.

CURTIN: (*shakes his head again*) If you think that, I can't see any way out but to tie you up every night.

DOBBS: (*sneering*) Come on and try to tie me up.

CURTIN and DOBBS sit looking at each other. Both men are exhausted after the hardship of the day. CURTIN knows he is in for a night of horror. He cannot afford to go to sleep even if DOBBS does, for how is he to know if DOBBS is really asleep? Or, on the other hand, if DOBBS is not feigning, what is to keep him from waking up? CURTIN yawns.

DOBBS: (*laughs*) I'll make you a bet. Three times thirty-five is a hundred and five. I bet you a hundred and five thousand dollars you go to sleep before I do.

He laughs again.

DISSOLVE TO:

EXTERIOR—THE TRAIL—DAY

The pack train on the move, DOBBS in the lead. CURTIN walks like a man in a trance, stumbling every so often out of exhaustion brought on by the sleepless night.

Now his eyes are actually closed. He is holding on to one of the burros' packs, letting the animal guide his steps. Observing this, DOBBS halts and stands aside on the trail, letting the train pass. Some instinct causes CURTIN to open his eyes just before coming abreast of DOBBS.

CURTIN: (*reaching for his gun*) Get up there ahead of the train.

Grinning, DOBBS obeys.

DISSOLVE TO:

CAMPFIRE OFF THE TRAIL—NIGHT

As on the night before the two men sit a few feet apart, facing each other. CURTIN's eyes finally begin to blink. He gets up, walks back and forth. DOBBS never stops looking at him. Presently CURTIN sits down again. It is not long before his head drops forward. DOBBS starts to crawl over to him. CURTIN jerks awake and draws his gun. DOBBS laughs.

DOBBS: A born night watchman. I have to hand it to you. You should try for a job at a bank.

DOBBS stretches out full length, lies on his side, looking at CURTIN. CURTIN's eyes start blinking again. Each time he opens them it is a greater effort. It is as though heavy weights are attached to each lid. Finally they remain closed. Not that CURTIN is asleep—it is simply that his eyes need a few seconds' rest. He is determined not to go to sleep—determined. Both fists are clenched with the effort. Even after his head has dropped forward on his chest the knuckles show white.

When CURTIN's breathing is deep and regular, DOBBS gets up, goes over to him, and relieves him of his gun. Then he kicks CURTIN hard in the ribs.

DOBBS: The cards are dealt once more—another way, and this is the last time. No more shuffling.

CURTIN: (*tries to rise; mumbles*) What cards do you mean?

DOBBS: Stay where you are. I'm going to finish things up right now. No more orders from you such as I had to swallow today. Get me?

CURTIN: (*he is too sleepy to comprehend all that is going on about him; voice thick*) You mean you're going to murder me?

DOBBS kicks him again to arouse him.

DOBBS: No, brother, not murder. Your mistake. I'm doing it to save my life which you'd be taking the first instant I stopped looking at you.

CURTIN: Don't forget the old man. He'll catch up with you. Just wait and see.

DOBBS: Yeah? Will he? Well, I got the answer for that when the time comes. You want to know what I'll tell him? I'll tell him you tied me to a tree and made your getaway with all the goods—yours, mine, and his. Then he'll be looking for you, not for me.

He laughs as if this were the best joke he'd ever heard. CURTIN, fighting to keep awake, tries to shake the sleepiness out of his system, but fails. DOBBS kicks him again.

DOBBS: Up now, and march where I tell you. Today I had to march to your music—now you're to march to mine.

CURTIN: (*lurches upright*) Where to . . . march?

DOBBS: To your funeral.

CURTIN moves in a dream. DOBBS grabs him brutally by the collar, pushes him ahead into the brush.

DOBBS: Keep going.

CURTIN: Please, let me have just another hour's sleep. I'm all in. I can't march any longer. And let the burros have another hour too. The poor beasts—they're all overworked and their backs are sore. (*He falls.*)

DOBBS: (*kicks* CURTIN) Get up. Keep going. You'll have time enough to sleep in a minute.

CURTIN staggers again, with DOBBS close behind, pushing and kicking. When they are far enough in the bush to suit DOBBS, he draws his pistol and shoots.

CURTIN goes down like a felled tree. DOBBS stands over him for a few seconds, pistol in hand. Then he bends down and listens briefly. Hearing no sigh and no moan, he rises and, putting his pistol back in the holster, returns to the campfire where he sits and stares into the flames. Presently he turns his face around toward the bush where CURTIN is. It's as though he expected CURTIN to appear out of the darkness.

DOBBS: (*to himself*) Maybe I didn't bump him off. Maybe he only staggered and dropped to the ground without being hit.

His eyes turn back to the fire where they remain staring. Suddenly he jumps up, takes a thick piece of burning wood out of the fire to use as a torch, and rushes back into the bush.

CURTIN is lying motionless in the same spot where DOBBS had left him. DOBBS leans over, goes to put his hand against the breast of his victim, then jerks his hand away. He holds the burning stick near CURTIN'S face, moving it back and forth, but there is not even the flicker of an eyelash.

DOBBS straightens up and turns away again, but before he goes ten feet he pulls out his gun, squares around, and lets CURTIN have another shot to make absolutely sure. Having fired the gun, he looks at it.

DOBBS: (*to himself*) It'll look better this way. (*He throws the gun toward where* CURTIN *lies, mutters.*) It's his anyhow. (*Then he goes back to the fire and resumes his former position; he shivers.*) This fire don't give any real heat. I'd ought to've brought more sticks in before dark. I won't go back into the bush now and get them. (*He gets his blanket and rolls up in it.*) They won't find him. I'll dig a hole first thing in the morning.

He closes his eyes. Suddenly they are open and he is sitting up, staring into the surrounding bush; then he laughs to himself.

DOBBS: Conscience. Conscience. What a thing. If you believe you've got a conscience, it'll pester you to death. But if you don't believe you've got one, what can it do to you? Makes me sick so much talking and fussing about nonsense. (*assuming a matter-of-fact tone*) Time to go to sleep.

He closes his eyes, but not for long. After a few seconds they're open again and he is staring into the fire.

DISSOLVE TO:

MORNING

DOBBS is just finishing the loading of the burros which is not easy without the help of a second man. His shirt is drenched with sweat and his impatience amounts to rage. He kicks one of the beasts savagely when a pack slips, as though it were the burro's fault. By the time the pack train is ready to start, the sun is high in the heavens. But there is one more task awaiting DOBBS. He has left a spade on the ground in anticipation of it. He picks up the spade and starts into the bush, but he only goes a step or two before stopping.

DOBBS: Might be better to leave him where he is. Ain't very likely anybody would happen on him in there. If they did they'd just as like to find a grave as a body. Bandits wouldn't have buried him. In a week's time the tigers and wild pigs and the buzzards and the ants will have done away with him entirely.

While he is standing thus, irresolutely arguing with himself, there is a CRY from not far distant, shrill as a woman's scream. It cuts into DOBBS like a knife. His hands start trembling and he totters in his tracks.

DOBBS: What's getting into me? That was only a tiger.

He pulls himself together and, in an attempt to shake off his fear, takes another step forward into the bush. Again he falters.

DOBBS: No. What if his eyes were open. I don't dare look at his eyes. Best thing is to hurry and try and reach the railroad soon as possible.

He leaves the bush, goes back to the burros, shouts at them. The train is once more on its way. But immediately trouble begins. A burro goes out of his way to scrape against a rock. The pack shifts on his back so that its weight is all on one side of the animal, who staggers, then falls. DOBBS must unhitch the burro, get him back on his feet, and do the whole job of packing him up over again. While he is about this, the other animals scatter. At last he succeeds in rounding them up and getting them all onto the trail again. But his difficulties have only started. When he marches at the head of the train, the animals in the rear stray off and when he is at its rear, the leader either stops or goes off the trail. He has to run up and down the train like a dog keeping a flock of sheep together. But presently, through DOBBS's strenuous efforts, the animals are all in single file and going in the right direction.

DOBBS: (*resuming the argument with himself*) Better not to bury him. I did right. Yeah. The chance of anybody happening on him inside a week is a mighty slim one . . . and there won't be much of anything left of him by then. Only his clothes . . . What I should've done maybe . . . undressed him and buried his clothes and left him for the wild pigs and the ants and the buzzards.

He stops suddenly. An appalled expression comes over his face.

DOBBS: . . . buzzards! They'll be seen circling overhead. Everybody around'll know something's dead . . . something bigger'n a coyote. (*He looks up at the sky then groans with relief.*) They ain't spotted him yet. Lucky for me.

He is some time in getting the animals turned on the trail and headed back toward last night's campsite. Upon reaching it he ties a rope around the neck of each burro, fastens it to the burro ahead. Then he ties the lead burro to a tree. He takes the spade out of one of the packs and moves quickly to the task before him. Reaching the bush, he hesitates again briefly, then plunges ahead. CAMERA DOLLIES ahead of DOBBS as he pushes his way through, disregarding the brambles which tear his face and hands. When he gets to the place, CURTIN's body isn't there. DOBBS cannot believe his eyes. He rubs them, then looks again.

DOBBS: This was the place right here. I know it was.

Nevertheless, he begins to look around, crawling through the underbrush, spreading open the foliage, peering left and right and becoming more excited every second.

DOBBS: He couldn't have flown away!

His nervousness mounts to the point of hysteria.

DOBBS: (*calls*) Curtin. Where are you? Curtin.

His voice comes bouncing back at him from a canyon wall—"Curtin. Where are? Curtin." The echo causes him a moment of real terror.

DOBBS: (*to himself*) I gotta get hold of myself. Mustn't lose my head. One thing, certain, he ain't here.

DOBBS'S mind delves gropingly into the problem. Finally he comes up with a solution.

DOBBS: I got it. The tiger. It dragged him off, that's what, to its lair. Very soon not even a bone will be left to tell the tale. Done as if by order.

The CAMERA PANS with him, laughing delightedly, as he starts out of the bush on back toward the campsite.

PACK ANIMALS

as DOBBS comes up. Miraculously no accident has occurred in his absence. They are all in line waiting for the kicks that will set them in motion. These DOBBS delivers.

DOBBS: Curtin didn't cry when I shot him. Not a sound out of him. He just dropped like a tree falls. (*After a moment.*) Funny the way his legs and arms were twisted around. I could have laughed right out. (*He chuckles*) Just to think, one slug and finished. A whole life. (*He chuckles again; after a moment.*) Tiger got him all right. Took him up in his jaws and carried him off. Must have been a big tiger—a royal tiger. They can jump over a fence with a cow in their mouths. (*Suddenly*) His gun—it wasn't there either. No tiger would've taken that gun away . . . Maybe he's crawling around in the bush. If he reaches a village . . . nearest village is twenty miles. Take him two days anyway. That's all the start I need—. Vamos! Vamos! Pronto!

(*Note:* This excerpt contains an abundance of possible scenes and monologues. Taken as one whole, the excerpt constitutes an extraordinary "one act," but one which for studio use, requires some means of conveying time lapse—perhaps lights that can fade to black—and some physical activities/circumstances requiring the degree of focus and exertion needed in tending fires and burros.)

EAST OF EDEN

A Warner Bros. presentation of an Elia Kazan production. Director, Elia Kazan. Screenplay by Paul Osborn. Based on the novel *East of Eden* by John Steinbeck. Director of Photography, Ted McCord. Art Directors, James Basevi, Malcolm Bert. Editor, Owen Marks. Sound, Stanley Jones. Dialogue Director, Guy Thomajau. Music, Leonard Rosenman. Assistant Directors, Don Page, Horace Hough. Running time, 105 minutes. 1955.

CAST

CAL TRASK	James Dean
ARON TRASK	Richard Davalos
ADAM TRASK	Raymond Massey
KATE	Jo Van Fleet
ABRA	Julie Harris
SAM	Burl Ives

East of Eden is where Cain is sent by the Lord to dwell, in Chapter 4 of Genesis, after he has killed his brother Abel, who had occupied a halo, a deep favor, in their father's eyes that Cain for some reason had been denied. The story of *East of Eden* takes place from March to August of 1917 in an America trying to decide whether or not to go to war. Two brothers, Aron and Cal, live with their father in Salinas, California. They've been told that their mother died when they were just infants. Aron's passionate pacifism is shot to hell when Woodrow Wilson, who he'd believed would keep America out of "the European conflict," declares war. What so shatters this young pacifist that he actually *enlists* is the sudden knowledge that his mother is not dead, but has been living quite prosperously all this time in Monterey running the town's principal brothel.

Cal surprises Aron with this knowledge, and he does so brutally. Why? Because Cal cannot tolerate the incessant gnawing of Aron's moral superiority, Aron's assumed alliance with their father which always excludes and humiliates Cal. Aron conducts himself with the assurance of a paragon because that is how his father, Adam Trask, sees him. It is codified into this family triangle that Cal is in trouble, or is a problem. Even when Cal is prompted by the right motives, his actions bring things crashing down into disorder or disaster or disgrace. For example, when anti-German feeling rises to the point that the town gangs up on an innocent immigrant, Aron jumps to the man's defense. Aron is being beaten. When Cal sees this he enters the fray swinging wildly at whatever moves. Afterwards, instead of thanking Cal for coming to his aid, Aron scolds him for escalating the violence. His brother's displeasure renders Cal so confused and crazy that he slugs Aron. What's breaking Cal's heart is that he honors and loves his father, and his father cannot see that Aron's virtue is a pose. Since Adam cannot see it, Aron can hardly sense it in himself. Aron constantly reinforces the point of view that Cal needs to learn this or that, or stop behaving in this or that way, even if Cal is perfectly *fine* at the moment.

Aron is even posing when he's with Abra, the girl he's been engaged to since they were kids. But Abra knows there is a difference between playing at being good little grown-ups and actually living one's own real life from adolescence into adulthood. The feelings she'd expected to experience as a "grown-up" are triggered in her by *Cal,* not by Aron. She tries to explain it to Cal: she and Aron lived in a story they made up; she grew out of it and Aron didn't. At the very end of *East of Eden,* after Aron has enlisted, Adam Trask suffers a stroke and lies paralyzed, unable to communicate. Abra, in the final excerpt below, pleads with Adam to show Cal some sign of his love, so that the son can know himself as loved and whole in his father's sight. Without that, she explains, he will never be able to love anyone back.

While *East of Eden*'s themes trace back to the Bible, the

plot is embedded in the specifics of time (WW I) and place (Salinas Valley). Adam Trask wants to do something before he dies "for progress, for people, maybe.". He's made a study of refrigeration and has the idea that the local lettuce crop, if shipped on ice, could survive longer and fresher than ever believed possible. He says he's just a man with a good idea—neither scientist nor inventor nor capitalist. The emphatic self-definition in renunciations—what one isn't—characterizes Adam's stern piety, as does his decision to tell his sons their mother is dead to save them the pain of understanding who and what she really is. Adam is walking so fully in the paths of righteousness there is hardly any room for anyone else. Cal sees the war coming, and with it sky-high prices for produce less perishable than lettuce—such as beans or corn. Adam reminds his son that he isn't interested in money. Once again, what Cal can contribute only bewilders and irritates his father. Adam loses his temper at Cal and calls him bad, through and through. Cal answers, as usual, directly from deepest vulnerability: "I *am* bad. I knew that for a long time. . . . Aron's the good one. . . . I guess there's just a certain amount of good and bad you get from your parents and I just got the bad." When the lettuce shipment is delayed, the ice melts, the lettuce rots, and Adam's investment is wiped out. Cal borrows money to raise a highly profitable crop of beans, the profits of which he turns over to his father as a gift at a surprise birthday party he has planned for him with Abra's help. Adam is so exhausted from his Draft Board duties that he has forgotten it's his birthday. Aron gives as his gift the announcement of his marriage to Abra, and it totally upstages Cal as the party-giver. Then Adam learns where Cal got the money for *his* gift, and the father refuses to even accept the second son's offering, explaining to Cal that war profits are immoral. Adam tells Cal that the boy has robbed the farmers and must return their money. Cal finally breaks, sobbing to his father that he hates him. Abra comforts Cal, and when Aron sees this, his hatred for his brother breaks water. He commands Cal never to get near Abra, and rages on about how Cal has always been wild and vicious, and about how much "we" (Adam and Aron) have been put through by Cal. Finally Cal cannot stand it any longer, and he busts wide open the lie about their mother. He screams to Adam the secret that has been twisting him so badly for so long: for "all your goodness and your rightness you never gave either of us an inch—*ever*—from what *you* thought was right! You kept

on forgiving us, but you never really loved us!'' Cal then drags
off Aron to meet their mother.

Cal had learned about his mother Kate at the very beginning
of the film, when we'd seen him following her, barging into her
office, begging *please* to just be allowed to *talk* to her, and
getting beaten by her bouncer in the process. Cal didn't tell his
father that he'd learned his mother was alive, but he did mention
to Adam that he wanted to know more about her. Adam revealed
little: ''She wasn't like other people. There was something she
seemed to lack. Kindness, maybe. Conscience.'' Cal is so
horrified by who he thinks he must be inside, with such a
mother, that he can barely tolerate himself. Other people inter-
pret his behavior to signify that Cal is angry at *them*, or just plain
mean. In the first scene below, Cal and Abra share a lunch at the
railroad yard where Cal is working to ship the ice-packed lettuce.
She tells him how she had to learn to forgive and once more love
her own father. In the second scene below, Cal finally gets to
meet his mother. The one beautiful thing about Kate which
Adam still remembers are Kate's hands. But now, when Cal
meets her, Kate's hands are crippled from arthritis, just as her
own mother's had been, just as she'd always feared hers would
become. However gnarled or hard or cold Kate may have
become, it has taken Adam twenty years to begin to get over her.
Her power of person is somehow so intense that Adam has
needed to call her ''dead''. But she's not dead. She's just beyond
the valley, in the city . . . east of Eden.

SCENE 1

EXTERIOR: RAILROAD YARDS—CAL—DAY*

He pushes a couple of more boxes up the chute and, as the men
start to their lunches, CAL walks toward the side where his own
lunch box is under a tree. As he comes along, we see:

A GIRL (LYDIA)

She is seated nearby, watching him. She half starts to rise.

---

* The following excerpts from *East of Eden* are from the final revised shooting script,
with occasionally interpolated indications from the Dialogue Continuity of the tone or
manner of certain dialogue—for example, ''(*laughing*)'' or ''(*overlapping*).'' (Please
see the Sample Scripts Appendix, Volume I, for a discussion of these various script formats.)

CAL

He makes a gesture to her and she rises and moves away. He passes her, and goes to his tree. He sits on the ground, picks up his lunch box, opens it and looks inside. ABRA comes over to him and sits silently. CAL looks up at her—grins a trifle embarrassed—and starts to eat. They say nothing for a moment. Then:

ABRA: Hi, Cal.

CAL: Aron's out in the field.

ABRA: I brought his lunch.

CAL: Well, okay, I'll take it to him.

ABRA: Cal.

CAL: Lydia vamoose! He'll be here in a minute.

ABRA: I've been fixing Aron's lunch. I'll fix yours, too, if you like after this.

CAL: No—thanks...

ABRA: Would you be eating with her if I weren't here?

CAL: Who? (ABRA *points.* CAL *looks up.*)

THE GIRL

seated at a new spot behind them, glaring at them.

ANOTHER CLOSER ANGLE—CAL AND ABRA

CAL: No—I didn't ask her to come up here.

ABRA: Girls follow you around, don't they?

CAL: Does she bother you?

ABRA: She doesn't bother me. Who is she?

CAL: (*with a grin*) Never saw her before in my life.

ABRA: (*smiling*) I'll bet. (*pause—*CAL *eats*) You're really work-ing at this lettuce business, aren't you, Cal? (CAL *shrugs*) Do you think it will turn out alright? (CAL *shrugs*) Your father will lose quite a lot of money if it doesn't, won't he?

CAL: Just about all he's got.

ABRA: I like your father.

CAL: Do you? (CAL *looks at her. There is a pause.* ABRA *steals a look at him.*)

ABRA: I threw away about three thousand dollars once.

CAL: (*looks at her, aghast*) Yeah?

ABRA: When I was thirteen.

CAL: You, you threw it away?

ABRA: (*nodding*) It was a diamond ring worth about that. At least my father told me that's what he paid for it. I threw it in the river. Made dad terribly angry.

CAL: I reckon it would.

ABRA: (*smiling*) But I forgave him. And it's been all right ever since.

CAL: (*overlapping*) You for—*You* forgave *him*?

ABRA: That's right.

CAL: Is there an egg in this basket? (*he looks into* ARON'S *lunch box*)

ABRA: You see, I thought he didn't love me, and that made me feel awful. Girls love their fathers terribly.

CAL: Do they?

ABRA: My mother died when I was thirteen and dad got married again not long after that. Did you know that?

CAL: No. I didn't know that.

ABRA: Are you interested in hearing about me? (CAL *looks at her slowly; she meets his gaze steadily; he reaches for a sandwich.*)

CAL: Yeah!

ABRA: When dad got married again it made me sick. I just hated everybody! I thought nobody in the world loved me. It was awful . . . Then I found the ring that dad gave . . . (*she hesitates*) . . . my new mother—and so I took it and threw it in the river.

CAL: (*grinning*) Good!

ABRA: (*smiling*) I thought you'd like that.

CAL looks at her, as though understanding her and liking her for really the first time.

CAL: (*grinning*) Did he ever find it?

ABRA: (*grinning*) Never. (ABRA *and* CAL *laughing*) They tried.

CAL: Well, what'd they do to you?

ABRA: Oh, dad punished me. Not badly, I guess—but I felt he shouldn't have punished me at all. I felt he should have loved me *more* because I did it. But he didn't. Isn't it funny. I'm grown up now—but I still understand kids better than I do grown-ups.

CAL: You're not so grown-up.

ABRA: I'm very grown-up.

CAL: That's a matter of opinion.

ABRA: I'm *very* grown-up. More than dad. Because I forgave him for not understanding. And the minute I forgave him in my mind I got better. Now, we get along fine—we love each other—not like we did when I was thirteen, of course— but enough to live together until I get married. He's just my father now . . . Nothing to rave about. I still don't like *her* much—but then she's a woman. (*pause*) My, that girl just hates me, doesn't she?

THE GIRL

glowering at them.

CAL and ABRA

ABRA: You'd better tell her I'm your brother's girl.

CAL: I don't have to explain anything to anybody.

ABRA: Well, I'll go now and leave the field to her. (*she rises, looks down at* CAL'S *head*) My, your hair's in a mess. (*she reaches down and smoothes his hair lightly, then looks up at the other girl*)

She smiles and turns lightly, to go.

SCENE 2

(*Note*: In this scene, Kate refers to several men by name. Sam is the sheriff who has known both Kate and Adam since their marriage, and who takes a kind interest in Cal. Joe is one of Kate's employees. Will Hamilton, Cal's business "partner," is a prosperous man who is both impressed and startled by Cal's determined energy, at one point regarding him thoughtfully and remarking, "You really take all the oxygen out of the air!" Although the first beats of this scene take place out on the street, they have not been bracketed out as pre-scene beats since the entire dialogue can take place inside Kate's office.)

EXTERIOR STREET WE FIRST SAW CAL ON—DAY

KATE AND CAL ON THE STREET

CAL is following her. KATE walks on, but she is conscious that CAL is there. Slowly CAL lessens the distance between them. KATE seems to pay no attention. CAL increases his pace and finally comes up alongside of her.

They do not look at each other, just walk on together.

Slowly KATE turns and looks at him. She looks him over carefully. CAL turns and looks at her closely. They both turn back and walk on. After a moment—

KATE: What does Cal stand for?

CAL: Caleb. It's in the Bible.

KATE: What's your brother's name?

CAL: Aron. Oh, that's in the Bible, too.

KATE: What's he like?

CAL: Oh, he looks like you.

KATE: Well, is he *like* me?

CAL: No. He's good. I'm more like you.

KATE gives him a quick, humorous look.

KATE: How's Adam? How's your father?

CAL: I don't want to talk about him.

KATE: Oh, you don't huh?

CAL: No.

They walk on in silence. Then—

KATE: I didn't know who you were when you were here before.

CAL: Yeah, I knew you didn't.

KATE: Aren't you afraid to come around here again?

CAL: Yeah—I am—no—well kinda—

They walk on in silence. Then—

KATE: What do you want? Just to look at me?

CAL: I want five thousand dollars.

KATE shows no emotion. They walk on for a moment.

They have come to the house.

KATE: All right, come on in.

He follows her up the steps onto the sagging porch and into the house.

DISSOLVE TO:

INTERIOR KATE'S OFFICE (WE HAVE SEEN BEFORE)—DAY

CAL stands looking around as KATE takes off her jacket.

KATE: Sit down. Come in. Try that chair. (CAL *sits. He watches her as she goes to her desk and sits facing him, looking at him. Pause.*) You've got your father's eyes. That's all I can see of him. You're a nice looking boy.

CAL: (*confused*) Yes ma'am.

KATE: I was very beautiful once. (*she arches her neck but covers it with her hand*)

CAL: (*embarrassed*) Yes ma'am.

KATE: (*with faint, amused scorn*) Caleb!

CAL: Yes ma'am.

KATE: Caleb and Aron. Your father still thinks he's living in the Bible, eh?

CAL: (*defensively*) Them's just names—

KATE: Joe says that you go to school in Salinas. Are you good in your studies?

CAL: Oh—I get by with them.

KATE: Does Aron get by with them?

CAL: He's bright.

KATE: What are you going to do when you finish? You going to college?

CAL: Maybe—

KATE: Or back to some ranch?

CAL: No, I don't like the ranch.

KATE: (*grimly*) Well, you take after me. Makes me mad just to think of a ranch. Now what do you want with five thousand dollars?

CAL: I want to go into business.

KATE: You're a little young for that, aren't you?

CAL: I'm old enough.

KATE: (*thinking back*) Ah, yeah, I guess you're right. I guess you are. What kind of business do you want to go into?

CAL: Beans. You see, they're up to three and a half cents now. They'll go up to ten or more if we get into the war.

KATE: (*overlapping*) Yeah, if we get into the war.

CAL: Well, that's a gamble you have to take. Now Will Hamilton says that if we—

KATE: (*overlapping*) Will. You going into business with Will Hamilton?

CAL: Yes. You see, my father lost about all he had in the lettuce business.

KATE: Yeah, I know. I heard about it.

CAL: I want to make enough to pay him back.

KATE: What's the matter with him. Can't he make any money?

CAL: (*defensively*) Yeah. Only—er—

KATE: Only he's too good to bother with money, huh? Okay. What makes you think I'll give you five thousand dollars?

CAL: Well, I don't know who else to ask.

KATE: You got a nerve coming to me.*

CAL: Why? I didn't do anything to you. Oh! Well, it's a good business venture. And I'll pay you back and I'll give you interest. You're a business woman, aren't you?

He looks around at her office.

KATE: (*dryly*) One of the best, son. (*she looks at him with grim humor*) You know Sam told me that you think I ought to be

---

* Although the shooting script does not detail any action of smoking, the dialogue continuity notes that Kate is exhaling smoke on this line and during her next speech. Given the year, and Cal's upbringing, this may be the first time he has ever seen, or been with, a woman smoking.

run out of town—you're afraid Aron and your father might find out about me. Is that it? (CAL *nods*) This five thousand dollars now. That wouldn't be any part of blackmail, would it?

CAL: (*suspicious*) Oh, I—I never thought about that.

KATE: (*laughing*) But now that you do it's a good idea, huh?

CAL: (*laughing*) I guess, maybe—

KATE: Well, it's not. I'm not going to hurt your precious father or brother. They don't know anything about me, do they?

CAL: (*shaking his head*) My father thinks you're in the East. Aron thinks you're dead.

KATE: Then there's no reason to think they'll ever find out about me. We don't exactly move in the same circles. What are you staring at?

CAL has been staring at her. He is suddenly very quiet.

CAL: How come you did it?

KATE: Did what?

CAL: Shot my father?

KATE: Did he tell you that?

CAL: How come you ran away from us? How come you shot him? Ran away? That kind of stuff?

KATE: (*overlapping*) What are you, a policeman? I shot him because he tried to stop me. I could have killed him if I'd wanted to, but I didn't. I just wanted him to let me go.

CAL: Why?

KATE: (*suddenly vehement*) Because he tried to hold me—he wanted to tie me down—he wanted to keep me on a stinking little ranch away from everybody and keep me all to himself! Well, *nobody* holds me.

CAL: But he loved you.

KATE: Love. He wanted to own me! Thought he could bring me up like some snot-nose kid and tell me what to do. Nobody tells *me* what to do. Always so right himself! Knowing everything. Reading the Bible at me!—What are you grinning at?

CAL: (*quickly*) Nothing.

KATE: Always so right himself. Maybe you know what I'm talking about, huh?

She stops. She has become very excited, stirring up memories, re-living her hatred, trying to explain to CAL.

CAL: Yeah.

KATE: Maybe like you said out there—maybe you're more like me. Yeah, you got sense. Maybe you don't fall for all that slop any more than I do. Maybe you know what people really are like and what they want. I've got the toughest house on this coast and the finest clientele. Half the stinking city hall go there. They sneak in at night—I walk in the front door in the daytime. And I built it up from nothing. And now you want five thousand dollars of *my* money to go into business to pay your father back what he lost. You know, that's funny. (*she chuckles, grimly*)

CAL: Oh, well, I don't think he'll know where I got it.

KATE: No. But it's funny just the same. Your father's the purest man there is, isn't he? He thought he had me all tied up with his "purity". And now I give you five thousand dollars, the money that *I* made—to save him his "purity". If you don't think that's funny, you better not go to college.

Suddenly she turns to her desk, business-like, and picks up a pen in her crippled fingers and starts to write. CAL watches her, fascinated.

KATE: (*continuing*) You tell Will Hamilton to come and see me. He's a good business man. How'd he ever happen to let you in on this bean business, anyway?

CAL: Well, I don't know.

KATE: Well, I do. Maybe he likes you.

CAL: Maybe.

KATE: Yeah. You're a likeable kid. (*she writes him the note*) If he wants to gamble we get into war it's okay with me. (CAL *moves to take her hands in his—she looks at him a second, then turns her back to him abruptly, leaning over the desk, finishes writing*) Okay give this to him. Oh, go on, get out of here. Go on, get out of here. I'm running a business.

CAL looks at her back a moment, not knowing quite what to do, then turns and goes out.

MONOLOGUE

(*Note:* Immediately before Abra gives this speech to Mr. Trask, Cal has tried to beg his father's forgiveness, but Cal is so overcome that he cannot speak and flees the room. The Dialogue Continuity indicates Abra sobbing throughout the speech. As soon as she leaves Adam's bedside, the officious nurse reenters, scolding Abra for having tired the patient.)

Slowly ABRA goes to the bedside and looks at ADAM.

ABRA: (*softly*) Mr. Trask. (*she waits*) Mr. Trask—can you hear me? Is it just Cal you won't answer? Can you answer? (ADAM *makes no sign*) I think you can understand me, though. I think behind your eyes you're just as alert as ever and understand everything I say—only you can't show it. Mr. Trask, excuse me for speaking to you this way (*she pauses*) but, Mr. Trask, it's awful not to be loved. It's the worst thing in the world. Don't ask me how I know that. I just know it. It makes you mean—and violent—and cruel. And that's the way Cal has always felt. All his life! I know you didn't mean it that way—but it's true. You never gave him your love. You never asked for his. You never asked him for one thing. Cal is going away, Mr. Trask, but before he goes, well—(*she pauses.* ADAM *doesn't speak*) Cal did something very bad and I'm not asking you to forgive him—or bless him or anything like that. Cal has got to forgive you—for not having loved him—or for not having shown your love. And he has forgiven you. I know he has.

But you must give him some sign that you love him—or he'll never be a man. All his life he'll feel guilty and alone unless you release him. Please help him. (*she pauses*) I love Cal, Mr. Trask. And I want him to be strong and whole. And only you can do it. Try! Please try! Find a way to show him! If you could, if you could ask him for something. Let him help you, so that he knows you love him—Let him *do* for you—(*she looks at him a moment more*) Excuse me, Mr. Trask, for daring to speak to you this way, but I just had to!

Upset, she hurries out of the room to the hall outside of ADAM'S room.

THE THREE FACES OF EVE

A Twentieth Century-Fox presentation. Producer & Director, Nunnally Johnson. Screenplay by Nunnally Johnson. Based upon the book by Corbett H. Thigpen, M.D. and Hervey M. Cleckley, M.D. Director of Photography, Stanley Cortez. Editor, Marjorie Fowler. Art Directors, Lyle R. Wheeler, Herman A. Blumenthal. Sound, W. D. Flick, Frank Moran. Music, Robert Emmett Dolan. Set Decoration, Walter M. Scott, Eli Benneche. Assistant Director, David Hall. Running time, 95 minutes. 1957.

CAST

EVE	Joanne Woodward
RALPH WHITE	David Wayne
DR. LUTHER	Lee J. Cobb
DR. DAY	Edwin Jerome
SECRETARY	Alena Murray
MRS. BLACK	Nancy Kulp
MR. BLACK	Douglas Spencer
BONNIE	Terry Ann Ross
EARL	Ken Scott
EVE (AGE 8 YEARS OLD)	Mimi Gibson
NARRATOR	Alistair Cooke

The Three Faces of Eve is a film adaptation of a true story of multiple personality in a case formally presented to the American Psychiatric Association in 1953.

Mrs. Eve White is a worn and withdrawn, twenty-six-year-old housewife living in Georgia with husband Ralph and daughter Bonnie. Ralph is a decent but vehemently unimaginative man. Bonnie is four and a half, and the light of her mother's life. Eve White has been suffering from dreadful headaches and blackout spells. Flashy, expensive dresses arrive at the door, but Eve swears she never ordered them. One day, Ralph runs in to see his wife attempting to strangle his child with the cord of a venetian blind. Afterwards, with Bonnie safe, Eve White swears she didn't do it.

She didn't. Eve Black did. Eve Black is an alternate personality who comes and goes at will—the kind of will which Eve White does not possess. But it is Eve White who is left to deal with the consequences when Eve Black abandons the switch. Black is funny, provocative, and acts on complete, irresponsible impulse. She ordered the dresses. She's the one who'll disappear for days at a time to prance in and out of honky-tonk bars, getting herself picked up by strangers, and then when the "escort" begins to pressure her, disappearing "inside" and leaving a frightened Eve White to fend off the sloshy pawings of some indignant man she's never seen before. Right in the middle of one of Eve White's sessions for her headaches and blackout spells Eve Black emerges before the amazed psychiatrist.

Eve Black does not want to get "well." She just wants to get Bonnie and Ralph out of her way, though she *tsks* that she wasn't *really* going to strangle the child. She has complete contempt for Ralph, whom she would never allow to dominate her—let alone strike her—as he does Eve White. Eve White's psychiatrist, however, she finds rather cute.

Though Dr. Luther buys the premise of multiple personality, albeit with great amazement, Ralph does not. He sees the body of just one woman who is either cowering or taunting him. If it isn't deviltry and it isn't willful lying on his wife's part, what is it? The doctors insist she isn't "crazy." So she has to be faking. Ralph can't take it anymore, and leaves for a new job in Florida. Eve White remains in Dr. Luther's care. Bonnie is sent to live with the grandparents. Eve Black now has what she's always wanted, but it isn't enough. She's coming out more frequently and unexpectedly, making it impossible for Eve White to even function in a job. The woman who is married to Ralph wants more than anything to be a good mother to Bonnie. As Mrs. White comes to understand that she is being rendered unfit for that role by Eve Black, Eve White wants to die. Now Eve Black arrives at the therapy session as herself, rather than waiting to emerge during White's therapy. Black tells Dr. Luther about White's suicide attempt. And then, Dr. Luther almost cannot believe what he is seeing as a third personality, Jane, emerges.

As Eve White had to make way for Eve Black, so Eve Black must make way for Jane. Although Luther has enjoyed the flirtatiousness of Black, and even been touched by her birthday-party energy, he's understood for some time that neither the White nor the Black personality is capable of integrating "the roles of wife, mother, or even responsible human being. . . . A victory for either would be disastrous—no solution whatever." Jane is intelligent, attractive, articulate, self-respecting—the whole kit for a functioning personality—except she has no memory of a childhood. She knows she needs to connect to a childhood if she is going to be a whole person, and not merely an adult front for a personality. She has met a man named Earl Lancaster who loves her and wants to marry her, but she fears that any marriage for her would be impossible. And yet, when she tells Earl that she is that woman he has read about, the one with all the personalities, this news alters nothing in his love or his desire to marry her. In the scene below, Jane finds her way back to her childhood in Dr. Luther's office. At the end of the film, which flashes forward to one year later, Jane and Bonnie and Earl are all living happily together.

(*Note*: The scene between Dr. Luther and Eve White/Eve Black/Jane has been written to include a third character, Dr. Luther's associate, Dr. Day. In the event that a third actor is not participating in the scene and only the relationship between the multiple personality and Dr. Luther, her principal therapist, is to be explored, brackets enclose everything that would be cut. Some of Dr. Day's questions to Eve White/Eve Black/Jane cannot be excluded from the scene if it is to make full dramatic or logical sense, and in these cases, Dr. Day's lines are asterisked, to designate that they would belong to Dr. Luther if the scene is played with just one doctor.)

SCENE

DOCTORS' OUTER OFFICE—DAY

MRS. WHITE sits waiting for DR. LUTHER to call her in to his office. Her eyes and face are even sadder than usual, and her body slumps in great weariness. [The secretary is typing.

NARRATOR: Then on the afternoon of September 17, 1953, by which time both doctors had begun to ask themselves if there would ever be a resolution of this most complex and baffling of cases, Mrs. White came to the office for her regular treatment—and died there.

DR. LUTHER appears at the door of his office and she rises.]

DR. LUTHER: How are you, Mrs. White?

MRS. WHITE: (entering his office) I don't feel very well.

As he closes the door . . .

DR. LUTHER'S OFFICE—DAY

DR. LUTHER: (as they sit) You look tired.

MRS. WHITE: I'm very tired. I'm tired all the time now.

DR. LUTHER: Has the lively Miss Black been keeping you out late?

MRS. WHITE: I guess so. I seem to be forgetting more than ever now.

DR. LUTHER: That could also be Jane, you know.

MRS. WHITE: Yes, I know.

DR. LUTHER: What do you think of Jane?

MRS. WHITE: From what you've told me—I hope she'll be the one.

DR. LUTHER: The one to what?

MRS. WHITE: To live.

DR. LUTHER: Is that what you think's going to happen—that two of you will eventually—disappear?

MRS. WHITE: Don't you?

DR. LUTHER: I have thought so—at times.

MRS. WHITE: I think so—and I think it'll be Jane. I hope so, anyway.

DR. LUTHER: Rather than yourself?

MRS. WHITE: She's the strongest, isn't she?

DR. LUTHER: I don't know that she's stronger than Eve Black.

MRS. WHITE: It mustn't be Eve Black. She doesn't like Bonnie.

DR. LUTHER: Did you go up to see Bonnie Sunday?

MRS. WHITE: Yes.

DR. LUTHER: Did you have fun with her?

MRS. WHITE: I did for a while—and then I forgot for a while— and then I came out again—before I left.

DR. LUTHER: You think Jane will take good care of Bonnie?

MRS. WHITE: (*nodding*) From what you tell me. I'd feel better if—I knew it was going to be Jane. Has she ever said anything to you about Bonnie?

DR. LUTHER: Several times. She thinks she's very bright—and lovable.

MRS. WHITE: Did she think she was her child?

DR. LUTHER: No. She knew she was yours. But she liked her from the first time she saw her—and now she says she loves her.

MRS. WHITE: Not like she was hers, though.

DR. LUTHER: Not yet—but she will, I imagine.

MRS. WHITE: I hope so—because I'm so tired all the time now. When I was saying goodbye Sunday she said, don't come back the other way, mommy—I don't like the other way—

DR. LUTHER: Eve Black?

MRS. WHITE: (*nodding*) When I was up there last month, I guess. She must have come out and been cross with her—or slapped her or something. Then she said, come back this way, mommy, the way you are now—so I knew it must have

been Jane that was out this time—when I forgot—and that
she'd been sweet to Bonnie.

DR. LUTHER: So she's calling you mommy again.

MRS. WHITE: (*nodding*) I was glad of that, anyway. But then
when papa was driving me out of the yard and we were all
saying goodbye, all of a sudden I got this idea—I'm not
ever going to see her again—this is—the last time. (*after a
silence*) I wanted to go back and hug her again. I wanted to
say something to her—to try to make her understand. But
what could you say? How could you make a little girl
understand that her mommy wouldn't ever be back again—
but another woman—who just looked like her.

DR. LUTHER: If it turns out to be Jane—as you say you hope it
will be—maybe Bonnie'll never know.

MRS. WHITE: Maybe. I hope not. But it won't be me there—not
her real mommy.

DR. LUTHER: Why do you think YOU'LL be one of the ones to
go?

MRS. WHITE: Just the way I feel, I guess. But I don't really
care much any more. I'm not really fit for her—not for
anything much any more. I know that now. But if it's
Jane—if she'll understand how much little girls need love—
and understanding—I won't mind dying—not if she'll take
good care of her for me.

DR. LUTHER: May I speak to Jane now?

MRS. WHITE: Of course.

DR. LUTHER: Jane?

There is a clenching of the eyes, a deep sigh, and then the
transition to Jane takes place—Jane straightening up and smiling
pleasantly.

JANE: She's a darling little girl.

DR. LUTHER: You heard us?

JANE: Yes—and it WAS me that came out up there. She and her mother were playing with a ball—bouncing it back and forth in the back yard—when a very curious thing happened—that I think you may be interested in.

DR. LUTHER: What was that?

JANE: She and her mother were bouncing this ball between them when . . .

DISSOLVE TO:

[BACK YARD OF THE BLACK FARMHOUSE—DAY

This is a FLASHBACK. BONNIE and MRS. WHITE, listless and weary, are bouncing the ball to each other.

MRS. WHITE: That's very good, sugar. Now catch this one.

But it goes past BONNIE and under the house, which sits on brick pillars.

MRS. WHITE: Oh my.

BONNIE: (looking under the house) Yon it is.

MRS. WHITE: I'll get it.

As she approaches the side of the house, she puts her hands to her temples and pauses a moment, and the transition to JANE takes place.

JANE: I'll get it, dear.

BONNIE: (as JANE goes under the house) Can you see it?

UNDER THE HOUSE—DAY

JANE: (crawling) I think I see it.

She comes straight toward the camera, which is shooting out toward BONNIE looking under the house. JANE comes straight to the ball, which is in the immediate foreground, and sits down and looks back at BONNIE.

JANE'S VOICE: That's when I looked back,] a strange thing happened. Suddenly—I was littler.

[REVERSE ANGLE—DAY

By the use of an improportionate set, the house higher off the ground, etc., JANE is no larger than a little girl.]

JANE'S VOICE: I was a little girl under the house. (*as she looks around*) I could smell the odor of fresh earth—like a long time ago—and morning glories—though there are no morning glories growing around there now.

[BONNIE: (*out of scene*) Did you find it?

As she picks up the ball and looks up and around at the size of the space she is in . . .

DISSOLVE TO:

DR. DAY'S OFFICE—DAY

The FLASHBACK is over and] JANE is looking gravely at DR. LUTHER.

JANE: It was a—very—odd—experience.

DR. LUTHER: Why was it?

JANE: Feeling so little under there.

DR. LUTHER: Did it remind you of anything—that you can remember?

JANE: Not that I can remember.

DR. LUTHER: You still can't remember anything at all about your childhood?

JANE: No—not even of being a child.

DR. LUTHER: Do you think Eve White might be able to remember something about it?

JANE: I have no idea.

DR. LUTHER: May I speak with her?

JANE: Of course.

DR. LUTHER: Mrs. White?

There is the familiar tightening of the features, the closing of the eyes, and now MRS. WHITE sits primly opposite him, too lifeless to take much interest in whatever it may be.

DR. LUTHER: Jane tells me that when she came out up there on Sunday—when you were playing catch with Bonnie—the ball rolled under the house—and she went under after it—and when she got under there she had a feeling of being very small—no larger than a little child—a very curious and somehow frightening feeling—as if she'd been there before—and it had some kind of meaning for her. Can you remember—when you were very little—any experience like that—of any kind?

MRS. WHITE: (*after thinking*) No.

DR. LUTHER: Will you think back to when you were—say—five—or six—or seven—something like that?

MRS. WHITE: (*presently*) I'm sorry. I can't remember anything like that—under the house.

DR. LUTHER: Under hypnosis—would you mind?

MRS. WHITE: I don't mind.

DR. LUTHER: All right, close your eyes. Now relax—your whole body—heavier and heavier. . . .

She submits to hypnosis easily and quickly and is soon asleep in the chair.

DR. LUTHER: Now I'd like you to think back to when you were five years old—just a little girl on the farm—a very little girl—just five years old. You're just five years old now—playing around in the back yard. Sometimes you play under the house, don't you?

MRS. WHITE: (*almost inaudibly*) Yes.

DR. LUTHER: Did you ever go under there for a ball?

MRS. WHITE: I don't remember.

DR. LUTHER: Was it dark under the house?

MRS. WHITE: Yes—very dark.

DR. LUTHER: Did it scare you?

MRS. WHITE: No.

DR. LUTHER: It never scared you when you went under there?

MRS. WHITE: No.

DR. LUTHER: All right—now you're six. Six years old—still playing around the house—in the back yard. Do you still go under the house sometimes?

MRS. WHITE: (*with a choke*) Yes!

DR. LUTHER: Do you remember—one particular time—that something happened to you—when you were under the house? (*she begins to mumble something*) Did a ball go under the house?

MRS. WHITE: (*incoherently*) Oh, no! No!

Then she begins to show signs of desperate agitation, struggling against some memory, mumbling things that he cannot understand, except now and then a few words together. The few words are "blue cup—blue china cup—I had a blue china cup"—all sorts of variations of these words. DR. LUTHER simply listens. Then the struggle becomes more intense, and she is protesting. "No, mamma! No, no, mamma, please! . . . I don't want to, mamma! . . . Don't make me, mamma! . . . I don't want to, mamma! Don't make me,—please!" Tears come into her eyes, of terror, and she sobs deeply. "All the people! . . . Please, mamma! . . . All the flowers. . . . Please don't, mamma! Please don't! . . . Flowers—and chairs—all the flowers! . . . Please don't, mamma! Please! Please! PLEASE!" The agony of the recollection is so intense that she comes out of hypnosis spontaneously, her face drenched with tears, still sobbing deeply.

DR. LUTHER: Mrs. White?

She looks up at him, her eyes appealing to him, and then she gasps, clutches her head with her hands, and the transition takes place and it is EVE BLACK, grinning through the tears.

EVE BLACK: What were you doing to her?

DR. LUTHER: (*puzzled*) Eve?

EVE BLACK: What were you trying to get at?

DR. LUTHER: Are you Eve Black?

EVE BLACK: Of course. What were you asking her those questions for?

He is very alert and sharp now, pretty sure that he is on to something important.

DR. LUTHER: I'm interested in something that Jane told me—about being under the house—your mother's house—probably when you were about six years old. It upset Mrs. White very much. Can you remember what it was?

EVE BLACK: No, I never paid much attention to things then.

DR. LUTHER: You came out then, didn't you?

EVE BLACK: (*grinning*) I came out when I wanted to do something she didn't want to. Didn't she tell you how she used to get lickings for things she didn't do?

DR. LUTHER: That you did do?

EVE BLACK: (*proudly*) I used to do anything I wanted to.

DR. LUTHER: How did you get out here now? I didn't call you.

EVE BLACK: (*growing sober*) I don't know. I just had to, I guess.

DR. LUTHER: You remember anything about that blue china cup?

EVE BLACK: (*impatiently*) I don't remember ANYthing about anything like that! I told you that! How long you gonna keep this up?

DR. LUTHER: Until we find out what's the trouble, of course.

EVE BLACK: How long you think that'll be?

DR. LUTHER: I have no idea.

EVE BLACK: You know what I think?

DR. LUTHER: What?

EVE BLACK: (*slouching but unwontedly sober*) I think—I think I ain't having much fun any more.

DR. LUTHER: You're still getting out, aren't you?

EVE BLACK: Yes, but—not like I used to. Is it Jane that's doing that to me?

DR. LUTHER: I don't know. What do YOU think?

EVE BLACK: I wish I knew more about her.

DR. LUTHER: What do you want to know about her?

EVE BLACK: I don't know. But it's not like it used to be—when I knew all about Eve White—and she didn't know anything about me—and they wasn't nobody else. That's the way I liked it. But it's changed now, hasn't it?

DR. LUTHER: Yes. There's Jane now.

EVE BLACK: You like her?

DR. LUTHER: Very much.

EVE BLACK: More'n you do me?

DR. LUTHER: No. I don't like anybody more than I do you really.

EVE BLACK: But you never would go out funning with me, would you?

DR. LUTHER: A psychiatrist can't go out with a patient. That's against the rules.

EVE BLACK: Would you go out with me if you wasn't a doctor?

DR. LUTHER: Any time you'd let me.

EVE BLACK: (*presently*) She know all about what I do?

DR. LUTHER: Unhunh.

EVE BLACK: And she tells you?

DR. LUTHER: When I ask her.

EVE BLACK: Like—about that sergeant?

DR. LUTHER: Yes, she told me about that.

EVE BLACK: That's what I mean—having somebody around like that—telling on you.

DR. LUTHER: You tell me about Mrs. White, don't you?

EVE BLACK: Yeah, but she don't DO anything! You know something, Doc?

DR. LUTHER: What?

EVE BLACK: You know that red dress? The low-cut one?

DR. LUTHER: How could I forget it!

EVE BLACK: I want you to have it.

DR. LUTHER: A low-cut dress for ME?

EVE BLACK: (*soberly*) I want you to have it—if anything happens.

DR. LUTHER: What do you mean, if anything happens?

EVE BLACK: Something's the matter, Doc. I don't know what it is—but something's the matter. You don't think we'll ever get well, do you.

DR. LUTHER: Of course I do.

EVE BLACK: (*beginning to sob*) I don't think we will. I think we're gonna die—all of us.

DR. LUTHER: (*uncertainly*) Eve?

EVE BLACK: (*grinning through her tears*) You didn't think I could cry, did you!

DR. LUTHER: You never have before.

EVE BLACK: (*in a state of melancholia*) I remember the first time I seen you.... You was the first one I ever said who I was.... You the first one ever knew me.... But you never would go out with me, would you!

DR. LUTHER: I couldn't, Eve. You know that.

EVE BLACK: You liked that red dress, didn't you?

DR. LUTHER: Very much indeed. It's a beautiful dress.

EVE BLACK: I want you to have it. Because you're the only one knows what it's meant to me. You're the only one.

DR. LUTHER: I know of nothing that's going to happen to you,

but I do appreciate the dress. Believe me. Now may I speak
to Jane?

EVE BLACK: Of course.

DR. LUTHER: Jane?

EVE BLACK: Goodbye, Doc.

DR. LUTHER: Goodbye, Eve.

She closes her eyes and the transition takes place to JANE.

DR. LUTHER: You heard her?

JANE: (*soberly*) Yes.

DR. LUTHER: What do you think she meant?

JANE: I don't know.

DR. LUTHER: Have you remembered anything about that blue
china cup—and under the house?

JANE: No.

DR. LUTHER: (*sharply*) Mrs. White?

The reaction to this frightens him. There is a long strangulated
gasp and then, her hands over her face, trying to smother her
voice, she begins to scream over and over again. He rises
quickly and comes around to her chair. [Then the door opens and
DR. DAY comes in.]

JANE: (*incoherently*) Please don't, mamma! Please don't!

DR. LUTHER: Jane?

JANE: Don't make me! Please don't make me!

DR. LUTHER: Tell me what happened, Jane—under the house.

JANE: She made me! She made me kiss her! I was playing
under the house! I was playing under the house with
Florence—with a blue china cup! I was filling it with
sand . . .

[DISSOLVE TO:

UNDER THE HOUSE—DAY

Two little girls six years old are pouring sand into a bucket. One is EVE as a child. The other is FLORENCE, her cousin. It is foolish, meaningless play, but it pleases them and they're enjoying it.

MRS. BLACK: (*off*) Evie?

As they look up . . .

REVERSE ANGLE—DAY

Over them to show MRS. BLACK, a young woman at this time, dressed in funereal black, bending down to look under at them.

MRS. BLACK: Come on, sugar. Time to get your clothes on.

EVIE: I be there in a minute, mamma.

MRS. BLACK: Come on, Evie. I don't want to come under there after you. You come on this minute.

Reluctantly EVIE starts crawling toward her mother as . . .

BACKYARD—DAY

MRS. BLACK takes her by the hand as she comes out from under the house and leads her around to go into the house through the back door.

MRS. BLACK: You have to kiss gramma goodbye, sugarpie. Then you won't miss her so much—if you kiss her goodbye.

As they enter the back door . . .

DISSOLVE TO:

PARLOR—DAY

The camera is on the door as MRS. BLACK APPEARS LEADING LITTLE EVIE by the hand. The child is now in her best clothes. They stop in the door as MRS. BLACK looks past the camera, tears in her eyes.]

EVIE: (*a whisper*) Please, mamma!

[MRS. BLACK: (*moving forward*) You've got to, sugar.]

EVIE: Please, mamma!

[The camera moves back before them until in the foreground is an open coffin; inside, the body of EVIE'S grandmother, a very old woman. Seated and standing around the parlor watching are country people in their best clothes. As they stop at the coffin, EVIE clings to her mother frantically.]

EVIE: I don't want to, mamma!

[MRS. BLACK: (*gently*) You got to, honey. Then you won't miss her so much.]

EVIE: Please, mamma! Please! Please!

[MAN: (*quietly*) Somebody help her.

2ND MAN: (*stepping forward*) Come on, honey. All you got to do—

MRS. BLACK: Give her to me.

EVIE is now struggling and crying incoherently in her mother's arms.]

EVIE: Please don't make me!

[MRS. BLACK: (*holding her down to the corpse*) Kiss her cheek, darling—so you won't miss her so much.]

EVIE: (*a scream*) Pleeeeeeeeease, mamma!

[As her mouth is pressed against the cheek of the corpse . . .

DISSOLVE TO:]

DR. LUTHER'S OFFICE—DAY

JANE lies back in the chair, her eyes closed. DR. LUTHER [and DR. DAY sit] watching her. There is a long silence. Then JANE opens her eyes and looks [at them] without much comprehension. Then she lies back and closes her eyes again. Finally she speaks.

JANE: (*wearily*) I didn't want to do it.

[But now the two doctors detect] a new inflection in her voice, a new normality, [and they exchange a questioning glance.]

JANE: She didn't mean wrong. That was just what people thought in those days. If we kissed—the dead face—it was a sweet goodbye—and we wouldn't miss her so much.

DR. LUTHER: (*gently*) You remember it very distinctly now, don't you.

JANE: Yes. Even the flowers—and the chairs—and who was there.

DR. LUTHER: You remember the funeral?

JANE: No.

DR. LUTHER: You don't remember the cemetery?

JANE: No.

DR. LUTHER: You remember the preacher?

JANE: Yes. Dr. Murray. Dr. Henry G. Murray.

DR. LUTHER: You remember what he said at the grave?

JANE: No. . . . I don't remember that.

DR. LUTHER: You remember anything else at all that happened that day?

JANE: I couldn't sleep that night. I had bad dreams—nightmares.

DR. LUTHER: Do you remember what any of them were about?

JANE: No—just that they scared me.

DR. LUTHER: Do you think about death a great deal now?

JANE: No. (*her eyes still closed*) Only that—"Life's a city full of straying streets, And death's the market-place where each one meets." Just that—some day it'll happen.

*DR. DAY: Who wrote that? That poem?

JANE: Shakespeare—isn't it?

*DR. DAY: Where did you learn it?

JANE: At high school. Mr. Montgomery recited it to us one day.

*DR. DAY: Who was Mr. Montgomery?

JANE: He was the English teacher.

DR. LUTHER: [(*picking up* DR. DAY'S *cue*)] Who was your first teacher—the very first—when you first started to school?

JANE: That was in Fortsville. Miss Bates.

The doctors wait, watching her. She starts to say something else, and then her eyes open. For a moment she stares at them, and then she begins to smile, her eyes shining with excitement, and it is an effort for her to keep her exultation under control. It is as if someone who had been blind a long time is now seeing again.

JANE: Miss Bates in the first grade. Miss Griffith in the second. Miss Stewart in the third. And then we moved to Richmond and we had Miss Patterson in the fourth grade . . .

DR. LUTHER: You remember all of 'em?

JANE: May I say 'em?

DR. LUTHER: Go on.

JANE: We lived on Fifth Street in Richmond—237 Fifth Street—next door to the Thompsons—Rick and Mary Lou Thompson. Mr. Thompson worked at the railroad. He was in the machine shop. He took all of us to the shop one Sunday morning—to see the machines—Rick and Mary Lou and Florence and me. Florence is my cousin . . . I can remember! I can remember—EVERYTHING!

DR. LUTHER: (*sharply*) Mrs. White!

Jane's smile vanishes. This was a part of her that she had forgotten in her excitement. And suddenly she is terrified.

JANE: Do you have to?

DR. LUTHER: Mrs. White?

With a long sigh of sadness, she sinks back in the chair, all of the joy and excitement gone.

DR. LUTHER: Mrs. White?

And then, when there is still no response, she begins to smile again, and now her excitement and happiness are even greater than before.

JANE: They're gone!

DR. LUTHER: Eve?

JANE: They're gone, I tell you!

DR. LUTHER: Eve Black?

JANE: They're BOTH gone! I know it! I can feel it! There's nobody now but me! (*rising*) Just me! And I can remember everything!—and everybody!—papa!—and mamma!—and —(*she begins to laugh and cry at the same time*)—Bonnie!

She throws back her head and begins to laugh almost hysterically as . . .

DISSOLVE

BREAKFAST AT TIFFANY'S

A Paramount Pictures, Inc. presentation. Producers, Martin Jurow and Richard Shepherd. Director, Blake Edwards. Screenplay by George Axelrod. Based on the novel *Breakfast at Tiffany's* by Truman Capote. Director of Photography, Franz Planer. Editor, Howard Smith. Process Photography, Farciot Edouart. Art Directors, Hal Pereira, Roland Smith. Sound, Hugo Grenzbach, John Wilkinson. Song, "Moon River," Johnny Mercer and Henry Mancini. Music, Henry Mancini. Set Decoration, Sam Comer and Ray Moyer. Assistant Director, William McGarry. Running time, 115 minutes. 1961.

CAST

HOLLY GOLIGHTLY	Audrey Hepburn
PAUL VARJAK	George Peppard
DOC GOLIGHTLY	Buddy Ebsen
O.J. BERMAN	Martin Balsam
"2-E"	Patricia Neal
JOSE DA SILVA PERRIERA	Vilallonga
TIFFANY'S CLERK	John McGiver
SALLY TOMATO	Alan Reed
RUSTY TRAWLER	Stanley Adams
MAG WILDWOOD	Dorothy Whitney
CAT	Putney

Lulamae Barnes. She was one of those wild, starved mountain kids, just a rag-on-a-stick, with a kid brother named Fred. Orphaned, Lulamae finds a home for them with Doc Golightly, the local horse doctor who is thirty years her senior and quite seriously in love with her. He weeps when he proposes. In a voice which will remain, as Truman Capote described it, "silly-young and self-amused," this fourteen-year-old girl asks, "What you want to cry for Doc? 'Course we'll be married. I've never been married before."

She grows plump under his adoring care, but soon runs away, unable to tolerate being contained or caged in any way. *We* first meet this girl two months shy of her nineteenth birthday. She is living in New York City, now she is called Holly Golightly, and she prides herself on being "top banana in the shock department." Were Doc not suddenly to succeed in locating her, and tell his story to one of her neighbors in the first monologue below, one would not deduce from merely looking at Holly Golightly that there had ever been a Lulamae Barnes. True, she's skinny again, and very simply dressed, only now it's New York drop-dead chic—an immaculate "soap and lemon" radiance, dropped into the most expensive, plain, little black dress, and nothing else but sometimes pearls and always the hugest sunglassess, completely masking very wide, multicolored, myopic eyes. She's "the Kid." Everyone is so taken with Holly that even she can't stop watching herself. Sometimes she's enthralled with the performance, sometimes dangerously bored, and almost always plotting or executing some caper of escape to what she envisions as freedom.

Between Doc and New York, Holly spent a few years in Hollywood. On the eve of what should have been her big break, she blew town. Her reasons? As she explained long-distance to O.J. Berman, her flabbergasted agent: she is in New York because she has never been there. To be good at being a movie star, she consoles O.J., you have to want it, and she doesn't. As soon as she knows what she does want, she promises O.J. that he'll be the first to know. O.J. is pissed off and impressed. He knows Holly is a consistent, spectacular liar, who is also capable of telling abruptly brilliant, even poetic truths. O.J. remains an enthusiastic fan, if a wary and irritable one. Holly helped him win $10,000 one night, and while he may be crass, he is nonetheless loyal. It was under his career-guidance that Holly's hillbilly accent was smoothed out with French lessons when mere English lessons didn't make a dent. Holly's present speech makes a knowing fun out of all these cosmopolitan influences and improvements which a bright young thing is expected to absorb. (For example, in the second of the scenes below, Holly escapes from her own apartment via the fire escape into her neighbor's, in the middle of the night, explaining as she crawls in that she's got the most terrifying man downstairs: "I mean he's sweet when he isn't drunk, but let him start lapping up the vino, and oh, golly, quel beast!") Holly is self-consciously styled, and extremely so, fanciful and willful; Lulamae, though never acknowledged, is also still there—dreamy, romantic, quick and brave when she needs to be, and it saves Holly from tipping entirely over into affectation. Holly's apartment, despite its toney East Side address, is decorated in crates, empty shelves, suitcases on the floor, and shoes under the bed. She is waiting for the place where it all fits together, before *putting* any of it together. There's a cat, usually addressed as "poor slob" because its only name is "Cat," lest over-naming impose too much on its independence. The contents of the refrigerator: a container of milk, a bottle of champagne, penicillin nose drops, and a pair of ballet slippers. The empty apartment is ideal for sudden, mass cocktail parties, populated principally by male strangers.

What Holly wants is to find "a place where nothing very bad could ever happen," someplace vast and outdoors, where Fred, who's presently off in the army, can raise horses. He's very good with them ... and not with too much else; or, as Holly describes him, "Vague and sweet and terribly slow." To secure this future, Holly will eventually succeed at fascinating (and ultimately lose at marrying) the handsome, wealthy, elegant diplomat who is planning to be the future President of Brazil. Before him, there is a false try named Mr. Rusty Trawler, embarked upon in the tipsy bravado of the third monologue below, just after Holly has placed Doc back on the bus. Marrying a millionaire doesn't happen overnight, however, and meanwhile a girl needs cash. Before going exclusively matrimonial, Holly could pick up "$50 for the powder-room" from the men on expense accounts who would take her out to top-dollar restaurants and clubs, hand her a $50 bill to cover her tip for the powder-room attendant, and not expect change. What *do* they expect, these make-believe barons with their polite vulgarities? And do they get it, these "rats" and "super-rats," as Holly calls them? Underneath all the glib glamour, the playgirl is a vibrating wreck. Half the time she is pretending to be shocked, and the rest of the time she's pretending that what actually does shock her, doesn't. She suffers from the "mean reds," depressions that go far beyond the generic "blues." (And this is all happening on constant martinis.) One of the best cures is to go to Tiffany's, the fine, solid, proud Fifth Avenue store for jewels, silver, china, crystal, gold, *and* personal stationery. But more than anything *in* the store, it is the store itself, the *establishment* of it, that drenches Holly in a calm certitude. As for the diamonds themselves, she confesses she finds them a bit tacky on anyone under forty, but marvelous on the really old girls. (And she means it.) The film begins with Holly, still dressed from a long, hard night out, sipping coffee and nibbling a danish, standing in front of Tiffany's windows, as dawn lights up Manhattan.

The other regular means of easy income, for which Holly is scrubbed *and* sober, is a weekly visit to Sing Sing, where she spends an hour's pleasant conversation visiting with Sally Tomato, a convicted mobster who'd never actually met, but had certainly seen and admired Miss Golightly before his incarceration. She's touched by all the wives and kids, in their best clothes and smiles, coming to visit the other prisoners. She's touched by how cheerful and sweet and grateful Mr. Tomato is for the visit. And she is paid $100 upon her return by Sally's "attorney", to whom she repeats Sally's "weather report" (such as "it's snowing in Peru"), which is a message in code. Holly has no idea what the weather report means and couldn't care less. Unfortunately, she is involved in a narcotics ring, and when it's busted she's indicted and splashed over all the front pages. The notoriety sends her Brazilian running, and she decides to jump bail: her brother Fred has died in action; she's already got the ticket to Brazil, which surely must have other millionaires; and as far as New York is concerned, "certain shades of limelight can wreck a girl's complexion."

Deep inside Holly, deeper even than Lulamae, is a hunger for open space, and an intrinsic lonely yearning to fly directly into it. She can be heard singing, and playing beautifully on a guitar, lonely prairie melodies of traveling and wandering, as she sits on her fire escape while her wet hair dries in the city sun. Holly had tried to explain it to Doc:

You mustn't give your heart to a wild thing. The more you do, the stronger they get. Until they're strong enough to run into the woods. Or fly into a tree. And then to a higher tree. Then to the sky....It's better to look at sky than to live there. Such an empty place...the sky...Just a country where thunder goes and things disappear....

The two scenes below introduce Holly to her new upstairs neighbor, Paul Varjak. By leaning out his front door, Paul can look down and see Holly, late at night, trying to squeeze *her* front door between herself and the belligerent super-rats who don't agree with her that the evening is definitely over. Paul is very handsome. Since the publication of his first collection of short stories, he's also been very blocked. Everything in Paul's apartment, from sweaters to rent, is provided by a wealthy, soignée woman who keeps him...and who keeps her marriage entirely separate. Significantly, the only thing Paul's newly outfitted apartment lacks is a ribbon in the typewriter. Holly leaves him one as a gift (following the second scene below), along with an invitation to one of her cocktail parties. Here, Paul will listen to O.J. Berman deliver his analysis of Holly as "a *real* phony" (in the second of the monologues below). But Paul will fall in love with Holly, quit his patroness, and begin to write again. At the end of the movie, Holly is holding Cat, and Paul is holding them both, and Holly is not afraid to be a permanent part of either one of them. Although the two scenes below come more or less from the book, there is no Paul Varjak in the novel *Breakfast at Tiffany's*. Rather, it is the novel's narrator who moves into the apartment upstairs. In the story that *he* tells, Holly becomes pregnant by the Brazilian diplomat, but her rough-house arrest results in a miscarriage. Then, with the exception of one postcard, Holly Golightly disappears, true to her own predictions, off into the sky.

From both versions, the character Holly Golightly, with her dream breakfasts at Tiffany's, emerged to take permanent root in the popular imagination as a cultural archetype: a fragile, self-amazed high-wire act of sophisticated youth with a hillbilly artful dodger tucked inside, too worldly and too innocent for its own good, utterly irresistible, but concealing an overwide wingspan, and possessing a deep, absolute faith in true love...but for herself only as a last resort, as an ambulance.

SCENE 1

INTERIOR. VESTIBULE—(DAY)

PAUL puts down his stuff, takes a key out of his pocket. It is tagged 3A. He looks over at the bells and card slots.

CLOSE SHOT—CARD SLOTS

CAMERA PANS DOWN: "Yunioshi," a blank, "Miss Holly Golightly" with the word: "Travelling" engraved in the corner, "Spanella".

INTERIOR. VESTIBULE—(DAY)

He is amused by MISS GOLIGHTLY'S card. He takes out a piece of paper and a pencil, writes something, tears it to the correct size, then inserts it into the empty slot.

CLOSE SHOT—CARD SLOTS

His slot now reads: PAUL VARJAK and in the corner the word "Arrived."

INTERIOR. VESTIBULE—(DAY)

Still grinning he tries his key in the door. It does not fit. Annoyed, he tries the door. It is locked. He hesitates for a moment . . . decides to ring one of the other bells . . . glances at his watch . . . decides it's not too early . . . then presses HOLLY'S bell.

INTERIOR. HOLLY'S LIVING ROOM—(DAY)

Begin on close shot of the cat asleep in HOLLY'S fallen evening dress. The buzzer sounds. The cat's head pops up. Pan to open bedroom door and move into—

INTERIOR. HOLLY'S DARKENED BEDROOM

The blinds have been drawn against the daylight. The bedroom (or what we can see of it) is unfurnished in the same manner as the living room except for an elaborate double bed. The buzzer sounds a second time and HOLLY'S head arises from the sea of pillows. She has on a sleep mask and ear plugs. She mumbles an unintelligible protest and sinks back. The buzzer sounds a third time. Reluctantly she sits up and lifts the eye shade. She sighs

and a bare arm reaches out and begins to grope under the bed.
The camera pans with the arm as it rummages around under the
bed. Under the bed is a jungle of shoes, underwear and assorted
articles of clothing. The arm finally settles on something that
turns out to be a man's dress shirt. The dress shirt is pulled up
and out of the picture.

INTERIOR. BEDROOM

HOLLY struggles into the dress shirt, hauls herself out of bed and
makes her way into—

INTERIOR. HOLLY'S LIVING ROOM—(DAY)

She crosses the room, kicking the evening dress out of sight in
the general interests of neatness. She pushes the clicker and
opens the door and peers sleepily out.

INTERIOR. HALLWAY—(DAY)

SHOOTING over HOLLY's shoulder we can see PAUL coming up
the stairs. He appears to be speaking but his lips move silently.
HOLLY strains to hear what he is saying. It is not until he reaches
her door that she catches on and removes her ear plugs. His
voice cuts in sharply in mid-sentence as she does so.

PAUL: . . . moving into Apartment 3A, but they only sent me
    the upstairs key so I couldn't get the downstairs door open.
    I hope I didn't wake you . . .

HOLLY: Quite all right . . . Could happen to anyone . . . very fre-
    quently *does* . . . Well, goodnight . . .

PAUL: Look, I hate to . . .

But HOLLY has replaced the ear plugs cutting his voice off
sharply once again. His lips continue to move. She notices and
reluctantly takes the plugs out again.

HOLLY: What?

PAUL: I said I hate to bother you, but I wonder if I could ask
    one more favor . . . if I could just use your phone . . .

HOLLY, now wide awake, sighs.

HOLLY: Sure. Why not...

She opens the door and motions him in. He enters, leaving his luggage in the hall.

INTERIOR. HOLLY'S LIVING ROOM—(DAY)

PAUL comes in followed by HOLLY. He is, out of a certain embarrassment, making conversation with more charm and brightness than is absolutely necessary.

PAUL: Thank you... Well, nice little place you have he—...

He gets a load of the "nice little place" and his remark more or less peters out.

PAUL: ...Uh, yes... Well... You just moving in, too?

HOLLY: No. I've been here about a year.

PAUL: Oh.

They both look around at the shambles for an uncomfortable moment.

HOLLY: The phone's right over there.

They both look at the spot she has indicated. The phone is *not* right over there.

HOLLY: Well, it *was*... Oh, no. I remember... I stuck it in the suitcase... it kind of muffles the sound...

She goes to the suitcase, opens it, rummages around among brassieres, etc., and finally finds the phone which she removes and hands him almost triumphantly. He starts for it and en route trips over the cat.

PAUL: Sorry! Didn't see him there... Is he all right?

HOLLY: Sure... Sure he is... You're okay, aren't you, Cat? Poor old Cat... (*She picks him up.*) Poor slob. Poor slob without a name. The way I look at it, I have no right to give him one.

PAUL listens to this with growing fascination.

HOLLY: We don't belong to each other. We just took up by the river one day. He's an independent and so am I . . . (*indicating room*) I don't even want to own anything until I've found a place where me and things go together. I'm not sure where that is. But I know what it's like. It's like Tiffany's . . .

PAUL: (*amused*) You mean the jewelry store?

HOLLY: That's right. I'm crazy about Tiffany's . . . Listen. You know those days when you've got the mean reds?

PAUL: The mean reds? You mean like the blues?

HOLLY: No. The blues are because you're getting fat or maybe it's been raining too long. You're sad, that's all. But the mean reds are horrible. Suddenly you're afraid, but you don't know what you're afraid of. You ever get that feeling?

PAUL: Sure.

HOLLY: Well, when I get it, the only thing that does any good is to jump in a cab and go to Tiffany's. It calms me down right away. The quietness and the proud look of it. Nothing very bad could happen to you there. Not with those kind men in their nice suits, and all the solid silver wedding presents waiting there so patiently for someone to propose . . . if I could find a real-life place that made me feel like Tiffany's, then I'd buy some furniture and give the cat a name . . .

She suddenly becomes aware that she has been rambling on.

HOLLY: I'm sorry. You *wanted* something—what was it? Oh, yes. The phone . . .

She hands it to him. He takes it and starts to dial.

PAUL: It's just that someone was supposed to meet me here . . . this *is* ten o'clock Thursday morning, isn't it? I just fell off a plane from Rome and . . .

HOLLY: (*an anguished squeal*) Thursday! Is this Thursday?

PAUL: I think so . . .

HOLLY: *Thursday!* Oh, no, it can't be! It's too gruesome!

She dashes wildly into the bedroom. He looks after her in some astonishment. Then, before he can pursue the matter, someone at the other end of the phone answers.

PAUL: Good morning. Is Mrs. Falenson at home? Oh. She has? I see. Thank you. No. No message.

He hangs up the phone. He stands holding it for a moment, looking for someplace to put it. He finally puts it back in the suitcase. As he does so, he calls into the bedroom:

PAUL: Hey, what's so gruesome about Thursday?

INTERIOR. BATHROOM—(DAY)

THE CAMERA IS SHOOTING OVER HOLLY'S bare shoulders, into the mirror as she frantically brushes her teeth.

HOLLY: (*through the toothpaste*) Nothing! It's just that I can never remember when it's coming up ... Wednesday nights I generally just don't go to bed at all ... because I have to be up to catch the ten-forty-five. They're so particular about the visiting hours!

INTERIOR. BEDROOM—(DAY)

PAUL stands in the doorway. He stares, somewhat bewildered, as HOLLY appears in the bathroom door, vaguely holding a bath towel in front of her.

HOLLY: Would you be a darling and look under the bed and see if you can find a pair of alligator shoes?

PAUL: Sure ...

Somewhat bewildered, but game, he crosses to the bed and kneels down.

HOLLY: I've got to do something about the way I look. I mean a girl just *can't* go to Sing Sing with a green face!

PAUL, down on his hands and knees, reacts rather violently to the words: Sing Sing.

PAUL: Sing Sing?

HOLLY dashes out of the bathroom, fetchingly attired in a half-slip which is pulled up to the arm-pits.

HOLLY: That's right. I always thought it was a ridiculous name for a prison . . . Sing Sing, I mean . . . it sounds more like it should be an opera house or something . . . *Brown* alligator . . .

She is now rummaging through still another unpacked suitcase.

HOLLY: And if you come across a black brassiere I can use that too . . . No really . . . all the visitors make an effort to look their best. It's only fair. Actually it's very touching, all the women wearing their prettiest things . . . I just love them for it. I love the kids too. I mean the kids the wives bring. It should be sad seeing the kids there—but it isn't. They have ribbons in their hair and lots of shine on their shoes, you'd think there was going to be ice cream and sometimes that's what it's like . . . a party.

PAUL has found the black brassiere. Somewhat astonished to find himself drafted into service as a ladies' maid, he nevertheless presents it . . . albeit a trifle timidly.

PAUL: As I understand this—what we're doing is getting you ready to visit somebody at Sing Sing?

With her back to him, she pulls the half-slip down to its normal position and hooks herself into the brassiere.

HOLLY: That's right. And now the shoes . . .

She is rapidly doing her face in a mirror that sits on a packing case. PAUL returns to beneath the bed in search of the shoes.

She selects a garish pair of earrings and tries them on. She studies the effect in the mirror.

HOLLY: You can always tell what kind of a person a man really thinks you are by the kind of earrings he gives you.

She studies her reflection, grimaces, and takes off the earrings.

HOLLY: I must say, the mind reels . . . garter-belt, garter-belt, garter-belt, garter-belt . . .

She has risen and is looking wildly around.

HOLLY: I think maybe it's hanging in the bathroom . . . would
you mind . . .

PAUL, hypnotized, sets off in search of the missing item. A
moment later he reappears with it and hands it to her.

PAUL: May one ask whom?

HOLLY: Whom what? Oh, who I go to visit, you mean?

PAUL: I guess that's what I mean.

HOLLY: I don't know if I should even discuss it . . . but . . . well
they never *told* me not to tell anyone . . . only you've got to
cross your heart and kiss your elbow . . .

PAUL: I'll try.

HOLLY: (*pulling on stockings*) You probably read about him. His
name is Sally Tomato.

PAUL: *Sally Tomato?*

HOLLY: Don't look so shocked. They could never prove for a
second that he was even *part* of the Mafia . . . much less the
head of it, my dear . . . the only thing they *did* prove was
that he cheated on his income tax a little . . . anyway, all I
know is, he's a darling old man. Oh, he was never my lover
or anything like that. In fact, I never knew him until after
he was in prison. But I adore him now. I mean I've been
going to see him every Thursday for seven months. Now I
think I'd go even if he *didn't* pay me . . . what about the
shoes?

PAUL: I could only find one . . . He *pays* you?

But this time they are both down on their hands and knees,
searching under the bed for the missing shoe.

HOLLY: That's right. Or anyway his lawyer does. If he *is* a
lawyer, which I doubt since he doesn't seem to have an
office, just an answering service and he always wants you to

meet him at Hamburg Heaven. (*Finding the shoe*)...there you are, you sneak!

During the following, HOLLY finds her scarf, which she puts over her head to avoid getting make-up on the dress which PAUL assists her into, via the over-the-head route.

HOLLY: Anyway, about seven months ago this so-called lawyer— Mr. O'Shaughnessy—asked me how I'd like to cheer up a lonely old man *and* pick up a hundred a week at the same time. I told him: Look, darling, you've got the wrong Holly Golightly. You can do as well as that on trips to the powder room. Any gentleman with the slightest chic will give you a fifty dollar bill for the girl's john...

She is into the dress by now and is piling things into a purse as PAUL zippers up the back of her dress.

HOLLY: And I always ask for cabfare, too. That's another fifty. But then he said his client was Sally Tomato. He said dear old Sally had seen me at Elmer's or somewhere and had admired me *a la distance* so wouldn't it be a good deed if I went to visit him once a week. Well, how could I say no? It was all so wildly romantic...

The dressing operation is now complete. Astonishingly enough, out of the terrible shambles, HOLLY has emerged looking neat, chic and altogether immaculate.

HOLLY: Well, how do I look?

PAUL: Very good. I must say, I'm amazed. Awed, actually.

HOLLY: You were a darling to help. I could never have done it without you...

PAUL: Call on me any time. I'm right upstairs. Or I will be as soon as I get moved in.

By this time they have moved through the living room and out into—

EXTERIOR. HALLWAY—(DAY)

HOLLY is locking the door behind her. We still get the sense of her being on the dead run. She starts down the stairs. PAUL, intrigued by what he has heard, follows.

PAUL: You mean for an hour's conversation he gives you a hundred dollars?

HOLLY: Well, Mr. O'Shaughnessy does. As soon as I meet him and give him the weather report.

PAUL: It's none of my business, but it sounds to me like you could get into a lot of trouble . . . And what do you mean, *weather report*?

They have now reached—

INTERIOR. VESTIBULE—(DAY)

HOLLY opens her mail box, inspects the mail, puts it all back, and closes the box again.

HOLLY: Oh, that's just a message I give Mr. O'Shaughnessy so he'll know I've really been up there. Sally tells me things to say like . . . Oh . . . "There's a hurricane in Cuba" . . . "It's cloudy in Palermo" . . . things like that. (*Nothing but bills.*) You don't have to worry. I've taken care of myself for a long time . . .

They move out to the—

EXTERIOR. BROWNSTONE—(DAY)

PAUL: Taxi! Oh, taxi!

A cab goes by but it already has a passenger. HOLLY puts two fingers in her mouth and whistles. Another cab goes by.

(*Note*: At the end of this scene, Holly will have to find something else requiring her last minute attention inside the apartment for the last few beats where the script has her moving down the steps of the brownstone to the street outside. But the beautifully rhythmic dialogue can be played uninterrupted straight through to Paul's call, "Taxi! Oh, taxi!" capped by the sound of Holly's whistle, by moving these lines offstage.)

SCENE 2

[EXTERIOR. HOLLY'S FIRE ESCAPE—(NIGHT)

The camera is shooting through the window into HOLLY'S bathroom. There is the sound of another crash. The bathroom door opens and HOLLY enters, wearing an evening dress. She quickly locks the door behind her.

INTERIOR. HOLLY'S BATHROOM—(NIGHT)

There is still another crash. She shrugs, sighs a little—she is, however, more amused than alarmed, then opens the window and attempts to climb out. But the tight dress prohibits this. Another crash. HOLLY quickly removes the dress, slips into a large terry cloth robe and climbs out onto the fire escape.

EXTERIOR. HOLLY'S FIRE ESCAPE—(NIGHT)

The camera follows HOLLY as she climbs the fire escape mounting to—

EXTERIOR. PAUL'S FIRE ESCAPE—(NIGHT)

HOLLY peers into the window.

INTERIOR. PAUL'S APARTMENT—(HOLLY'S P.O.V.)—(NIGHT)

PAUL is asleep on the bed. In the single light from the bed lamp we can see that he is smiling benignly in his sleep.

EXTERIOR. HOLLY ON FIRE ESCAPE—(NIGHT)

Her features take on the same benign smile. She starts to open the window and enter. Then she sees something that stops her.

INTERIOR. PAUL'S APARTMENT—(HOLLY'S P.O.V.)—(NIGHT)

2E dressed for the street, is coming out of the bathroom. She moves about the room, straightening up. Emptying ashtrays and clearing away glasses.

EXTERIOR. HOLLY ON FIRE ESCAPE—(NIGHT)

HOLLY, resigned, seats herself on the fire escape. She settles in to wait.

INTERIOR. PAUL'S APARTMENT—(NIGHT)

2E, her domestic chores finished, goes to the bed and lovingly pulls the covers up around the sleeping PAUL. She kisses him very gently. He does not awaken. She starts to go—then, almost as an afterthought—opens her purse and takes out three hundred dollars in fifty dollar bills which she places on the desk. She kisses PAUL once more and tiptoes out, closing the door softly behind her.]

EXTERIOR. HOLLY ON THE FIRE ESCAPE—(NIGHT)

Now the coast is clear. HOLLY raps on the window. PAUL does not stir. She raps again louder. This time his eyes open.

INTERIOR. PAUL'S APARTMENT—(NIGHT)

Aware of the rapping at the window, PAUL startled sits up. HOLLY opens the window and enters.

HOLLY: It's all right. It's only me . . .

PAUL: Now wait a minute, Miss . . .

HOLLY: Golightly. Holly Golightly. I live downstairs. We met this morning, remember?

PAUL looks anxiously around for 2E.

HOLLY: That's all right. She's gone. I must say, she works late hours . . . for a decorator. The thing is, I've got the most terrifying man downstairs. I mean he's sweet when he isn't drunk, but let him start lapping up the vino and oh, golly, quel beast! It finally got so tiresome down there that I just went out the window.

There is another crash from below. PAUL looks at her questioningly. She shrugs.

HOLLY: Look, you can throw me out if you want to . . . but you *did* look so cozy in here . . . and your decorator friend *had* gone home . . . and it *was* beginning to get cold out there on the *balcon.* . . .

PAUL: And I always heard people in New York never get to know their neighbors. How was Sing Sing?

HOLLY: Fine. I made the train and everything . . .

PAUL: And what's the weather report?

HOLLY: Small craft warnings Block Island to Hatteras . . . whatever that means . . . (*making a decision*) You know, you're sweet. You really are. And you look a little like my brother Fred. Do you mind if I call you Fred?

She seats herself at his desk.

PAUL: (*lighting a cigarette*) Not at all . . .

HOLLY: When I was little, we used to sleep four in a bed. Fred was the only one who would let me hug him on a cold night . . . (*casually, she picks up the money* 2E *left on the desk; rapidly counts it*) Three hundred? She's very generous . . . Is that by the week, the hour . . . or what?

PAUL: (*suddenly angry*) Okay. The party's over. Out!

He starts to get out of bed to throw her out. Realizes in time that he has no clothes on and, frustrated, glowers at her from the bed. HOLLY, realizing she has been rude, rushes to him, kneeling beside the bed.

HOLLY: Oh, Fred, darling Fred, I'm sorry. I didn't mean to hurt your feelings. Don't be angry. I was just trying to let you know I understand . . . I understand completely.

PAUL: (*after a moment*) That's okay. Stick around . . . Make yourself a drink . . . or throw me my pants and I'll get up and make you one . . .

HOLLY: You stay right where you are! You must be absolutely exhausted . . . I mean it's very late and you were sound asleep and everything . . .

She pours two drinks and brings one to him and then, finally settles back in the chair at the desk.

HOLLY: I suppose you think I'm very brazen. Or *tres fou*. Or something.

PAUL: I don't think you're any *fou*-er than anybody else . . .

HOLLY: Yes, you do. Everybody does. I don't mind. It's useful being top banana in the shock department. What do you do, anyway?

PAUL: I'm a writer, I guess . . .

HOLLY: You guess? Don't you *know*?

PAUL: Okay. Positive statement. Ringing affirmative. I'm a writer.

HOLLY: (*thoughtfully*) The only writer I've ever been out with is Benny Shacklett . . . He's written an awful lot of television stuff . . . But quel rat! Tell me, are you a *real* writer? I mean does anybody buy what you write? Or publish it or anything?

PAUL motions toward the cardboard carton that is now resting open on the floor beside the desk. It contains a dozen copies of a book. She starts to take them out.

HOLLY: Yours?

PAUL: Uh-huh . . .

HOLLY: *All* these books?

PAUL: Well, it's just the one book. Twelve copies of it . . .

HOLLY: (*reading the title*) "Nine Stories" by Paul Varjak. They're stories?

PAUL: Nine of them.

HOLLY: Tell me one.

PAUL: They're not the kind of story you can really tell . . .

HOLLY: Too dirty?

PAUL: Well, I suppose they're dirty, *too*. But only incidentally. Mostly they're "angry," "sensitive," "intensely felt" and that dirtiest of all dirty words, "promising." At least that's what the *Times* book review said on October 1st, 1956.

HOLLY: 1956?

PAUL: That's right.

HOLLY: I suppose this is kind of a ratty question . . . but what have you written lately?

PAUL: Lately I've been working on a novel.

HOLLY: Lately since 1956?

PAUL: A novel takes a long time. I want to get it exactly right.

HOLLY: And so no more stories?

PAUL: The idea is I'm not supposed to fritter away the talent on little things. I'm supposed to be saving for the big one.

HOLLY: Do you write every day?

PAUL: Sure.

HOLLY: Today?

PAUL: Sure.

HOLLY: It's a beautiful typewriter.

PAUL: Of course. It writes only very sensitive, intensely felt, promising prose . . .

HOLLY hits a few keys at random.

HOLLY: There's no ribbon in it.

PAUL: There isn't?

HOLLY: No.

PAUL: Oh. (*pause*) Something you said this morning . . . it's been worrying me all day.

HOLLY: What's that?

PAUL: Do they really give you fifty dollars whenever you go to the powder room?

HOLLY: Of course . . .

PAUL: You must do very well . . .

HOLLY: I'm trying to save. But I'm not very good at it. You *do* look a lot like my brother Fred . . .

She comes over and sits down on the edge of the bed.

HOLLY: I haven't seen him, of course, since I was fourteen, that's when I left home, and he was already six-feet-two. I guess it must have been the peanut butter that did it. Everybody thought he was dotty the way he gorged himself on peanut butter. But he wasn't dotty. Just sweet and vague and terribly slow. He'd been in the eighth grade three years when I ran away. Poor Fred. He's in the army now. That's really the best place for him . . . until I can get enough money saved . . .

PAUL: And then?

HOLLY: Then Fred and I . . . I went to Mexico once. It's a wonderful country for raising horses. I saw one place . . . near the sea. Fred's very good with horses . . . but even land in Mexico costs something . . . and no matter what I do there never seems to be more than a couple of hundred dollars in the bank . . .

She notices the alarm clock on the bed table.

HOLLY: It *can't* be four-thirty! It just can't!

The first light is beginning to filter into the room. HOLLY suddenly looks terribly young and terribly tired . . . like a transparent child.

HOLLY: Do you mind if I just get in with you for a minute?

She slides into bed beside him.

HOLLY: (*sleepily*) It's all right—really it is. We're friends, that's all . . . We *are* friends, aren't we?

PAUL: Sure . . .

She snuggles her head against his shoulder and closes her eyes.

HOLLY: Okay . . . Now let's don't say another word . . . Let's just go to sleep . . .

He looks down at her . . . in a moment she is almost asleep.

Moving gently, he reaches over to turn out the lamp. Morning begins to fill the room. In her sleep now, HOLLY stirs and holds his arm.

HOLLY: Poor Fred . . . where are you, Fred? Because it's cold. There's snow in the wind . . .

PAUL looks more closely and sees that she is crying.

PAUL: What is it . . . what's the matter? Why are you crying?

HOLLY, suddenly wide awake, springs out of bed.

HOLLY: If we're going to be friends, let's get one thing straight right now! I *hate* snoops!

And with this, she starts for the window and fire escape.

MONOLOGUE 1

[EXTERIOR. PARK—EXTREME LONG SHOT—(LATE AFTERNOON)

PAUL coming across a large section of grass, the man following him in far b.g.

MOVING SHOT—MAN

Still following.

MOVING SHOT—PAUL

He glances back over his shoulder, quickens his pace.

DISSOLVE TO:

EXTERIOR. CENTRAL PARK—AT MALL—(LATE AFTERNOON)

The man, enters shot, looks around, spots PAUL O.S.

MAN'S P.O.V.

PAUL seated in one of the rows of empty chairs. Only one other person is present, a man seated in the back row sleeping.

ANOTHER ANGLE

PAUL in f.g. The man who has been following PAUL crosses and seat himself next to PAUL.

PAUL: Okay. What do you want?]

MAN: Son, I need a friend.

[PAUL watches with mounting curiosity as] the man reaches into his pocket and withdraws a wallet—it is as worn and leathery as his hands—almost, in fact, falling to pieces. From it he takes an equally worn snapshot [which he hands to PAUL.]

THE MAN: That's me. That's her. And that's her brother Fred.

[PAUL takes the snapshot and looks at it curiously.

INSERT—THE SNAPSHOT

There are seven people in the picture, all grouped together on the sagging porch of a stark wooden house. And all are children except for the man himself who has his arm around the waist of a plump little girl who stands with her hand shading her eyes against the sun. The little girl has a clear, if embryonic resemblance to HOLLY.

BACK TO SCENE—(LATE AFTERNOON)

PAUL continues to study the snapshot. Then he looks up amazed.

PAUL: You're Holly's *father*?]

THE MAN: Her name's not Holly. She was Lulamae Barnes. Was...'til she married me. I'm her husband...Doc Golightly. I'm a horse doctor. Animal man. Do some farming too. Near Tulip, Texas.

[PAUL laughs. But it is a nervous laugh, completely without humor.

DOC: This here's no humorous matter, son.] Her brother Fred's getting out of the army soon. Lulamae belongs home with her husband, her brother and her churren . . .

[PAUL: *Children?*]

DOC: (*indicating the snapshot*) Them's her churren . . .

PAUL sits for a moment, staring wide-eyed at DOC.

DOC: Now, son, I didn't claim they was her natural-born churren.

Their own precious mother, precious woman, passed away July 4th, Independence Day, 1955. The year of the drought. When I married Lulamae she was going on fourteen. Maybe an ordinary person, being only fourteen, wouldn't know their own mind. But you take Lulamae, she was an exceptional person.

[He offers PAUL the crackerjack box.]

DOC: I tell you, son, she plain broke our hearts when she ran off like she done. And she just plain had no cause. All the housework was done by her daughters. Lulamae could just take it easy. Fuss in front of mirrors and wash her hair. That woman got positively fat . . . while her brother, he growed into a giant. Which is a sight different from how they come to us. Two wild young'uns, they was. I caught 'em outside the house stealing milk and turkey eggs. Lulamae and her brother'd been living with some mean no-count people a hundred miles east of Tulip. She had good cause to run off from that house. She didn't have none to leave mine.

[PAUL: What about her brother? Didn't he leave too?]

DOC: No sir. Fred was with us till they took him in the army. That's what I got to talk to her about. I had a letter from him. He gits out of the army in February. That's why I got on the Greyhound bus and come all this way to git her. Her place is with her husband and churren and brother.

[Through this, PAUL has located the prize in the box of crackerjacks, in this case a plain, gold-looking metal ring. He proffers it to DOC.

DOC: (*noticing the proffered ring*) Huh?

PAUL: The prize in the box of crackerjacks. You want it?

DOC shakes his head. PAUL starts to toss it away, then, for no reason whatever, puts it instead in his pocket. He hands the box to DOC, who begins, casually, paying no real attention to what he is doing, to toss a few kernels of crackerjack on the ground in front of him.]

DOC: Never could understand why that woman run off. Don't tell me she wasn't happy. Talky as a jay bird she was. With something smart to say on every subject. Better than the radio. The night I proposed I cried like a baby. She said: "What you want to cry for, Doc? Course we'll be married. I've never been married before." Well, I had to laugh and hug and squeeze her. *"Never been married before!"*

[As he talks now, the crackerjack has begun to attract pigeons. It is clear that DOC has a way with them. In a moment or two they are eating out of his hand, climbing on his shoulders. He works with them, almost automatically as he talks. He seems completely at home with them and they with him.]

DOC: We all doted on that woman. She didn't have to lift a finger, except to eat a piece of pie. Except to comb her hair and send away for all the magazines. We must've had a hundred dollars worth of magazines come to that house. Ask me, that's what done it. Looking at show-off pictures. Reading dreams. That's what started her walking down the road. Every day, she'd walk a little further. A mile and then come home. Two miles and come home. One day, she just kept on . . .

[He turns to PAUL with some intensity.]

DOC: Listen, son, I advised you, I need a friend. Because I don't want to surprise her or scare her none. Be my friend. Let her know I'm here. Will you do that for me, son?

[After a moment:

PAUL: Sure, Doc. If that's what you want. Come on.

They rise and move off toward Fifth Avenue.]

MONOLOGUE 2

[INTERIOR. HOLLY'S APARTMENT—(LATE AFTERNOON)

A smattering of guests, O.J. BERMAN, a brisk, tough-talking little man, pours himself a drink and reacts to a knock at the door. O.J. crosses to the door, opens it disclosing PAUL.

O.J.: Kid's in the shower. . . You expected?

PAUL: I was invited. If that's what you mean...

With that, he ushers PAUL into the room.

O.J.:   Okay. So don't get sore. It's just a lot of characters come
here they're *not* expected. That's all. You know the kid
long?

PAUL: Not very. I live upstairs.

O.J.:   (*with some horror*) In this building?

PAUL: That's right.

O.J.:   What a dump! Look at it. Unbelievable!]

He pauses for a moment and then, very suddenly and dramatically hurls a question.

O.J.:   Well—what do you think? Is she—or isn't she?

[Before PAUL can come up with a suitable reply, the bedroom
door bursts open and HOLLY, fresh from the shower, splashes
into the room, a towel more or less wrapped around her and her
wet feet dripping foot marks on the floor.

HOLLY: Fred, darling—I'm so glad you could come—

PAUL: I brought you a house present—something for your
bookcase. (*He hands her the book.*)

HOLLY: You *are* sweet—(*She puts it on the shelf where it sits in
solitary splendor.*) It does look nice there, doesn't it—Light
me a cigarette, will you? Not you, O.J. You're such a
slob...

She reaches down and deftly scoops up the cat and places it on
her bare shoulder. PAUL lights her a cigarette. Through this,
HOLLY's line of chatter does not lose a beat.

HOLLY: O.J. is a slob but he's a great agent and he knows a
terrific lot of phone numbers. What is Jerry Wald's phone
number, O.J.?

O.J.:   ...Come on now. Lay off...

HOLLY: Darling. I want you to call him up and tell him what a
         genius Fred is. (*she indicates book on the shelf*) See—nine
         stories—by Paul Varjak. Now you just stop blushing, Fred.
         You didn't say you were a genius. I did. So quit stalling,
         O.J. Just tell me what you're going to do to make Fred rich
         and famous . . .

O.J.:   Suppose you just let old Fred-baby and me settle that,
         huh, kid?

There is another KNOCK at the door. HOLLY moves off to answer
it, calling over her shoulder as she goes:

HOLLY: Okay. But just remember. I'm his agent. He's already
         got a decorator—but I'm his agent.

O.J.:   Well, okay, Fred-baby . . .

PAUL: (*correcting him*) *Paul*-baby . . .

O.J.:   Okay, Paul baby . . .] So answer the question. Is she—or
         isn't she?

[PAUL: Is she what?]

O.J.:   A phony.

[PAUL: I don't know. I don't think so . . .]

O.J.:   Well, you're wrong! She *is* a phony! But on the other
         hand, you're right. Because she's a *real* phony. You know
         why? Because she honestly believes all this phony junk she
         believes! Mind you, I like the kid. I do. I sincerely like the
         kid. I'm sensitive, that's why. You got to be sensitive to like
         the kid. A streak of the poet . . .

[PAUL: Have you known her long?]

O.J.:   Me! O.J. Berman! I'm the one *discovered* her. On the
         coast, a couple of years ago. Just a kid . . . but stylish. Even
         though when she opens her mouth, you don't know if she's
         a hillbilly or an okie or what. One year it took to smooth
         out that accent. How we finally did it, we give her French
         lessons. Once she could imitate French it wasn't so long

before she could imitate English. Finally, when I think she's ready, I set her up a screen test . . . I could kill myself . . . the night before . . . wham! the phone rings! She says: This is Holly. I say: Baby, you sound far away. She says: I'm in New York. I say: What kind of New York? You got a screen test here tomorrow. She says: I'm in New York because I've never been to New York. I say: You get yourself on a plane and get back here. She says: I don't want it. I say: You don't want it? She says: I don't want it. I say: What *do* you want? She says: When I find out, you'll be the first one to know. So listen, [Fred-]baby . . .

[PAUL: *Paul*-baby . . .]

O.J.:   Don't stand there and try and tell me she ain't a phony!

Having made his point, O.J. moves off into the thickening crowd—leaving PAUL to his own devices.

MONOLOGUE 3

EXTERIOR. 52ND STREET—(NIGHT)

HOLLY and PAUL are walking up the street. HOLLY clings to him ever so slightly for support. They are now passing the iron gate of Twenty-One. HOLLY stops.

HOLLY: ''Twenty-One'' . . . world famous rendezvous of the great . . . meeting place of the famous . . . haunt of movie stars . . . account executives and . . . (*considers for a moment*) . . . international polo players . . . [Shall we pop in for a quick one . . . just to see who's there . . .

PAUL: I think better not. Personally not being an international polo player . . . are you *sure* polo players?

HOLLY: Figure of speech.

PAUL: That's what I thought . . .]

HOLLY: Exactly . . . aphorism . . . or eupheumism or some kind of mism . . . anyway, it may be Twenty-One to you . . . but you know what it is to me . . . the mess hall . . . that's what I

call it . . . the mess hall . . . and you want to know why I call
it the mess hall . . . because I have dinner there every night
of my life. Every Tom, Dick and Harry . . . no . . . correction
. . . every Tom, Dick and Sid . . . Harry was his *friend* . . . also
in the machine tool business, however . . . Anyway, every
Tom, Dick and Sid thinks if he takes a girl to Twenty-One
for dinner she'll just curl up like a kitten in a little furry ball
at his feet . . . Right?

[PAUL: If you say so. You're an authority . . .]

HOLLY: I have by actual count been taken to Twenty-One by
twenty-six different rats in the last two months. Twenty-
seven, if you include Benny Shacklett, who is, in many
ways, a *super*-rat . . . and do you know something funny? In
spite of the fact that most of these rats . . . or, in the case of
Benny Shacklett, *super*-rats, fork up fifty bucks for the
powder room like little dolls . . . I find I have, again by
actual count, nine dollars less in the old bank account than I
had six months ago . . . so, my darling [Fred], I have this
night made a very serious decision . . . no longer will I play
the "Field" . . . "The Field" stinks . . . both economically
and socially and I am giving it up . . .

[PAUL takes her firmly by the arm and attempts to lead her
away . . .]

HOLLY: Goodbye "Field" . . . goodbye all you rats . . . and/or
super-rats as the case may be . . . Goodbye . . . goodbye . . .
goodbye . . .

[PAUL is leading her, still babbling, up the street as we

DISSOLVE TO:

EXTERIOR. BROWNSTONE—(NIGHT)

HOLLY is leaning even more heavily on PAUL than before. He
leads her up the steps.]

HOLLY: And as Holly Golightly sinks slowly into the West, she
bids a fond Aloha . . .

[He has, by now, led her to the top of the steps and into—

INTERIOR. VESTIBULE—(NIGHT)]

HOLLY: . . . To Tom, Dick and Harry . . . no . . . Tom, Dick and *Sid* . . . Harry was his *friend* . . .

[Through this, PAUL searches for his key. He cannot find it. HOLLY does not bother to look for hers but simply pushes MR. YUNIOSHI's bell, keeping her finger on it until the door finally clicks open and HOLLY and PAUL move into—

INTERIOR. STAIRWELL—(NIGHT)

As they weave up the stairs we hear the irate cries of MR. YUNIOSHI.

YUNIOSHI'S VOICE: *(O.S.)* Miss Golightly, this time I will call not only the police but the Fire Department, the New York State Housing Commission and if necessary the Board of Health . . .

HOLLY: And, my friend, Miss Golightly further announces . . . *(She suddenly becomes aware of* MR. YUNIOSHI'S *voice. She bellows sternly up at him)* Quiet up there! You want to wake the whole house!

HOLLY gets her key from under the mat, then struggles with it. PAUL takes it away from her and opens the door and hastily pushes her into—

INTERIOR. HOLLY'S LIVING ROOM—(NIGHT)

PAUL closes the door behind him. He switches on the light. The cat is sitting on a packing case watching them. During the next speeches, HOLLY takes off her raincoat and drops it on the floor. PAUL picks it up, looks for somewhere to hang it, realizes there is no such place, and folds it neatly over a packing case. HOLLY, lurching a little, finds the whiskey bottle and pours herself a drink.

HOLLY: As Miss Golightly was saying before she was so rudely interrupted] . . . Miss Golightly further announces her intention to devote her not-inconsiderable talents to the immediate capture, for the purposes of matrimony, of Mr. Rutherford

("Rusty" to his friends, of whom I am sure he has many)
Trawler...

[PAUL: Who?]

HOLLY: Rusty Trawler. [You met him at my party a couple of
weeks ago. He came with Mag Wildwood...not the beautiful latin-type. The other one. The one] who looks like a
pig.

She puffs out her cheeks by way of illustration.

HOLLY: [Remember?] The ninth richest man in America
under fifty-five?

[She starts to pour more whiskey into her glass but the bottle is
empty—a fact she does not immediately notice.

HOLLY: Ah! Do I detect a look of disapproval in your eye?
Tough beans, buddy. Because that's the way it's going to
be.

PAUL: You're drunk.

HOLLY: True. Absolutely true. True but irrelevant.] So let's have
a drink to the new Mrs. Rusty Trawler. Me. What's the
matter? Don't you think I can do it?... Tell me. I'm
seriously interested. Don't you think I can?

[PAUL: I'm sure you can.

HOLLY: You were there...you heard the Doc...my brother
gets out of the army in February and the Doc won't take
him back...so it's a-l-l-l up to me...and I need money
and Rusty's got money and if I marry him then he'll have to
buy a ranch for Fred and me...you're supposed to be so
smart with your nine stories...I don't know why you don't
understand...I need money and I'll do whatever I have to
do to get it...so-o-o...by this time next month I'm going
to be the new Mrs. Rusty Trawler...and...I think we
should have a little drink to that.

She attempts to pour again and this time realizes the bottle is
empty.

HOLLY: All gone. Isn't that too bad? Got any whiskey upstairs?

PAUL: Sure . . . but you've had enough.

HOLLY: I asked a simple question, requiring only a simple yes or
no. What I did *not* ask for was advice, counsel or the
benefit of your opinion. Go ahead get the whiskey. I'll *pay*
you for it.

PAUL: Holly! Come on!

She opens her purse, fumbles in it and finally takes out a ten-
dollar bill.

PAUL: Holly! Stop it!

HOLLY: No, no . . . you disapprove of me . . . and I do not accept
drinks from gentlemen who disapprove of me . . . I can pay
for my own whiskey and don't you forget it.

She tries to force the money into his hand, but he manages to
push the bill back into her purse.

HOLLY: I do not accept drinks from disapproving gentlemen . . .
especially dispproving gentlemen who are kept by other
ladies . . . so take it . . . you should be used to taking money
from ladies by now.

She throws the ten-dollar bill to the floor at his feet.

PAUL: If I were you, I'd be more careful with my money.
Rusty Trawler is too hard a way of earning it.

HOLLY: It should take you exactly four seconds to cross from
here to that door. I'll give you two.

He hesitates a moment, then turns and goes.]

(*Note*: From Holly's opening words, "Twenty-One" straight
through to ". . . Tell me. I'm seriously interested. Don't you
think I can?" presents a monologue which Holly can speak alone
onstage. If the actress wishes to perform the material beyond this
point to the end of the excerpt, she will need an onstage Paul. He
may be silent if she wishes to use the material as monologue, or
he may speak if the material is to be used as a scene. Whether
Paul is silent or speaking, however, his presence will be essential
if Holly's transition based on his disapproval is to play properly.)

JUDGMENT AT NUREMBERG

A United Artists release of a Roxlom Production. Producer & Director, Stanley Kramer. Screenplay by Abby Mann. Associate Producer, Philip Langner. Camera, Ernest Laszlo. Editor, Fred Knudtson. Production Designer, Rudolph Sternad. Music, Ernest Gold. Sound, James Speak. Production Manager, Clem Beauchamp. Assistant Director, Ivan Volkman. Running time, 190 minutes. 1961.

CAST

JUDGE DAN HAYWOOD	Spencer Tracy
ERNST JANNING	Burt Lancaster
HANS ROLFE	Maximilian Schell
COLONEL TAD LAWSON	Richard Widmark
MME. BERTHOLT	Marlene Dietrich
IRENE HOFFMAN	Judy Garland
RUDOLF PETERSEN	Montgomery Clift
MRS. HALBESTADT	Virginia Christine
CAPTAIN BYERS	William Shatner
SENATOR BURKETTE	Ed Binns
JUDGE KENNETH NORRIS	Kenneth MacKenna
JUDGE CURTISS IVES	Ray Teal

The Heisenberg Uncertainty Principle: measuring anything alters the substance being measured; inserting the thermometer heats up the surrounding substance. Periodically since 1957,

---

Abby Mann has written a drama for television about an actual trial. (*Judgment at Nuremberg* was the first.) What gets measured in these dramas is justice—guilt, the law, the court system, the police, responsibility, human decency and human evil. These are always extremely tense dramas, and each one, like the Heisenberg thermometer, always increases the social/political temperature of its day. Each one always upsets a lot of people. In the foreword to the published script for the movie version of *Judgment at Nuremberg*, Abby Mann recalls:

> When I first began writing *Judgment at Nuremberg* in the fall of 1957, it was considered a breach of good manners in polite society in America as well as in most quarters in Europe to bring up the subject of German guilt or the victims of the Third Reich during the period of the years 1935 to 1942. . . . It struck me as fantastic that perhaps the most significant trial in all history had never been treated artistically and little journalistically. Casual research unearthed an even more startling fact. Of the ninety-nine men sentenced to prison terms in the second of the Nuremberg trials, not one was still serving his sentence.

The second trials—after the stars, architects, and masterminds had been dealt with—included the judges who during the Third Reich had carried out laws that violated not only the Constitution of Germany, but also the human rights of more victims than history had ever recorded. Nuremberg had been an ancient seat of learning and the law. It was also the site of the overwhelming Nuremberg rallies, where the sheer physical might of thousands of "Heil Hitlers!" cried out together was intended to last a thousand years. Here were enacted the "Nuremberg Laws," which made anyone with "impure" blood the enemy of the Reich. Anyone who mixed with these enemies could be imprisoned, sterilized, or killed. Ernst Janning, perhaps the greatest legal mind of his generation, was already mature and on the bench when Hitler was given the reins. Despite the loyalty oaths and overturned laws, many were thankful that Janning *stayed* in the Ministry of Justice, to fight for what little justice could be preserved. Until the Feldenstein case, in which Janning allowed a sixteen-year-old girl to be imprisoned for a nonsexual, innocent sit-in-the-lap of an old Jewish man who'd been kind to her. The old man was killed. By 1942, Hitler threw Janning off the bench.

Now, years later, the Third Reich crushed, Nuremberg mostly bombed rubble, Janning's defense attorney is badgering the woman from the Feldenstein case with the same questions heard in the court the first time the case was "tried." Until now, Janning has refused to even speak. He has not recognized the legitimacy of this Tribunal to charge him. But suddenly he wants to make a statement. He cannot believe that he is listening to this woman, all over again, being rendered hysterical by lawyers trying to pervert her testimony. Janning had rationalized allowing it once, years ago, because he'd let himself believe it would happen only once. This time he stops it. He claims his guilt, issuing in the first monologue below an opening and closing statement, incriminating himself. (Somehow, however, he still maintains some corner of retreat in himself. At the film's conclusion he will ask Judge Haywood, who has sentenced him to life imprisonment, to assure him that it is understood between the two of them that Janning had no idea how massive the evil would grow. He is told, "Herr Janning. It came to that the first time you sentenced to death a man you knew to be innocent.")

The second monologue belongs to Rolfe, the defense counsel assigned to Janning. Rolfe answers Janning's self-incrimination with the argument that if Janning is guilty, then so are all the Allied leaders who knew as much as Janning, perhaps more, perhaps earlier. Rolfe is described in the script as "a vital-looking man in his late twenties . . . He was once a Hitler youth leader. His studies as a law student were interrupted when he had to join the Army at a very early age. His manner is one of decorum and politeness before the Tribunal. Underneath, one sees his scorn of the trials. His conviction that they are unfair, that they are no more than the trial of the vanquished by the victors, covered by hypocritical, high-sounding verbiage. Very much apparent in his action, too, is his intention of taking the game at its own price, to hoist the trials up by their own petard. But he is even more deeply involved than that. He is, himself, on trial, although he is not fully aware of it."

MONOLOGUES 1 AND 2

INTERIOR. PALACE OF JUSTICE, COURTROOM—DAY

JANNING is on the stand. HAYWOOD is looking over at him. The courtroom is in silence. Electric silence.

[HAYWOOD: Ernst Janning. Do you wish to make a statement?
     (*pause*)

JANNING: I do.

HAYWOOD: Proceed.]

This is a moment. JANNING'S eyes seem to go to every face in the courtroom. JANNING is a Junker, and to understand this, is to understand how difficult it is for him to speak to the Tribunal. It means the casting off of his reserve. It means the opening up of a wound that it has been his main profession not to tamper with these last ten years. He speaks finally. The NEWSMEN take down every word.

JANNING: I wish to testify about the Feldenstein case because it was the most significant trial of the period. (*pause*) It is important not only for the Tribunal to understand it, but the German people. (*pause*) But to understand it, one must understand the period in which it happened.

He tries to bring the period into words. This is not easy.

JANNING: (*continuing*) There was a fever over the land. A fever of disgrace, of indignity, of hunger. We had a democracy, yes, but it was torn by elements within. There was, above all, fear. Fear of today, fear of tomorrow, fear of our neighbours, fear of ourselves. (*pause*)

THE BENCH—CLOSE-UP—HAYWOOD

He understands. The last few days since the Berlin crisis have brought fear home to him.

CLOSE-UP—JANNING

JANNING: Only when you understand that can you understand what Hitler meant to us. Because he said to us: Lift your

heads! Be proud to be German! There are devils among us!
Communists, Liberals, Jews, Gypsies—Once the devils will
be destroyed, your miseries will be destroyed!

Pause. JANNING smiles sardonically.

JANNING: (*continuing*) It was the old, old story of the sacrificial
lamb. (*pause*)

He seems to look inside himself. The words are hard to come.

JANNING: (*continuing*) What about those of us who knew bet-
ter? We who knew the words were lies and worse than lies?
Why did we sit silent? Why did we participate? (*pause*)
Because we loved our country!

THE BENCH—CLOSE-UP—HAYWOOD

The revelation is a bombshell to him which is self-explanatory.
The last meeting he had had with SENATOR BURKETTE and IVES
has made it self-explanatory.

FULL SHOT

JANNING: What difference does it make if a few political ex-
tremists lose their rights? What difference does it make if
a few racial minorities lose their rights? It is only a
passing phase. It is only a stage we are going through. It
will be discarded sooner or later. Hilter himself will be
discarded sooner or later. "The country is in danger."
We will "march out of the shadows." "We will go
forward."

He looks toward people in Press section.

JANNING: (*continuing*) And history tells how well we succeeded,
Your Honour! (*looks at* HAYWOOD) We succeeded beyond
our wildest dreams. The very elements of hate and power
about Hitler that mesmerized Germany, mesmerized the
world! (*remembering with sardonic bitterness*) We found
ourselves with sudden powerful allies. Things that had been
denied us as a democracy—were open to us now. The world
said, go ahead, take it! Take Sudetenland, take the Rhineland—
re-militarize it—take all of Austria, take it! (*pause*) We
marched forward. The danger passed. (*pause; simply*) And

then one day we looked around and found we were in an even more terrible danger. The rites began in this court-room, swept over our land like a raging, roaring disease! What was going to be a passing phase had become a way of life.

There is a moment. He speaks quietly.

JANNING: (*continuing*) Your Honour, I was content to sit silent during this trial. (*dryly*) I was content to tend my roses. I was even content to let counsel try to save my name. (*pause; looks over at* ROLFE) Until I realized that in order to save it, he would have to raise the spectre again. (*pause; as he looks over at* ROLFE) You have seen him do it. He has done it in this courtroom. He has suggested that the Third Reich worked for the benefit of people. He has suggested that we sterilized men for the welfare of the country. (*dryly*) He has suggested that perhaps the old Jew did sleep with the sixteen-year-old girl after all. (*pause; sardonically*) Once more it is being done out of love of the country. (*looks over at* ROLFE)

CLOSE-UP—ROLFE

CLOSE-UP—JANNING

Pause. His eyes seem to reach out to every German in the audience.

JANNING: (*continuing*) It is not easy to tell the truth.

Looks out into audience.

FULL SHOT

JANNING: (*continuing; with emotion*) But if there is to be any salvation for Germany those of us who know our guilt must admit it no matter the cost in pain and humiliation. (*pause*) I had reached my verdict on the Feldenstein case before I ever came into the courtroom. I would have found him guilty whatever the evidence. It was not a trial at all. It was a sacrificial ritual in which Feldenstein the Jew, was the helpless victim—

[There is a bombshell of noise. ROLFE is on his feet. He is making this one last attempt to reach JANNING.

ROLFE: Your Honour, I must interrupt. The defendant is not aware of what he is saying—he is not aware that—

JANNING: I am aware. I am aware. (*turns to* HAYWOOD)] My defense counsel would have you believe that we were not aware of concentration camps. (*pause; cries out*) Not aware? (*pause*) Where were we? Where were we when Hitler began shrieking his hate in the Reichstag? Where were we when our neighbours were being dragged out in the middle of the night to Dachau? Where were we when every village in Germany had a railroad terminal where cattle-cars were filled with children who were being carried off to their extermination? Where were we when they cried out into the night to us? Were we deaf, dumb and blind?

[ROLFE: (*again on his feet*) Your Honour, I must—]

JANNING: My counsel says we were not aware of the extermination of millions. He would give you the excuse we were only aware of the extermination of the hundreds. Does that make us any the less guilty? (*pause; looks around the room; scathingly*) Maybe we didn't know the details. But if we didn't know, it was because we didn't want to know.

[ROLFE stands motionless. JANNING has flung his final rationalization back in his teeth. ROLFE is powerless to answer it, although he refuses to accept it emotionally. But HAHN rises to his feet.

HAHN: Traitor! Traitor!

THE BENCH

HAYWOOD: Order! Order! There will be order! (*losing his New England temper*) Put that man in his seat and keep him there!

HAYWOOD gestures to a husky, coloured SOLDIER who stands close to HAHN, his truncheon ready.

FULL SHOT]

JANNING: (*looking at* HAHN *steadily*) I am going to tell [them] the truth. I am going to tell the truth if the whole world conspires against it. I am going to tell [them] the truth about their Ministry of Justice. (*looks at men in dock*) Werner Lammpe.

THE DOCK——CLOSE-UP——LAMMPE

JANNING'S VOICE: Werner Lammpe. An old man who cries into his Bible now. An old man who profited by the property expropriation of every man he sent to the concentration camp.

FULL SHOT

JANNING: Friedrich Hoffstetter, the good German who knew how to take orders. Who sent men before him to be sterilized like so many digits.

THE DOCK——CLOSE-UP——HOFFSTETTER

FULL SHOT

The excitement in the courtroom is rising.

JANNING: Emil Hahn—

[EMIL HAHN's defense attorney rises to his feet and shouts.

DEFENSE ATTORNEY: Your Honour—!]

JANNING: (*continuing*) The decayed, corrupt bigot, obsessed by the devil within himself.

THE DOCK——CLOSE-UP——HAHN

CLOSE-UP——JANNING

JANNING: (*finally*) And Ernst Janning, worse than any of them because he knew what they were and went along with them.

There is a moment. There is shouting in the courtroom but JANNING does not hear it. He continues.

JANNING: (*continuing*) Ernst Janning who made his life . . . excrement because he walked with them.

[The noise in the courtroom mounts and grows into the thundering, overwhelming crescendo of sound. But ERNST JANNING does not hear it. He is spent now. Spent now with the release and with the shame. He sits there shivering inwardly at the sight of himself that he has presented to the courtroom. The roar continues. JANNING gets up finally. He goes to his seat.

CLOSE-UP—HAYWOOD

CLOSE-UP—GENERAL MERRIN

Sitting in audience. He looks over at COLONEL LAWSON.

CLOSE-UP—COLONEL LAWSON

There is a moment. ROLFE rises finally from defense table. All eyes in the courtroom are on him. He walks slowly to the stand. He carries, as though by habit, his portfolio with him. He stares at the judges a moment, thinking. He opens the portfolio. He looks down at all the carefully arranged affidavits, arguments, etc. Then he closes them. Then begins to speak quietly.]

ROLFE: Your Honours, my duty is to defend Ernst Janning. And yet Ernst Janning has said he is guilty.

He pauses. Turns to look over at ERNST JANNING in the dock.

ROLFE: (*continuing*) There is no doubt he feels his guilt.

THE DOCK—CLOSE-UP—JANNING

He is steadily looking at ROLFE.

FULL SHOT—COURTROOM

ROLFE: He made a terrible mistake in going along with the Nazi movement, hoping it would be good for his country. But . . .

He finds within himself the strength for what he feels he must say.

ROLFE: (*continuing*) If he is to be found guilty, there are others who also went along who must also be found guilty. Herr Janning said we succeeded beyond our wildest dreams. Why did we succeed? (*bends forward*) What about the rest of the world, Your Honours? (*smiles scathingly*) Did they not know the intentions of the Third Reich? Did they not hear the words of Hitler broadcast all over the world? Did they not read his intentions in *Mein Kampf,* published in every corner of the world? (*pause; bends forward*) Where is the responsibility of the Soviet Union who in 1939 signed a pact with Hitler and enabled him to make war? Are we now to find Russia guilty? (*pause*) Where is the responsibility of the Vatican who signed the Concordat Pact in 1933 with Hitler, giving him his first tremendous prestige? Are we now to find the Vatican guilty? (*bends forward*) Where is the responsibility of the world leader, Winston Churchill, who said in an open letter to the London *Times* in 1938—1938, Your Honours! "Were England to suffer a national disaster, I should pray to God to send a man of the strength of mind and will of an Adolf Hitler." Are we now to find Winston Churchill guilty? (*bends forward; smiles a little*) Where is the responsibility of those American industrialists who helped Hitler to rebuild his arms and profited by that rebuilding? Are we to find the American industrialists guilty? (*pause; smiles a little*) No, Your Honour. Germany alone is not guilty. The whole world is as responsible for Hitler as Germany. It is an easy thing to condemn one man in the dock. It is easy to condemn the German people—to speak of the "basic flaw" in the German character that allowed Hitler to rise to power—and at the same time comfortably ignore the "basic flaw" of character that made the Russians sign pacts with him, Winston Churchill praise him, American industrialists profit by him!

There is a moment. ROLFE stands with dignity before the Tribunal.

ROLFE: (*continuing*) Ernst Janning says he is guilty. If he is, Ernst Janning's guilt is the world's guilt. No more and no less.

[He collects his papers from stand and goes back to defense table. Camera goes to faces of German people in the audience. There is no applause but we see the applause in their eyes. There are tears of emotion in some of their eyes. There is no need for them to rationalize any further. ROLFE has done it all for them.]

DR. STRANGELOVE, OR: HOW I LEARNED TO STOP WORRYING AND LOVE THE BOMB

A Hawk Films, Ltd. Production. Released through Columbia Pictures. Producer & Director, Stanley Kubrick. Associate Producer, Victor Lyndon. Screenplay by Stanley Kubrick, Terry Southern, Peter George. Based on the novel *Red Alert* by Peter George. Photography, Gilbert Taylor. Film Editor, Anthony Harvey. Production Designer, Ken Adam. Art Director, Peter Murton. Special Effects, Wally Veevers. Music, Laurie Johnson. Sound, John Cox. Running time, 94 minutes. 1963.

CAST

GROUP CAPTAIN LIONEL MANDRAKE	Peter Sellers
PRESIDENT MUFFLEY	Peter Sellers
DR. STRANGELOVE	Peter Sellers
GENERAL "BUCK" TURGIDSON	George C. Scott
GENERAL JACK D. RIPPER	Sterling Hayden
COLONEL "BAT" GUANO	Keenan Wynn
MAJOR T.J. "KING" KONG	Slim Pickens
AMBASSADOR DE SADESKY	Peter Bull
LIEUTENANT LOTHAR ZOGG, BOMBARDIER	James Earl Jones
MR. STAINES	Jack Dreley
LIEUTENANT H.R. DIETRICK	Frank Berry
LIEUTENANT W.D. KIVEL, NAVIGATOR	Glenn Beck

CAPTAIN G.A. "ACE" OWENS, CO-PILOT	Shane Rimmer
LIEUTENANT B. GOLDBERG, RADIO OPERATOR	Paul Tamarin
GENERAL FACEMAN	Gordon Tanner
ADMIRAL RANDOLPH	Robert O'Neil
MISS SCOTT	Tracy Reed

The opening narration of *Dr. Strangelove* explains "Operation Dropkick":

> America's Strategic Air Command maintains a large force of B-52 bombers airborne twenty-four hours a day. Each B-52 can deliver a nuclear bomb-load of fifty megatons, equal to sixteen times the total explosive force of all the bombs and shells used by all the armies in World War II. Based in America, the Airborne Alert Force is deployed from the Persian Gulf to the Arctic Ocean but they have one geographical factor in common. They are all two hours from their targets inside Russia.

Operation Dropkick is set in motion by General Ripper, the Base Commander of Burpleson Air Force Base. He is acting under Plan R, "an emergency war plan in which a lower echelon Commander may order nuclear retaliation after a sneak attack if the normal chain of command has been disrupted." There has been no sneak attack, but General Ripper is convinced that one day there *will* be. He decides to save the Free World by getting the "Commies" before they get him. He telephones Group Captain Mandrake, an Englishman on the Exchange Officer Program, who is in the control tower. He instructs Mandrake to put the base on Red Alert, which includes trusting no one, despite the uniform he may be wearing, unless you know him personally, and firing on anything approaching within two hundred yards of the base. So that the Russians cannot plant false radio transmissions, Ripper instructs Mandrake to have all radios confiscated and to lock all radio communications to the B-52s into a special code preceded by a special prefix.

Ripper has effectively sealed the base against any interference and set into motion the end of the world. In the War Room,

the President of the United States places a call to the Premier of
the Soviet Union in the excerpt below. The President finally
decides to send the 23rd Airborne Division, seven miles away
from Burpleson, to attack and penetrate Burpleson, locate General Ripper and reverse Operation Dropkick. It is too late. The
final image of *Dr. Strangelove*'s black, black comedy is that of
the mushroom-shaped cloud.

(*Note*: Please see Volume I for the scenes in which Mandrake tries to get the recall code from Ripper, and in which
Mandrake tries to get through to the President on a pay phone.)

MONOLOGUE

INTERIOR WAR ROOM

[LS War Table, everybody in position.*

PRESIDENT: Tell him where you are and that you'll enter the
        conversation if I say anything that's untrue but please don't
        tell him anything more than that.

CS DE SADESKY looking L. to PRESIDENT.

PRESIDENT: (*off*) Alexi, Alexi, please, I beg you.

DE SADESKY: But I don't have a 'phone.

MCS DE SADESKY & PRESIDENT at table.

PRESIDENT: Give him the 'phone, Frank.

FRANK leans in L to hand receiver to DE SADESKY.

LS War table, everybody in position.

DE SADESKY: (*not to be translated*) Tovarishch predsedatel?
        Govorit Desadsky. Ya s Prezidentom Merkin Muffley v
        Pentagone. On prosit menya skazat, chto yesli on skazhoot

---

*This excerpt is taken from the continuity script, not from the shooting script. (Please
see the source appendix at the end of Volume I for a discussion of these terms.) The
"action" as it appears here is not the writing of the screenwriters, but a kind of log or
map of where the bodies on the screen, and where the camera, are moving. The
dialogue is actual to the soundtrack. ("MCS" means Medium Close Shot, "LS", Long
Shot, etc.)

chto-nibud ne tak . . . da, da . . . ya dolzhen yevo prervat.
Da. Khorosho, ponyatno, tovarishch predsedatel.

CS DE SADESKY looking L. to PRESIDENT.

DE SADESKY: I've done as you asked. Be careful, Mr. President,
I think he is drunk.

CS PRESIDENT. DE SADESKY retires up of frame L.]

PRESIDENT: (*on telephone*) Hello . . .

MCS DE SADESKY & PRESIDENT.

PRESIDENT: (*on telephone*) Eh, hello, Dimitri. Listen, I can't
hear too well, do you suppose you could turn the music
down just a little. Ah, ah, that's much better.

MS OFFICER, TURGIDSON across table. Others BG. CAMERA
L & R.

PRESIDENT: (*on phone*) Yes, huh, yes. Fine, I can hear you
now, Dimitri, clear and plain and coming through . . .

MCS DE SADESKY & PRESIDENT.

PRESIDENT: (*on phone*) . . . fine. I'm coming through fine too,
aye? Good, then, well, then as you say, we're both coming
through fine. Good. Well, it's good that you're fine . . .

LS War table, everybody in position.

PRESIDENT: (*on phone*) . . . and, and I'm fine. I agree with you,
it's great to be fine.

MCS DE SADESKY & PRESIDENT

PRESIDENT: (*on phone*) Now then, Dimitri, you know how
we've always talked about the possibility of something
going wrong with the bomb.

MCS TURGIDSON reacting, holding receiver to his ear.

PRESIDENT: (*on phone*) The bomb Dimitri, the Hydrogen bomb.

MSC DE SADESKY & PRESIDENT

PRESIDENT: (*on phone*): Well now, what happened is that, eh,
one of our base commanders, he had a sort of, well, he

went a little funny in the head. You know, just a little funny.
And he went and did a silly thing. Well, I'll tell you what
he did. He ordered his planes to attack your country. Well,
let me finish Dimitri . . .

MCS TURGIDSON reacting.

PRESIDENT: (*on phone—off*) . . . let me finish Dimitri . . .

MSC DE SADESKY & PRESIDENT.

PRESIDENT: (*on telephone*) . . . well, listen, how do you think I
feel about it? Can you imagine how I feel about it Dimitri?

MLS section of table.

OFFICIALS seated in position reacting.

PRESIDENT: (*on phone—off*) Why do you think I'm calling you?

MCS DE SADESKY & PRESIDENT.

PRESIDENT: (*on phone*) Just to say hello? Of course I like to
speak to you . . . of course I like to say hello . . . not now, but
any time Dimitri. I'm just calling up to tell you something
terrible has happened. It's a friendly call, of course it's a
friendly call. Listen, if it wasn't friendly you probably
wouldn't have got it.

MCS TURGIDSON reacts.

PRESIDENT: (*on phone—off*) They will not . . .

MCS DE SADESKY & PRESIDENT.

PRESIDENT: (*on phone*) . . . reach their targets for at least another hour. I am, I am positive Dimitri.

MCS TURGIDSON looking towards Maps on wall, off.

PRESIDENT: (*on phone—off*) Listen, I've been all over this with
your Ambassador. . . .

MS Map on wall showing targets and approaching aircrafts.

PRESIDENT: (*on phone—off*) . . . it is not a trick. Well, I'll tell
you. We'd like to give your Air Staff a complete run down

on the targets, the flight plans and the defensive systems of
the planes.

MCS TURGIDSON reacting.

PRESIDENT: (*on phone—off*) Yes, I mean . . . if we're unable to
recall the planes then I'd say that, eh, well, we're just going
to, eh, have to help you destroy them, Dimitri. I know
they're our boys.

MCS DE SADESKY & PRESIDENT.

PRESIDENT: (*on phone—off*) All right. Well listen, now who
should we call. Who should we call Dimitri what was—
the . . . people—sorry you faded away there. The People's
Central Air Defence Headquarters. Where's that, Dimitri?
In Omsk. Right. Yes . . . Oh, you'll call them first will you?
Uhhh. Listen, do you happen to have the phone number on
you, Dimitri? Well . . . what? I see, just ask for Omsk
Information. Uhhhmmm.

MS. OFFICER, TURGIDSON across table, Others BG. CAMERA
L & R.

PRESIDENT: (*on phone—off*) I'm sorry too, Dimitri, I'm very
sorry. All right, you're sorrier than I am, but I am sorry as
well.

MCS DE SADESKY & PRESIDENT.

PRESIDENT: (*on phone*) I am as sorry as you are, Dimitri, don't
say that you're more sorry than I am because I'm capable of
being just as sorry as you are. So we're both sorry, all
right?

[LS War table, everybody in position.

PRESIDENT: (*on phone*) All right. Yes, he's right here. Yes, he
wants to talk to you, just a second.

DE SADESKY: (*not to be translated*) Tovarishch predsedatel . . .

DE SADESKY: (*over these four scenes*) . . . govorit Desadsky. Da,
da. Chto? Oni oozhe nachali? Net, (ne) mozhet byt! Dooraki!
Dosvidanya.

MCS DE SADESKY.

MCS PRESIDENT looking off L to DE SADESKY.

MCS TURGIDSON reacting.

LS War table, everybody in position.

PRESIDENT: What? What is it? What.

DE SADESKY: The fools. The mad fools!

PRESIDENT: What's happened?

DE SADESKY: The Doomsday Machine!

MCS PRESIDENT looking off L to DE SADESKY.

PRESIDENT: The Doomsday Machine, what is that?

MCS TURGIDSON reacting.

DE SADESKY: (*off*) A device which will destroy all human and animal life on earth.

PRESIDENT: (*off*) All human and animal life?]

THE LOVED ONE

Metro-Goldwyn-Mayer and Filmways presentation of a Martin Ransohoff Production. Producers, John Calley and Haskell Wexler. Director, Tony Richardson. Screenplay by Christopher Isherwood and Terry Southern. Based on the novel *The Loved One* by Evelyn Waugh. Director of Photography, Haskell Wexler. Supervising Editor, Antony Gibbs. Editors, Hal Ashby, Brian Smedley-Aston. Music, John Addison. Sound, Stan Fiferman. Associate Producer, Neil Hartley. Production and Costume Designer, Rouben Ter-Artunian. Assistant Director, Kurt Neumann. Running time, 116 minutes. 1965.

CAST

DENNIS BARLOW	Robert Morse
WILBUR GLENWORTHY	Jonathan Winters
HARRY	Jonathan Winters
AIMEE THANATOGENOS	Anjanette Comer
MR. JOYBOY	Rod Steiger
MOM	Ayllene Gibbons
SIR FRANCIS HINSLEY	John Gielgud
SADIE BLODGETT	Barbara Nichols
MR. KENTON	Milton Berle
MRS. KENTON	Margaret Leighton
GENERAL BRINKMAN	Dana Andrews
IMMIGRATION OFFICER	James Coburn
D.J., JR.	Roddy McDowall

MR. STARKER	Liberace
SIR AMBROSE ABERCROMBIE	Robert Morley
THE GURU BRAHMIN	Lionel Stander
THE GURO BRAHMIN'S ASSISTANT	Bernie Kopell
GUIDE	Tab Hunter

Dennis Barlow is an aspiring English poet. He reads a great deal of literature and handles the language with facility, but as for originality, he's no great Shakes (peare). When he falls passionately in love with Aimee Thanatogenos, he borrows freely from his heroes. He never actually says to Aimee that he, personally, wrote the poems he is reciting and sending to her. But Aimee is *very* innocent, and that is just what she believes.

Dennis had won a free trip to America by being the ten millionth person to see off a friend at a London airport. He arrives in Los Angeles with no definite source of income or plan, beyond contacting his uncle, Sir Francis Hinsley, a celebrity portrait painter who thirty-one years ago became head of the Art Department of Megalopolitan Pictures. Partly because he is broke, Sir Francis is only reluctantly a member of the chauvinistic English Club; but he's also genuinely tolerent of the southern California natives, whom he characterizes as "very decent and generous. They talk entirely for their own pleasure and *they do not expect you to listen.*" Coldly and abruptly dropped by the studio, Sir Francis hangs himself from the diving tower of his cracked, empty swimming pool. The responsibilities of burial are assigned to Dennis by the English Club. They send him through the giant gates into the world of Whispering Glades, a Disneyland-concept mortuary/cemetery. Here, Aimee Thanatogenos works in the Nightshade Room as the cosmetician in charge of hair, skin and nails. She counsels Dennis through all the possibilities of "inhuement, entombment, inurnment, immurement." She leads him to the other counselors who handle the decisions about caskets (silk-lined is better because rayon chafes), corpse facial expressions ("Judicial and Determined," "Serene and Philosophical," or "Laughing Child"), and eternal flames (eight-hour "standard eternal" vs. twenty-four-hour "perpetual eternal," propane vs. butane). Aimee escorts Dennis on a tour of the park's various zones—The Falls of Xanadu, Neptune's Cradle,

The Poets' Corner—each appropriately decorated with rotating, larger-than-life statuary. Aimee is enraptured with Whispering Glades and enthralled with its creator, the Reverend Wilbur Glenworthy. The whole park is just as he'd dreamt it, a sugarcoated eternity, "where Grief became Gladness, where Sorrow became the Friendly Mewing of Tiny Kittens, and the Splash of precious Duck Babies at play." There is an overwhelming purity and naivete in Aimee that allows her to solemnly adore this, and that just knocks Dennis head over heels.

Fired from the studio along with Sir Francis is Harry, a desperate mogul-manqué. His brother, Reverend Glenworthy, hears Harry's plea for help over the telephone in his private black helicopter, and offers him a take-it-or-leave-it, last chance job—the management of Happier Hunting Ground, an extremely tacky pet cemetery side business, with which Glenworthy must not be publicly affiliated. Harry has no choice but to accept. For deceased pet pickups, he hires Dennis, who has fumbled every crumb tossed him by the English Club and is now desperate for a job. To further augment his income, Dennis has become a nonsectarian minister so he can also officiate at the pet funerals. Aimee loathes the Happier Hunting Ground; it mocks everything she holds sacred. In crisis, she goes to her Blessed Reverend Glenworthy. She wants spiritual guidance. He wants sex. Now, Aimee is a young woman whose strength of faith has been so intense and trusting that she has lived in an unfinished, condemned house hanging off a cliff in a slide area, because she found the open view inspiring. Glenworthy's attentions, dripping with dishonor, send her over the edge. The newly named First Lady Embalmer of Whispering Glades hooks herself up to the embalming machine and commits suicide.

Reverend Glenworthy is described in the script as "a figure of brusque and ruthless authority." In the conglomerating of a corporate empire, he's run into a problem with Whispering Glades: soon it will be filled to its maximum with bodies. For a piece of developmental real estate, this is a definite limitation. In the first monologue below, Reverend Glenworthy presents to his Board of Directors the urgency for cleaning out Whispering Glades and making the land reusable. As he will later declare to Aimee, "Death has become a *middle-class* business. There's no future in it." Harry will bring his brother a solution that is being researched by a ten-year-old boy genius working at the

Happier Hunting Ground: the corpses can be loaded into rockets and sent out into orbit.

Aimee's horror at this blasphemy helps drive her to suicide. The Mortuary Chief is so fearful that Glenworthy will discover her body on the premises and hold him responsible that he accepts Dennis's offer to remove the body in exchange for a plane ticket back to England. But at the last minute, Dennis puts Aimee's body in the casket designated for Tod "The Condor" Blodgett, the late, great astronaut. Blodgett's casket was scheduled as the first launch of Glenworthy's program, so Aimee Thanatogenos is hurled into space. Clearance for awarding this posthumous honor to Captain Blodgett had been obtained from his widow, Sadie, described in the script as "a dyed blonde in a whorish dress—attractive in a jaded and brittle way." Having located her in a run-down motel room which turns out to be her place of business, Harry and Dennis learn her story of how Tod, a national hero, *really* died, in the third monologue below.

The Mortuary Chief, Mr. Lafayette Joyboy, and his Mom are the crowning grotesqueries of *The Loves One*'s black comedy of consumer death. Mr. Joyboy is treated by his staff as if he were Leonardo. He adores Aimee, and he sends her assigned corpses to her with their mouths set in huge smiles, as a kind of valentine. In honor of Aimee's promotion, he takes her home to meet Mom. Aimee stares in sick fascination at Mom, a gigantic obesity, collapsed in a bed, frantically following the food commercials on television by using a remote control. These food commercials engender a sort of sexual experience, and at the conclusion of each, "Mom sighs like an exhausted swimmer," and then continues to gorge more food. Mom instructs Aimee to feed live mealworms to an ill-tempered mynah bird that hops around the room screeching, "There is no death! There is no death!" Joyboy takes a break from preparing dinner to rescue Aimee. He proudly shows her his bedroom, with musclemen pictures covering the walls. He shares with her his most intimate dream of how he'd like to make Mom happy, in the second monologue below.

When the mynah bird dies, Joyboy takes it to the Happier Hunting Ground, meets Dennis and realizes that this is his rival for Aimee. Joyboy exposes Dennis to Aimee, and Dennis counters by exposing Glenworthy to Aimee. Then, it is only a matter of time until Aimee, as they say at Whispering Glades, changes from a Waiting One into a Loved One.

MONOLOGUE 1

[EXTERIOR HELIPORT—DAY—KIRKEBY BUILDING, WESTWOOD

The black helicopter lands, and THE BLESSED REVEREND steps out, walks toward entrance.]

INTERIOR CONFERENCE ROOM—KIRKEBY BUILDING RESTAURANT

with windows overlooking the city. Seated at a table are four (or more) of THE BLESSED REVEREND'S financial advisors—BLAKE, VREEMAN, DAVIDSON, ROBERTS, etc. All rise as THE BLESSED REVEREND enters. He takes his place at the head of the table. The others sit down after he does. THE BLESSED REVEREND appears to be deeply concerned.

GLENWORTHY: (*curtly*) Gentlemen. (*turns to nearest advisor*) Blake, the report.

BLAKE hands him a slender sheath of onionskin paper, black with figures.

GLENWORTHY: (*gravely*) Gentlemen, these quarterly figures have distressed me greatly. (*taps the report*) Poor *gains,* gentlemen, reflect poor *planning* . . . and (*ominously, as he looks at each face*) *dead wood* where there should be *green!* Glenworthy Enterprises will tolerate neither. (*pounds the table*) Glenworthy Enterprises, gentlemen, is *not* a philanthropic organization! (*pauses, drinks a glass of water*) Now then, let's go straight to the purpose of this meeting—namely, the status and future of our beloved Whispering Glades . . . as a financial proposition. (*to* BLAKE) Blake, the projection.

BLAKE hands him another paper.

GLENWORTHY: (*referring to it*) According to our projection, at the present rate of burial, the total remaining acreage will be depleted in *seven years'* time. Whispering Glades, as an operational enterprise, will then cease to exist. (*pause*) Gentlemen, this is a challenge which must be met with force and wisdom. As of this moment the most feasible possibility which has yet been suggested is to convert this acreage into a Retirement City—a haven for our senior citizens. (*to* BLAKE) Blake, the views.

BLAKE switches on small slide projector.

GLENWORTHY: (*to the group*) Now here are some views of one of
the more successful retirement communities, the "Shangri-
Lodge Tropicana." (*with views*) Here we see our senior
citizens at work . . . (*appropiate views: to* BLAKE) Okay, kill
it.

BLAKE switches it off.

GLENWORTHY: (*continuing*) The annual net is placed at twenty-
five thousand per acre . . . with the distinct advantage of not
depleting itself . . . since the, uh, turnover among retirement-
city clientele is, ahem, fairly *brisk*. Suffice it to say that our
over-all projection figures indicate a twelve thousand per-
cent gain in the immediate conversion of this acreage into a
retirement city—a haven for our senior citizens. [(*pause*)
Well, gentlemen, any comment?

This elicits frowns of puzzlement from the others.

ROBERTS: (*incredulously, after a pause*) You aren't thinking
of . . . *disinterment*?]

GLENWORTHY: (*firmly*) It's a first-rate problem, gentlemen, and
let me say this to you . . . (*with great feeling*) the man who
can solve it will find himself in a very strong position with
Wilbur Glenworthy!

[VREEMAN: (*stunned*) But . . . but surely it's out of the question,
Wilbur. I mean, after all, it *is* consecrated ground, and—]

BLESSED REVEREND interrupts by smashing his hand to the table
and rising.

GLENWORTHY: (*with tremendous authority*) [No!] There has *got* to
be a way of *getting those stiffs off my property*!

MONOLOGUE 2

They stop at his room. It is small and depressing; the walls
are covered with photos of body-builders. He glances at AIMEE
shyly.

JOYBOY: It's...my room, Aimee.

AIMEE stares at the bed, averts her glance demurely; it rests on a picture of a nude muscle-man.

JOYBOY: I just wanted you to...I don't know...to *see* it. (*anxiously searches her face*)

AIMEE looks confused. JOYBOY hurries on.

JOYBOY: I'm going to partition the room...(*indicates*) here...so we can put in a big tub for Mom.

[AIMEE: (*puzzled*) A big tub?

JOYBOY: Yes, a big tub for Mom.] You see, Aimee, I've always given her spongebaths...(*explains*) Oh I don't say I'll stop those but I *have* saved up now and I've ordered this big tub for her.

He stops suddenly, dabs with the apron at his eye, shakes his head, continues in a choked voice.

JOYBOY: She's such a *queen*, Aimee! (*sighs*) Sometimes it almost breaks my heart...that we can't afford to give Mom all the darn Big Boy Crabs and King Chicken she can eat!

He raises his eyes to AIMEE, gives her a brave smile, continues in a wistful tone, a la a Stanley Kramer hero:

JOYBOY: You know, Aimee...I used to have this *dream*...Oh, I suppose it sounds crazy...but there I would be, in the Supermarket, the one on La Brea Street—*buying lobsters for Mom!* The biggest, juiciest lobsters you can imagine! I bought them by the dozen—the way most people buy *eggs*. "Here comes the lobster-man!" they'd say. And then I would do this, well, I know it sounds darn silly to tell it, but I would do this sort of funny *dance*, and I'd sing: "Momma's little Joyboy wants lobster, lobster! Momma's little Joyboy wants lobster for Mom!" (*happily*) And the next thing I knew I'd be walking into Mom's room, carrying the biggest darn platters of sweet yummy, baked lobster you can imagine! And boy, would Mom be glad to see *me*! (*pauses; the childlike smile clouds over; shrugs*) And then, . . . well, I don't know, then the dream became a kind of *nightmare* . . . because I'd put the big platter down in front of Mom, and the lobsters would still be *alive,* just like they hadn't been cooked at all, and I'd . . . (*chokes up*) I'd start crying because, well, because I knew I'd let Mom down again! (*brave smile, eyes glistening*) But Mom would say: "It's all right, Laf . . . *I'll have them like this!"* (*happily*) And by golly, Mom would tear right into those live lobsters, claws and all! (*pause, face becomes troubled again*) But those darn things fought back. They begin to . . . to *pinch* Mom and everything . . . and then, well, it got just . . . (*shakes his head hopelessly*) *terrible*! (*grimaces*) I don't even want to think about it. I mean, they wouldn't *stop,* and finally—

The narrative is abruptly broken by MOM'S shout from the other room.

[MOM: Laf! Channel seven's on the blink! Laf!]

JOYBOY: (*calls*) Right, Mom! Be there in a second! (*turns back to* AIMEE, *shudders*) Gosh, I don't know how I got on to that darn dream again! Say, we'd better run! [(*leads* AIMEE *back to room*)

MONOLOGUE 3

INTERIOR SADIE'S ROOM

HARRY, DENNIS and SADIE have settled down to drinking and listening to her story. All appear slightly drunk.

SADIE: (*bitterly*) So don't talk "hero" at *me,* Jack. I mean, I was *there,* right? Well, he fell off a bar stool and broke his neck, *that's* what happened. (*cynical laugh and wave of her hand*) Oh, don't worry, I'm not going to do any broadcasting. (*takes a big drink*) I'm just glad to be out of the whole lousy mess. Right after Tod's first spin, *Love* Magazine was going to do this picture story—you know, "A Day With the Blodgetts." So the Base Commander calls up and says he's sending someone over to have a look at our place—wanted to make sure there weren't too many bottles around, I guess. Anyway, this fruity lieutenant shows up and starts taking down the *curtains*. My curtains! Can you imagine that? "They don't give the right *image*" he said, "there's too much *New York* in them." "But we *are* from New York" I told him. "No, no," he kept saying, "it's the *Iowa* image we want to put across." So he throws up some chintzy cornball stuff, with big, hideous flowers on it—then he heads for the *bedroom,* and he nearly blows his stack. We had these great sheets—you know, *black satin.* "Out of the question!" he says, "—and get that *mirror* off the ceiling!" Well, I kicked him right the hell out of my home! And that killed the picture story—not just for Tod, but for the whole Base. The C.O. was so mad he nearly went off his rocker. So Tod came home that night and started juicing it up big, and raising hell with me for not being more "cooperative." Well, by about three o'clock he was loaded right out of his mind, and I went in to bed. A few minutes later I hear this terrific KLUNK, and sure enough he had fallen off the bar stool, right on his noggin. Of course they sort of hushed it up ... and naturally everybody said it was *my* fault. But I don't see it that way—I think it was the fault of the *system* ... don't you?

BLOW-UP

A Bridge Films Production for Metro-Goldwyn-Mayer Pictures. Distributed by Premier Productions. Producer, Carlo Ponti. Director, Michelangelo Antonioni. Screenplay by Michelangelo Antonioni and Tonino Guerra; English dialogue in collaboration with Edward Bond. Inspired by a short story by Julio Cortázar. Executive Producer, Pierre Rouve. Director of Photography, Carlo de Palma. Editor, Frank Clarke. Art Director, Assheton Gorton. Music, Herbie Hancock; "Stroll On" featured and conducted by the Yardbirds. Assistant Director, Claude Watson. Running time, 111 minutes. 1966.

CAST

THE PHOTOGRAPHER, THOMAS	David Hemmings
THE GIRL	Vanessa Redgrave
PATRICIA	Sarah Miles
BILL	John Castle
RON	Peter Bowles
THE BLONDE	Jane Birkin
THE BRUNETTE	Gillian Hills
THE FIRST MODEL	Verushka

Michelangelo Antonioni, the director and co-author of *Blow-Up*, had once written that in his process of filmmaking, "An idea almost always comes to me through images ... with restricting the accumulation of these images, with digging into them, with recognizing the ones that coincide with what interests me at the time." This is exactly how the film's central character, a successful photographer named Thomas, falls into the story. He takes a sequence of still shots of a couple in the distance; something about them has caught his visual interest as he is walking through the park. The "Girl"—we never learn her name—notices Thomas. She is willing to go so far as to bite his hand to get the camera and the pictures, but because he wants the rest of the film, he doesn't let go. When he develops, enlarges, arranges, rearranges, and re-enlarges the images, it appears that he has witnessed a murder.

One of the most pervasive aspects of *Blow-Up*'s world is its newness, its conscious turning from the structures and obligations of the past. There are no parents with children, or families, in the story, just young adults like Thomas, living through *these* twenty-four hours in London in 1966. Everything in Thomas's life seems to be orbiting quickly and successfully, and getting *younger*, so there is an innocence to his arrogance, and something almost pristine about his disengagement. *Innovation* is the new tradition. Thomas is far more fascinated by the story his photos seem to reveal than he is shocked along any traditional lines of morality. Though the Beatles may still all be wearing the same suit and haircut, other rock musicians in *Blow-Up* are already trashing their instruments onstage. It's 1966, when skirts are becoming so short that pantyhose have to be invented. The city streets in *Blow-Up* suddenly fill with unexpected, surreal theater as students, both in mime acts and in political demonstrations, enact alternate views of reality. It's London in 1966, when casual social behavior suddenly includes activities such as sex without relationship, or the smoking of marijuana. Antonioni felt the irony of Thomas's world was that it was completely regulated by a relentless search for freedom: "The pursuit of freedom gives man his most exciting moments. Once it's conquered, once all discipline is discarded, then it's decadence. Decadence without any visible future." Thomas is no more interested in envisioning a future than he is in upholding any particular past. When the Girl from the park comes to Thomas's studio to get the pictures in the scene below, she faces a man who is willing to spend the full content of his worth in an impatient and restless present tense.

During the filming of *Blow-Up*, Antonioni said, "Love today is weaker, paler than in the past." Thomas's relationships to women are tenuous, and governed by his work, to which he seems truly dedicated. When he is photographing a model who creates something out of herself, who gives *him* something, he devours her with his camera, physically intimate and demanding: "Come on, more of that. More of that. Now give it to me. Really give it to me. Come on, now!" But it is not personal, and he is not transformed by his passion. Even while having a raucous romp with a pair of young groupies who force themselves into his studio, Thomas quickly shelves the fun as soon as a detail in a photo distracts him. Should the female models dare become unimaginative or lazy (even when he has kept them waiting for hours), he can swerve out of amused indifference into contemptuous abuse. Thomas is deeply *unattached*. When he is not working with his photographs, he seems to spend most of his time jumping in and out of his very expensive car, buying what interests him, wishing he had even more money. The only focus with the power to still him is the collection of photographs he has taken of derelicts and decay, which he is assembling into a book. These photographs have a resonance beyond the merely trendy. With all his contradictions—aloof/obsessive, confident/doubt-fearing, the involved voyeur, the fashion photographer indifferent to his own clothing—Thomas is one who, according to Antonioni, had "chosen to take part in the revolution which has affected English life, customs and morality. . . ." This "revolution" was one of the early blasts of an entire social explosion which would eventually be called "the Sixties."

At the time of the scene below, Thomas has not yet developed the photographs, so neither he nor we have any idea who this girl is or why she so desperately wants them. After she has left, Thomas will continue to work with the film until the images finally reveal a corpse. Thomas goes to the park, and he finds the corpse. When he tries to telephone the girl, the number which she'd given him (in the scene below) turns out to be fake. Before the following morning, both the corpse and the photographs have disappeared.

(*Note*: This scene is virtually a one-act. If it reads somewhat like a blueprint or diagram, this is partly because Antonioni has described his shooting scripts as never definitive—"It's notes about the direction, nothing more"—and partly because the excerpt is also collated from the cutting continuity of the final screen version, and a continuity *is* a kind of diagram of what is said, and where it's said, on the screen. Certainly, in order for the scene to play inside the acting studio, some of the set, blocking, and direction must be adapted to the specific actors and to the restrictions of space. The set will require at least two entrances.)

SCENE

THOMAS comes out of the phone booth. A few more steps—and he is home. He pulls out his key and is about to unlock the door. The clatter of a woman's hurried footsteps drawing near makes him turn round. A GIRL runs towards him. It is the GIRL from the park. She is out of breath, and for a moment can hardly speak. THOMAS looks at her in surprise. Finally she says:

GIRL: I...I've come...I've come for the photographs.

THOMAS eyes her curiously.

THOMAS: Well, how did you manage to find me?

The GIRL avoids his eyes.

GIRL: Do you live here?

THOMAS: Mmm.

THOMAS opens the door and lets her in.

Through a partially open door in the foreground we see first the GIRL, then THOMAS coming into the studio through the front door. She comes through the second door, followed by THOMAS. Camera follows them as they go through the receptionist's office.

They come through the door into the large studio.

At the other end of the studio THOMAS closes the door. The GIRL comes forward, looking about with interest. She seems on edge. THOMAS joins her and we follow them as they walk behind the smoked glass panels and up the steps at the back of the studio.

The GIRL and THOMAS come up the stairs to the upper studio.

Camera moves with her as she comes forward, stooping under photographic equipment and ostrich plumes. THOMAS switches on a few scattered lights, motions to her to sit down, and switches on the record player. The music is a very slow guitar.

THOMAS: Drink?

She wanders about as if looking for something.

Without waiting for her answer he pours two whiskeys, and turns in her direction with the glasses.

THOMAS: What's so important about my bloody pictures?

Camera follows THOMAS as he goes up to her, now settled on the couch, to give her the glass. She holds him with her eyes. Doesn't take the glass.

GIRL: That's my business.

THOMAS puts her glass down. She gets up and stands stiffly opposite him. Both are obscured by an overhead beam.

Close-up of THOMAS, drinking and saying as if recollecting a pleasant memory:

THOMAS: The light was very beautiful in the park this morning. Those shots should be very good. Anyway, I need them.

Close-up of the GIRL leaning against a cross-beam. She is tense, insisting . . .

GIRL: My private life's already in a mess. It would be a disaster if . . . (*She moves away.*)

THOMAS comes across to the beam where she is standing and stares at her.

THOMAS: So what—nothing like a little disaster for sorting things out.

The GIRL starts at his reply. She paces up and down in front of the long polythene-covered window, growing more and more restless. Camera moves back to reveal THOMAS watching her with a professional eye through the beams of the low ceiling, then moves in again to the GIRL.

THOMAS: (*off*) Have you ever done any modelling? Fashion stuff, I mean?

The GIRL shrugs and sighs impatiently.

THOMAS: (*off*) You've got it.

Camera moves back to reveal THOMAS as she begins to wander about again. He studies her from head to toe, then moves across to the plastic-covered window. He motions her to come closer, pulling down a lilac-coloured back-drop in front of it. He stands her against the back-drop.

THOMAS: Hold that. (*He hurries away, leaving her standing rather bewildered.*)

THOMAS watches the GIRL standing impatiently in front of the screen.

THOMAS: Not many girls stand as well as that...

She comes towards him.

GIRL: No thanks, I'm in a hurry.

THOMAS takes off his coat, and heads for the couch.

THOMAS: You'll get your pictures. I promise. I always keep my word.

He falls onto the couch.

THOMAS: Come here. Show me how you sit.

Close-up of the GIRL. She sighs, but complies.

She goes and sits beside him.

THOMAS doesn't take his eyes off her. They sit side by side and he is relaxed and confident, just staring at her, satisfied that he has at least made her sit down. The telephone rings. He looks round at the sound but does not make a move. It goes on ringing.

THOMAS sit on the sofa, ignoring the telephone. He is seen from above, over one of the beams. Suddenly he hurls himself across the floor and dives for the telephone. He has to crawl behind an armchair to find it and bumps his head on a corner of the chair's wooden frame in the process.

THOMAS: (*into phone, rubbing his head*) Who is it?

Close shot of THOMAS.

THOMAS: (*remembering his earlier call*) Oh yes, that's right. Hold on a second.

He stretches up and holds out the receiver.

THOMAS's hand holds the receiver out from behind the chair. He is otherwise invisible. Seen reflected in a large pane of glass, the GIRL sits forward, shocked.

GIRL: Is it for me?

She goes over to him and sits in the armchair, camera moving with her. Hesitantly she picks up the receiver.

THOMAS: It's my wife.

Close-up of the GIRL, hurriedly putting the receiver down, and starting to rise.

GIRL: Why should I speak to her?

Close-up of THOMAS. He takes the receiver back and addresses the person at the other end of the line, as the GIRL walks away in front of him.

THOMAS: Sorry, love, the bird I'm with won't talk to you. (*He hangs up.*)

The GIRL stands with her back to him, looking out of the window. THOMAS moves over to her, but she moves away, ducking under a beam. Camera moves in to close-up as she turns and taps her knuckles impatiently on the beam.

THOMAS goes up to a painting in the living area, runs his finger over it, then turns back to the GIRL, explaining:

THOMAS: She isn't my wife really. We just have some kids . . . No . . . No kids. Not even kids. Sometimes, though, it . . . it feels as if we had kids. She isn't beautiful, she's . . . easy to live with.

He sits down in close-up and lights a cigarette.

THOMAS: No she isn't. That's why I don't live with her.

He breaks off, and drops a match on the lace mob-cap of a marble bust on his right. It's a girl's head, and he gazes at it, patting it thoughtfully as though reflecting on his personal problems.

The GIRL stands behind some lighting equipment. She shows a first minimal sign of interest in him. A moment of silence. The GIRL goes and sits down on the couch again.

THOMAS gets up and goes on speaking, turning in her direction.

THOMAS: But even with beautiful girls you . . . you look at them and . . . that's that. That's why they always end up by . . . (*He sighs*) . . . Well, I'm stuck with them all day long.

THOMAS stands looking down at the GIRL on the sofa.

GIRL: It would be the same with men.

He shrugs. A new track is playing. This one has a fast beat.

THOMAS: Have a listen to this!

He moves up to the record player, and turns up the volume.

Close-up of THOMAS as he straightens. Pan and track with him as he moves with the music.

The GIRL listens. Instinctively she starts swaying with the rhythm. THOMAS goes and sits down beside her.

THOMAS motions her to listen to the music.

THOMAS: No, keep still. Keep still! Listen. Keep still.

A pause. He hands her the cigarette he is smoking.

THOMAS: You can smoke, if you like.

The GIRL takes the cigarette and in the same movement raises it to her mouth, still swaying in time to the music.

THOMAS: Slowly, slowly. Against the beat.

The GIRL tries to smoke moving slowly, swaying sensuously.

THOMAS: (*off*) That's it.

For a few minutes the GIRL stays with the game. She even seems a little amused. She returns the cigarette to THOMAS's hand, laughing.

THOMAS, in turn, draws on the cigarette very slowly, his eyes fixed on her, then gives it back to her.

Resume on the GIRL. She is about to take it, but changes her mind.

The GIRL gets to her feet abruptly: her nerves cannot stand such an artificial game. THOMAS gets up, too.

GIRL: Ohhh . . . I can't stand it. I'm nervous enough as it is.

She sits down again. Rummages in her bag. Then in a different voice she says:

GIRL: Can I have some water?

THOMAS: Sure. (*He goes off to the kitchen.*)

She watches him disappear into the kitchen, and immediately her eyes light on the camera lying on the film storage cabinet in the extreme foreground.

An instant's pause. She looks furtively towards the kitchen door, and then she is on her feet. She picks up her bag, then tiptoes over to the camera and picks it up.

She hurries past the ostrich feathers on tiptoe and rushes down the stairs leading through the great ground floor room towards the entrance hall.

The door downstairs is flung open and the GIRL bursts through. She stops dead in her tracks.

In front of her is the PHOTOGRAPHER. He is leaning against the wall, smiling slyly. He comes up to her at once, holding out his hand.

THOMAS: And I am not a fool, love.

The GIRL hands him back the camera. She leans against a counter top at the end of the big studio. Beside her is a huge blow-up of a girl doing a parachute jump.

GIRL: Can I have the photographs?

They stand looking at one another silently for a few moments.

THOMAS: Of course. Later.

They move towards the stairs again. She is front, he following.

THOMAS: Your boyfriend's a bit past it.

The GIRL goes on up the stairs without reacting, camera moving up with her.

No sooner are they in the studio than she turns and looks THOMAS straight in the face. It is obvious she resents his previous remark.

GIRL: Why don't you say what you want?

They stand looking at one another, the rack of ostrich feathers between them. THOMAS avoids having to answer. The GIRL puts down her bag and starts undoing her blouse.

The GIRL stands behind the ostrich plumes and takes off her blouse. She is not wearing a bra and stands there bare-topped, but with her black scarf still knotted round her neck.

Close up of the YOUNG MAN, gazing at her with amusement and admiration in his eyes, from over the top of the plumes.

Resume on the GIRL. She puts her blouse down and stands waiting. They look at each other, suddenly serious and tense.

Camera moves with THOMAS as he goes up to her, ducking under the plume rack, and places his hands on her shoulders. He looks at her silently.

Reverse angle shot of them looking at one another. He moves
away and she turns to look at him.

THOMAS: Get dressed. I'll cut out the negatives you want.

He goes off down the gangway leading to the darkrooms. He
opens the purple door of the first one.

Inside the darkroom the door slides open, revealing THOMAS in
close-up. Camera follows him as he goes to the table and takes
the reel from the camera. He toys with it, as if still undecided
whether to give it to her or not. Then he puts it out of sight and
picks up another roll of film, and turns back to the door.

He comes back into the studio and looks round, toying with the
film still in his hand. At first glance it seems the GIRL has
disappeared. The music is now cool, quiet jazz.

The GIRL's legs are visible, but the rest of her body is obscured
by the lilac back-drop. He pulls it away from the wall and looks
behind it. She is standing still, half-naked, with her arms folded
across her breasts. THOMAS comes towards her behind the purple
paper, holding it back, then letting it fall, obscuring them both
from view.

THOMAS comes up to the GIRL and tosses her the roll of film. She
takes it and moves away, camera following her. But after one or
two steps she stops and turns back. She looks at THOMAS almost
tenderly. Then gives him a kiss. A fleeting kiss. And again
moves away.

This time it is his turn to follow her. She stands in close-up
against the purple screen, and he takes her in his arms, holds her
tight and kisses her. This, too, is brief.

Then, with an arm round her shoulders, he leads her gently
towards the bedroom. As they pass, camera tracks in rapidly to
the GIRL's blouse as she tosses the reel of film onto it.

They reach the doorway to the bedroom. She wraps her arms
round his neck . . . when the doorbell rings. They both pause.

THOMAS: (*taking off his shirt*) They'll go.

He tosses the shirt into the bedroom and stands bare-chested. The bell rings again.

GIRL: But they're not going.

THOMAS makes a move to go and open the door. But it is she who holds him back, with a hand on his shoulder.

GIRL: Don't go.

THOMAS gives her hand a kiss and goes down the stairs.

THOMAS crosses the receptionist's office and opens the front door. A DELIVERY BOY stands outside.

DELIVERY BOY: Have you bought a propeller?

THOMAS: What?

DELIVERY BOY: You bought a propeller this morning. Right?

THOMAS: Oh, yes.

DELIVERY BOY: You'll have to give us a hand with it.

THOMAS steps outside to see, then comes back inside to get the key to the big garage door from a chest of drawers in the hall. He picks it up and goes outside.

Outside in the street the DELIVERY BOY unties the propeller from the top of his van, while THOMAS unlocks the garage door.

From the platform overlooking the studio we see the two of them coming in carrying the propeller.

They put it down on the floor near the smoked glass panels.

DELIVERY BOY: All right?

THOMAS: Fine. Yes. (*The* DELIVERY BOY *goes off.*)

We see THOMAS's reflection in a mirror as he turns to go back to the GIRL, going up the steps.

GIRL: (*off*) What's it for?

He hurries up the narrow stairs, but she has already come out onto the platform above. She is still half-naked, with her arms folded across her body, as she bends down, looking down at the propeller.

THOMAS: Nothing. It's beautiful.

GIRL: If I had a big room like this I'd hang it from the ceiling like a fan.

THOMAS leads her back into the studio.

THOMAS: Do you live on your own?

Camera pans as THOMAS come back into the studio.

GIRL: (*off*) No.

She follows him up the steps, ducking under the ostrich plumes. A pause. They move towards the end of the room.

THOMAS: (*gesturing*) Perhaps I'll put it there like a piece of sculpture.

GIRL: It'll look good there. It'll break up the straight lines.

THOMAS takes two cigarettes out of a packet and offers one to the GIRL, who is standing with her hands resting lightly on a beam above her head. The accepts. He gives her a light.

Now the GIRL is sitting in an armchair, still without her blouse on. She laughs, leaning back against the arm of the chair. When she leans her head forward her glance falls on the watch on her wrist. She turns serious, and gets up, hurrying off.

THOMAS: (*off*) Are you going?

GIRL: It's late.

THOMAS moves towards her.

Close-up of THOMAS as he comes up to the GIRL.

THOMAS: Do I see you again?

The GIRL shrugs her shoulders. She is slipping on her blouse. Again she is on edge.

THOMAS: Well, at least tell me your name . . . your phone number.

The GIRL looks in her bag for a piece of paper. While THOMAS is getting her one, she puts the reel into her bag.

THOMAS finds some paper and a pencil and gives them to her.

She scribbles something on the paper and starts for the door, tucking in her blouse. Halfway down the stairs she turns round and looks up.

GIRL: Thank you. (*Then she disappears.*)

THOMAS is alone in the studio. We see him standing at the top of the stairs. He folds the slip of paper and puts it in his pocket. We can see him, partially obscured by the ostrich plumes. He turns off the record player, pours himself another drink and sits down, tapping his knee. He sips some wine. He doesn't really know what to do. Suddenly, he puts his glass down, gets up and runs out.

THOMAS comes into the passage, and camera pans with him as he tucks in his shirt and rolls up his sleeves, going into the first darkroom. He picks up the reel exposed in the park that morning and sets it up for developing. Then he slides the door shut behind him, shutting himself in. Camera moves across the red warning light outside flashing on.

BEDAZZLED

A Twentieth Century-Fox release. Producer & Director, Stanley Donen. Screenplay by Peter Cook and Dudley Moore. Based on a story by Peter Cook. Cinematography, Austin Dempster. Editor, Richard Marden. Art Directors, Terence Knight, Ted Tester. Sound, John Purchase, Doug Turney. Music, Dudley Moore. Assistant Director, John Quested. Running time, 107 minutes. 1967.

CAST

GEORGE SPIGGOT	Peter Cook
STANLEY MOON	Dudley Moore
MARGARET SPENCER	Eleanor Bron
LUST	Raquel Welch
GLUTTONY	Parnell McGarry
VANITY	Alba
ENVY	Barry Humphries

The screenplay of *Bedazzled* opens with the director of the film strolling towards the camera and announcing directly to the audience his decision to withdraw the film from distribution because everyone who has previewed it unanimously agrees "that it might cause irreparable damage to unformed personalities. I refer of course to you." The Devil tiptoes onto the screen and over to the director's ear, reminding him that the film cost millions and that if it's withdrawn, the director will go bankrupt.... "With great pride and pleasure," and without missing a beat, the director spins 180°, and presents *Bedazzled*.

Having set its tongue-in-cheeky tone, *Bedazzled* jumps into a droning Sunday English church service. As the Vicar leads the congregation in prayer, we hear (in voice-over) the silent thoughts of one of the congregants, Stanley Moon. He is an overworked short-order fry cook at the Wimpy Hamburger Bar, where for six excruciating years he has longed to speak to the most exciting woman in his world, the waitress, Margaret Spencer. In the monologue below, Stanley asks God to grant him the courage. But he knows his schlumpiness is terminal; he's a dishrag of Destiny, and he returns to his pathetic bed-sit and attempts suicide. He fails.

Enter the Devil in the first scene below. Bubbling with charm and assurance and dressed in an exuberant whirl of funk and chic, he has arrived to make his typical Faustian bargain with Stanley—seven earthly desires in exchange for his immortal soul. But Stanley wants proof first that Spiggott, as he calls himself, is who he claims to be. Spiggott asks Stanley what he'd like to eat. Stanley says a raspberry ice lolly, so Spiggott escorts Stanley out to the store, orders one, and then asks Stanley to pay, as all Spiggott has is a million pound note. If Stanley Moon were smarter than he needed to be, he'd recognize right here the catch to the whole deal. Instead, he objects that he certainly didn't need the Devil to buy himself an ice lolly, to which Spiggott tsks, "You're just like all the rest; no proof is good enough. God has the same trouble." Later, Spiggott will confide to Stanley that he's finding the whole job tedious; making parking meters expire and cutting off telephone conversations just doesn't hold the same kick for him it once did. For the moment, however, Stanley needs convincing, and in a snap of Spiggott's fingers, they are transported to his London headquarters, the Rendezvous Club. Stanley is introduced to Spiggott's staff—Anger, Sloth, Lust, etc. The little fry cook realizes he is indeed in the presence of the Dark One. He signs the contract. Spiggott cheerfully confirms the deal: "Well done. You'll always regret this."

As with the ice lolly, each of the seven wishes granted Stanley contains a hidden betrayal. His first wish is to be articulate with Margaret so that he can tell her how he feels about her. Courtesy of Spiggott, Stanley's resplendent new vocabulary backfires on him in the second scene excerpted below.

Stanley figures out Spiggott's game and starts to add protective stipulations to each wish, but Spiggott is always one double cross ahead of him. For example, when Stanley wishes for a fantasy in which he and Margaret are married to each other and so rich they couldn't have a care, Spiggott grants it, but he pops up in the fantasy as Margaret's lover. Stanley then wishes for he and Margaret to be alone together, and specifies that this time they must be in love with each other. Spiggott grants them this wish, but with both Stanley and Margaret as nuns trapped in a convent. But at the very last moment, it turns out that Spiggott has finally damned enough souls to win his wager with God and is free to return to heaven. In a farewell gesture of generosity, Spiggott cancels Stanley Moon's contract. Stanley returns to Wimpy's, and maybe...

MONOLOGUE AND SCENE 1

[EXTERIOR CHURCH. DAY

We hear the muffled voice of the VICAR leading the congregation in the Creed.

INTERIOR CHURCH

OMNES: I believe in God the Father Almighty Maker of heaven and earth: And in Jesus Christ his only Son our Lord, Who was conceived by the Holy Ghost, Born of the Virgin Mary, Suffered under Pontius Pilate, Was crucified, dead and buried, He descended into hell; The third day he rose again from the dead, He ascended into heaven, and sitteth on the right hand of God the Father Almighty: From thence he shall come to judge the quick and the dead. I believe in the Holy Ghost: the Holy Catholic Church; The Communion of Saints; The Forgiveness of sins; the Resurrection of the body, And the life everlasting. Amen.

The congregation kneels. The VICAR and the people begin the Lord's prayer:

VICAR: Our Father, which art in heaven, Hallowed be Thy name etc.......]

STANLEY MOON. His lips continue to move but we don't hear what he is saying. We hear this thoughts.

STANLEY: (V.O.) Dear God. . . . there's something I want to ask You. . . . Of course you know what it is because You know everything that's going to happen before it happens, so there's really no need to ask You but I thought I'd ask You in any case; now you know that I believe in You but I was wondering if You could give me just a little sign . . . not that I need it but I thought that if You gave it to me I would believe in You even more. I'm not saying that if You don't give me the sign that I won't believe in You. . . . I'm not threatening You or anything like that. . . . but You remember when I had that nasty dose of 'flu when I was seven and I couldn't breathe properly and I told You that if You made me better I'd always believe in You . . . well, I got better in a week but I couldn't be sure if it was You or whether I would have got better in any case. Do you think this time You could do something clearer; if You do I promise I'll be a better person; please please give me enough courage to speak to Margaret Spencer and get to know her. . . . just do that and I'll know You exist. . . .

[VICAR: O God make clean our hearts within us.

CONGREGATION: And take not Thy Holy Spirit from us.

INTERIOR WIMPY BAR (COOKERS, GRILLS, ETC.)

A hamburger is placed on a fiery grill. The flames leap about it. The air is filled with fire and sizzling noises. Potatoes are lowered into boiling oil. Eggs seethe on a griddle. Steam pours from a machine. The coffee bubbles in the machine.
STANLEY MOON, a chef in the Wimpy Bar. He is a sad figure who wipes the sweat from his brow with his white sleeve. He works feverishly.

From time to time he glances at the cool efficient figure of MARGARET SPENCER a waitress who is serving the customers: she is smiling, attractive, on the surface a rather bright girl whose outward poise disguises an extremely ordinary mind. STANLEY has been infatuated with her for years but has never dared speak to her. As they both go about their work we hear STANLEY'S thoughts.]

STANLEY: (V.O.) Miss Spencer . . . I wonder if I could have a word with you. . . there's something I've got to tell you . . . something I've got to bring out into the open now. I have been bottling it up inside me too long and there's no point hiding it any more. For six years now, ever since you came to Wimpy's I have been in love with you. I only live to hear your voice.

[MARGARET: (*V.O.*) One king sized Cheeseburger, french fries.]

STANLEY: (*V.O.*) Each time you speak it's like a thousand violins playing in the halls of heaven. I have watched you every day and wanted to tell you of my love but I've never had the courage to say more than good morning and good night. . . but now I can contain myself no longer.

[He pours a bucket of potato chips into a vat of sizzling fat.]

STANLEY: (*V.O.*) I love you Miss Spencer . . . I love everything about you . . . the way you walk . . . your sweet smile . . . your easy grace and charm.

[MARGARET: Wimpeyburgers twice, one MR, one well, heavy on the onions.

She collects the cheeseburger.]

STANLEY: (*V.O.*) I wish I could take you away from all this . . . I'd like to be able to give you everything you want.

[During the above MARGARET serves the cheeseburger to GEORGE SPIGGOTT who is sitting at a table.]

STANLEY: (*V.O.*) I know with you beside me I can achieve so much; I'd give anything to have you. I'd like us to start a new life together, emigrate to New Zealand. . . . a little house of our own, a car, the two of us against the world, gaining strength from each other . . . joined forevermore in holy wedlock.

[He pours runny cheese onto a sizzling Hamburger.]

STANLEY: (*V.O.*) I've wasted six whole years in futile longing. . . . I know what I've got to say and I'm going to say it. . . .

[EXTERIOR WIMPY BAR

MARGARET emerges buttoning up her coat. STANLEY bursts through the door in hot pursuit.]

STANLEY: Miss Spencer.

[MARGARET: (*not being rude but hardly hearing*) Did you say something?

STANLEY: No, nothing.

MARGARET gets into a waiting bubble car and drives off with a young man, STANLEY'S eyes follow the departing vehicle with despair. It is a most miserable look.]

INTERIOR STANLEY'S DEPRESSING BED SITTING ROOM.

He enters with a brown paper parcel, sits down and writes a brief note. He addresses the envelope "Miss Spencer" and places it on top of a cellophane topped cardboard box that houses his collection of moths, all uniformly grey. He undoes the parcel and takes out a length of rope. He goes to his bookshelf that contains a meagre collection of Teach Yourself books; he takes out "Teach Yourself Knots" and fashions a noose. He fastens the rope to a pipe that runs across the ceiling, places his chair beneath it, climbs up, puts the noose round his neck and jumps off; the pipe breaks, a small steady stream of water comes out.

The door opens and GEORGE SPIGGOTT enters. He is dressed in a double breasted dinner suit, red socks and black sneakers.

SPIGGOTT: Ah, good evening, I couldn't help noticing that you were making an unsuccessful suicide bid.

STANLEY: What are you doing in my room? What do you want?

SPIGGOTT: (*helping undo the noose*) I've come to help you Mr. Moon.

STANLEY: I don't want any help; just get out please.

SPIGGOTT: You don't understand; I've got some good news for you.

STANLEY: You must have the wrong bloke.

STANLEY climbs on the chair and tries to staunch the flow.

STANLEY: Can't you see I'm busy? Please go away.

SPIGGOTT: Just as you like Mr. Moon; I thought you might be interested in a small matter of a million pounds.

SPIGGOTT makes for the door. STANLEY rushes after him.

STANLEY: A million pounds?

SPIGGOTT: That's right, but don't let me interfere with your doing away with yourself.

STANLEY: Hold on a minute; what do you mean, a million pounds?

SPIGGOTT: May I sit down.

STANLEY: Please.

SPIGGOTT: Very nasty little place you've got here.

STANLEY puts his finger in the pipe.

STANLEY: Yes... what about this million pounds?

SPIGGOTT: Well you remember your great, great, great grandfather? Well of course you don't, he was a bit before your time.

STANLEY: I never even met my father.

SPIGGOTT: I know, how sad; suffice it to say, your great, great, great grandfather Ephraim Moon sailed to Australia in 1782 and set himself up as an apothecary.

STANLEY: A what.

SPIGGOTT: A chemist; the business flourished and by the time he died it was worth two thousand pounds; your great great grandfather Cedric Moon, by careful management and shrewd investments increased that sum a hundredfold.

STANLEY: Yes, yes.

SPIGGOTT: This money he left to your great grandfather Thomas

Moon, who in turn diversified, expanded until he had accumulated a personal fortune of well over a million pounds which when he died was inherited by your grandfather Harold Moon who returned to London and squandered every penny on wine women and loose living.

STANLEY: And where does that leave me?

SPIGGOTT: Destitute, and on the brink of suicide.

STANLEY: You get out of here before I . . .

SPIGGOTT: Before you what?

STANLEY: Before I call the police.

SPIGGOTT: You realise of course that suicide is a criminal offence; in less enlightened times they'd have hung you for it.

STANLEY: I wish you'd stop making fun of me and just leave me alone.

SPIGGOTT: Seriously Mr. Moon, I want to help you; tell me what's the matter; unburden yourself; it does you good to share your problems.

STANLEY: What interest is it to you; please go away.

SPIGGOTT: I'm interested in everyone; now what made you try and kill yourself?

STANLEY: I'll tell you what; I'm miserable, penniless, got no friends, I can't get to know anyone and nobody wants to get to know me and everything's hopeless and if you want to help me, get me something for this pipe.

SPIGGOTT: But suicide Mr. Moon, a man with your opportunities, that's the last thing you should do.

STANLEY: That's what I was counting one . . . I thought I'd get it over with while I've still got my health . . .

SPIGGOTT: But that's taking the easy way out.

STANLEY: Easy way out; what's easy about it? Look, the bleeding pipes broke. Nothing's easy for me; I can't even manage to kill myself.

SPIGGOTT: Let's face it Mr. Moon; you are a complete failure.

STANLEY: Yes.

STANLEY sits. The water starts to flow again.

SPIGGOTT: I'll fix that. (*He gets a cork from a bottle and inserts it*) You know that million pounds I mentioned; it wasn't a joke; I could give you that and more.

STANLEY: Don't be stupid.

SPIGGOTT: All the things you've ever seen on the advertisements, fast white convertibles, blonde women, their hair trailing in the wind, wafer thin after dinner chocolates; if I could give you all that, would that make you any happier?

STANLEY: Of course it would, but you can't.

SPIGGOTT: But I can; would the words Prince of Darkness mean anything to you? The Horned One, Beelzebub, Mephistophiles?

STANLEY: I know; you've escaped from somewhere.

SPIGGOTT: Far from it. I am the Horned One; the Devil; let me give you my card.

STANLEY: Don't give me that rubbish; you're a nut case.

SPIGGOTT: They said the same of Jesus, Freud and Galileo.

STANLEY: They also said it about a lot of nut-cases.

SPIGGOTT: You're nobody's fool Mr. Moon; supposing I granted you your dearest wish here and now, would that convince you?

STANLEY: Do leave off.

SPIGGOTT: What about that girl at Wimpy's?

STANLEY: (*surprised*) Margaret Spencer?

SPIGGOTT: Yes.

STANLEY: How do you know her?

SPIGGOTT: I know most people intimately. Would she by any chance be your dearest wish?

STANLEY: Yes she is.

SPIGGOTT: Would you like to kiss her and make love to her. And press her taut brown frame against yours and have her for your very own.

STANLEY: Yes yes, that's it.

SPIGGOTT: Well you can if you agree to my little proposition . . .

STANLEY: I'm not agreeing to anything.

SPIGGOTT: I understand Mr. Moon . . . let me give you a demonstration . . . to prove who I am and help you make up your mind . . . no obligation on your part. Isn't there anything in the world you wish for?

STANLEY: Margaret Spencer?

SPIGGOTT: Ah . . . not until we've made our bargain . . . how about something more modest, something to eat, something comestible.

STANLEY: A Frobisher and Gleason raspberry flavoured ice lolly, I wish I could have one of those.

SPIGGOTT: Very well, to prove beyond any shadow of a doubt that I am indeed The Unholy One, a Frobisher and Gleason raspberry flavoured ice lolly shall be yours in a trice.

He snaps his fingers dramatically.

CUT TO:

EXTERIOR LODGING HOUSE. DAY.

STANLEY and SPIGGOTT emerge and get onto a bus.

CUT TO:

INTERIOR SHOP. DAY

SPIGGOTT: One Frobisher and Gleason raspberry flavoured ice lolly, please.

SHOP ASS.: Here you are, sir.

SPIGGOTT: (*patting his pocket*) Have you got 6d. Mr. Moon, I only have a million pound note?

STANLEY hands the shop assistant 6d. and they go out.

CUT TO:

EXTERIOR STREET DAY

SPIGGOTT: Convinced?

STANLEY: I could have done that myself. I thought you were going to conjure it up.

SPIGGOTT: You're just like all the rest; no proof is good enough. God has the same trouble.

STANLEY: Well at least He did something big, parting the Red Sea, magic writing on marble tablets, virgin birth, pillars of fire, walking on water.

SPIGGOTT: And does that make you believe in Him?

STANLEY: All I'm saying is that I don't believe in you just because you buy me or rather I buy me this rotten ice lolly.

SPIGGOTT: I thought that was what you wanted.

STANLEY: I'd like a real miracle. A rain of toads.

SPIGGOTT: What's it to be then, wine into water, stick into serpent, how about travelling through space at the speed of light?

STANLEY: Yes and how about you checking in to the nearest loony bin for a few weeks holiday?

SPIGGOTT: Oh ye of little faith; you're not wearing nylon underwear are you?

STANLEY: No.

SPIGGOTT: It disintegrates at high speeds; now then . . . the magic word ELLBEEJAY.

He snaps his fingers and they disappear.

(*Note*: The first time that Spiggott snaps his fingers, in the acting studio the ice lolly will unfortunately have to come to the flat, rather than the actors taking a bus to get to the ice lolly. Perhaps an ice-cream vendor's melodic bell is heard on cue at the front door of the flat, where a silent vendor stands ready with ice lolly.

As written in the script, the second time Spiggott snaps his fingers, the actors are teleported in a jump-cut to his London lair. Upon arrival, Stanley is convinced, marveling, ''My ice lolly's melted. Ere, you really are The Devil.'' ''Incarnate,'' Spiggott confirms. The actors may wish to ''tag'' the scene with this exchange heard in the darkness a moment after the blackout.

''ELLBEEJAY,'' the magic words, are the initials of Lyndon Baines Johnson, the President of the United States in 1967, the year the film was made. In 1967, an ice lolly could still be purchased in England for 6d, a ''sixpence.'')

SCENE 2

EXTERIOR ZOO. DAY.

MARGARET and STANLEY are at the Monkey House.

MARGARET: Aren't they sweet? I could watch them all day.

STANLEY: I mean by studying them we can learn a great deal about ourselves.

MARGARET: They have such beautiful hands.

STANLEY: Don't they; a fantastic delicacy combined with praeternatural strength; do you know that the Simius Tetrolacus can lift objects seventeen times his own weight.

MARGARET: Seventeen times! Do they do it often?

STANLEY: It's difficult to say; its only happened once under properly controlled laboratory conditions; there's a man

working on the subject in Zurich. . . . you've probably heard
of him . . . Einstetter . . . Heinrich Einstetter . . .

MARGARET: I think I know who you mean.

STANLEY: He made that incredible film on the mating rituals of
land snails . . .

MARGARET: Of course, I've heard so much about it; does it
make you sad to see animals caged up like this.

STANLEY: In a way, but you know they're really no worse off
than most of us.

MARGARET: How do you mean?

STANLEY: Well metaphorically speaking and in a very real sense
society creates its own cages, cages of the mind, a curious
kind of cerebral captivity.

[They pass SPIGGOTT who is selling poppies.

SPIGGOTT: Buy a flower.

MARGARET: What is it for?

SPIGGOTT: Depraved criminals.

MARGARET: Oh good. (*She hands over a coin and pins the
poppy to* STANLEY.)]

INTERIOR LONDON BUS. DAY.

STANLEY: You see civilisation has had the effect of inhibiting our
deepest natural animal instincts; the conventions of an
ordered society have made us lose what Freud calls our
"Urmenschgefuhlnaturlichkeit."

MARGARET: Is that what he called it. He must have been a
marvellous man.

STANLEY: One of the seminal forces.

MARGARET: I mean to have thought up the unconscious and all
that; I would love to have met him.

STANLEY: And I'm sure he'd have been delighted to meet you; but as I was saying, this loss of Urmenschgefuhlnaturlichkeit means that we've eroded our capacity for real happiness; to be happy you have to be free, uninhibited.

MARGARET: Free as a bird... that's what it is isn't it... birds are free... that's where the expression comes from... free as a bird.

STANLEY: You're a very perceptive girl you know... it's almost as if our superior brains destroy our naturalness... we become ashamed of our primitive drives and this creates neurosis... man should forget all his logic and learning and simply be... in the animal sense...

MARGARET: You're so right.

STANLEY: As Rousseau said... we must learn to unlearn, because only by unlearning can we really learn to be...

MARGARET: The noble savage.

STANLEY: Exactly... but modern urban orientated man has trapped his basic spontaneity in the spider's web of his self imposed conformist behaviour patterns.

MARGARET: We must rip that spider's web away.

INTERIOR STANLEY'S BOOKLINED FLAT.

STANLEY opens the door.

STANLEY: Why don't you... would you like to come in...

MARGARET: What a fabulous room... it's marvellous.

STANLEY: Do you like it....

MARGARET: I love it.... it's so right... I mean it's you... the moment I walked in I knew everything about it says Stanley... this room is you...

STANLEY: I'm afraid it's a bit of a mess.

MARGARET: (*She sees some records and screams.*) Oohhh... Brahms! I can't believe it... you too.

STANLEY: I adore him. He has a muscular romanticism that I find irresistible.

MARGARET: Brahm is just so fantastic . . . whenever I feel tense or anything I put him on and just sprawl on the carpet and let him flow all over me and get swept away into a wonderful world where everything is so mmmmmmmmm. . . .

STANLEY: Would you like some now?

MARGARET: Please . . . not that I'm tense or anything . . . It would just make everything even more marvellous (*He puts on music.*) oh yes . . .

STANLEY: Go on lie down . . . let it happen . . . (*She does*)

MARGARET: Mmmmmmmmm . . . it's gorgeous . . . (*He lies beside her.*)

STANLEY: I know what you mean about letting it overwhelm you . . .

MARGARET: One is at one with it. I love the way he brings the flute in there.

STANLEY: Yes . . . it's an organ actually . . .

MARGARET: How silly of me.

STANLEY: Not silly at all . . . an organ can sound incredibly like a flute . . . in fact they often sound more like a flute than flutes do. Not many people notice the flute like qualities of an organ.

MARGARET: It's so sensuous and evocative.

STANLEY: Yes yes . . . you can almost see the trees and the sunlight dappling through . . .

MARGARET: And a little brook.

STANLEY: Ah yes yes . . . and what's that . . . a young deer darts into the clearing raises his antlers and edges closer to his doe . . . (*The record is scratched and makes a ghastly noise.*) That was new this morning . . .

MARGARET:　Isn't it strange that the same country that gave birth to such beautiful music could also produce an Adolf Hitler?

STANLEY:　That's a very profound thought.

MARGARET:　(*her eyes boggling with excitement*) Where did you get that fantastic thing?

STANLEY:　It is nice isn't it. . . .

MARGARET:　It's beautiful . . .

STANLEY:　I got it off a stall . . . I just saw it and had to have it . . . I'm like that, if I see something I want, I have to have it.

MARGARET:　Me too.

STANLEY:　Yes you too . . . here.

MARGARET takes the marble object. She rubs it against her face.

MARGARET:　Ooooh, it's so smooth and cool.

STANLEY:　That's the extraordinary thing about marble; it's always eleven degrees cooler than the air that surrounds it; fahrenheit of course.

MARGARET:　Do you like feeling things?

STANLEY:　Oh yes, I'm a very tactile person.

MARGARET:　I just love touching things, sometimes I go out into the forest and shut my eyes and just wander around touching trees and grass and boulders . . . you should try it . . . do it in here . . . go on shut your eyes.

STANLEY and MARGARET both shut their eyes and begin wandering round the room touching objects.

MARGARET:　Now feel something hard.

STANLEY:　I am feeling something hard, it's fantastic.

MARGARET:　You see when your eyes are closed the other senses are heightened.

STANLEY: My how they're heightened. This chair, it's so beautiful . . . I can feel its whole essence . . . I can almost sense the vibrations of the wood, the very life of the chair, in a kind of osmotic fusion.

MARGARET: Now try something soft.

STANLEY: Yes yes. (*He begins to stroke his silk tie.*) Oh it's unbelievable . . . the contrast . . . I've never felt anything so exciting . . . I love it . . . feel my tie.

She comes over, her eyes still shut and langorously feels his tie.

MARGARET: It's delicious . . . silk is so wild . . . it really does something to me.

Their hands meet in the middle of the tie and they jump apart.

STANLEY: Would you like a drink?

MARGARET: Thank you.

STANLEY: What would you like?

STANLEY and MARGARET (*simultaneously*) Cinzano.

STANLEY: Fantastic.

MARGARET: One sip of cinzano and I'm in Italy . . . the freedom of it . . . the sun beating down . . .

STANLEY: The incredible thing about the Italians is the way they touch each other.

MARGARET: Yes. I was in Rimini for two weeks.

STANLEY: Have you noticed that.

MARGARET: Yes.

STANLEY: They touch each other all the time . . . and there's so much warmth and love . . . the Anglo-Saxons have lost the art of touching each other . . . if somebody wants to touch somebody else they should go right ahead and touch them . . . it's a healthy human thing to do . . .

MARGARET:　You're right . . . there's a tribe in Africa who never speak a word . . . they just touch each other . . . and that's the way they communicate . . . and in a way you know I think that language creates a sort of barrier between us . . . well not us but other people . . .

STANLEY:　Life is far too complicated. We should get down to basic elements . . . I mean for example if you were a girl . . . which you are . . . but I mean if you were and I wanted to touch you . . . I wouldn't feel restrained . . . I'd just touch you . . . that's how I am . . . (*He is very close.*)

MARGARET:　I feel the same way . . . I mean if two adult human beings want to touch each other they should touch each other . . . why hold back . . . This whole afternoon has been so perfect. The Cinzano, the Zoo.

STANLEY:　The music. The touching.

MARGARET:　Such immediate rapport . . . and you're so right about the animals . . . I mean that's what we are, deep down beneath our civilized sophistication and we should behave like they do, instinctively, naturally.

STANLEY:　The fact that it's seven minutes past three in the afternoon shouldn't make any difference.

MARGARET:　A goat doesn't stop to think what time of day it is . . . it goes right ahead and does what it feels like.

STANLEY:　Learn to unlearn.

MARGARET:　Feeling, touching, being, doing . . .

Inflamed unbearably STANLEY hurls himself against her. She screams in horror.

MARGARET:　(*screaming*) Rape! Rape! Help! Get off me you beast . . . oooh I hate you . . . I hate you. (*She cringes against the headboard.*) You're just like all the others.

STANLEY:　But Margaret, really . . . (*He advances*)

MARGARET:　Rape! Help!

Footsteps are heard running, there is a banging on the door, whistles blow and in terror STANLEY blows a raspberry.

(*Note*: The dramatic structure of the material offers an uninterrupted build, in continuous conversation, but in three locations—the monkey house of the zoo, a moving bus, and Stanley's fantasy flat. But how much, if any, of the dialogue in the first two could be played in the third? In other words, when Margaret declares that they must rip the spider's web away, is her first rip to declare the room that she's already in suddenly "fabulous" and "marvelous"? The gush of her enthusiasms probably *requires* that she enter this part of the flat for the first time in the conversation, but could Margaret and Stanley have been in the kitchen for the *first* parts of their conversation? A stunning kitchen, with an outside entrance, connected to the book-lined living room by a swinging door? A kitchen in which Stanley has been assembling with outrageous expertise an assortment of hors d'ouevres . . . in which Margaret has come across the monkeys in a National Geographic-type magazine . . . or on a National Geographic-type show playing on the little countertop television set. . . . After all, the scene *is* a fantasy . . .

On the other hand, the actors may wish to study the entire conversation, rehearse and improvise around the first two parts in their actual locations, and then bring only the third part, the part that takes place in the flat, into class. Wherever they enter the scene, they will need to create an exit, probably for Margaret first, leaving Stanley onstage alone. The raspberry he is blowing is a signal to Spiggott that he wants out of the wish, and in the film it will jump cut Stanley into a new scene.)

CATCH-22

A Paramount Pictures release of a Paramount Pictures-Filmways, Inc. Production. Producers, John Calley, Martin Ransohoff. Director, Mike Nichols. Screenplay by Buck Henry. Based on the novel *Catch-22* by Joseph Heller. Cinematographer, David Watkin. Film Editor, Sam O'Steen. Associate Producer, Clive Reed. Production Manager, Jack Corrick. Production Designer, Richard Sylbert. Art Director, Harold Michelson. First Assistant Director, Harold A. Teets. Sound Recording, Lawrence O. Jost, Elden Ruberg. Running time, 121 minutes. 1970.

CAST

CAPTAIN YOSSARIAN	Alan Arkin
COLONEL CATHCART	Martin Balsam
MAJOR DANBY	Richard Benjamin
CAPTAIN NATELY	Art Garfunkel
DR. DANEEKA	Jack Gilford
MAJOR MAJOR	Bob Newhart
CHAPLAIN TAPPMAN	Anthony Perkins
NURSE DUCKETT	Paula Prentiss
LIEUTENANT DOBBS	Martin Sheen
LIEUTENANT MILO MINDERBENDER	Jon Voight
GENERAL DREEDLE	Orson Welles
GENERAL DREEDLE'S WAC	Susanne Benton
HUNGRY JOE	Seth Allen
CAPTAIN ORR	Robert Balaban
CAPTAIN MCWATT	Peter Bonerz

AARDVARK   Charles Grodin
LIEUTENANT COLONEL KORN   Buck Henry
COLONEL MOODUS   Austin Pendleton

Yossarian is an American soldier stationed in Italy during World War II. Were war not absurdity enough, the base on the isle of Pianosa is a whole world of insanity all unto itself. What keeps it spinning is that war *is* enough for the general and his colonel and the mad, brilliant lieutenant who are stationed there to all make money and have fun. Yossarian, on the other hand, is worried about being killed.

If the lieutenant were *really* nuts, he'd get kicked out... wouldn't he? If you're really crazy, you can get out, can't you? Yossarian, who has had a man's shot-up body pour right through his hands, insists that *he* is crazy. How could he be otherwise, to still be flying missions when he has almost been killed so many times? The doctor tells him that since he has asked to be grounded, he is obviously not crazy anymore, and therefore he must follow orders and keep flying. That's Catch-22.

Lieutenant Milo Minderbender is a venture capitalist who begins as a mess sergeant and trades up. He will swap anything that he can profitably trade on, no matter what. Able to get a good deal for silk, Milo trades away the parachutes, and when the flyers go to use them, they find instead a note issuing them a single share of M & M Enterprises. At his most inventive, Milo is chocolate-coating a surplus in cotton, expecting to use it as food. This does not work, but the Germans (who are incidentally the enemy), are willing to absorb the excess cotton in return for a bombing of Milo's base. By this time M & M Enterprises is a multinational conglomerate, and this is a deal that is simply too good to be refused. At one point or another, whoever you are and whatever you are doing, you are actually working for Milo.

Colonel Cathcart has no problem with the Lieutenant's operations; Cathcart is working by his own private set of rules, anyway. After a certain number of missions, his men are supposed to be sent home. The Colonel keeps upping the number, since he is so proud of (and will no doubt become famous for) commanding the outfit that averages more combat missions than any other. He pads the numbers further by ordering bombings of extra towns, even those with no tactical or strategic value. In charge of the whole shebang is General Dreedle. He is always accompanied by his personal WAC, a khaki undulation who sets the men moaning en masse. General Dreedle is actually quite surprised when he learns that he is not allowed to shoot whomever he wants. The chaotic command becomes so wildly and smugly inefficient, and the self-serving outrages against human life and welfare become so huge and careless, that one of the men who tries to kill Colonel Cathcart tells Yossarian, "This is the first sane thing I've ever done." Yossarian is eventually wounded seriously, and then offered a deal: he can be sent home a hero if he'll do PR for the unit once he's back in the States. He refuses. In the end, Yossarian steals a raft and rows away across the sea.

When the squadron commander had been shot down over Perugia, it was said, "That'll teach him to go fooling around on bombing missions when he's supposed to be working in his office." Colonel Cathcart nonetheless needed to choose a replacement. As if this weren't enough, Cathcart was further nettled by some captain with a bothersome name blocking the path of his jeep. This is how Cathcart became aware of Captain Major, a dull and dutiful sort assigned to billeting and laundry. Greatness is suddenly thrust upon Captain Major when the Colonel promotes him officially to squadron commander Major Major. At first, Major is in total bewilderment as to what he's supposed to do. (If he is just the butt of a bad joke, this is nothing new. His own father named him Major Major Major.) Major figures out, with perfect Catch-22 logic, that he is only going to see people in his office during the hours when he is not in his office. He explains to his assistant how business will be handled now that he is in charge (scene 1 below).

Chaplain Tappman feels himself just as ineffectual, over-his-head, and nerve-wracked as the Major. In scene 2 below, Tappman has been summoned to Colonel Cathcart's office—though it feels more like he's under arrest—to learn a plan which Cathcart has no doubts can ultimately result in a cover story on himself in the *Saturday Evening Post*.

(*Note*: The way in which one image or scene displaced the previous one was one of the most striking stylistic characteristics of the film *Catch-22*. Both scenes below begin with conversation already directly underway. Since both scenes have exits, for classroom study the actors playing Towser and Tappman may also wish to provide themselves with entrances at the top of their scenes. Towser's entrance might logically come on his second line, after Major Major has donned his disguise.)

SCENE 1

INTERIOR MAJOR MAJOR'S OFFICE—ANGLE ON MAJOR MAJOR AND SERGEANT TOWSER

TOWSER: (*sympathetically*) I know that, sir. But we all have to do our part, I guess.

MAJOR MAJOR: Well, I don't like my part. I'm going to take the rest of the afternoon off and go lie down in my tent and think about things.

MAJOR MAJOR goes to his desk, opens a drawer and takes out a pair of dark glasses and a false moustache.

TOWSER: Sir—there's someone waiting to see you.

MAJOR MAJOR: Now?

TOWSER: Yes, sir.

MAJOR MAJOR: Who is it?

TOWSER: Captain Tappman, sir. The group chaplain.

MAJOR MAJOR: What does he want?

TOWSER: I don't know, sir. Something to do with Captain Yossarian.

MAJOR MAJOR: Look Sergeant, the job that I have to do is tough enough without having to deal all the time with a lot of people who want something. Do I make myself clear?

He puts on the false moustache.

TOWSER: Yes, sir.

MAJOR MAJOR: I suppose you wonder about this? (*indicating his moustache*)

TOWSER: No, sir. It's not my place to wonder.

MAJOR MAJOR: It's just that I don't like people staring at me. People stare at me. Did you know that?

TOWSER: No, sir.

MAJOR MAJOR: That's because they're thinking who is that Major Major that he gets to be squadron commander without ever having flown in a plane.

TOWSER: I don't think people are thinking that, sir.

MAJOR MAJOR: Well, they are. But when I've got this on they don't know who I am. Did you know that in the middle ages a lot of princes and kings used to put on disguises and walk around their subjects?

TOWSER: No, sir. I didn't.

MAJOR MAJOR: Then I guess you don't know everything, do you?

TOWSER: No, sir. Why did they do that?

MAJOR MAJOR: Why did who do what?

TOWSER: Why did those princes and kings walk around in disguise?

MAJOR MAJOR: How the hell should I know? I'm not some historian or anything. I'm just a guy who's trying to do his job. Good afternoon, Sergeant.

MAJOR MAJOR goes to the open window. He starts to climb out.

TOWSER: Sir?

MAJOR MAJOR: What is it now?

TOWSER: What do you want me to do about the chaplain?

MAJOR MAJOR: Sergeant—from now I don't want anyone to come in and see me while I'm in my office. Is that clear?

TOWSER: Yes, sir. What shall I say to the people who come to see you while you're in your office?

MAJOR MAJOR: Tell them I'm in and ask them to wait.

TOWSER: For how long?

MAJOR MAJOR: Until I've left.

TOWSER: And then what shall I do with them?

MAJOR MAJOR: I don't care.

TOWSER: May I send them in to see you after you've left?

MAJOR MAJOR: Yes.

TOWSER: But you won't be there then, will you?

MAJOR MAJOR: No.

TOWSER: I see, sir. Will that be all?

MAJOR MAJOR: I also don't want you coming into my office while I'm there to ask me if there's anything you can do for me. Is that clear?

TOWSER: Yes, sir. When *should* I come in to find out if there's anything I can do for you?

MAJOR MAJOR: When I'm not there.

TOWSER: Yes, sir. And what should I do then?

MAJOR MAJOR: Whatever has to be done.

TOWSER: Yes, sir.

MAJOR MAJOR: I'm sorry to have to talk to you this way, Sergeant, but I have to. Goodbye.

He reaches out his hand. The SERGEANT salutes. MAJOR MAJOR changes the attempted handshake to a salute and climbs all the way out the window. He holds on to the window sill for a moment.

TOWSER: Goodbye, sir.

MAJOR MAJOR: (*holding on to the sill*) And thank you. For everything.

MAJOR MAJOR drops to the ground outside and starts off. TOWSER turns and goes through the door to the outer office.

SCENE 2

INTERIOR CATHCART'S OFFICE—CATHCART—DAY

sitting behind his desk. He stands.

CATHCART: Well, Chaplain—we don't see much of you around lately.

TAPPMAN: Well, sir—I try and stay out of the way as much as possible. I have the feeling that I make many of the men uncomfortable.

CATHCART: Nonsense! I can't imagine any man not enjoying the benefits of your—uh—presence. Unless, of course, they're atheists. (*he laughs*) And I guess there's not much chance of that. Is there?

TAPPMAN: Well, I don't know, sir.

CATHCART: What do you mean, you don't know? Atheism is against the law, isn't it?

TAPPMAN: No, sir.

CATHCART: IT ISN'T? Then it's un-American, isn't it?

TAPPMAN: I'm not sure, sir.

CATHCART: Well, I am! And if I find any lousy atheists on this base, you can bet your ass they'll soon start believing in *something*.

TAPPMAN looks uncomfortable and tries to smile. CATHCART takes a deep breath and smiles.

CATHCART: Well—that's not why I called you in, Chaplain. I want you to take a look at this.

The COLONEL picks up a magazine from the desk and throws it to TAPPMAN who catches it clumsily.

CATHCART: Page forty-seven.

TAPPMAN opens to page forty-seven as CATHCART lights a cigarette and watches him carefully. TAPPMAN looks at the page and looks up.

CATHCART: You don't have to read the whole thing, Chaplain. But I think you can get the point from the photographs. There's a full page color picture of a Colonel in England whose Chaplain conducts prayers before every mission.

TAPPMAN: Yes, I see.

TAPPMAN looks at the COLONEL. They look at each other for a few minutes.

CATHCART: Well?

TAPPMAN clears his throat and looks away. He looks in the direction of a huge basket of peaches that sits on a chair near the desk.

CATHCART: Would you like a peach, Chaplain?

TAPPMAN: No, thank you, sir.

CATHCART: Lieutenant Minderbender shipped them in just today. There's a tremendous profit to be made in fresh peaches.

TAPPMAN: Is there?

CATHCART: (*picking one of the peaches up and fondling it*) Notice how firm and ripe they are. Like a young girl's breasts.

SHOT—TAPPMAN

He blinks and looks away in embarrassment.

SHOT—CATHCART

He looks at TAPPMAN. His smile disappears. He puts the peach down quickly and turns icily to TAPPMAN.

CATHCART: However we were speaking about something else. We were *not* speaking about the firm ripe breasts of young girls. Were we?

TAPPMAN: No, sir.

CATHCART: We were speaking about conducting prayers before missions. Is there any reason why we can't stick to the subject?

TAPPMAN: No, sir.

CATHCART: All right, then, I see no reason why the *Saturday Evening Post* shouldn't be interested in the story of *my* outfit. I want you to think up some nice snappy prayers that will send the officers out feeling good. Can you do that?

TAPPMAN: I'll try, sir. Now—what about the enlisted men?

CATHCART: What about them?

TAPPMAN: Well—I assumed you would want them to be present also since they would be going along on the same mission.

CATHCART: What for? They've got a God and a Chaplain of their own, don't they?

TAPPMAN: No, sir.

CATHCART: Hold on a minute. Are you telling me that the enlisted men pray to the same God that we do?

TAPPMAN: Yes, sir.

CATHCART: And he listens?

TAPPMAN: I think so, sir.

CATHCART: I'll be damned.

CATHCART stands and looks out the window, shaking his head.

CATHCART: (*continuing*) Look—don't get me wrong. It isn't that I think the enlisted men are dirty, common or inferior. But there are limits. (*turning suddenly*) You wouldn't want your sister to marry an enlisted man, would you?

TAPPMAN: My sister *is* an enlisted man, sir.

CATHCART: Just what do you mean by that remark, Chaplain? Are you trying to be funny?

TAPPMAN: Oh, no, sir. My sister is a Master Sergeant in the Marines.

CATHCART: Oh?

TAPPMAN: (*reaching into his pocket*) Would you like to see a picture of him? *HER*.

CATHCART: No no no. Look, Chaplain, I'm going to leave this thing in your hands. I'll give you a minute and a half at this afternoon's briefing. I'd like you to keep it light and snappy. None of your morbid negative Kingdom of God or Valley of Death stuff.

TAPPMAN: Like the Twenty-Third Psalm?

CATHCART: How's that one go?

TAPPMAN: The Lord is my Shepherd—I shall not—

CATHCART: *That's* the one I was referring to. It's *out*. What else have you got?

TAPPMAN: Uh—"Save me, O God; for the waters are come in unto—"

CATHCART: No waters! Something musical—with some *zip* in it. What about that harps on the willows thing?

TAPPMAN: Oh, yes, sir. That's very nice. "Yea, we wept when we remember Zion."

CATHCART: ZION? Let's forget about *that* one right now. I'd like to know how that one even got in there. Haven't you got anything humorous that stays away from waters and valleys and—God?

TAPPMAN: I'm sorry, sir, but just about all the prayers I know do make at least some passing reference to God.

CATHCART: Then let's get some new ones. Let's stop rubbing in this God thing and take a more positive approach. Let's just stay away from the subject of religion altogether. Let's all pray for something good—something worthwhile—like a tighter bombing pattern. Is there any reason we can't pray for a tighter bombing pattern?

TAPPMAN: No, sir—I suppose not.

CATHCART: Good. Let's get to it.

TAPPMAN doesn't move.

CATHCART: Is there something else?

TAPPMAN: Sir—it may be none of my business, but I think some of the men are particularly upset about the fact that you keep raising the number of missions they have to fly.

CATHCART: You're right, Chaplain.

TAPPMAN: I *am*, sir?

CATHCART: You're right that it's none of your business. And it's none of their business either. Their business is to fly missions. And your business is to think of some short catchy prayers that will get me into the *Saturday Evening Post*. Good afternoon, Captain.

CATHCART presses a button on his intercom.

TAPPMAN: Yes, sir.

TAPPMAN goes to the door and opens it.

CATHCART: Chaplain.

TAPPMAN: (*turning*) Yes, sir.

CATHCART: Tell the men to trust in God.

TAPPMAN exits.

    •   •   •   •   •

PATTON

A Twentieth Century-Fox release. Producer, Frank McCarthy. Director, Franklin J. Schaffner. Screen story and screenplay by Francis Ford Coppola and Edmund H. North. Based on factual material from *Patton: Ordeal and Triumph* by Ladislas Farago and *A Soldier's Story* by Omar N. Bradley. Music, Jerry Goldsmith. Director of Photography, Fred Koenkamp. Film Editor, Hugh S. Fowler. Art Directors, Urie McCleary, Gil Parrando. Set Decorators, Antonio Mateos, Pierre-Louis Thevenet. Associate Producer, Frank Caffey. Assistant Directors, Eli Dunn, Jose Lopez Rodero. Sound supervisor, James Corcoran. Running time, 170 minutes. 1970.

CAST

GENERAL GEORGE S. PATTON, JR.	George C. Scott
GENERAL OMAR N. BRADLEY	Karl Malden
CAPTAIN CHESTER B. HANSEN	Stephen Young
BRIGADIER GENERAL HOBART CARVER	Michael Strong
GENERAL BRADLEY'S DRIVER	Cary Loftin
FIELD MARSHAL ERWIN ROMMEL	Karl Michael Vogler
GENERAL PATTON'S DRIVER	Bill Hickman
FIELD MARSHAL SIR BERNARD LAW MONTGOMERY	Michael Bates
SOLDIER WHO GETS SLAPPED	Tim Considine

General George S. Patton was a soldier who loved combat. He'd grown up a child of great wealth, studying the lives of the legendary commanders such as Napoleon and Caesar; but unlike these models, fighting for Patton did not comprise a segment of a larger career. He was neither politician nor diplomat, believing instead that the noblest glory was achieved by man in war. If confronted by what he judged cowardice in his subordinates, he was so deeply offended, for himself or for the others in his command, that he literally slapped it down. He was brilliant in battle and incorrigible elsewhere in the war. If he had doubts, he kept them to himself.

And yet... he was married with three children, wrote poetry, believed in reincarnation (and that he'd been present when Rome defeated Carthage), read the Bible daily, proclaiming, "I don't yield to any man in my reverence to the Lord but Goddammit! no sermon needs to take longer than 10 minutes." He was nicknamed "Blood and Guts," but he designed his own uniform complete with riding crop, gold-buckled holster, and twin ivory-handled pistols. In World War II, after brilliant victories in Africa, Patton was made head of the Seventh Army for the invasion of Sicily, but it was his personal rivalry with his ally, Field Marshal Montgomery, which seemed to really spur him on, and may have led to an unnecessarily high cost in American lives. While his slapping of soldiers on two occasions became national scandals and contributed to the decision to keep him out of D-Day, it was not long afterward that the speed and daring with which he raced the Third Army across France made him again a popular favorite. And this was when he was fifty-nine years old, after having spent the years between the two World Wars riding polo ponies and living in privileged leisure on various American army bases. Still to come would be what many considered his finest hour, the Battle of the Bulge, although afterwards his very public dislike of the Soviet Allies led to still more controversy.

When General Patton was killed in an automobile accident just after the end of World War II, *The New York Times* described him as "Spectacular, swaggering, pistol-packing, deeply religious and violently profane, easily moved to anger because he was first of all a fighting man, easily moved to tears because underneath all his mannered irascibility he had a kind heart, he was a strange combination of fire and ice.''

The following monologue opens the film:

MONOLOGUE

CLOSE SHOT—PATTON

The anthem concludes and he completes his salute. Now this twenty-eight-star general scans us carefully. In a vibrant voice, and with a cold, mean look, he speaks directly at us:

PATTON: At ease, men. I want you to remember that no bastard ever won a war by dying for his country. He won it by making the other poor dumb bastard die for his country... Men, the stuff we heard about America not wanting to fight, wanting to stay out of the war, was a lot of horsedung. Americans traditionally love to fight. All real Americans love the sting of battle. When you were kids you all admired the champion marble player, the fastest runner, the big league ballplayers, the toughest boxers. Americans love a winner and do not tolerate a loser. Americans play to win all the time. I wouldn't give a hoot in hell for a man who lost and laughed. That's why Americans have never lost, and will never lose a war, for the very thought of losing is hateful to Americans. An army is a team. It lives, sleeps, eats, fights as a team. This individuality stuff is a lot of crap. The bilious bastards who wrote that stuff about individuality for the *Saturday Evening Post* don't know any more about real battle than they do about a sock full of silt. We have the finest food, equipment, the best spirit and men in the world. Why, by God, I actually pity those poor bastards we're going against—by God, I do. We won't just shoot the bastards. We're going to cut out their living guts and use them to grease the treads of our tanks. We're going to murder those lousy Hun bastards by the bushel. Many of you boys are wondering whether you'll chicken out under fire. Don't worry about it; I can assure you you will all do your duty. The Nazis are the enemy. Wade into them and spill their blood. Shoot them in the belly. When you stick your hand into a bunch of goo that a moment before was your best friend's face... you'll know what to do. There's another thing I want you to remember. I don't want to get any messages saying: "We are holding our position." We're not holding anything. Let the Hun do that. We are advancing constantly and are not interested in holding anything, except onto the enemy. We're going to hold onto him by the nose and kick him in the ass. We'll kick the hell out of him all the time. We'll go through them like crap through a goose. (*pause*) There's one thing you men will be able to say when you get home. You may all thank God for it. Thirty years from now, when you are sitting around the fireside with your grandson on your knee and he asks what you did in the great World War II, you won't have to say, "I shoveled shit in Louisiana." (*pause*) All right—now you sonsuvbitches know how I feel. I will be proud to lead you wonderful guys into battle anytime, anywhere.

He stares sincerely, almost wet-eyed at us for a moment.

PATTON: That is all.

LAST TANGO IN PARIS

A United Artists presentation of a co-production of PEA Produzioni Europee Associate S.A.S. & Les Productions Artistes Associes S.A. Producer, Alberto Grimaldi. Director, Bernardo Bertolucci. Screenplay by Bernardo Bertolucci and Franco Arcalli. Director of Photography, Vittorio Storare. Film Editor, Franco Arcalli (in collaboration with Roberto Perpignani). Music, Gato Barbieri. Sound, Michael Billingsley. Assistant Directors, Fernand Moskowicz, Jean David Lefebvre. Color. Running time, 129 minutes. 1972.

CAST

PAUL	Marlon Brando
JEANNE	Maria Schneider
TOM	Jean-Pierre Leaud
MARCEL	Massimo Girotti
ROSA'S MOTHER	Maria Michi
PROSTITUTE	Giovanna Galletti
CONCIERGE	Darling Legitimus
CATHERINE	Catherine Allegret

Paul is an American in his forties who lives in Paris. He used to work as an actor and then as a journalist, but for many years now he has been sponging off his French wife who owned and ran a cheap hotel. She has just committed suicide.

Jeanne is a French girl of twenty. She lives in ample bourgeois comfort with her widowed mother; her father was a colonel. In a week she's to be married to her fiancé, who loves her and loves making improvisational *verité* films. He combines both of his loves by relentlessly following her around with a movie camera and documenting her real life, all the while directing her to make it more cinematic.

Paul and Jeanne know none of this about each other. They meet while looking at a vacant flat for rent. They are violently attracted to each other; they have sex. Paul rents the apartment, and they meet there for three days. Paul's need to escape from his own life is so overpowering that he demands ground rules of total anonymity: they are not to speak their names; they are not to share their outside lives, either present or past. He insists on an isolation chamber that extracts sex from love or personality or previous experience. They enter a private limbo so hypnotically and erotically compelling that Jeanne, despite her growing confusion, keeps returning for more. He needs to imprison her in the psychological jungle-gym of an American machismo myth, but his brutality is made of grief and self-rage. He finally sits beside his wife's body, which is now laid out on a bed of flowers, ready for burial. In the monologue below, he releases his hate and his love for her, to her corpse.

Paul will then want to take his relationship with Jeanne into the "real world." He is ready to come out of their sexual soldier closet. But when he does, she sees him as the middle-aged failure he believes himself to be. She tries to just leave, but he is ready to live with her for the rest of their lives. She tells him she's getting married. He keeps repeating that one thing ends and another begins. She starts screaming at him. He chases her down the street and back to her mother's flat. He pushes his way in. There is no one else in the flat. Nothing can deflect his absolute, impenetrable plea. Jeanne is not screaming, just crying, as she pulls out her father's pistol. He does not stop: "This is the title shot, baby, we're going all the way . . . Now I've found you. And I love you. I want to know your name." She fires the gun and tells her name.

(*Note*: Please see Volume I for the scene in which Paul and Jeanne come back to the flat for the first time since their initial meeting and for the scene in which Paul goes to his wife's lover's room after the suicide and discovers that she has put the same robe on the outside, and the same bad liquor on the inside, of both of her men.)

MONOLOGUE

INTERIOR—WALL AND STAIRWAY, HOTEL—NIGHT

What appeared to be a quiet, third-rate hotel seems completely transformed, now, in the middle of the night. Shadows decorate whole walls. The corridors seem endless. Everything that looked like a quaint relic in daylight—everything dusty, old crooked—recovers its unconscious geography at night. The flavor of places explored long ago. A journey into the subconscious, the *déjà-vu*.

PAUL moves around like the guardian of a labyrinth, making the rounds of some strange prison. He turns corners. He disappears into shadows. He reappears in a pool of light, there, at the end of the hall, near the stairway: and he spies.

He spies through a series of peepholes that in the wallpaper's leafy patterns are like tiny eyes hidden behind innocent and anonymous landscapes, hidden at the back of empty closets, hidden in the shadows of dead corners.

The hotel is a sort of spider's web. A hole there, another here; through them, it is possible to oversee every being living there, dying there.

PAUL sees bodies lost in sleep, figures falling apart in the heat of the night, eyelids of soft stone that seem to shut forever, mouths slack with uncontrolled grimaces, lips sunk in nothing but parched air, asses that are only the negation of fleshy roundness, breasts that are old and pale, breasts young and pale, throats that rasp out sudden invocations in sleep, incoherent phrases, spit that dribbles down to the jaw and dries up, old bodies curled in fetal positions. The vision is hallucinating, nightmarish, because sleep has invented anatomies that are definitive and absolute.

All is well in the hotel. Everyone is asleep. And yet, it is with suffering and disgust that PAUL recognizes familiar faces. Recognizing them there is like identifying them on a slab in the morgue.

With a certain anxiety PAUL turns the key in the lock and enters a somber room. He relocks the door carefully and goes to sit down. He lights a last cigarette and throws the empty packet away. He is tired.

PAUL: I just made the rounds. I haven't done it in a long time.

He speaks to someone in front of him, someone we can't see.

PAUL: Everything's fine. Quiet.

[He tries to search for something on the wall with his fingertips. It is another peephole.

PAUL: Here it is. These walls are like Swiss cheese.]

Now his eyes are used to the dark. The room is not his room. It is the one decked with flowers and a big bed.

ROSA'S corpse lies in the open coffin in a beatific pose. She seems to be laughing in a little lake of flowers. Flowers all along her body, flowers in her hair, in little minuscule bouquets.

PAUL: You look ridiculous in that make-up. Like the caricature of a whore. A little touch of mommy in the night. Fake Ophelia drowned in a bathtub. I wish you could see yourself. You'd really laugh. You're your mother's masterpiece. Christ, there are too many fucking flowers in this place, I can't breathe... You know, on top of the closet I found a cardboard box. Inside I found all your little goodies. Pens, key chains, foreign money, French ticklers, the whole shot. Even a clergyman's collar... I didn't know you collected all these little knickknacks left behind.

He speaks to her as if she were alive.

PAUL: Even if the husband lives two hundred fucking years, he's never going to be able to discover his wife's real nature. I mean, I might be able to comprehend the universe but I'll never discover the truth about you, never. I mean, who the hell were you? Remember that day, the first day I was there? I knew that I couldn't get into your pants unless I said—what did I say? Oh yes—"May I have my bill please? I have to leave." Remember? Last night, I ripped off the lights on your mother and the whole joint went bananas. They were all your—your guests, as you used to call them. I guess that includes me, doesn't it? It does include me, doesn't it? For five years I was more of a guest in this fucking flophouse than a husband, with privileges of course. And then to help me understand you, you let me inherit Marcel. The husband's double whose room was the double of ours. And you know what? I didn't even have the guts to ask him. Didn't even have the guts to ask him if the same numbers that you and I did were the same numbers you did with him. Our marriage was nothing more than a foxhole for you. And all it took for you to get out was a thirty-five cent razor. And a tub full of water.

Now he puts his hands together as if he is praying.

PAUL: You cheap, goddam fucking Godforsaken whore—hope you rot in hell! You're worse than the dirtiest street pig that anybody could ever find anywhere and you know why? Because you lied. You lied to me, and I trusted you. You lied. You knew you were lying. Go on, tell me you didn't lie. Haven't you got anything to say about that? You can think up something, can't you? Go on, tell me something. Go on, smile, you cunt. Go on, tell me—tell me something sweet. Smile at me and say it was—I just misunderstood. Go on, tell me you pig-fucker. You goddam fucking pig—fucking liar.

Suddenly he gets up and takes a towel from the bathroom. He wets a corner of it with saliva and gently rubs it on her lips.

PAUL: (*sobbing*) I'm sorry. I just can't stand to see these goddam leaves in your face. You never wore make-up—all this fucking shit. I'm going to take this off your mouth. Lipstick.

The rouge disappears little by little, and the lips pale. PAUL caresses ROSA's cheek with the palm of his hand, then, as if his energy is diminishing rapidly, he lets himself slide onto his knees; he leans his elbows on the coffin and buries his face in his arms. He cries, his face hidden.

PAUL: Rosa, my love . . . forgive me . . . I don't know why you did it. I'd do it too if I knew how. I just don't know. I need to find a way.

A ringing bell is superimposed on his voice. The sound seems very far away. PAUL remains immobile for a few minutes, then gets up slowly. The bell continues with a kind of desperate insistence. PAUL begins to dress, every gesture tired and mechanical.

PAUL: What? All right, I'm coming. I have to go. I have to go, sweetheart baby, someone's calling me.

Two silhouettes in the shadow behind the windows of the locked door. PAUL looks at them, they look at him, waiting for him to open up. It is a man and a woman. Impossible to tell more than that, the street is so dark and shadowy. As is the hotel entrance. PAUL doesn't turn on the lights . . . .

AMERICAN GRAFFITI

A Universal presentation. Producer, Francis Ford Coppola. Co-producer, Gary Kurtz. Director, George Lucas. Screenplay by George Lucas, Gloria Katz, Willard Huyck. Visual Consultant (Supervising Cameraman), Haskel Wexler. Directors of Photography (Operating Cameramen), Ron Eveslage, Jan d'Alquen. Film Editors, Verna Fields, Marcia Lucas. Design Consultant, Al Locatelli. Art Director, Dennis Clark. Set Decorator, Douglas Freeman. Sound Montage & Rerecording, Walter Murch. Sound Editing, James Nelson. Production Sound, Arthur Rochester. First Assistant Director, Ned Kopp. Running time, 110 minutes. 1973.

CAST

CURT	Richard Dreyfuss
STEVE	Ron Howard
JOHN	Paul Le Mat
TERRY	Charlie Martin Smith
LAURIE	Cindy Williams
DEBBIE	Candy Clark
CAROL	Mackenzie Phillips
DISK JOCKEY	Wolfman Jack
BOB FALFA	Harrison Ford
JOE	Bo Hopkins
CARLOS	Manuel Padilla, Jr.
ANTS	Beau Gentry
BUDDA	Jane Bellan
BLONDE IN T-BIRD	Suzanne Somers

American Graffiti takes place in a small California town during one end-of-summer night in 1962. This circumscribed unity of space and time reflects something of the limited horizons and innocent conformity which govern most of the adolescent characters' lives. The film nostalgically documents an American youth culture which would soon vanish with the advent of the "swinging sixties" and all that it would bring, from acid rock to assassinations to the Vietnam war. For the moment of *American Graffiti,* however, the girls are still in ponytails and the guys in ducktails. Everyone still takes off his or her shoes for a sock hop in the gym, and the smokes that are sneaked are tobacco. Nice kids go steady, and if they do more than "make out," they stop being nice. The great tribal teenage ritual consists of cruising in cars down the town's main drag, and since the seducing and the challenging of each other are done from inside the cars, one's social status is virtually determined by the car one drives. This "metallic ballet" of social traffic is choreographed to the ceaseless blast of rock and roll coming in over AM radio. And the raucous, growling, yowling master of ceremonies is disc jockey Wolfman Jack, making dedications and choosing the tunes— Buddy Holly, the Platters, the Big Bopper, etc.

The central meeting place from which the night's activities emanate is Mel's drive-in. As the principal characters gather at the beginning of the film,

> Suddenly, there's an ear-splitting roar and they turn as a yellow '32 Ford deuce coupe—chopped, lowered and sporting a Hemi-V8—bumps into the lot. The low slung classic rumbles and parks at the rear of the drive in.

> Big John Milner, twenty-two, sits in his Ford, tough and indifferent, puffing on a Camel. He wears a white T-shirt and a butch-haircut molded on the sides into a ducktail. A cowboy in a deuce coupe—simple, sentimental, and cocksure of himself.

John reminisces about how it was five years ago, when it took a full tank of gas and several hours just to make a single round of his nightly vehicular promenade. The other kids, all younger, look up to him, but they already seem to know they don't want to end up like him, "seventeen forever." Still, it is John

Milner whom you dare to insult, and challenge to race, if you've a hot set of wheels and you're up-and-coming in this town, or if you're visiting from rival turf. The girls in cars who drive by and call out to him seem to do so on a dare, zooming off all scared and giggly.

At a red light, he invites any occupant from a Studebaker packed with females to come ride with him. They send over Carol Morrison, who turns out to be one of their kid sisters. Carol is cute and obnoxious and plucky as befits her thirteen years, and John wants to get rid of her immediately. But she's too thrilled with where she is to allow herself to be returned or taken home. She threatens to scream "rape" if he tries to drop her off. When he sees friends, he is so embarrassed at Carol's presence that he tells them he is just babysitting. She is appalled, acts up badly, and leaps out of his hot rod. Unfortunately, some punks are following her, so John reluctantly follows her, too. He pulls up beside her, and she jumps back in. In the following scene, which is excerpted for John's monologue, he begins to soften towards her, feeling the beginning of what will grow, against his better judgment, into a fond enjoyment of this sweet, spirited, exasperating kid.

MONOLOGUE

AUTO WRECKING YARD

JOHN's '32 deuce coupe crunches to a gravelly stop in front of a dark auto-wrecking yard. JOHN and CAROL get out and climb over the fence. They walk through a valley of twisted, rusting piles of squashed, mashed and crushed automobiles. JOHN sticks his hands into his pockets moodily and stops and looks at one of the burnt-out cars.

JOHN: That's Freddy Benson's Vette . . . he got his head on with some drunk. Never had a chance. Damn good driver, too. What a waste when somebody gets it and it ain't even their fault.

[CAROL: Needs a paint job, that's for sure.

JOHN doesn't hear her and walks on.]

JOHN: That Vette over there. Walt Hawkins, a real ding-a-ling.

Wrapped it around a fig tree out on Mesa Vista with five kids in it. Draggin' with five kids in the car, how dumb can you get? All the ding-a-lings get it sooner or later. Maybe that's why they invented cars. To get rid of the ding-a-lings. Tough when they take someone with them.

[CAROL: You never had a wreck though—you told me.]

JOHN: I come pretty close a couple of times. Almost rolled once. So far I've been quick enough to stay out of here. The quick and the dead.

[CAROL: I bet you're the fastest.]

JOHN: I've never been beaten—lot of punks have tried. See that '41 Ford there? Used to be the fastest wheels in the valley. I never got a chance to race old Earl. He got his in '55 in the hairiest crash ever happened around here. He was racing a '54 Chevy, bored and loaded, out on the old Oakdale Highway and every damn kid in town was out there. The Chevy lost its front wheel doing about 85. The idiot had torched the spindles to lower the front end and it snapped right off. He slammed bam into the Ford and then they both of them crashed into a row of cars and all those kids watching! Jesus, eight kids killed including both drivers, looked like a battlefield. Board of Education was so impressed they filmed it. Show it now in Drivers Education, maybe you'll see it. Anyway, since then street racing's gone underground. No spectators, I mean. Too bad.

[CAROL: I'd love to see you race.]

CAROL takes his hand and they walk a bit, until JOHN realizes what he's doing, and drops her hand and pulls away.

JOHN: Come on! None of that.

CAROL: Whadaya mean? I'm the one who's supposed to say that. Whadaya afraid of? I'll keep it above the waist.

JOHN: Funny... (*he looks at her for a moment*) Who knows, in a few years—but not now, bunny rabbit.

CAROL: Bunny rabbit! Oh brother, you are such a drip.

She stomps off and gets back into the coupe, quickly rolling up all the windows. JOHN saunters up and finds the door locked.

JOHN: Come on, open the door.

CAROL: If you say "Carol's not a bunny, she's a foxy little tail."

JOHN grins and starts to pull his keys out of his pocket. He stops grinning: CAROL grins and dangles his keys inside the car. JOHN leans against the window, closes his eyes, a defeated man.

JOHN: (*quietly*) Carol's not a rabbit, she's a foxy little tail.

He hears the button click up and slowly opens the door.

CAROL: You say the cutest things.

JOHN gets into the car.

WOLFMAN: (*voice over*) Sneakin' around with the Wolfman, Baby.

The WOLFMAN's gravelly voice whispers over the airwaves as JOHN and CAROL drive out of the shadowy car grave-yard.]

(*Note*: In a postscript to the film, we are told, "John Milner was killed by a drunk driver in June 1964.")

DOG DAY AFTERNOON

A Warner Bros. presentation of An Artists Entertainment Complex Production. Producers, Martin Bregman & Martin Elfand. Director, Sidney Lumet. Screenplay by Frank Pierson. Based on a magazine article by P.F. Kluge & Thomas Moore. Associate Producer, Robert Greenhut. Director of Photography, Victor J. Kemper. Film Editor, Dede Allen. Production Designer, Charles Bailey. Art Director, Doug Higgins. Sound Mixer, James Sabat. Assistant Directors, Burtt Harris, Alan Hopkins. Technicolor. Running time, 130 minutes. 1975.

CAST

SONNY	Al Pacino
SAL	John Cazale
MULVANEY	Sully Boyer
SYLVIA	Penny Allen
MARGARET	Beulah Garrick
JENNY	Carol Kane
DEBORAH	Sandra Kazan
MIRIAM	Marcia Jean Kurtz
MARIA	Amy Levitt
HOWARD	John Marriott
EDNA	Estelle Omens
BOBBY	Gary Springer
SHELDON	James Broderick
MORETTI	Charles Durning
VI	Judith Malina
VI'S HUSBAND	Dominic Chianese
ANGIE	Susan Peretz
LEON	Chris Sarandon

The first look we get of Sonny Abramowicz is at 2:15 P.M. on August 22, 1972, the day on which almost all of the events depicted in *Dog Day Afternoon* actually took place. He is described as "in his mid-twenties, dark, with a mobile face, merry eyes, a mouth with a tough defiant twist. Right now he's looking at himself in the mirror, and with a little spit on his finger adjusts his already tidily combed hair, pasting a lock back in place." It is 94°F outside in Flatbush, Brooklyn, and Sonny's wife, Angie, and two little kids, to whom he is a wonderful father, are lying out on the beach. A baseball game is in progress at Shea Stadium. The Americans have just unleashed the heaviest bombing of the war in Indochina. This can all be seen on the television that Sonny's parents watch in their apartment, which he provides for them. Sonny has to get downstairs and over to the bank before it closes at three. He is going to rob the bank. His parents will be able to see all this on television as well.

As a bank robber, Sonny knows all of his lines, but his timing is totally off. He delivers his opening "this-is-a-stickup" speech long after everyone already knows. Having worked in a bank, Sonny has been able to plan carefully, right down to the spray paint he brings to black out the lenses of the surveillance cameras. But when he burns the registers in a wastebasket, so that there will be no record of the bills' serial numbers, the smoke is sucked up through the air-conditioner and is visible outside the "slightly seedy little branch bank." Soon a call comes in for Sonny. It's Moretti from the police.

The police are jammed into the barbershop directly across the street where they've set up a direct phone line into the bank. During the next several hours, huge crowds of spectators and vendors will mass into the street for a live game of Pass the Hostage, a thrilling entertainment for those stuck in the city on a miserable summer day. Others will prefer to watch on television, and another ring is added to the circus with the television lights, camera crews, and helicopters. A newscaster calls for a live interview but refuses to answer Sonny's questions, at which point Sonny demands that if he is going to be used as entertainment, then the television station will have to pay him. What started out as a little heist has mushroomed totally out of control.

On one level, *Dog Day Afternoon* is the story of a bank robbery that goes haywire. A terrifying standoff ensues between those trapped inside the bank and the police and FBI on the outside. Sonny and his partner Sal get as far as the airport, but they don't make it onto the plane that they've been promised will fly them to freedom in return for all the employees they've been holding hostage. The driver of their car is a plainclothesman with a gun. Sal is shot dead, and Sonny's last lines are screamed to the police, begging them to kill him, too. On another level, however, the story is a chaotic farce about a couple of nice, overstrung guys who try to pull off a simple, friendly holdup and get involved way over their heads in the colliding incongruities that characterize American life on one sweltering August day in 1972. While Sonny may be roaring, "We're Vietnam veterans so killing don't mean nothing to us," he is horrified by a crank call urging him to kill all the hostages. He's the one who's been helping them on and off with their jackets, holding doors open for them, patiently calming away their terror. When the police cut the air conditioner and Mulvaney the manager collapses, it's Sonny who insists that a doctor be admitted. Neither the doctor nor a pizza delivery boy will accept Sonny's payment, so he tosses the money to the crowd outside, and he and Moretti share a moment of contemptuous disbelief as the police join in the diving for dollars. The crowds cheer Sonny as he plays directly to them, screaming about police brutality and stupidity. He ignites into a sudden media hero/punk—a brilliant, tragic, armed hostage of society.

The ultimate symbol of all these incongruities is Leon, Sonny's male lover, who suffers from suicidal depression stemming from his belief that he is a woman trapped inside a man's body. Sonny has married Leon in a church service because that is what Leon thought would make him happy. The only thing that will really help Leon is a sex-change operation, and it is in order to pay this bill that Sonny has decided to rob the bank. The first time we see Sonny's wife, Angie, we don't even know who she is. She is lying in an oiled, anonymous sea of sunbathing bodies, "just another pretty 175-pound Italian girl with two kids, Kimmy and Jimmy, about four and five years old." Leon, on the other hand, is given quite an entrance. A car is permitted through the police barricades. Grinning policemen open the back door. Out steps Leon: "She is spectacularly good looking in a lithe, cruel sort of way, like Lauren Bacall, but right now she is a mess." Moretti asks, "What's that?" and is informed that *this* is Sonny's wife. Leon has been pulled from the hospital and is still so doped up that he can barely comprehend where he is. At the sight of Sonny across the street jumping up and down and wishing Leon a happy birthday, he just faints dead away. Revived in the barbershop, with police crowding around him, Leon at first refuses to talk to Sonny, and then finally agrees when Moretti frightens him into it. Over the telephone, Sonny finally has to accept that Leon wants neither him nor his help. The hostages feel real sympathy for Sonny. They've all laughed together until the tears have run down their faces, until they've looked at each other in embarrassed bewilderment at how inappropriate their behavior is in their given roles and circumstances. They wish Sonny luck.

One of the hostages inside the bank is a notary, so Sonny dictates his will. He's a good boy, this bank robber, and he tries to make provisions for his mother, his children, and his wives. From his $10,000 life insurance policy, Sonny leaves $2,700 for the sex-change operation "to my darling wife Leon whom I love as no other man has loved another man in all eternity." Should there be any money left over, the will designates that it be given to Leon one year after Sonny's death, over Sonny's grave, at which time Leon will be "a real woman" with a "life full of happiness and joy." Sonny assigns $5,000 from the same policy to go to "my sweet wife Angie . . . You are the only woman I have ever loved, and I re-pledge my love to you in this sad moment." He asks his son to watch over the household. To his mother, Sonny leaves the remainder of the policy, his stamp collection, and the responsibility of seeing that he receives the free military funeral to which he is entitled. (Please see Volume I for the scene in which Sonny's mother has come down to the bank to talk to him, but her oblivious, inappropriate advice causes Sonny to send her home to watch the rest on television. He tells her she should, as his father has done, pretend she doesn't have a son.) Sonny's will concludes: "Life and love are not easy and we have to bend a lot. I hope you find the places and the people to make you all happy as I could not. God bless you and watch over you as I shall, until we are joined in the great hereafter."

In the first of the excerpts below, Angie tries to explain to the police that Sonny has changed and that the real Sonny could never have done what this Sonny has done. In the second excerpt, Angie and Sonny are on the telephone in a call which Sonny has had placed from the bank to his home so that he can say good-bye to his children and their mother before he leaves on what he expects to be his escape. (The excerpt is bracketed to present a monologue for Angie.) The third excerpt is Leon's attempt to explain to Moretti why, particularly now but even under the best of circumstances, it would be impossible for him to talk to Sonny and convince him of *anything,* let alone surrendering to the police. (This conversation is bracketed to present a monologue for Leon.) Moretti makes it clear to Leon that he has no choice. The final excerpt is the consequent telephone conversation between Sonny in the bank and Leon in the barbershop in which Sonny finally understands that it is over between them. (A telephone conversation has obvious restrictions as a scene for two actors to study and play together, but this excerpt is presented more for use as two telephone monologues, each one offering the actor an extraordinary character at one end of an extraordinary conversation.)

(As a postscript to the film, titles inform us that Leon is now called Lana, Angie and her two children are now on welfare, and Sonny is now serving a twenty-five year sentence in federal prison.)

MONOLOGUE 1

[EXTERIOR ROCKAWAY BEACH—DAY

There's ANGIE. Her body lies exactly as before, baking in the sun. The transistor RADIO plays . . . she seems to be asleep . . .

RADIO: . . . the leader of the pair, a Vietnam veteran, Sonny Abramowicz, has demanded in return for releasing one of the hostages that police allow his wife to visit him at the bank. Police spokesman . . .

ANGIE sits bolt upright, stares at the radio, which continues to blather on. Abruptly she begins to gather up her things, her children, in a characteristically scatter-brained and hyperactive sort of way. ANGIE is a one woman panic: she hustles away across the broiling sand carrying the radio wadded up in towels, and lugging a child, crying helplessly, by one elbow, as though it were a handle, a silhouette against the late afternoon sun, out of Fellini . . . meanwhile on the SOUND TRACK we are hearing her voice.] It is a breathless, harsh childish voice that pours out the words in a torrent:

ANGIE: (*V.O.*) The transistor goes Sonny *what*? I couldn't believe my ears, so I shut the transistor, get outta here, who needs this? I say Sonny didn't do it. It's not him to rob a bank. It's not him to hurt anybody, to threaten anybody, to steal or do anything wrong. 'Cause he's never done nothin' wrong from the day I know him.

[She is stumping off into the sunset as she says these words and we

                                                    CUT TO:

EXTERIOR—BROOKLYN STREET—DAY

Out of a subway crowd, she struggles, pulling the two kids by the hand, a very ordinary woman in a most ordinary New York scene . . .]

ANGIE: (V.O.) . . . Only he tells me this and he tells me that, he's with the Mafia, I say, Sonny, where do you get the money, you're on welfare, how can you rent a new Eldorado, red, you don't like the color you rent a yellow.

[EXTERIOR—ANGIE'S APARTMENT HOUSE—DAY

A working class block, dirty, shops in the first floor, three story walk-ups above . . . ANGIE appears and runs up the stoop. TWO COPS get out of a squad car where they've been staked out and move up to her. They never really get in a word edgewise. They follow her into the hall . . . Now as we CUT CLOSER to her, we will SEE ANGIE's mouth in SYNC with the words . . .]

ANGIE: So night before last we're at Coney Island, he's on the rides with the kids, an' I have this habit of goin' in glove compartments an' all, an' I see . . .

[INTERIOR—HALL—DAY

ANGIE struggles up the stairs, dragging the kids—the COPS following . . .]

ANGIE: —this gun with bullets in there, an' I go to myself, oh God, Sonny! That's all I had to see, I didn't say anything.

[She's got her door unlocked. Below and on the stairs behind the COPS, curious neighbors peer in . . .

INTERIOR—ANGIE'S APARTMENT—DAY

Chaos out of cut-rate furniture stores. Full of unwashed glasses, kids' clutter. Throughout, the children rush around unchecked. Neighbors enter without ceremony and listen. The COPS stand, trying vainly to communicate . . . As they enter . . .]

ANGIE: (*continuing*) And things are adding in my head, how crazy he's been acting, and in with a bad crowd, an' I look at him, he's yellin' at the kids like a madman. So inna car I said to him, Sonny, what you gonna do with the gun? You gonna shoot me and dump my body inna river or what? I was so scared of him, I never been scared of Sonny never. You know, his mother says the cops was always at our house, we was always fighting. I hit him with the jack in the car once, but I only missed and hit myself, you should of seen my leg. And all he would ever do is put on his coat and go out. So they say it's Sonny but I don't believe it.

[COP 1:   Lady, you saw him. You saw his gun.]

ANGIE: He might of done it, his body functions might of done it, but not he himself.

MONOLOGUE 2

[INTERIOR—BANK

SONNY hangs up, walks back toward rear of Bank and picks up receiver again on EDNA'S desk.

SONNY: (*into phone*) You cut off incoming, gimme a line. I want to talk to my wife, I want to say goodbye to my kids. (*line is connected, he begins to dial; anguished; to the group*) Here I am, I could call, and they'd put anybody on the phone, the Pope, an astronaut, the wisest of the wise and who do I have to call? (*to phone; as she answers*) Angie?

ANGIE'S APARTMENT—NIGHT

The TV is on, the kids up and racing around, neighbors pouring beer—An event!

ANGIE: (*on phone; excited*) Hey, Sonny! I'm watchin' it on TV!

ON SONNY

SONNY: What about the kids?

ON ANGIE

ANGIE: They don't know, I sent them to the neighbors.] Sonny, Jesus, it's not like you. I can't believe, because you never hurt anybody since the day I knew you.

[ON SONNY

SONNY: Angie, I'm dying.]

ON ANGIE

ANGIE: (*oblivious*) I blame myself, Sonny. I notice you been tense, like something is happening; the night before last you're yellin' at the kids like a madman, believe me. And then you wanted me to go on this ride with the kids, this caterpillar about from here to there—fulla one-year-old kids. It's ridiculous. I'm not about to go on this ride, so you yell right there, "You pig, get on the fuckin' ride!" Well, everything fell outta—me—my heart, my liver fell to the floor—you name it! Yellin' at me in front of all those people. Because you never talked like that. I was scared of you and I never been scared of you, never. I think: he's gonna shoot me and dump my body in the river.

[ON SONNY

SONNY: Angie for Christ sake, shut up! Will you shut your fucking mouth and listen?!

ON ANGIE

ANGIE: (*afraid*) See?] You're screaming with the language and all! A person can't communicate with you. You become a stranger in your own home . . .

[ON SONNY

he sits, dispiritedly listening to this rap: seeing her in a clear and unambiguous light as before he saw LEON: what a waste to live in the company of people like this!]

ON ANGIE

ANGIE: (*continuing*) . . . because you hurt me, God how you hurt me. Can you imagine, marrying another man? Did I do something to make you do that? Did I ever turn you down, or anything? The only thing I couldn't do, you're gonna laugh, is go on top—I got this fear of high places! (*giggles*) And I let myself get fat.

[ON SONNY

SONNY: Don't call yourself fat.]

ON ANGIE

ANGIE: I know you can't stand me to say I'm fat. Like I can't stand you being a bank robber. I guess that's what love is—huh, Sonny?

[ON SONNY

SONNY: (*weakly*) Angie—why didn't you come down here?

ON ANGIE

ANGIE: Jesus—what—I'm afraid—I'm gonna get shot or whatever. You oughta see it on TV, the guns, the cops, they got cannon, machine guns, they're loaded for bear.

ON SONNY

SONNY: They're not after you, they're after me.

ON ANGIE

ANGIE: Listen, it's late already when I realize it's not just a couple of ordinary faggots, it's just you and Leon. I couldn't get a baby sitter.

ANGIE goes on and on, but SONNY just drops the phone on the hook.

•   •   •   •   •

MONOLOGUE 3

INTERIOR—BARBERSHOP

[where MORETTI and COPS are trying to revive LEON. A COP at the phone turns to MORETTI.

COP ON PHONE: Moretti—he wants to talk to you.

MORETTI walks over to phone, takes receiver from cop.

INTERIOR—BANK

SONNY waiting for MORETTI to answer phone.

SONNY: Is he all right? Is he all right?

MORETTI: (*V.O.*) He's all doped up.

SONNY: I want to talk to him.

MORETTI: (*V.O.*) He's groggy, Sonny. Let me get him on his feet and he'll call you back. (*hangs up*)

INTERIOR—BARBERSHOP

as MORETTI hangs up phone and walks over to LEON, who now has a glass of water and a cold towel.

MORETTI: Leon? Whatsa matter? They give you a shot down the hospital or what?

LEON: Oh, God, they shot me with like unreal!

MORETTI: Well, you got to get hold of yourself. You got to talk to him, tell him to give himself up.

LEON: Oh no!

MORETTI: He's got eight people in there with him. He's got this kid with him . . . they're gonna shoot the people.]

LEON: I can't help it. I can't stop him from anything.

[MORETTI: If he won't listen to you, who will he listen to?]

LEON: He won't listen to anybody. He's been very crazy all summer. Since June he's been trying to kill me.

[MORETTI: You try calling the police?

LEON: What good is that? They couldn't stop him. And it'd just make him mad. They don't know him.

MORETTI: Somebody's got to stop him, Leon.]

LEON: He was under great strain: you don't understand, he's a very mixed up person.

[MORETTI: He's makin' threats in there.]

LEON: He's scared. It's crazy. I never met anyone like him. His wife, he's a wonderful father to his children. His mother— you should see her—his mother and father together are like a bad car wreck—he lets it all slide off his back, he sees them, he pays their rent. Unbelieveable. I wanted to get married . . . He didn't really want it . . . he's married already! But he did it. I don't know why. I thought it would help me but it didn't. I was just as confused and unhappy as before; I did terrible things.

[MORETTI: What kind of things, Leon?]

LEON: Ten days I spent in Atlantic City—Sonny was frantic—he knew I was drinking; he didn't know where I was . . . who I was with. I couldn't explain why I did the things I did. So I went to this psychiatrist who explained to me I was a woman in a man's body. So Sonny right away wanted to get me money for a sex change operation: but where was he to get that? 2500 dollars! My God, he's in hock up to his ears already.

[MORETTI: He needed money? For the operation for you?]

LEON: It made him crazy—so much demand, he'd fly into these rages. And I got more depressed than ever; I saw I'd never get the operation. So I tried to take my life—I swallowed about a half pound of pills . . . blues, reds, yellows, downers, uppers, screamers . . . you name it. But I just threw them up and wound up in the hospital. Sonny comes there and looks at me and just says: "Wow!"

So when I hear he's in the bank, I almost go crazy because I know he's doin' it for me.

[MORETTI: Well, don't you figure you owe to him to get him out of there?]

LEON: I can't talk to him.

[MORETTI: You're in it up to your ass, Leon. You're an accessory. You talk him out of there and they might be a little more understanding of your case.]

LEON: I'm afraid.

[MORETTI: How is he gonna hurt you on the telephone?]

LEON: I don't know what to say to him. I can't.

[MORETTI: You think it over, Leon.

MORETTI walks over to the wall phone, picks up the receiver, and waits to be connected with the bank and SONNY.

ON LEON

Terrified. He really can't do it.

ON MORETTI

waiting.]

MONOLOGUES 4 AND 5

INTERIOR—BANK

SONNY rushes in. The phone rings. He picks it up.

SONNY: Hello. Hello, Leon.

LEON: Hello, Sonny.

SONNY: How are you doing?

LEON: Well . . . I'm out of the hospital.

SONNY: (*pleased*) Yeah. You said . . . I thought you were never getting out?

LEON: I never thought I'd get out this way. I'll tell you.

SONNY: Well . . . huh . . .

LEON: Ooohh . . .

SONNY: Oh...huh...how you feeling?

LEON: I'm really shakey.

SONNY: Well, you know...Moretti told me before that you were drugged up.

LEON: Yeah. It was terrible.

SONNY: That...huh...they just shoot you with drugs.

LEON: You come in and they say, right away, that you are crazy. And they start putting things in your arm...you know. How do they expect you to get uncrazy if you're asleep all the time?

SONNY: Yeah...

LEON: You can't talk or do anything. You really feel...you know...I'm just sort of coming out of it now.

SONNY: (*pensive*) So...that sure is something.

LEON: Yeah. So how are you?

SONNY: (*chuckling*) Fine, thank you. I'm in trouble. That is...now I am!

LEON: (*chuckling*) Yeah...I know.

SONNY: I don't know what I'm gonna do...you know. Boy...I'm dying.

LEON: What? What are you talking about? *You* are dying? Did you ever listen to yourself when you say that?

SONNY: What are *you* talking about?

LEON: What do you mean...what am I talking about? Do you realize that you say that to me every day of your life? I am dying. Do you know...do you realize the death that you are spreading around to the people who are around you?

SONNY: Now don't give me that deep shit now. Don't start with that shit.

LEON: No really . . . I don't think that you realize what it means. The things that you do, Sonny. You put a gun to somebody's head . . .

SONNY: I don't know what I'm doing.

LEON: (*annoyed*) Yeah . . . obviously you don't . . . when you put a gun to somebody's head . . . and you say go to sleep so that it won't hurt when I pull the trigger. Death? Don't talk about death to me. I have been living with death for the last six months. Why do you think I'm in the hospital? I take a handful of pills to get away from *you*. And then here I am out of the hospital talking to you on the phone . . . again. I have no friends left. No job. I can't live. I have to live with people. This death business . . . I'm sorry!

SONNY: I'm not on the phone to talk to you about that. Well, I don't know what to say, Leon. When you gimme that . . . when you hit me with that shit. I mean, what am I supposed to say?

LEON: (*indifferent to* SONNY) I'm sorry . . .

SONNY: I told you. That I got a lot of pressures. You said to me that you needed money, and I knew that you needed money! I saw you there lying in the hospital like that . . . and I said . . . shit, man, I got to get this guy some money.

LEON: (*excited*) But I didn't ask you to go rob a bank.

SONNY: (*getting louder*) All right. I know you didn't ask me. You didn't ask me but I did it.

LEON: Well . . .

SONNY: I did it on my own. I did this all on my own. I ain't laying it on anybody. Nothing on anybody. I'll tell you something, though, it's about time that I squared away my accounts . . . you know. I am squaring away my accounts with life. Maybe this whole thing is gonna end, somehow. Maybe it'll just end! Maybe I'll just close my eyes and the whole fucken thing will be over. That would be all right too! I said . . . I thought I would square it away with you . . . you

know? That I would get you down here and that I would say
so long to you . . . or, if you wanted . . . you know, to take a
trip . . .

LEON: What trip?

SONNY: I'm getting out of here, man. I'm not going to stay here
and I'm not giving up. I mean, huh, they're going to kill
me, anyway. So fuck it! But, *if* I can get out of this . . . I
am going to get out. And, how I'm going to get out is to get
a jet out of here and I'm flying the fuck out . . . That's all,
Leon. If you want to come with me, then you're entitled
. . . you can come. You're free to do what you want.

LEON: I'm free to do what I want? And you think I would want
to go with you some place on a plane? Where? Where ya
going?

SONNY: I gotta jet coming here and we're gonna try to get the
fuck outta this thing. And we're gonna go, man!

LEON: You're crazy.

SONNY: That's it.

LEON: You're really crazy.

SONNY: I know!

LEON: Where you gonna go?

SONNY: Who the fuck knows? I think we're gonna go . . . we
worked it out to Algeria. So, I don't know. So I'll go to
Algeria.

LEON: Why you going to Algeria?

SONNY: Huh . . . I don't know. They got Howard Johnson's
there. I don't know why the fuck I'm going there for.

LEON: Howard Johnson's . . . you're warped. You know that?
You're really warped!

SONNY: I know that. I'm warped . . . I'm warped!

LEON: (*stuttering*) God, Algeria! Do you know there's a bunch of ... they walk around there ... God! People walk around with masks and things on their heads. They're a bunch of crazy people there.

SONNY: What am I supposed to do?

LEON: (*bitchy*) I don't know ... you could have picked a better place.

SONNY: Denmark? Sweden?

LEON: (*pleased*) I like that ... yeah!

SONNY: Sal wanted to go to Wyoming. I told him it wasn't a country. We gotta get outta the country! To hell with a guy who doesn't know where Wyoming is. Okay. Can you imagine what kind of a shape I'm in?

Laughter from both SONNY and LEON.

LEON: So! Sal is with you?

SONNY: Sal? Yeah ... Sal is with me.

LEON: Oh ... wow! Sonny, you're really into one mess now.

SONNY: I know I am. I know!

LEON: (*making fun of* SONNY) Sal ... Sal ... Naturale, oh boy!

SONNY: He ain't going out. And if I go out he's just gonna kill the people. There's a lot of lives that I'm responsible for ... that's all. So, I can't do anything. I got myself into this mess and I'll get myself out of it ... the best way I know how! One of the ways is not giving up. I'm telling ya!

LEON: Would you do something for me? Please?

SONNY: What?

LEON: These guys that got me down here, you know, huh ... they think that I'm ... they think that I'm part of this whole thing. They think I'm part of the plot to rob the bank!

SONNY: How did they think that? What are they ... crazy? What do you mean. That's bullshit, Leon. They're giving you a fucken story.

LEON: Well . . . they told me that I was an accomplice . . .

SONNY: Oh . . . they're fucken crazy. That's a snow job. Don't listen to that shit!

LEON: I gotta listen to it if they think . . .

SONNY: Shit . . .

LEON: I can't survive in prison, Sonny . . .

SONNY: All right. Then what do you want me to say?

LEON: Sonny, would you please just tell them . . . please . . .

SONNY: Where are they now? Just tell me . . . are they on the phone now?

LEON: (*meekly*) Yeah.

SONNY: (*annoyed*) That's great. Just terrific. You talk to me with them on the phone, right? That is really smart. And, you don't tell me?

LEON: I don't have a choice.

SONNY: You don't have a choice?

LEON: No! They're standing all around me. Seven thousand fucken cops . . . all around me.

SONNY: Look . . . who's on the phone?

LEON: Look . . . don't throw that on me.

SONNY: Who's on the phone, now? What do you mean . . . throw it on you? You knew it, right?

LEON: Yeah . . . I knew it. But, what choice do I have? I'm in the hospital; they drag me out of the hospital . . . bring me down here . . .

SONNY: All right, enough! Who the fuck is on the phone . . . anyway? Is that you Moretti? (*angrily into phone*) You on the phone? Will somebody talk to me?

LEON: They won't talk to you.

SONNY: Are they on the phone still?

LEON: Yeah . . . yeah!

SONNY: (*still angry*) All right! He didn't do it. All right? Now . . . would you get the fuck off the phone? I'll bet that really changed them, huh? (*calmly to* LEON) Anyway, Leon . . . did I do it for you?

LEON: Yeah . . . huh, thank you. I'm going to go back, Sonny, to the hospital. They're really nice people. They're really trying to help me.

SONNY: That's good then. You've found something.

LEON: Well . . . I don't know if I have or not.

SONNY: Do you still want the operation?

LEON: (*moody*) Yeah . . . yeah.

SONNY: Well, then . . .

LEON: It's my only chance!

SONNY: I don't know what to say to ya! I guess I just wanted to say I'll see ya . . . or whatever.

LEON: Thank you much . . . and huh, bon voyage.

SONNY: Right. See you sometime.

LEON: Yeah . . . see ya in my dreams, huh?

SONNY: Yeah . . . I'll write a song. Ha, ha. I don't know. Life is funny!

LEON: You said a mouthful . . . sweetheart!

FUNNY LADY

A Columbia Pictures and Rastar presentation of a Persky-Bright/Vista Production. Producer, Ray Stark. Director, Herbert Ross. Screenplay by Jay Presson Allen and Arnold Schulman, from a story by Arnold Schulman. Director of Photography, James Wong Howe. Editor, Marion Rothman. Production Designer, George Jenkins. Songs, John Kander and Fred Ebb, Vincent Youmans, Harry Warren, Billy Rose, and others. Conductor, arranger, Peter Matz. Assistant Director, Jack Roe. Running time, 140 minutes. 1975.

CAST

FANNY BRICE	Barbra Streisand
BILLY ROSE	James Caan
NICK ARNSTEIN	Omar Sharif
BOBBY	Roddy McDowell
BERT ROBBINS	Ben Vereen
NORMA BUTLER	Carole Wells
ELEANOR HOLM	Heidi O'Rourke
ADELE	Royce Wallace

Fanny Brice was born in 1891 and died in 1951. She first appeared in the fourth of Florenz Ziegfeld's Follies in 1910, and she headlined the majority of those to follow. To understand the quality of her radiance and appeal as a performer, remember that it was not an *image* of her that people watched on a television or

Funny Lady © 1974 Vista Productions. Reprinted courtesy of Columbia Pictures and with the permissions of Jay Presson Allen and Arnold Schulman.

a movie screen. People got dressed up, and paid, to go sit in the same room with Fanny Brice while she performed— *live*. Audience and star heard and saw one another; it was a human relationship. Before silent films had even learned to talk, Miss Fanny Brice was a household name: a top-billed, top-dollar, *beloved* American Star.

The photographs of her cutting-up freeze-frame a manic inner glee that makes mayhem out of her features and limbs. You see the same kind of exuberant anarchy in the press photos of her colleagues, such as Eddie Cantor and Beatrice Lillie and Bert Lahr: the eyes and grin wild with a glittering mischief that seems to have flung the body off the dollmaker's bench before the glue could dry. But then, there was a complete other side to Fanny Brice as a performer, in its way no less physical, but playing completely against this grain of the clowning, goofing girl with the skinny legs: Fanny Brice would sing and oh, your heart fell out. In a fragile, tragic soprano, she sang ''My Man'' about a masochistic devotion to a louse, and the same audience who had howled with laughter a few sketches back was now weeping. She'd be profoundly torchy in one number, profoundly hilarious in the next. To see Fanny Brice shimmy was to see sexy and goofy get all mixed up. But never, with Fanny Brice, was it vulgar. She just possessed and projected some inspired crisscross of urban, earthy, cuckoo-wiggle-zany, and audiences adored her.

Fanny Brice started out on Lower East Side streets that clattered with immigrant accents and pushcart peddlers. She auditioned first as a chorus dancer—not because she knew her left foot from her right, but because that was the audition she could get into, and she had to get in, somehow. Once she did, she took off. She acquired money (though the Depression would take her finances through quite a trough), and with it she educated herself about fabrics, furnishings, and art to such a point that she would eventually design the interiors of her friends' homes and offices. (And then she would be highly indignant if they tried to pay her.) From her beginnings she evidenced a taste as innate as her talent. She possessed that instinctive understanding (''in here,'' she'd say) about what went with what, as unerringly as she could walk onstage and know how to just *wait*, until that audience was ready to be hers. This inborn command of audiences, good taste, and proportion may have been just the combination that made Fanny Brice one of the first to ease the mainstream American audience into comfortable enjoyment of Yiddish dialect onstage. She was famous offstage for being exquisitely dressed, immaculately groomed, carrying herself with regal aplomb, and talking with the mouth of a truck driver. Early in her career she had kept the laughs coming by climbing up the curtain as the audience called for more bows. But later, as her sense of her own style became more highly cultivated, she would bow once, only once, and be gone. And still, she called everybody "Kid," from her pals in the chorus to government leaders, and she mixed freely among them all. After years of Follies and touring through exhausting performance schedules, she brought her "Baby Snooks" character to radio out in California. There she lived in a beautiful home where she hid her jewels in a hot water bottle under the bathroom sink.

The screenplay of *Funny Lady* chronicles, amidst other biographical detail, the arc of a woman's personal development in romantic relationship to men—two men, specifically, Nicky Arnstein and Billy Rose. In the back story (as dramatized in the musical *Funny Girl*), Arnstein begins as Fanny's prince in shining armor, her dream man. With marriage, family, and Fanny's blossoming celebrity, certain cracks in Arnstein's armor widen. He possesses enormous style and charm, but the only way he understands to finance all this style and charm is through high-stakes private poker games. When he really needs a job, he becomes entangled in a shady deal that lands him in prison. "I'm glad I know where he's spending his nights," Fanny reportedly remarked to Will Rogers. (She is also credited with the crack that giving birth was like shoving a piano through a transom.) Underneath the cheeky one-liners, however, is someone who grew up in a neighborhood where "nice girls" marry once and do not get involved in scandals. As her personal life became daily headlines, she faced the reporters as a funny, but very loyal, very loving wife. She was playing the truth. When Nick Arnstein comes out of prison, which is where *Funny Lady* begins, he is not a whit less courtly, but he has had it with being Mr. Brice. Fanny and Nick are divorced.

There's a Depression outside and in. Ziegfeld can't raise the money to produce a show, so Fanny is out of work, out of a marriage, and out of money. She first meets Billy Rose when he barges in on her appointment with her financial adviser, Bernard Baruch, who has just been telling her that her stock holdings have been decimated in the Crash. She starts to make the rounds of the clubs, looking for songs to build an act that she can tour.

She finds herself one night in Billy's club, somewhat surprised that he's anything more than Baruch's ex-office boy. She's even more surprised that he's the composer of a song, the beautiful "More Than You'll Know," which she'd like to record. But her surprise climbs into amazement when he offers it to her for half-price; fledgling songwriters usually pay *her* for the chance to have Fanny Brice record their material. Still, this is nothing compared to her astonishment when she reads in the trades a few days later that she is *starring* in the new Billy Rose show! In the first scene below, Fanny arrives at Billy's apartment/office/pigpen to read him the riot act, and ends up agreeing to appear in his show.

In many ways, Billy is the complete opposite of Nick. He begins as a shrewd, uncouth, very talented, highly ambitious "energy" wound up to an extremely high rpm. Whether speed-writing from a photographic memory, or staging massive aquacades, producing reviews, or writing hit popular songs, Billy Rose churns ceaselessly as a showman and a promoter. His chutzpah and willingness to work harder than anybody remind Fanny of herself before she became so famous and toney. Billy doesn't have time to shave or relax, but he does want to take the time to marry Fanny Brice. While showing her a scale-model of a massive arena theater he is masterminding, he points out that the finale of its inaugural show will be a wedding number. He abruptly asks her how she'd like "to star in the wedding bit." He shows her a bouquet with an engagement ring stuck in it and proffers his declaration of utmost vulnerability: "I paid retail."

In Billy, Fanny sees somebody who isn't freeloading, and who certainly isn't faking class, or even aspiring to it. After her previous marriage, it's a relief. She recognizes Billy is real and on the ball—he can even locate backing for a show when Ziegfeld can't. Billy openly admires and respects her as a pro and is happy to learn from her. He's even helpful with *her* career, writing and finding material when she must put together her own act. But there is a condescending edge to her attitude and tone with him and it continues after their wedding. On their honeymoon, onboard a train, they finally have a major blowout in the second scene below and Billy confesses to his wife that he loves her.

Although Billy keeps putting up his name ever bigger and

higher on the marquees as "producer" and "creator" and "presenter," too many people still regard him as that grubby little guy who married Fanny Brice. And Fanny's attachment to Nick still noodges at her. By the time she realizes it was Nick's polish that pulled her and not actually Nick, it is too late. Billy has met someone, the star of one of his aquacades, who seems to adore and admire him the way he's always known Fanny felt about Nick. Fanny and Billy's marriage, but not their friendship, ends in divorce. As Fanny Brice once remarked about herself, "I never liked the man I loved and I never loved the man I liked."

SCENE 1

[INTERIOR— BACKSTAGE—DAY

A WORKMAN is carefully stacking chairs on one side of the room. FANNY comes in, looks around, spots a stairway leading to the second story. She goes up the stairs. No one pays attention to her.]

INTERIOR—BILLY'S APARTMENT/OFFICE—DAY

BILLY, in rumpled, ill-fitting, inexpensive pajamas and grubby bathrobe, is talking to a big, equally rumpled man, DAVE, a painting contractor.

BILLY: (*pointing to a small ballroom type chair*) You paint the chair, Dave, and I'll hold the watch on you. However long it takes you to paint the chair, I multiply by two-hundred. So then we both know how long it takes you to paint two hundred chairs. And that's *exactly* the time I pay you for. Is that clear?

DAVE: (*blandly agreeable*) Sure, Mr. Rose. Where you want me to do the painting?

BILLY picks up a can of paint, and brush he has ready, hands them to DAVE.

BILLY: Right here, you goddam thief. Where I can watch you.

There is a KNOCK on the door. BILLY shouts "Come in," and FANNY walks in.

BILLY: (*continuing; to* FANNY, *whom he bows inside with a flourish*) What a pleasant surprise!

FANNY: I'll bet.

BILLY: (*to* DAVE) Move it out in the hall, Dave, but keep right in line with the door so I can see you . . .

FANNY, in the moments that BILLY is attending to DAVE, takes in the squalor of BILLY's living quarters.

To one side of the floor, beside the sofa, FANNY spots a pair of woman's shoes, one stocking, a bra . . . she glances toward the closed door leading to a bedroom. She knows what's inside it. Deliberately, she sits on the end of the sofa near the discarded clothing . . .

BILLY, satisfied with DAVE's position, checks his watch.

BILLY: (*continuing; to* DAVE) Okay. *Start.* (*moves back into room, addresses* FANNY) Painting contractor . . . you gotta watch the bastards every minute.

BILLY sits opposite FANNY, instantly sees the underwear on the floor beside her. He blanches, but doesn't know what he can do, except move his chair to an angle so that FANNY's head is forced to face away from the mess beside her.

FANNY, completely aware of his maneuver, smiles sweetly.

BILLY: I'm glad to see you, Fanny. I apologize you found me like this . . . I work late in the club.

FANNY: Sure. I appreciate you're a hard worker. What I *don't* appreciate is you're a *fast* worker. (*pleasantly*) You little creep. Where do you get the nerve using my name in your cockamamie news release?

BILLY: (*refusing to be hassled*) You interested in explanations?

FANNY: I'm interested in *retractions*.

BILLY: Maybe you're not going to want a retraction . . . maybe you're gonna agree to . . .

FANNY: ... to be in some half-assed sandlot, two-bit production scratched up by a tasteless crummy Johnny-come-lately hustler like you? Sonny, I was a Ziegfeld star when you were still sweating your way up to fifty words a minute in shorthand class, so don't try to hustle me, you bum.

BILLY: (*calmly*) I know where I can get fifty-thousand dollars. *Today.* I've got the songs. I know where I can get the sketches. And if I get *you,* I can pull in another star...Fields maybe, or Williams...(*catches her look*) But it's *you* I really want.

FANNY: Oh sure. (*eyes him up and down*) And *you* can get fifty thousand when Ziegfeld can't?

BILLY: That's right. (*checks his watch, calls to* DAVE) You can do better than that, Dave...three rungs in four and a half minutes, that's not good enough.

FANNY: *Where?*

BILLY: Where what?

FANNY: Where can you get fifty-thousand?

BILLY: (*hesitates only a moment, then shrugs*) Bolton.

FANNY: (*incredulous*) Buck Bolton? I don't believe you. Buck is Ziggy's bank.

BILLY: (*grimly*) He's mine now.

FANNY: *How?*

BILLY: (*disarmingly*) He *believes* in me.

FANNY stares long and hard at BILLY, then she sighs.

FANNY: Maybe I'm wrong. Maybe you're not just a nickel and dime hustler. Maybe what you are is a really big-time pimp. Buck's got a new girl. Right? (*as* BILLY *grins*) Does she get billing?

BILLY: Very *small*.

FANNY: And she also works sketches. Don't lie.

BILLY: (*nods*) Yes, she works sketches. But not *yours*.

FANNY stands, not speaking, obviously irresolute. BILLY lets out his breath carefully.

BILLY: (*continuing*) You need a show . . . why try to scrape up an act and play the Palace when you can do a show? You need me.

FANNY: Kid, you're full of it. *You* need *me*.

BILLY: Let me phrase it another way. *Use* me.

FANNY: *I'll* phrase it another way . . . ask me to help you. Go ahead. *Ask*. Ask *nice*.

BILLY: (*doesn't hesitate*) Help me, Fanny.

FANNY: And why do you want my help, kid?

She gestures "come on, come on!" with her fingers.

BILLY: (*swift to give her what she demands*) Because I need you.

FANNY: What'd you say? I didn't hear you.

BILLY: I said . . . I *need* you.

A beat . . . she visibly relaxes . . . but still eyes him coldly.

FANNY: Just don't aggravate me.

BILLY: You'll do it?

FANNY: (*philosophically*) What a crummy world . . . Why don't you ever get a manicure? It only costs a buck.

BILLY: Yeah, but it takes twenty minutes.

DAVE: (*from hallway*) I'm done. Finished, Mr. Rose.

BILLY checks his watch, then gets up and walks toward hall.

BILLY: Excuse me, Fanny. I got to check this guy out . . .

When BILLY is past her, FANNY gives a quick look down at the underwear, gets up and goes to the bedroom door, makes sure the door is already open before she calls . . .

FANNY: Gotta use your john, kid . . .

BILLY whirls about, rushes back into the room and into position to see FANNY walking slowly through his bedroom, giving full points to the long, blonde, beautiful SHOW GIRL in BILLY's bed. The girl's eyes widen when they see FANNY.

FANNY: (*continuing*) Hello, there . . . this the door to the john?

SHOW GIRL: (*open-mouthed*) You're Fanny Brice! I don't believe it!

FANNY: What? That Fanny Brice goes to the can?

SHOW GIRL: (*grabbing sheet around her*) My God, Miss Brice! I see all your shows . . . every chance I get . . . I like to *die* laughing! Why, sometimes I laugh so hard I . . .

FANNY: (*serenely*) Fall right out of bed?

She goes into bathroom, shuts door gently.

CLOSE-UP—BILLY

He has watched this scene. He doesn't make a sound, but we feel his tremendous conviction of triumph.

DAVE: (*V.O.*) Okay, Mr. Rose? Eight minutes a coat per chair. You want two coats?

BILLY: (*as he walks jubilantly back toward* DAVE) Yeah, two coats. That's sixteen minutes a chair for two hundred chairs, that's 3200 minutes . . . makes exactly fifty-three hours and thirty-three minutes. I'll pay you cash on the line for forty-five hours, take it or leave it.

DAVE: (*equably*) Sure, Mr. Rose. That's okay with me. Glad to get the work. (*smiles*) And congratulations you got a show going.

BILLY: (*softening*) Thanks, Dave.

(*Note*: The scene is written for four actors. If studied by just two, Fanny and Billy, the painter and the show girl must at least be present as offstage voices. Billy needs to be keeping an eye on that workman and his watch *while* he's negotiating with Fanny; one of the things she likes best about him is that he never stops working. She, on the other hand, knows that her ace in the hole is that girl in the bed, and she would never forgo playing it. If the area where Dave is working and the bedroom are both moved offstage, they should be in distinctly separate directions.)

SCENE 2

INTERIOR—TRAIN DRAWING ROOM—NIGHT

The drawing room is made up for the night. Two single beds, head to foot. On one of the beds is a satin comforter, clearly not the property of the Santa Fe line. There are also two small and prettily covered pillows. There are books, magazines, a bowl of fruit, and flowers . . . an ice bucket and glasses.

The room is empty. FANNY emerges from the W.C. She sits down at an improvised dressing table. She slips the robe and the straps of her gown down around her shoulders.

Taking a bottle of lotion, she pours some into her hands and begins to spread it soothingly on her neck and shoulders . . . At the SOUND of the door opening, she quickly shrugs her shoulders back into her robe. BILLY enters, dressed in a suit. He smiles faintly, then moves rather restlessly to a chair next to a window and sits. FANNY continues her toilette. BILLY watches her.

FANNY: No action in the club car?

BILLY: How many times I have to tell you? I'm not a gambler.

Silence as FANNY now takes half a lemon and rubs it first into her elbows, then onto the back of her heels. Her concentration totally on what she is doing.

BILLY: (*continuing*) You done your knees yet?

FANNY: No. I'm coming to them.

BILLY: I thought you did the knees before the heels.

FANNY: No. I do the heels first. Then the knees.

BILLY: (*a statement*) Every night.

FANNY: Every night.

Finished with the heels, she proceeds to take another lemon half and rub her knees. BILLY continues to watch. Finished with the lemon, FANNY now takes cream to her knees, and to the *backs* of her knees.

BILLY: You know, by the time you finish that production I'm all mixed up.

FANNY: Mixed-up what?

BILLY: Mixed-up I don't know what part I'm supposed to go for. I figure, Jesus, maybe there's something I don't know about . . . like something I ought to be doing like to your goddamn heels or knees or something.

FANNY doesn't answer, just proceeds now with perfume, starting with the backs of her knees. BILLY stares.

BILLY: (*continuing*) You put perfume behind your knees? You didn't do that before.

FANNY: Yes I did.

BILLY: Then I'm right! I *am* supposed to go for the knees!

FANNY: Forget the knees. We're gonna hit Fort Worth at seven in the morning. Let's get some sleep.

BILLY rises abruptly and gets out his pajamas. They are rather startling. FANNY gives them an enigmatical look, then turns back to finish up.

BILLY removes his coat and vest, and then unbuttons his shirt, removes his belt. FANNY's back is to him. He gives it a look, obviously trying to make up his mind about something . . . does. It is to make the crucial change inside the W.C. He goes in, closes the door behind him. Not too gently.

FANNY gets up from the dressing table, removes her robe and gets into the bed with the pillows and the comforter. She picks up a magazine, a copy of *L'Illustration*. She chooses a pear from the bowl of fruit and settles cozily in.

The faint SOUND of flushing; after a moment, BILLY comes out in his pajamas, carrying his clothes which he flings down carelessly.

FANNY: (*continuing; without looking up from her magazine*) Hang up your pants, Billy. You're gonna land in Fort Worth looking like two bits.

BILLY: I'll get 'em pressed.

FANNY: Why pay a buck to get your pants pressed when all you've got to do is hang 'em up?

BILLY: Nick always hang up his pants?

FANNY looks up from the magazine ... her eyes slightly narrowed.

FANNY: (*a beat*) Yes.

BILLY: (*looks at his rumpled clothes*) I'll pay the buck.

FANNY: Flinging your clothes all over ... it makes the place look like a dump.

BILLY grabs up his pants and throws them under the bed.

BILLY: So I never been three days on a train with goddamn royalty.

Both his action and his words are so obviously hostile, that FANNY sits up, looks at him. BILLY glares at her.

BILLY: (*continuing*) And how come *you* never go to the can? When you were at the theatre you went to the can.

FANNY: It's none of your damned business when I go to the can.

BILLY: How come now we're married and spend three days cooped up together you never go to the can? How do you think that makes me feel? Cooped up and *always* having to go to the *can*!

FANNY: (*suddenly furious*) Listen, kid, you don't like being "cooped up" with me, there's an empty compartment down the car. Hire it! You can spend the whole goddamned night in the can. And I won't have to look at your crummy pajamas any more which will be strictly okay with me.

BILLY: (*outraged*) What's wrong with my pajamas?

FANNY: You got terrible pajamas. I hate your pajamas.

BILLY: (*yelling*) Yeah? Well, I hate your . . . *lemons*! And your . . .

He yanks the comforter off her bed, slings it across the room:

BILLY: (*continuing*) . . . fancy bed junk and your . . . your . . . (*slaps the magazine out of her hand*) . . . where do you get off reading French magazines on our honeymoon for Chrissakes!? I know you can't read French!

FANNY throws her half-eaten pear at him.

FANNY: (*equally furious*) I look at the pictures, you creep! I learn what's good and what goes. And I tell you one thing that won't ever go and that's your pajamas!

BILLY: (*starting to tear his pajamas, ripping the buttons*) Screw the pajamas! And screw you, lady! When I get off this . . .

Suddenly grabs at his nose, pulls the torn pajama tops up to his face.

FANNY: What? What's the matter with you?

FANNY: (*muffled through the pajama fabric*) Nosebleed . . . you give me a goddamn nosebleed . . .

Quickly, FANNY gets out of bed, moves efficiently to the wash basin and dampens a cloth, firmly leads BILLY to his bed and forces him to lie down. She puts the cloth to his nose.

FANNY: Hold it till I get some ice . . .

She reaches for the ice bucket and takes a hunk of ice, wraps the damp cloth around it and holds it to BILLY's nose. He glares up at her. She returns the look in spades. He tries to move his head; she holds it forcefully in place.

FANNY: (*continuing*) If you bleed on my good gown, I'll . . .

BILLY: Fanny, when my nose stops bleeding, I'm gonna belt you a good one. You really got it coming.

Their mutual tension and outrage holds their eyes locked for a long moment, then, the foolishness of the entire scene breaks over FANNY, and she begins to smile.

FANNY: Kid, you're some nut.

Soothingly, she rubs around BILLY'S nose. BILLY continues to look up at her, his expression slowly softening. At last he speaks:

BILLY: You know the trouble? The trouble is, Fanny . . . I think I love you.

Startled, embarrassed, FANNY gets up, moves to basin. BILLY starts to move.

FANNY: Stay put.

She rinses out the cloth, comes back to BILLY.

FANNY: (*continuing*) You're not so bad. Why didn't you ever tell me? I mean you could've put your best foot forward now and then . . . just for the hell of it.

BILLY just looks at her. She hesitates, then leans over and kisses him, gently. Then, when she starts to withdraw, to rise, he puts a firm hand on her neck, holds her mouth to his. When she finally struggles free, she stands, looks down at him for a moment. Then she moves to retrieve the comforter and put it back on the other bed. BILLY watches her, then gets up from his own bed.

BILLY: I'll come over there.

FANNY doesn't speak, just climbs into bed. BILLY hesitates, looking down at his pajama pants.

BILLY: (*continuing*) You don't like 'em, I'll take 'em off.

FANNY: (*quietly*) Just turn off the light, Billy.

CUT TO:

[LONG SHOT—TRAIN—NIGHT (STOCK SHOT)

SONG: *ISN'T THIS BETTER*

FANNY AND BILLY

lying very close to one another in the dark. BILLY is asleep. FANNY, in a conflict of emotions, is wide awake.

BILLY stirs.

FANNY: . . . Billy. . . listen, Billy. When we get back to New York I'm going to take you to Sulka's and have some pajamas made for you.

BILLY: (*opens his eyes in astonishment*) *Made* for me? They make *pajamas* for you?

FANNY: Sure. Just like shirts. Underwear, too. So it fits.

BILLY: Lady, you're not getting me measured for BVDS. Pajamas, maybe, but not BVDs. I draw the line.

He closes his eyes, a faint scowl of resistance on his face. FANNY looks at him, smiles, then sighs, turns her face to the dark window.

FANNY: (*whispering*) Fanny. . . you're some nut.

Complete *ISN'T THIS BETTER* to end scene.]

MIDNIGHT EXPRESS

A Columbia Pictures presentation of a Casablanca Filmworks Production. Executive Producer, Peter Guber. Producers, Alan Marshall and David Puttnam. Director, Alan Parker. Screenplay by Oliver Stone. Based on the true story of Billy Hayes from the book *Midnight Express* by Billy Hayes with William Hoffer. Camera Operator, John Stanier. Lighting Cameraman, Michael Seresin. Editor, Gerry Hambling. Production Designer, Geoffrey Kirkland. Art Director, Evan Hercules. Music, Giorgio Moroder. Song, "Istanbul Blues," David Castle. Sound Mixer, Clive Winter. Production Manager, Garth Thomas. First Assistant Director, Ray Corbett. Running time, 123 minutes. 1978.

CAST

BILLY HAYES	Brad Davis
SUSAN	Irene Miracle
TEX	Bo Hopkins
RIFKI	Paolo Bonacelli
HAMIDOU	Paul Smith
JIMMY BOOTH	Randy Quaid
ERICH	Norbert Weisser
MAX	John Hurt
MR. HAYES	Mike Kellin
YESIL	Franco Diogene
STANLEY DANIELS	Michael Ensign
CHIEF JUDGE	Gigi Ballista
PROSECUTOR	Kevork Malikyan
AHMET	Peter Jeffrey

Billy Hayes is described in the opening of the script as possessing "an aura of innocent and youthful arrogance." It was for him a toxic combination. This twenty-one-year-old American, on October 7, 1970, taped tightly pressed plaques of hashish all over his body and attempted to pass by Turkish authorities onto a plane back home. He almost made it, back to an almost-completed journalism degree at Marquette University and his family in Babylon, Long Island. But in 1970 the recent spate of Palestinian hijackings had suddenly made airport security a major part of getting onto an airplane all over the world. Not that the Turkish authorities even detected the bulges beneath Billy's clothing, but at the last moment before boarding, a guard did notice and placed a hand over the American college kid's wildly racing heart. The soldiers were relieved and amused to find out that it wasn't a bomb, just "hashish . . . smuggler . . . hippie."

Billy had paid $200 to a cab driver in Istanbul for two kilos of hash which would bring between $3,000 and $4,000 back in the States, enough to pay off his college loans. To Turkish authorities, however, Billy Hayes was a useful example, whose punishment should satisfy the American government's growing demands that Turkey exert control over its heroin traffic. Billy was thrown into the unspeakably deranged, violent, sickening nightmare of Sagmalcilar Prison, "a large and eerie, ancient Byzantine structure . . . built by some mad Arab architect . . . transformed by an equally mad Turkish bureaucracy into a prison." Its courtyard is a black market bazaar. Behind its walls every last particle of human decency must be bought or stolen. Prisoners range from people who've never committed crimes to specially privileged ones who have guns they shoot at the guards and the guards are nothing more than "inanimate lumps of boredom" earning a dollar a month in wages. Rape and torture are incessant; the "wardens" feed on body-tearing cruelties. At first Billy keeps himself drugged constantly, but the time comes, as he writes in a letter to his girlfriend Susan, when even "dreams don't seem to work anymore. Because the outside doesn't seem real anymore. It's not even a fantasy because there is no fantasy." Somehow, Billy Hayes learns to subsist in the oases of trust and self-discipline he locates within himself via yoga, letter-writing, and the personal growth he finds through a few inmate relationships.

His sentence of 4 years and 2 months for possession has only 53 days left remaining when the Turkish High Court decides to make an international example of this "Vil-helm Hay-ees" and re-sentence him to life imprisonment on the more serious charge of smuggling. The U.S. Consul assures Billy that the Lower Court judge likes Billy and is sure to do the best possible under the law—the sentence will be reduced to no more than thirty years. Billy is brought into court for re-sentencing, and delivers the monologue excerpted below.

(It was after this second sentencing that Billy Hayes eventually took the "Midnight Express"—the prison slang for escape— and made his way out of Turkey to freedom.)

___

MONOLOGUE

BILLY, in the prisoner's dock, addresses the Court; as he speaks, a Turkish TRANSLATOR drones underneath his voice level:

BILLY: . . . What is the crime? And what is the punishment? The answer seems to vary from place to place, and from time to time. What's legal today is suddenly illegal tomorrow 'cause some society says it's so; and what's illegal yesterday all of a sudden gets legal today because everybody's doing it and you can't throw everybody in jail. Well I'm not saying this is right or wrong. It's just the way things are . . .

YESIL the lawyer; DAVIS the Consul.

THE PRESS GIRL from the previous trial in the short skirt.

BILLY

BILLY: (*continuous*) But I spent the last 3½ years of my life in your prison and I think I paid for my error and if it's your decision today to sentence me to more years, I . . . I . . . (*a break*) You know my lawyers told me "be cool Billy—don't get upset, don't get angry, if you're good I can maybe get a pardon, an amnesty, an appeal, this that and the other thing." Well that's been going down now for 3½ years . . .

YESIL looks over, surprised he is talking like this. Looks at
DAVIS.

BILLY

BILLY: (*continuous*) . . . and I been playing it cool and I been
good and now I'm damn tired of being good 'cause you
people gave me the belief that I had 53 days left. You hung
53 days in front of my eyes and then you took those 53 days
away, and Mister Prosecutor! I just wish you could . . .

PROSECUTOR looks over, through his dark green glasses.

BILLY: (OVER) . . . stand right here where I'm standing and feel
what that . . .

BILLY

BILLY: (*continuous*) . . . feels like, 'cause then you'd know something you don't know—you'd know what Mercy means,
Mister Prosecutor—and you'd know the concept of a society is based on the quality of its mercy, of its sense of fair
play, its sense of justice . . . but (*shrugs and scoffs at himself*) I
guess that's just like asking a bear to shit in a toilet . . .

TRANSLATOR STOPS, LOOKS PUZZLED.

BILLY

BILLY: (*same self-mocking tone*) For a nation of pigs, it's funny
you don't eat them. Fuck it, give me the sentence. Jesus
forgave the bastards, but I can't. I hate you. I hate your
nation. I hate your people. And I fuck your sons and
daughters.

Sits down, disgusted; under his breath:

BILLY: . . . 'cause you're all pigs.

SILENCE in the courtroom. People looking at each other
uncomfortably.

DAVIS looks down. [YESIL flips some pages abstractedly.

TRANSLATOR, scared:

TRANSLATOR: (Would your honor like me to translate?)

THE OLD CHIEF JUDGE, the same one as before, shakes his head.

JUDGE: (That won't be necessary.)

ANOTHER ANGLE—THE JUDGE turns to BILLY in foreground, rises, and unexpectedly crosses his wrists out in front of him.

JUDGE: (*emotionally*) (My hands are tied by Ankara!)

Makes the gesture of the hands forcefully, with anger.

TRANSLATOR: (*off*) "My hands are tied by Ankara."

BILLY watching.

JUDGE: (*off*) (I must sentence you, Vilyum Hi-yes . . .)

JUDGE

JUDGE: (. . . to be imprisoned at Sagmalcilar for a term no less than thirty years . . . Getchmis olsun.)

TRANSLATOR: (*off*) "I must sentence you, Vilyum Hi-yes, to be imprisoned at Sagmalcilar for a term no less than thirty years . . . Getchmis olsun."

As he translates, the JUDGE unable to control his emotion exits rapidly, not looking at BILLY, followed by the TWO OTHER JUDGES.

TRANSLATOR: (*off*) "May it pass quickly."]

FAME

A Metro-Goldwyn-Mayer presentation. Producers, David de Silva and Alan Marshall. Director, Alan Parker. Screenplay by Christopher Gore. Director of Photography, Michael Seresin. Film Editor, Gerry Hambling. Music, Michael Gore. Lyrics to song "Fame," Dean Pitchford. Choreographer, Louis Falco. Production Designer, Geoffrey Kirkland. Art Director, Ed Wittstein. Set Decorator, George DeTitta. Sound Editors, Les Wiggins, Rusty Coppleman. Sound Mixer, Chris Newman. First Assistant Director, Robert F. Colesberry. Running time, 134 minutes. 1980.

CAST

LYDIA	Debbie Allen
ANGELO	Eddie Barth
COCO	Irene Cara
BRUNO	Lee Curreri
LISA	Laura Dean
HILARY	Antonia Franceschi
MICHAEL	Boyd Gaines
PROFESSOR SHOROFSKY	Albert Hague
MRS. FINSECKER	Tresa Hughes
FRANÇOIS LAFETE	Steve Inwood
MONTGOMERY	Paul McCrane
SHIRLEY	Carol Massenburg
MRS. SHERWOOD	Anne Meara
MISS BERG	Joanna Merlin
RALPH	Barry Miller
FARRELL	Jim Moody
LEROY	Gene Anthony Ray
DORIS	Maureen Teefy

"I want to live forever; Baby, remember my name . . ." The lyric is from the title song to this film musical which follows one class of students, from first audition to graduation four years later, at a performing arts high school in contemporary Manhattan (based on New York's High School of the Performing Arts and High School of Music and Art). Their thirst for celebrity and immortality is certainly not uncommon. What is uncommon, however, is for anyone, particularly at this age, to commit so fully to this dream via the often torturous but transforming disciplines of the trained professional performing artist. These are not just kids "taking lessons." As Miss Berg explains to the newly enrolled freshmen in the dance department (and it applies equally to music and acting as well): "Dancing isn't a way of getting through school. It's a way of life plus school. And the school part is easier. You can fail French or geometry and make it up at night or in summer school. But if you flunk a dance class, you're out."

At the auditions for the dance department we meet Shirley and Leroy, a pair of "inner-city black youths." Leroy is a tough and barely literate dropout who is partnering Shirley for her audition, but certainly has no plans to audition himself for *any* high school. Shirley cautions Mrs. Sherwood, the English teacher registering auditioners, not to attempt to have Leroy sign in, since he gets mad if anyone asks him to write. Mrs. Sherwood insists, however, that he at least check his knife. During the audition, Leroy breaks away from Shirley and rocks out. His performance staggers the auditors: he's a natural, a breathtaking, if untutored, revelation of why humans have bodies. He is invited into the school; a furious Shirley is not. Mrs. Sherwood demands that Leroy also learn how to read. She pushes and pushes until his shame explodes, and one day midway through freshman year he stomps out of her class, smashing glass all the way down the corridor. He visits Shirley, who is now working as a topless dancer in a crummy nightclub. In the first monologue below (which was cut from the film), Shirley's bravura doesn't hide from Leroy her unhealed, bitter resentment, and he eventually finds his way back to school.

The other two monologues belong to Raul Garcia, who calls himself Ralph Garcy. When Ralph auditions for the dance department, he glues bottle caps to the soles of his sneakers to make tap shoes. The dance department suggests he try the music department. The music department suggests he try the acting department. When asked in each audition where he was taught, he makes up outlandish answers all crediting a brilliant, imaginary father. Actually, Ralph lives in a South Bronx tenement, and it's he who holds together his fatherless family of mother and baby sisters. When he is not attending school full-time, or selling joints to businessmen on the subway to make money, he is trying to establish himself as a stand-up comic. His hero is Freddie Prinze, who was also Puerto Rican and also attended the same high school. Ralph is driven by great ambition and courage and power of invention, but it's all snared under lies and stoked by drugs.

At first, he is particularly snide to the two classmates who will become his special supporters, Doris and Montgomery. Doris is an overly protected girl from the Bronx whom Ralph labels as "Irishy-Jewish, paranoid." Montgomery has a mother who is a famous actress who's always on tour, and always stays with friends so she can send home her per diems to pay for Montgomery's analyst. Montgomery tries hard to accept himself as homosexual; he's been struggling with it since he was a child. Ralph's sneering taunts don't help. But Ralph needs Montgomery, whose analyst prescribes him drugs that he then passes on to Ralph. And Ralph comes to need Doris, whose innocence eventually commands his affection. It is not immediate, however; early on in the script, we are told "Ralph doesn't trust silences," and until he can stop insulting these two, he cannot see or hear what they might have to offer him beyond being objects of his mockery.

In the second monologue below, Ralph is trying to fulfill the first acting exercise of his sophomore year—"to re-create a difficult memory, a painful moment when you first realize something about yourself." Ralph talks to his class about the death of Freddie Prinze. In the third monologue, Ralph is with Doris in the apartment where Montgomery lives alone. Ralph's little sister has just been molested by a junkie while Ralph was at a rehearsal, and in her ignorance and fear, their mother has taken his sister not to a doctor, but to the priest. We've never seen Ralph so devastated or vulnerable as now, when he reveals who his real father was and what the father did to one of Ralph's baby sisters; he then tells Doris about the parade of "stepfathers" who followed.

Monologue 1

INTERIOR THE METROPOLE—NIGHT

It is early evening. Disco music. SHIRLEY is dancing to it.
We see only her face. She is talking to someone very close.

SHIRLEY: His name is Mr. Sands. I don't know his first name.
Anyway, he's been real good to me. He says I got potential
and he's gonna take me to all these parties, see, and I'm
gonna meet some real heavy people.

C.U. LEROY, listening to her and nursing a beer.

Well, anyhow . . . he comes in here one night in these fancy
threads and talks about buyin' me dresses and shoes and I
say, "Don't shit me, Mister! I know what you want." But
he says he wants to be my business partner and how easy
real talent gets ripped off in this town and he wants to look
after my interests.

The CAMERA has pulled back and we see that SHIRLEY is dancing
topless, as are three other TOPLESS DANCERS. She turns away
briefly, giving other PATRONS a front view. Then, turning back to
LEROY . . .

Only thing is I gotta quit my job an' I'm real happy here.
I get to dance and I get good tips. They drop them in the
basket there see. Yeah, and respect. They call me *Miss*
Mullholland and I like that. They even let my friends in,
if they look old enough. They think I'm eighteen, see. I
told 'em I just got outta school an' that ain't no lie! Fact
is . . . that's the sweetest thing whatsever happened to me.
I near but shit four years of life away in some fool
classrooms. Who needs it? Look at me, Leroy Johnson . . .

SHIRLEY shakes her breasts frantically from side to side.

I got it made!

LEROY looks at her thoughtfully, and then to the other girls dancing topless on the bar, he gets up and throws a tip into the basket.

Monologue 2

INTERIOR THE AUDITORIUM—DAY

A few minutes later. RALPH's turn. For once he looks quite vulnerable astride a bentwood chair. Centre stage.

RALPH: I come home from school, you know, like always. I'm late because I got one or two little pieces of business to attend to and it's January and Santa Claus has just ripped everybody off and split for Toy Town or Igloo City or somewhere. So anyway . . . I find this note and it says my chicks are in church and it's Thursday night, I think, and I wonder who died . . . that's a joke. That's supposed to be a joke. And then I drop a little incense like always to relax and I switch on the TV and some dude is on talkin' about Freddie . . . sayin' Freddie Prinze put this gun in his mouth . . . and makin' noise like he *meant* to kill himself— and everybody knows it was an accident.

Pause. The CAMERA moves in tight.

He was jokin', you know. He was always jokin'. You had to laugh. He didn't even have to say anything . . . and sometimes you didn't even *want* to laugh . . . and you laughed anyway, you know. Like it was a gift he had. All you had to do was look in that man's eyes to know he was not into death. The world wanted his ass 'cause he didn't think livin' was such a heavy trip and he was workin' its case real good. So they had to get him. Had to say he was depressed and suicidal 'cause the world gotta take itself real serious, you know. We can't have happy people walkin' around this planet. It doesn't pay. There's gotta be somethin' wrong with us . . . somethin' seriously wrong so the plastic surgeons and the witch doctors and the underarm deodorant people stay in business and we all gotta suffer and go to church on Sunday and be sorry to the asshole god that fucked it up in the first place!

[FARRELL cuts in.

FARRELL: ` Does all this make you realize anything about yourself?

RALPH: (*still in outer space*) What?

FARRELL: How does it affect you?]

RALPH: I'm here. In his school. Fuckin' it back. For Freddie.

[The bell rings. They begin to disperse. MONTGOMERY looks at RALPH for a moment, then he leaves. After a moment, FARRELL goes up to RALPH.

FARRELL: Take it easy, Ralph. You want them laughing with you, not at you.

RALPH: (*almost bitterly*) I want 'em laughin'.

Pan up to ceiling. We mix in F.X. of thunder. The sound of feet.]

MONOLOGUE 3

INTERIOR MONTGOMERY'S APARTMENT—NIGHT

It is the next evening. Early. DORIS and RALPH are talking. He is very down. The room is dark as always. The light from the Times Square neon. Rain beats at the window.

[DORIS: Is she alright?

RALPH: You aren't attacked by some creep at five years old and alright.

Pause. He takes a drink of wine, from a glass on the table. There are two other glasses.

DORIS: I'm sorry.

RALPH: I wasn't there. I wasn't even fuckin' there!

DORIS: What about your father?

RALPH: (*a little hesitant*) We're between fathers.

DORIS: What does *that* mean?]

RALPH: (*beginning to open up*) See, you gotta understand. A
Puerto Rican woman . . . she thinks of the kids, you know?
And how they gotta have a father. Love and stuff, that's got
nothin' to do with it. We got an extra room and my mom
rents it and next thing you know . . . a new father. My sister,
Theresa . . . she's eleven years old . . . I tell her it's her fault.
Mammi asked her what she wanted for Christmas once, and
she said she wanted Papa back. Well, "Papa can't come
back right now," she said. "He's doin' work for the
government . . . but if you pray to the Virgin, maybe she'll
send you a new Papa for Christmas." I guess someone got
the message 'cause our stockins' been full of fathers ever
since.

They laugh. Their first nice shared moment. RALPH takes another
drink . . . continues.

They're alright, mostly. They stay a few months and help
out with the rent and keep the rats out . . . and I don't mean
the animal-type rats . . . I mean the real thing. The junkies
and the winos and the creeps that set fires . . . and beat up on
little girls . . .

He is silhouetted against the window. He takes another drink.
This is difficult for him.

I got three sisters, see. One of 'em . . . Maria . . . she's in a
special place. We see her a couple times a year. She had
some sorta birth defect.

RALPH leans his head against the glass. The neon bleeds through
the beads of rain that run past his face.

No, that's a lie. My father . . . my real, first, ever-fuckin'
father . . . who ain't no special shit . . . who's off doin' a
dime in the New York State Penitentiary . . . he got bothered
one night because she was laughin'. I was tellin' some
stories . . . just kid stuff, you know . . . flyin' carpets and
dragons . . . and he got mad. He always said I was lyin'
see . . . and I was just tellin' stories and makin' my little
sisters laugh. And this one night, he just comes down on me

like always and while he's beatin' on me I keep sayin' I don't tell lies...I tell stories...and I make people laugh and that's a gift, not a goddamn lie...and *he* can't do it. And he says, alright, if he can't do it, he can stop it, and my little sister, she's in the way all of a sudden, and he puts her head inside a wall.

He begins to cry. [DORIS goes over to him, takes his hand.]

It wasn't a hard wall. Me and my fat head, I'da been okay. But Maria...well...she wasn't.

Pause. [DORIS squeezes his hand.]

But she laughs a lot. She's got the prettiest little laugh...

He starts sobbing. [DORIS holds him. He just lets go. All the pain. DORIS kisses his face with great tenderness. We cut to MONTGOMERY, standing in the doorway watching...after a while he puts on his old mackintosh and walks to the door. He throws the door keys onto a chair, and leaves them alone.]

RESURRECTION

A Universal presentation. Producers, Renée Missel, Howard Rosenman. Director, Daniel Petrie. Screenplay by Lewis John Carlino. Director of Photography, Mario Tosi. Film Editor, Rita Roland. Production Designer, Paul Sylbert. Music, Maurice Jarre. Special Visual Sequences by Tony Silver, Richard Greenberg, Robert Greenberg. Art Director, Edwin O'Donovan. Set Decorator, Bruce Weintraub. Sound, John Kean. First Assistant Director, Craig Huston. Running time, 103 minutes. 1980.

CAST

EDNA	Ellen Burstyn
CAL	Sam Shepard
ESCO	Richard Farnsworth
JOHN HARPER	Roberts Blossom
GEORGE	Clifford David
MARGARET	Pamela Payton-Wright
JOE	Jeffrey DeMunn
GRANDMA PEARL	Eva Le Gallienne
KATHY	Lois Smith
RUTH	Madeleine Thornton-Sherwood
EARL CARPENTER	Richard Hamilton
HARVEY	Lou Fant

To experience physical death and to return from it is a known phenomenon. People describe the cold sensation, and the view from above, down onto one's own physical body. Then comes the movement through a hazy, converging tunnel, in toward a vast light visible at the end, but too bright to see into. The tunnel is lined with clearly to faintly familiar people, all of whom have left this life before you. And then, as you are moving into that light, you pivot on whatever gyroscope it is that swings you through your soul's itinerary, and you regain consciousness back in this realm. When you do return, it is in a state of some sort of grace. In the case of Edna McCauley, this is manifest in the gift of healing through the laying-on of hands. Somehow, Edna is now able to escort *something* out of the sick, crippled and damaged human form, which releases it into a state of wellness.

Edna is accused of doing the Devil's work because she won't claim this gift in the name of Jesus Christ. To a gathering in a meadow, she tries to explain just how much of this power she can actually trace or understand (monologue 1 below). Though there certainly may be something Christ-like in leeching the suffering from the sufferer and passing it out through oneself, Edna herself can claim no ideological identification for what happens. All she *can* identify is a concentration of herself into a channel through which pain is able to travel back out into Love.

She first learns she has this gift by using it on herself. She'd bought a sports car for her husband's birthday present, and it seemed the perfect exclamation point to the funny, easy, sexy pleasure of their marriage. A beautiful Southern California drive ends in a fatal crash. Joe is dead. Edna is "legally" dead for seven minutes, during which time she experiences being in the tunnel with the beckoning guides and the light. When she regains consciousness, her legs are paralyzed. She moves back to her family home in a Kansas of wheat fields and "bleached and weathered turn-of-the-century buildings . . . with a look of forlorn surrender to time and the elements." Here, she remeets her stern father, whom she still holds responsible for the complications that had left her sterile after he insisted, when she was living under his roof, that she abort her first pregnancy. But also at home is her maternal grandmother, a beacon of love and courage. Edna makes friends with a dog, and she uses the companionship of this relationship as a kind of lever on herself, to open herself up out of mourning and paralysis, ultimately to make nerve contact with her lifeless legs. She succeeds. And, eventually, she discovers she can do this for others.

The one whom Edna cannot heal is Cal, the wild and broken son of the fundamentalist Christian who is challenging the source of her ability. One night in the simple bunkhouse in which Edna lives at the back of her father's property, she and Cal become lovers. But what Cal feels for Edna and the doctrine he's inherited from his father are irreconcilable in him and eventually tear him apart. He tries to kill her, but she survives.

When Edna's father has a stroke, she's able to know it without anyone having told her. By the time she reaches his bedside, he is lying helpless, unmoving. For the first time, she is able to sit with him and actually tell him of her sorrow and fury over the abortion and its consequences. And, she is also able to tell him what she's seen and learned of death, so that rather than fearing it, he may welcome it (the second monologue below).

MONOLOGUE 1

EXTERIOR MEADOW—DAY

About twenty trucks and cars are parked in the meadow. CAL'S beat-up Harley is here as well. EDNA stands in the center of about thirty people. Among them are GRANDMA PEARL, DOCTORS BAXTER and HANKINS, and CAL who stands on the periphery of the crowd surrounding EDNA. There is an assortment of about ten sick and injured. A hush falls over the crowd.

EDNA: Before we get started, I've got something to say. Last week Earl Carpenter asked me in whose name am I doing this healing. I've been thinking about that and thought I'd tell you what I feel when this thing happens. There's this person in front of me, see, sick and hurting and scared . . . an' in some way . . . don't ask me how . . . I just begin to feel what they're feeling. I get scared. I hurt. Seems like I just go inside them and . . . *become* them for a little while. But there's still this other me, outside, and this other me has to reach out to make the pain better, to say it's gonna be all right. You know like a mother does when her little one gets hurt? Kind of a kiss-it-and-make-it-better thing. I can't help thinkin' if we could just take that feeling and give it to each other, why I bet dollars to donuts we could all heal each other, of all kinds of hurt. Do you know what I'm saying? Doc Lurkins told me a story about a patient a'his; a little girl that was dying over in Clark county. She needed a special type of blood. They searched all around, but nobody seemed to have it, until they found out her seven-year-old brother did. So Doc asked the boy if he'd give his blood to save his sister. The little boy was scared... scared as hell, but Doc told him how important it was and that it was the only way his sister could live, and finally the boy agreed. Well, while they were takin' the blood, the little boy lay there so scared, he was shakin' all over, and Doc talked to him, tried to calm him, telling him everything was gonna be all right, and that what he was doin' was gonna make his sister live. The boy calmed down some and he looked up, watchin' his blood running into the tube and he said to Doc, "Will I die, pretty soon?" See? He thought he had to give up *all* his blood, he thought he had to die so his sister could live. That was what he thought he had *agreed* to.

A silence.

EDNA: I guess that's the kind of love I'm talkin' about. That boy's folks weren't what you might call church folks. Nobody'd ever read the Bible to him. He didn't need to know about Jesus, to love like him. Now I don't deny God, or Jesus, or any other name you want to give to this thing. All I'm sayin' is that they don't speak to me personally. I wish they would. I think it would be beautiful. So if one of you ask me in whose name I do this, then I've gotta say in the name of caring... and loving... in the name of me being you. I don't know how the power comes to me. All I know is we touch the place of caring in each of our hearts.

A moment. Heavy silence.

EDNA: (*laughs*) Hell, I didn't mean to make a speech. Let's get to what I'm here for.

MONOLOGUE 2

INTERIOR JOHN HARPER'S BEDROOM—DAY

JOHN is in bed suffering the effects of a massive stroke. An oxygen tube leads into his nose, an IV into his arm. EDNA sits in a chair next to the bed. He stares straight ahead, seemingly not seeing or hearing her. EDNA leans close to him.

EDNA: (*there are tears in her eyes*) I wanted that baby. I didn't see any shame in not being married . . . But *you* made me feel dirty and ashamed. And, God help me, I let you bring that old horse doctor in here to kill that little girl, to scrape me out so that no life could ever grow inside me again. What happened to make you so hard? What hurt you? What made you stop loving? God, Daddy, you drove us all away from you; Mama into her silence where she stayed grieving until she died, me to California, Sam to Viet Nam where they killed him. *All* of us. I wish you could tell me what it was. I wish I could've helped you. I loved you so much. Daddy, listen . . . I want you to know I still love you . . . and I can help you now. I can. Honest. I know you know you're dying. I know you're afraid . . . but you don't have to be. See, when I had the accident, I died for a little while and I saw it. It's wonderful! Oh, Daddy, it's so wonderful. Everybody's there, Mama, and Sam and Joe and Mr. Condon the grocer and Mr. Stratton. You remember him? And my friends, Jody and Cora . . . and Uncle Amos and Casper and Aunt Mildred. They're all there. And Daddy, there's a music, like chimes . . . and little bells, and you feel like you're beginning to understand everything. It's all clear and right. You don't feel your body any more . . . or pain . . . or anything bad. There's no you you can touch, or see or anything. It's just you in the idea of you . . . in the way of knowing the idea of you is forever. Oh, Daddy, it's so beautiful. And there's this light. Oh . . . oh, my. It is so bright and loving, you can hardly look at it. But you can. And it feels like it's reachin' out to you. And everybody, Mama, and Joe, and Sam helps you toward it. And pretty soon, you begin to feel like you're made of the same light. Daddy. I promise you, it's all there. I *promise* you. (*a silence*) Hey, you know what? Grandma Pearl and Uncle

Ely and Aunt Carrie and everybody are downstairs. I've been telling them about it, and listen, Daddy...they all wanna come up and say good-bye. Can you hear me? Can you?

ARTHUR

An Orion Pictures/Warner Bros. release of a Rollins, Joffe, Morra, and Brezner Production. Executive Producer, Charles H. Joffe. Producer, Robert Greenhut. Director, Steve Gordon. Screenplay by Steve Gordon. Director of Photography, Fred Schuler. Editor, Susan E. Morse. Production Designer, Susan Hendrickson. Sound Editor, Sandford Rackow. Sound Mixer, James Sabat. Music and Lyrics, Burt Bacharach, Carole Bayer Sager, Peter Allen, Christopher Cross. Assistant Directors, Robert Greenhut, Thomas Reilly. Running time, 97 minutes. 1981.

CAST

ARTHUR BACH	Dudley Moore
LINDA MAROLLA	Liza Minnelli
HOBSON	John Gielgud
MARTHA BACH	Geraldine Fitzgerald
STANFORD BACH	Thomas Barbour
SUSAN JOHNSON	Jill Eikenberry
BURT JOHNSON	Stephen Elliott
BITTERMAN	Ted Ross
RALPH MAROLLA	Barney Martin
GLORIA	Anne De Salvo

Arthur is the Little Tramp all dressed up as Little Lord Fauntleroy. He's sweetly, sadly, enormously charming and polite.

Falling down drunk quite regularly, he's still funnier (and richer) than anybody else. From the back seat of his chauffeured Roll-Royce, he apologizes to a pair of streetwalkers as the car glides up, "I know this is last minute . . ." And once he's got company in his playpen-on-wheels, he burbles, "Isn't this fun! Isn't fun the best thing to have! Don't you wish you were me? I know I do!" Arthur is so rich he's never even had to throw anything *out*—his bedroom features everything from a throne to bathtoys. Arthur's father, who owns quite a bit of everything, has decided it is high time the boy grew up and settled down. He wants Arthur to marry Susan Johnson, and if he won't, he's to be cut off without a cent. Arthur's grandmother, who adores him, nonetheless concurs. "We are ruthless people. Don't screw with us." Susan is so good, pure, uninterruptedly faithful, and so sure of her power to redeem Arthur that he knows if he does marry her, he'll be dead within six weeks. (And, redeem him into *what*? Her own father is a caricature of a Great White Hunter from Scarsdale.) One day, while Arthur is buying a dozen of everything at Bergdorf Goodman, he bumps into Linda Marolla. She is an actress working as a waitress, shoplifting a tie for her father's birthday present. She gets caught, he pretends they are together and the tie is for him. They improvise to the hilt. Linda hasn't a penny, and lives with her unemployed but good-hearted father out in Queens. What she does have is enough wit, vulnerability, playfulness, and energy to keep up with Arthur, and not get run over by his style. They fall in love.

Arthur is a fairy tale. Even rich people get sick if they, as Arthur does, stay drunk *all* the time. At the end of the story, the girl gets the boy, and they both get the money. But Arthur has to earn it by first losing his security and learning how to take care of someone else, how to love another. This happens through the death of Hobson. Arthur has had a fairy godfather, a Yoda, a Merlin—a valet, Hobson. He's been with the boy since the beginning. Though Hobson's martinis and his wit are absolutely the dryest, his love for Arthur and Arthur's love for him is the warmest, most tender relationship in the entire story. Arthur has been impressed by the way he's seen Linda looking after her father. Arthur wants to take care of someone, too. When Hobson must be hospitalized, Arthur moves in with him, has special food brought in, special toys. Sweet though Arthur's ministrations may be, Hobson still must die. It is time to grow up.

Arthur tries to get sober, serious, and married. He tries to go through with the plans to marry Susan . . . until the very last moment when he just has to call it off, almost at the altar. He'd thought Hobson wanted him to go through with it; Hobson had advised him, "Marry Susan, Arthur. Poor drunks do not find love, Arthur. Poor drunks have very few teeth. They urinate outdoors. They freeze to death in the summer. I can't bear to think of you that way." Before he died, however, Hobson realized that Arthur had fallen in love with Linda, so he arranged for Linda to crash Arthur and Susan's engagement party. As he'd foreseen, once Arthur and Linda see each other again, it's only a matter of time and plot complications until they choose true love over money. And then just before the final credits, the grandmother relents, restores Arthur's inheritance, and orders them to produce another little Bach, pronto.

The screenplay of *Arthur* went through a number of polishings and tinkerings. The three selections below are each excerpted from different drafts. The first selection, in which Arthur's father tells him it's time to get married, is from the Final Draft. It appears, in part, in the film. The second selection, consisting of two scenes back-to-back, is from an earlier Third Draft and does not appear in the film. Its first half takes place in the Palm Court of the Plaza Hotel. Arthur and Linda have just left his engagement-to-Susan party. This scene is a study of two people making a drunken spectacle of themselves in public, unable to stop, as Arthur and Linda realize that this thing is bigger than both of them. We then cut immediately to the Bach family suite upstairs in the hotel. Arthur and Linda are now sobering up to the reality of Arthur's no play/no pay status—if he doesn't marry Susan, he doesn't get the Bachs' $750 million. The third excerpt is from an even earlier draft. Instead of jilting Susan inside the church, with Linda waiting for him outside, as in the film, Arthur here plays out the whole scene from inside Linda's apartment in Queens, simply *calling* Susan on the telephone with his regretful news. For cinematic purposes this may not have proven preferable; for the purposes of playing the scene in a single space, it's a blessing.

(Don't worry. In all the drafts they get the money.)

SCENE 1

INTERIOR—STANFORD BACH'S ENORMOUS OFFICE—DAY

STANFORD BACH sits behind his gigantic desk. Trim. Tough. About 55. Good looking. Smart. And not the nicest man. ARTHUR stands in the middle of the office. MR. BACH looks up from his reading and they face each other. On the wall and desks are pictures of STANFORD BACH with practically every luminary of the past thirty years. Roosevelt, Truman, Kennedy, Nixon, Ford and others. The whole office speaks of power. This is a powerful man. There is a long pause as ARTHUR and his father face each other.

MR. BACH: (*finally*) Sit down, Arthur.

ARTHUR: How long will this take, sir?

MR. BACH: (*reading*) I don't know. Do you have any pressing appointments?

ARTHUR: No.

MR. BACH: I wouldn't think so. Sit down please.

ARTHUR sits on a couch rather distant from his father. His father continues to read the report in his hands.

MR. BACH: (*continued*) Pardon me for a moment, Arthur. I have to read this. It's important.

ARTHUR: Father . . .

MR. BACH: (*reading*) Yes, Arthur . . .

ARTHUR: It's good to see you.

MR. BACH: Really, Arthur?

ARTHUR: Yes. Somehow . . . no matter what . . . it's always good to see you. I don't know why. I tell people I hate you.

MR. BACH: (*smiling*) You've always been honest. It's good to see you too, Arthur . . . Let me read this . . .

ARTHUR: I used to hide in your closet . . .

MR. BACH: Pardon?

ARTHUR: I just remembered . . . I used to hide in your closet.

MR. BACH: Why?

ARTHUR: You went to work and your clothes stayed home. Remember that huge closet in your bedroom in Harrison? Before I was sent away? I used to hide in there.

MR. BACH: From what?

ARTHUR: Lions . . . tigers . . . Indians . . . the main thing was . . . nobody could see me . . . and I used to put on your suits . . . and your shirts . . . and your ties . . . and I would become you . . . and I would want to come home from work and play with my son Arthur . . .

MR. BACH: You're too gentle to live in this world, Arthur . . .

ARTHUR: Yes. May I get a drink?

MR. BACH: Help yourself.

ARTHUR rises. He crosses to the elaborate bar and prepares himself a drink. He drinks. MR. BACH puts down what he is reading and picks up a rather large folder. He pulls out several press clippings.

MR. BACH: The press has a good time with you, Arthur . . . millionaire drunk playboy.

ARTHUR: Yes . . .

MR. BACH: You're the weakest man I've ever known! I despise your weakness!

ARTHUR: (*pouring himself a drink*) What weakness?

MR. BACH rises. He starts to cross to ARTHUR at the bar.

MR. BACH: (*on the cross*) Arthur . . . I'm afraid we have to talk.

ARTHUR: (*almost to himself*) I'll be good. I'll be good.

MR. BACH reaches ARTHUR at the bar. He pours himself a drink.

MR. BACH: Arthur . . . surely you realize that we can't let you go on like this . . .

ARTHUR: Yes. Shall we sit down and discuss this? I'm glad
we're talking. I have been excessive.

ARTHUR crosses to the couch. His father follows.

ARTHUR: (*continued, almost to himself*) I'm in such trouble. . . .

MR. BACH: You're going to marry Susan Johnson. One month
from today. We want this marriage, Arthur. We want your
children. If you do nothing else with your life . . . you're
going to father a Bach!

ARTHUR crosses back to the bar. His father sits on the couch.

ARTHUR: (*on the cross*) Excuse me a moment. (*to himself*) This
is big trouble.

He turns to his father.

ARTHUR: (*continued*) I'm not going to marry her. I've told you
that a thousand times.

MR. BACH: Fine. Arthur . . . if that is your decision, then the
family has no choice. I'm sorry, Arthur . . . very sorry, but
as of this moment, you are cut off.

ARTHUR: (*very nervous*) Do you mean . . . cut off from you and
grandmother and the family?

MR. BACH shakes his head no.

ARTHUR: So you mean that I'm cut off from the uh . . . the . . . uh . . .

MR. BACH: The money, Arthur.

ARTHUR: May I have another drink? I don't need it . . . but it's
something to hold in my hand.

MR. BACH: Your grandmother and I have had the papers drawn
up. We want this marriage, Arthur. I want it. Burt Johnson
wants it.

ARTHUR: Burt Johnson is a criminal!

MR. BACH: We all are, Arthur. And as you know, we usually
get what we want.

ARTHUR: (*drawing himself up*) So . . . that's it, is it? I marry a woman I don't love . . . or lose the money? Well, father . . . I'd rather starve. And I will.

ARTHUR starts for the door.

ARTHUR: (*continued*) I'll get married when I fall in love with somebody.

MR. BACH: Fine. I respect your integrity. You just lost 750 million dollars.

There is a long silence.

ARTHUR: Actually . . . Susan is a very nice girl.

MR. BACH: Very nice.

ARTHUR: Have you ever seen her when the light hits her face just right? She looks very beautiful. Of course, you can't depend on that light. And she does wonderful things with a chicken. I love a chicken made at home.

MR. BACH: (*overlapping*) The wedding's one month from today. The invitations will be mailed tonight.

ARTHUR: (*overlapping*) I love that Susan.

MR. BACH goes to his desk and opens a drawer. He crosses back to ARTHUR. He carries a ring box.

MR. BACH: Arthur . . . this is the engagement ring your grandfather gave to your grandmother. She wants you to give it to Susan.

He opens the box, revealing an enormous exquisite diamond ring.

ARTHUR: (*looking at the ring*) This is to marry one girl? Father— please don't do this to me.

MR. BACH: Arthur, I've waited for you to grow up. I can't wait any longer. There will be an engagement party at our summer house in Southampton next Wednesday. Everything is taken care of, Arthur. All you have to do is show up . . .

ARTHUR: You win, father. Congratulations.

MR. BACH: I had every intention of winning. Congratulations to you, Arthur. You're going to be a wealthy man for the rest of your life.

ARTHUR: Good.

SCENE 2

INTERIOR—THE PALM COURT AT THE PLAZA—NIGHT

Very swank. A violin player strolls and plays. ARTHUR and LINDA sit together drinking. They're both drunk. A waiter comes over.

ARTHUR: (*to the waiter*) I'll have another Scotch . . . and you can bring a pot of coffee for her. The woman is inebriated.

LINDA: If you don't mind . . . I'll have a vodka and tonic.

ARTHUR: (*to the waiter*) Bring it. There's no use in trying to reason with her.

The waiter exits.

ARTHUR: (*to Linda*) I hate to see a woman drunk.

LINDA: Just what the world needs. A chauvinist lush.

The waiter returns with the drinks. He puts them in front of LINDA and ARTHUR. He withdraws. ARTHUR and LINDA drink. There is silence. Both are drunk.

ARTHUR: (*finally*) So . . . would you like to go to Acapulco tonight?

LINDA: No.

ARTHUR: Good.

They drink again. Again there is silence.

ARTHUR: (*finally*) My family has a suite in this hotel.

LINDA: Forget it.

ARTHUR: It never entered my mind. Like another drink?

LINDA: Yes.

ARTHUR waves at the waiter.

LINDA: (*continued*) How would we get to Acapulco?

ARTHUR: (*casually*) I have a plane.

LINDA: Four planes would impress me.

The waiter puts a drink in front of each of them. Again there is silence.

LINDA: (*continued, toasting*) Well . . . here's to you and Susan . . . and me and Harold . . .

ARTHUR: You should never have come to the party. You knew I was engaged.

LINDA: I looked too good to be alone. Know what I mean? (*pause*) I think I'm drunk.

ARTHUR: I hate amateurs. Stop drinking.

LINDA wiggles her finger to bid ARTHUR to come forward. He does. Their faces are very close.

LINDA: In spite of everything . . . this is kind of like Prom night. I mean . . . it keeps going . . . You have the face of a boy who shaves.

ARTHUR: Would you consider having sex with me on this table?

LINDA:.   Why on the table?

ARTHUR: The place where I usually make love is closed. The delicatessen.

LINDA: We can't make love. You're engaged. Move your face back.

They move back to their original positions. The waiter brings another drink. LINDA leans back and puts her foot on another chair.

LINDA: (*continued*) Do you love her at all? Susan?

ARTHUR: I like her a lot. Want to see how I kiss her?

LINDA: Yeah.

They lean forward.

ARTHUR: You're Susan. I'm kissing you goodnight.

LINDA: I know my part.

He kisses her lightly on the lips.

LINDA: (*continued, after the kiss*) I see. It's not as bad as you
    think.

They are close together.

ARTHUR: Now . . . would you like to see how I once screwed a
    nurse in Philadelphia?

LINDA: (*laughing*) Yeah. You got slides?

ARTHUR: You make me smile. Don't we have fun together?

ARTHUR caresses LINDA'S hair.

ARTHUR: (*continued*) I'm fooling around with your hair. Why
    should I lie to you?

LINDA: Arthur . . . don't.

ARTHUR kisses her on the forehead. The cheek. The eyes.

LINDA: (*continued*) You do nice work.

ARTHUR kisses her hard on the lips. LINDA throws her arms
around him. It is lingering. It is passionate. They stay close.
They keep kissing.

LINDA: (*continued, after the kiss*) Is everyone looking at us?
    They probably think we can't get a room.

ARTHUR: Nobody's looking at us. Although . . . the violin player
    is jerking off. I think we have to get out of here. Linda . . .

LINDA: Arthur... don't ask me. Take me.

ARTHUR: Okay.

LINDA: You know... you're taking advantage of me...

ARTHUR: Because you're drunk?

LINDA: No... because I'm crazy about you.

CUT TO:

INTERIOR—HUGE ORNATE PLAZA HOTEL SUITE—NIGHT

LINDA and ARTHUR enter the room.

LINDA: (*looking around*) Look at this room! It's not easy to feel cheap here.

ARTHUR sits on the bed.

ARTHUR: You want something to drink? Or eat.

LINDA: No.

She walks to the window and looks out.

LINDA: New York...

ARTHUR: You were expecting Pittsburgh?

LINDA: I feel like we're a young couple from the midwest on our first trip to New York.

ARTHUR: (*lying back on the bed*) Come here.

LINDA goes to the bed and lies next to him. He puts his arm around her. They lie like that for a beat.

LINDA: What are we waiting for?

ARTHUR: The other girl will be here in a minute. You didn't think this was just going to be you and me did you? You'll like her.

LINDA laughs.

LINDA: (*laughing*) Why do I feel so comfortable with you?

ARTHUR: Because we are that couple from the midwest. And we're very nice people.

He kisses her. Light at first. Then it quickly turns to passion.

ARTHUR: (*breathing heavily*) You're a nice girl . . . but you don't turn me on physically.

LINDA: You're not going to marry that girl. And you know it.

ARTHUR kisses her again.

ARTHUR: Let's not talk anymore. Okay?

LINDA starts to unbutton **ARTHUR'S** shirt. She kisses his chest. They are both very excited.

LINDA: (*while kissing his chest*) I know you're not going to marry her.

ARTHUR: She's talking. Linda . . . let's not talk.

He rolls over and kisses her again. After the kiss:

LINDA: Let's talk for a second . . .

ARTHUR: I'm having sex here! Do you mind!

LINDA: Why would you marry a woman you don't love?

ARTHUR: I have to. Can I help you with that zipper?

LINDA: What do you mean . . . you have to?

ARTHUR: Linda . . . there's not a shower in the world cold enough to fix what's going on here. Now . . . could we talk about this later?

LINDA: Just tell me what you mean . . . you *have* to?

ARTHUR: My family is forcing me to marry her.

LINDA: You asshole! Nobody gets married like that! That hasn't happened since 1850!

ARTHUR: They'll cut me off if I don't! Without a cent!

LINDA: So! You'll get a job like everybody else! How much money is it?

ARTHUR: 750 million dollars.

LINDA: Try it with her for a few years. Maybe it'll work out.

ARTHUR: Linda . . . you see this suite? I have to be in suites like
this.

LINDA: Why?

ARTHUR: Because . . . that's who I am. I'm Arthur Bach. I've
got nothing but the money.

LINDA: Me. You got me.

ARTHUR: (*touching her face*) Yeah. We have each other. How
would you like to share the money with me?

LINDA: And Susan?

ARTHUR: Yes. I have to marry Susan.

LINDA: We're not that nice young couple from the midwest, are
we? I'll get a cab.

LINDA crosses to the door. ARTHUR sits on the bed. She stops.

LINDA: (*continued*) You can't have everything, Arthur. If you
get the potato you don't get a vegetable.

ARTHUR: Would you turn down this money?

LINDA: Are you crazy? Of course not! I steal ties for Christ
sakes! But when you look for a mistress . . . make it a
mistress! She should speak French and give back rubs.
Don't come to me. I want to get married. What do I know
about being a mistress? You'd get me an apartment and I'd
want to know if it's near a good school.

ARTHUR: Goodbye, Linda.

LINDA: Don't pout. You're lovely. I'll remember you the rest of
my life.

LINDA exits. ARTHUR goes to the bar and pours a drink. [The
phone rings. ARTHUR picks it up.

ARTHUR: (*into the phone*) Hello . . . Bitterman? . . . oh no. (*he looks at his watch*) I'll meet you there in an hour.]

(*Note*: This excerpt may of course be used as written, as two separate scenes. But since playfully clever improvisation is the very stuff of Arthur and Linda's delight, particularly when egged on as it is here by lots of booze, the temptation may become irresistible to consider how to make sense of *all* the dialogue in a single location . . . or at least have fun trying.

From the point in the dialogue where Linda wonders if everyone is looking at them, to the point where she wonders why she feels so comfortable with Arthur—this is the section wherein the actors will have to (1) internally edit the dialogue to bridge the missing elevator ride, and (2) invent behavioral transitions to accommodate the shift in tone and topic when there has been no accompanying shift in time or setting.

If it all takes place in the Palm Court, it is possible to enter the last kiss in the Palm Court scene and simply cut to where Linda and Arthur come out of their first kiss in the suite, excising all the dialogue in between. But most of the dialogue between these two points *could* be played if Arthur and Linda do decide to go upstairs, but before they can get the check, get it paid, and get to the exit, their conversation has taken its irreversible turn to the topic of Susan. They become so engrossed in their arguing that they never get out the door. [Perhaps they *almost* get out the door, but return to the table to leave a tip or retrieve a coat, talking all the way. By this point, though, they've become so involved in what they're saying that they just sit right back down. They're both so drunk it's entirely possible they wouldn't at first notice or care that the waiter had completely cleared and reset the table in the interim. Or perhaps even that they're reseated at a different table, maybe even one that already has people!] The scene will have to be carefully rehearsed with a waiter. When it is brought into class, the other students could be seated at surrounding tables, the audience for Arthur and Linda— which is precisely what the other Palm Court customers become.

If it is all to play as one scene in the suite, there are no other people present. All their concern for the surrounding customers would be grand put-on. The bar would be running low, so the fresh drink orders would be placed with room service over the phone. Though all the action this time is transpiring in the suite, it's the same section of dialogue, between the two kisses, wherein the actors will need to edit text and invent transitions if both scenes are to play as one.)

SCENE 3

INTERIOR—LINDA'S APARTMENT—LATE MORNING

The door bell rings. LINDA crosses to answer it. ARTHUR is at the door in top hat and tails. He is incredibly drunk and furious. She opens the door.

ARTHUR: (*mad and drunk*) God damn you!

LINDA: Oh Jesus. What are you doing here? Are you doing a musical?

ARTHUR: (*weaving*) I'm getting married in two hours. You're not invited.

LINDA: Are you dangerous?

ARTHUR: I came here to tell you a few things! Later... I'm marrying Susan. Who it turns out... I'm crazy about! Get me a drink.

LINDA: Go screw yourself.

ARTHUR: I thought you'd say that! It's so like you! How have you been?

LINDA: Fine.

ARTHUR: Who asked you? I hate you! Where's your telephone?

LINDA: Right there.

ARTHUR goes to the telephone and throws it on the floor.

ARTHUR: That's what I think of your telephone. (*softer*) Hobson died three weeks ago. He weighed less than a hundred pounds.

LINDA: I'm so sorry Arthur...

ARTHUR: Sorry! Where the hell were you? I had to go through it all by myself.

LINDA puts her hand on ARTHUR'S face.

LINDA: I wish you had called me.

ARTHUR: I don't call you for anything! I'm marrying Susan! In 90 minutes! Susan... who I cherish!

LINDA: Can I get you some coffee?

ARTHUR: I've got 250 million dollars! I don't need your coffee! Do you love me?

LINDA: Yes.

ARTHUR: (*screaming*) God damn you! If you love me... Why are you just standing there? I'm getting married in 20 minutes. You got a pencil?

LINDA hands him a pencil. ARTHUR throws it across the room.

ARTHUR: (*throwing the pencil*) I'm throwing around everything because I'm furious! You're ruining my life!

LINDA: Do you love me?

ARTHUR: I hate you! I was a kid... growing up.

He makes a sign with his hand to show how small he was.

ARTHUR: (*continued*) I went to school. I was rich. I drank. I was happy. I screwed the upstairs maid. I didn't have you bothering me! Then I got bigger. I went to Europe. I drank. I was rich. I was happy. That was before I met you! Then... I got bigger. I drank. I met you! Now... I drink. I screw nobody! I may lose all my money! And for what? Forget it! (*losing control*) Yes! Yes! I love you!

He grabs her and holds her.

ARTHUR: (*holding her*) Oh shit! My life is in the toilet!

LINDA: Was that a proposal?

ARTHUR: Actually... that was a nervous breakdown.

LINDA: You're getting married soon.

ARTHUR: I know. To Susan... who is no bargain either.

LINDA: What would we live on?

ARTHUR: Who?

LINDA: You and I.

ARTHUR: Am I marrying you?

LINDA: Yes. This nonsense has got to stop.

ARTHUR: Oh shit!

LINDA: So... what are we going to live on?

ARTHUR: Welfare. Listen... that's your department. You have a job.

LINDA: And you'll get a job.

ARTHUR: Don't push me, Linda. This is a tremendous mistake we're making. Luckily... I'm drinking again. Hobson's last words to me were, "Marry Susan... poverty sucks."

LINDA: I think you should call Susan and tell her.

ARTHUR: You're right. Will you call her?

LINDA: (screaming) Get on that phone!

ARTHUR picks up the phone and starts to dial.

ARTHUR: (while dialing) I don't enjoy being screamed at. If that's the way you intend to communicate with me... What am I going to say to her? Women hate this kind of crap.

LINDA: Just tell her the truth.

ARTHUR: (into the phone) Hello Susan. Arthur. Well... it's not bad luck to *talk* to the bride before the ceremony.

ARTHUR laughs gaily. LINDA indicates to him to get on with it. ARTHUR indicates for LINDA to stay out of it.

ARTHUR: (*continued, into the phone*) Yeah . . . I'm a little nervous. I did have a few drinks. Uh Susan . . . I hate to uh . . . (*pause*) Sure . . . we can take a side trip to Berlin on the honeymoon . . . sure if your brother's going to be there . . .

LINDA almost faints. She indicates to ARTHUR to tell her.

ARTHUR: (*continued, into the phone*) But the thing is Susan . . . and I feel terrible . . . I can't do it. The wedding. I can't (*pause*) Susan . . . that isn't it. Well . . . I guess . . . between Hobson and everything else . . . I'm just not ready. You should hate me. (*pause*) I know. But Susan . . . if you're humiliated today . . . imagine what it would be like to be married to me every day and be humiliated like this. I wish I could say something. I've never felt so sorry about anything, Susan. Yeah. Can I call you ever? Okay. Goodby. I'm very sorry.

He hangs up.

ARTHUR: (*to* LINDA) Well . . . I hope you're happy.

LINDA: I'd feel sorry for her . . . but I'm the one who's getting him.

ARTHUR: I'm poor.

LINDA: You'll be happy. I promise. Our sex life will be wonderful! I make great food.

ARTHUR: Really?

LINDA: Really. And we'll have kids.

ARTHUR: They'll be poor too.

LINDA: But happy. I promise. Come on . . . cheer up.

She puts her arms around him.

ARTHUR: We'll be one of those young couples! We'll ride the subway! We'll hold hands. How much is the subway?

LINDA: Fifty cents. A dollar for a couple. If you spit . . . it's five hundred dollars. Nobody spits.

ARTHUR: Can we go into the bedroom now?

LINDA: Yes.

ARTHUR: This better be good.

(*Note*: An actress scored a particular triumph in class when she brought in this scene playing the Arthur role herself. She arrived at her true love's front door drunk and furious and in her bridal gown, telephoned the groom, and called the whole thing off!)

ATLANTIC CITY

A Paramount Pictures release of an International Cinema Corporation presentation of a John Kemeny-Denis Heroux Production. Producer, Denis Heroux. Director, Louis Malle. Screenplay by John Guare. Director of Photography, Richard Ciupka. Editor, Suzanne Baron. Music, Michel Legrand. Sound, Jean-Claude Laureux. Production Designer, Anne Pritchard. Executive Producers, Joseph Beaubien, Gabriel Boustany. Associate Producers, Justine Heroux, Larry Nesis. Production Coordinator, Vincent Malle. Assistant Director, John Board. Running time, 104 minutes. 1981.

CAST

LOU	Burt Lancaster
SALLY	Susan Sarandon
GRACE	Kate Reid
DAVE	Robert Joy
CHRISSIE	Hollis McLaren
JOSEPH	Michel Piccoli
ALFIE	Al Waxman
FELIX	Moses Znaimer
WAITER	Wally Shawn
SINGER	Robert Goulet

The opening shot of *Atlantic City* is a piece of art come to warm, glowing life——a beautiful woman (Sally) washing herself in lemons to the gorgeous sound of a Bellini opera. Then the camera pulls back to include a man, in a darkened adjacent apartment, watching her. His name is Lou Paschall and he is smoking an unfiltered cigarette. Sally's admiring neighbor is a has-been, would-be high-toned gangster who seems to have mastered the gentlemanly gestures, but lacks the raw nerve, or so his old nickname, "Numb Nuts," would suggest. The next time we see Lou, he is alone in his undershirt in the very spare, tidy apartment he has occupied for thirty years. He's over sixty now, but still quite fit. He is ironing his tie. He ignores the insistent ringing of a makeshift bell, which is being yanked on by Grace, who lies upstairs in her satin-quilted boudoir. A life-time ago, Grace came to Atlantic City for a beauty pageant and stayed to marry Cookie Penelli, Lou's boss. Now that Cookie is dead, Lou looks after Grace. She keeps him on a small wage for such demeaning responsibilities as escorting her yappy dog Peppy to the groomer's, where Lou is also known in his own right, as a numbers runner. From some old, deep place Lou is in love with Grace, and at the end of the story he will win her respect; but when we meet them, she still has Lou on a steady diet of humiliating "Don't-you-ever-forget's."

Lou, Grace, and Sally all live in the Vermont, just one more of the old apartment buildings in Atlantic City soon to be demolished to make way for the shiny, new, state-controlled casino redevelopments. Enter Dave, Sally's ex-husband. He arrives with Sally's sister, "one of the Last Roses of the flower generation" who is eight months pregnant by Dave. He's also got a lot of stolen cocaine he wants to sell. Sally wants them *out*. Lou is passingly polite to the kid and is rebuffed. But when Dave's big plans don't pan out, he turns on his little lost surfer-boy charm, flattering Lou with made-up reports of Lou's extensive reputation in Las Vegas. As Lou and Dave walk along the boardwalk, a huge old building collapses, but for Lou this is an ordinary occurrence. He ignores it as he reminisces about how things used to be in the old days. He has, after all, the wisdom of experience—for example, "Never let anyone badmouth you at a funeral." Lou Paschall speaks with that certain loopy grandeur and boomerang eloquence that is the special province of John Guare's characters.

Monologue

EXTERIOR—FURTHER DOWN THE BOARDWALK. END OF DAY.
A police car cruises on the boardwalk. DAVE and LOU leave the
boardwalk and walk down a side street past an automatically
controlled garage that looks like a large moving erector set or,
more to the point, a vertical ferris wheel. You park your car in
the bottom rung, get out, a button is pushed and your car moves
up one slot. The garage is the height of eight cars stacked on top
of each other.

LOU: The name Capone mean anything to you?

[DAVE: Al Capone? The Godfather?]

LOU: Lucky Luciano, Dutch Schultz, Meyer Lansky.

[DAVE: You know them?]

LOU: You work for the people who work for the people. I was
taken a shine to.

[DAVE: Pardon me, but you don't look exactly like the King of
the Mobs.]

LOU: You make wrong turnings with the mobs, wrong affec-
tions, some mistakes. It's all shit now. Shame you didn't
see Atlantic City when it had floy-floy. You know the song
"Flatfoot Floogie with the Floy-Floy"?

DAVE doesn't know the song.

They walk around construction gear in the street.

[DAVE: No, I . . .]

LOU: A very hep cat in like a zoot suit, that's the floogie part.
But the somethin' special—that's the floy-floy. Atlantic City
had floy-floy out the ears. Now it's all so goddamn legal.
Howard Johnson runnin' a casino. Tutti frutti ice cream and
craps do not mix. Gambling should not be a place to bring

the family to. Playboy magazine. You got to be on the stock exchange to open a casino. Wall Street guarding the profits, state takin' taxes. It used to be beautiful here, what with the rackets and the whoring and the guns. Events would happen where I'd kill people. I'd feel bad for a while, but then you go in the ocean, swim way out, come back to the shore, feel all clean, start in again.

[DAVE: I never seen the Atlantic Ocean till right now.]

LOU: The Atlantic Ocean used to be somethin' then. You shoulda seen the Atlantic Ocean then.

DAVE jabs LOU's shoulder gently. LOU straightens his tie and adjusts his top coat. They enter the Trocadero Hotel lobby.

THE FRENCH LIEUTENANT'S WOMAN

A United Artists presentation of a Juniper Films Production. Producer, Leon Clore. Director, Karel Reisz. Screenplay by Harold Pinter. Based on the novel *The French Lieutenant's Woman* by John Fowles. Director of Photography, Freddie Francis. Editor, John Bloom. Music, Carl Davis. Production Designer, Assheton Gorton. Costumes, Tom Rand. Art Directors, Norman Dorme, Terry Pritchard, Allan Cameron. Sound Editor, Don Sharpe. Period Costumes, Cosprop. First Assistant Director, Richard Hoult. Associate Producers, Tom Maschler, Geoffrey Helman. Running time, 124 minutes. 1981.

CAST

SARAH, ANNA	Meryl Streep
CHARLES, MIKE	Jeremy Irons
SAM	Hilton McRae
MARY	Emily Morgan
ERNESTINA	Lynsey Baxter
MR. FREEMAN	Peter Vaughan
MRS. POULTENEY	Patience Collier
DR. GROGAN	Leo McKern
MRS. FAIRLEY	Liz Smith
MRS. TRANTER	Charlotte Mitchell

John Fowles's novel *The French Lieutenant's Woman* contained two prominent elements that would prove particularly challenging in its adaptation to a screenplay. One was that the novelist gave the story two possible endings and left the reader to choose: would Sarah Woodruff and Charles Smithson be ultimately reunited, or not? And second, while Sarah and Charles's story takes place in Victorian England, the narrator is reaching back to it from a modern perspective, and the hindsight is pivotal. For example, we now know that in Victoria's London one out of every sixty houses was a brothel and the prostitutes received clients at the rate of two million per week—which definitely colors one's understanding of a public morality so severe that an unmarried man and woman seen talking to each other could be ruined for that alone. Harold Pinter's solution was to create a screenplay that *added* a layer around the Victorian story, involving the present-day making of the film of the novel. Mike and Anna, the actor and actress who play Charles and Sarah, are having an affair. They are married, however, to other people, and there are children. The two of them are always trying to penetrate deeper into their characters' realities by basting the historical data in the juices of their own attraction, frustrations, secrecies, and passions. At the end of the film, Sarah and Charles reunite, but Anna and Mike do not.

When the story opens, Charles, a gentleman scientist, is just getting himself engaged to a sweet, silly, wealthy girl named Ernestina. They are out walking along the harbor in Lyme Regis when he notices way out at the far end of the rock-pile pier a woman looking out to sea. The wind is too high for it to be safe. He edges his way out to ask her to return. Sarah turns and just stares at him, her haunted, beautiful face framed by her wind-tossed hair and cloak. (She will later tell him, "I was lost from the moment I saw you.") Known to the locals in Lyme Regis as "Tragedy" or "The French Lieutenant's Woman" or "The French Lieutenant's Whore," Sarah gazes out to sea ostensibly in search of the lover who has abandoned her. In the eyes of everyone, she is a fallen, disgraced woman. Whilst out on one of his fossil hunts, Charles meets her and suggests she leave the town. What could keep her in a place where she must work as a barely paid companion to a vindictive, repressed gorgon, whose only pleasure seems to be in trying to break and humiliate Sarah?

She will be punished for even being out on such a walk. But Sarah says she cannot leave, even though she knows that the French lieutenant is married and will never return.

Accompanying the gorgon on a visit to Ernestina, Sarah slips Charles a note asking him to meet her that night in the churchyard. He does, but he is outraged at her impertinence. He demands to know why she will not leave and go to London, where surely, he hypothesizes, with her education and experience as a governess she could begin a new life. Sarah believes that if she goes to London, no matter how well she speaks French or how beautifully she draws, without any actual protector or sponsor, she will be forced into prostitution to survive. And Anna's research validates statistically the likelihood of a woman in Sarah's situation knowing precisely such a fate. What often appears to Sarah's critics as her obsessive melancholia can be viewed from Anna's vantage point as a very real understanding of a completely unacceptable, seemingly inescapable future. Sarah tells Charles, "You cannot imagine . . . my suffering. My only happiness is when I sleep. When I wake, the nightmare begins." When she asks why she was born to the life she is being forced to live, why she was not born Ernestina, Charles can do no better than to counsel, "That question were better not asked." Even if he knew what to do for her, at this point he does not yet want to help her. She begs him to meet her just once more so that she may tell him her story. She insists he is her only hope and that she will wait for him out where they had previously met by accident, on the Undercliff. They meet again in the excerpt below, bracketed for Sarah's monologue, in which she reveals to Charles how she forced her own undoing.

It will turn out later in the story that much of what Sarah tells Charles in this speech is not true. When she engineers an entire scene so that Charles will throw himself on her, and he does, he discovers to his shock that she is a virgin. Why had she lied? She only tells him years later, after having disappeared just when he'd wanted to marry her: "There was a madness in me . . . at the time, a bitterness, an envy. I forced myself on you, knowing that you had . . . other obligations. It was unworthy . . ." Having been dragged through the mud by Ernestina's father after breaking the engagement, and having spent years searching for Sarah before she'd let herself be found, Charles tells her that she has not only ruined his life, but she appears to have taken pleasure in doing so. She answers, "You misjudge me. It has taken me this time to find my own life. It has taken me this time . . . to find my freedom."

MONOLOGUE

EXTERIOR—UNDERCLIFF—DAY

A dell, high up, overlooking the sea.

SARAH and CHARLES emerge through the trees into the dell. She sits. He sits. She looks out to sea.

SARAH: I was working as a governess. At the Talbots. His name was Varguennes.

[EXTERIOR—BEACH—DAY—PRESENT

ANNA turns over suddenly onto her stomach and looks towards the Undercliff.

MIKE: What's the matter?

She is silent. He rolls over to look at her face.

MIKE: What's the matter? You look sad.

ANNA: (*softly*) No.

MIKE: Why are you sad?

ANNA: I'm not.

He lies under her, pulls her down gently, kisses her. Her eyes close, then open. She looks towards the Undercliff.

THE UNDERCLIFF—ANNA'S P.O.V.]

EXTERIOR—UNDERCLIFF—DAY

The dell. SARAH is sitting on a hummock. CHARLES is sitting on a flat-topped block of flint. She looks out to sea. Her face is in profile to him.

SARAH: His name was Varguennes. He was brought to the house after the wreck of his ship. He had a dreadful wound. His flesh was torn from his hip to his knee. He was in great pain. Yet he never cried out. Not the smallest groan. I admired his courage. I looked after him. I did not know then that men can be both very brave and very false. (*Pause*) He was handsome. No man had ever paid me the kind of attentions he did, as he... was recovering. He told me I was beautiful, that he could not understand why I was not married. Such things. He would... mock me, lightly. (*Pause*) I took pleasure in it. (*Pause*) When I would not let him kiss my hand he called me cruel. A day came when I thought myself cruel as well.

[CHARLES: And you were no longer cruel?

SARAH: No.

CHARLES: I understand.]

SARAH: (*fiercely*) You cannot, Mr. Smithson. Because you are not a woman. You are not a woman born to be a farmer's wife but educated to be something... better. You were not born a woman with a love of intelligence, beauty, learning, but whose position in the world forbids her to share this love with another. And you are not the daughter of a bankrupt. You have not spent your life in penury. You are not... condemned. You are not an outcast.

[CHARLES: Social privilege does not necessarily bring happiness.

SARAH: It brings the possibility of happiness.

EXTERIOR—DAY—BEACH—PRESENT.

MIKE and ANNA lying side by side. Her eyes are closed. He is looking at her. Over this, the voices of SARAH and CHARLES.]

SARAH: (*voice over*) Varguennes recovered. He asked me to go back with him to France. [He offered me...

CHARLES: (*voice over*) Marriage?

ANNA opens her eyes and looks at MIKE.

EXTERIOR—UNDERCLIFF—DAY

SARAH: Yes.] He left for Weymouth. He said he would wait there one week and then sail for France. I said I would never follow him, that I could not. But...after he had gone...my loneliness was so deep, I felt I would drown in it. (*Pause*) I followed him. I went to the Inn where he had taken a room. It was not...a respectable place. I knew that at once. They told me to go up to his room. They looked at me...and smiled. I insisted he be sent for. He seemed overjoyed to see me. He was all that a lover should be. I had not eaten that day. He took me...to a private sitting room, ordered food. (*Pause*) But he had changed. He was full of smiles and caresses but I knew at once that he was insincere. I saw that I had been an amusement for him, nothing more. He was a liar. I saw all this within five minutes of our meeting. (*Pause*) Yet I stayed. I ate the supper that was served. I drank the wine he pressed on me. It did not intoxicate me. I think it made me see more clearly. Is that possible?

[CHARLES: No doubt. (*Pause*)]

SARAH: Soon he no longer bothered to hide the real nature of his intentions towards me. Nor could I pretend surprise. My innocence was false from the moment I chose to stay. I could tell you that he overpowered me, that he drugged me. But it is not so. (*She looks at him directly.*) I gave myself to him. (*Silence*) I did it...so that I should never be the same again, so that I should be seen for the outcast I am. I knew it was ordained that I could never marry an equal. So I married shame. It is my shame...that has kept me alive, my knowing that I am truly not like other women. I shall never like them have children, a husband, the pleasures of a home. Sometimes I pity them. I have a freedom they cannot understand. No insult, no blame, can touch me. I have set myself beyond the pale. I am nothing. I am hardly human any more. I am the French Lieutenant's Whore.

[CHARLES stands, walks over to her, looks down at her. For a moment it seems that he will take her in his arms. He straightens.

CHARLES: You must leave Lyme.

Suddenly voices, laughter, from below, ascending. SARAH stands. She beckons to him silently and moves to the trees. He follows.

The laughter comes closer.

SARAH and CHARLES hide behind thick ivy. They look through it down to an ashgrove.

THE ASHGROVE—THEIR P.O.V.

A girl and a boy, coming up towards them. The boy has his arm round her waist. He turns her to him and kisses her. They fall to the grass. The girl lies back. The boy kisses her.

CLOSE-UP—SARAH SMILING AT CHARLES.

CHARLES.

He stares at her.

CHARLES and SARAH.

They are looking at each other. Her smile fades. Silence.

CHARLES: Please go. We must never meet alone again.

She turns away.

A shrill laugh from below. CHARLES turns to look.

THE ASHGROVE.

The girl running downhill. The boy chasing her. Their figures flash between trees; a laugh; a scream; silence.

CHARLES: Go. I will wait.

She moves past him, into the ashgrove.

CHARLES.

He watches her walk downhill through trees.]

PRINCE OF THE CITY

A Warner Bros. and Orion Pictures Co. presentation. Producer, Burtt Harris. Director, Sidney Lumet. Screenplay by Jay Presson Allen and Sidney Lumet. Executive Producer, Jay Presson Allen. Based on the book *The Prince of the City* by Robert Daley. Director of Photography, Andrzej Bartkowiak. Production Designer, Tony Walton. Film Editor, John Fitzstephens. Supervising Sound Editor, Peter C. Frank. Music, Paul Chihara. Associate Producer/Production Manager, Ray Hartwick. Art Director, Edward Pisoni. Assistant Directors, Alan Hopkins, Robert E. Warren. Running time, 167 minutes. 1981.

CAST

DANIEL CIELLO	Treat Williams
GUS LEVY	Jerry Orbach
JOE MARINARO	Richard Foronjy
BILL MAYO	Don Billett
DOM BANDO	Kenny Marino
GINO MASCONE	Carmine Caridi
RAF ALVAREZ	Tony Page
RICK CAPPALINO	Norman Parker
BROOKS PAIGE	Paul Roebling
SANTIMASSINO	Bob Balaban
CARLA CIELLO	Lindsay Crouse
RONNIE CIELLO	Matthew Laurance

Prince of the City screenplay based on the book *The Prince of the City* © 1978 by Robert Daley. Published by Houghton Mifflin Company. Reprinted by permission of Houghton Mifflin Company, by permission of The Sterling Lord Agency, Inc., and with the permissions of Jay Presson Allen and Sidney Lumet.

When we first meet Danny Ciello in 1971, he is thirty-one years old, and not only the youngest member of his Special Investigating Unit of the New York Police Department's Narcotics Division, but its head. (As a boy in school, Danny had always been the one to carry the flag.) The S.I.U. are called "Princes of the City" because they choose their own targets, report to no one, punch no time clocks. They just produce spectacular arrests. Achieving such ends, however, involves questionable means. If junkies, for example, are to provide information that busts their source, you must offer them at least what their source does, if not better. Since there is no way to adequately pay these police for the danger, fear, and stress of their work, it begins to seem almost logical to them to retain a small amount of the mountains of cash they seize in dramatic raids, so that after the complimentary headlines are over, they can at least go home and carpet their kids' bedrooms. As the head of the anticorruption unit of the U.S. Attorney's office explains, "No cop joins the force with the idea of becoming a crook. The process is gradual and when it happens the conflict is terrible. In the suicide statistics, cops are at the top of the list."

City and federal prosecutors investigating police corruption begin to court Danny. He's invited to dinner at one prosecutor's apartment and it is the kind of place he wishes he could afford; and they do seem to be inviting him to become one of them, saying they need him because they want to start with the best and the brightest. Danny explains in the speech below why even if there were any question about the integrity of his fellows, which there is not, he would never betray them: your partners are the only ones who'll protect you.

Eventually Danny breaks this rule and goes undercover within the Department to expose the corruption inside it. Why does he do it? To prove to his father that a policeman's badge is not the only difference between himself and his brother, who is a coward and an addict? Or, as his wife Carla says, because "You want *everybody* to love you?" Or simply, according to one prosecutor, because, "In their hearts they want to admit their guilt. That's the way cops are"? As the investigation is subsumed by ever higher authorities, the attacks on Danny's credibility become ferocious. He is forced to choose: either reveal privileged information implicating his partners for long-ago sins, from which he is now immune, or lose all the indictments because his testimony has been discredited. His family now living under constant armed guard, his friends shunning him, his gums bleeding and his sleep ruined, Danny Ciello must decide whether or not to spend the rest of his life lying. Is he a tragic hero, or a crooked cop who got what he deserved, or something in between—someone who allowed himself to use illegal methods, such as wiretapping, because he couldn't figure out any other means to achieve highly decent ends? Sidney Lumet, the film's director and co-author, said the man on whom the character is based "fell into a classic trap. He knowingly tangled with powerful forces believing he could manipulate and control them. The results were catastrophic. From a body of 70 men . . . considered to be his friends and compatriots, 52 were indicted, 2 committed suicide, one went mad."

MONOLOGUE

INTERIOR—CAPPALINO'S APARTMENT—NIGHT

THREE MEN engaged in conversation.

CIELLO: All cops are like me. I'm no different.

[PAIGE: Oh, I think you are. That's why you're here.]

CIELLO: (*suddenly angry*) *You* don't know why I'm here. (*a beat*) Where'd you go to school, Paige?

[PAIGE: (*calmly*) I went to Harvard. And before Harvard, Andover. And before Andover, St. Bernard's.]

CIELLO: St. Bernard's. That's in the Twenty-Third Precinct. Little blond boys in blazers. Right? *Shit, Cappalino!* My own father can't understand the pressures on cops! What am I supposed to get from St. Bernard's? You people in the Chase Commission, focusing on the police department . . . you tell cops you're out to catch them taking meals, taking Christmas presents, *bastards*. It's you guys who run the whole fucking thing . . . starting with assistant D.A.'s who plea bargain murder one into a misdemeanor, lawyers wearing $400 suits that meet cops in the hallways and whisper, "This case doesn't mean anything, here's $50, $100, $500 . . . *$15,000* . . . forget it . . ." *We* know how you become a judge. You pay fifty thousand. Zap. You're wearing robes. You guys, you're in Westport or here on Central Park West and we're in El Barrio, 125th Street. You want us to keep everybody inside the barricades so you can stay outside. (*stops, stares out the window*)

[PAIGE: That's not true.

CIELLO: The fuck it's not true.] The first thing a cop learns is he can't trust anybody but his partners. Nobody loves him but other cops and not all of them. Shit, everytime we're getting set to make a bust, and I think about the guy I'm going after and I know he's going up for five ... (*a beat*) I wonder if some other cop is on some other stakeout and *his* target is *me*? You know? *Cops hunt cops.* So you don't trust nobody but your *partners*. I sleep with my wife, but I *live with my partners.* You people, you're just looking to hurt us. You only want to lay the fucked up system on us. *The only one who cares about me is my partner.* I see what kind of man you are, and you, and I see what kind of man my partner is, and there's just no comparison, see? It's me and him and whatever guy we caught. We're going to take him to jail and lock him up. We're going to take his money. Fuck him, fuck you, fuck them.

We are aware of PAIGE silently signaling CAPPALINO that CIELLO is out of control ... they should remain very passive, very *receptive*.

CIELLO: You're winning in the end anyway. We're selling ourselves, our families. These people we take from own us. Our family's future rests on the fact that some dope pusher is not going to give us up, or some killer, some total piece of shit, is not going to give us up. Between those bastards and you bastards ... I know what people like you think of us, but we're the only thing between you and the jungle!

DISSOLVE TO:

EXTERIOR—TERRACE—DAWN

The THREE MEN. They have talked all night. CIELLO is a wreck,

PAIGE unchanged. CAPPALINO rumpled and worn out, but *is* preternaturally alert, exhilarated. PAIGE looks as contained and collected as he did ten hours earlier.

CIELLO: (*hoarse*) . . . you've got the same kind of dirt under your fingernails as me. Sure I give my informants heroin. They've got nobody but me and they're sick and helpless and I feel responsible for them. But under the law, I give them junk that's no different than selling . . . a felony. So why don't you arrest me right now! Because you've got a use for me down the line just like me with my informants. You're the U.S. Attorneys . . . if you have guilty knowledge of a felony and don't move against me, *you're* committing a felony. So don't give me any shit. (*turns, stares the two men straight in the face*) Everybody's using everybody, right? So what I want is . . . let's be straight, okay? Like I decide to do this . . . I will not give up my partners. I would want you to break up my unit so they could be protected . . . (*stops*) I mean they're not doing anything but [I want . . .

CAPPALINO: We'll transfer them out of SIU. It's time for normal rotation anyway.]

CIELLO: There are lines I won't cross.

[CAPPALINO: Hold on. My name is Cappalino and every time an Italian crook is brought to trial I want it to be an Italian prosecutor. We're the same blood, Danny. How do *you* feel when you open the *Daily News* and see all the mob names ending in "IO" . . . a big piece in the Sunday *Times* on the Five Families? I tell you when I see a Jewish name in there, my heart sings! I personally hope I never have to go after Meyer Lansky . . . we *need* the son of a bitch.

CIELLO laughs. PAIGE essays a little smile. Then, after a beat, CIELLO speaks.

CIELLO: I got to think. I got to have more time.]

RICH AND FAMOUS

A Metro-Goldwyn-Mayer presentation of a Jacquet-William Allyn Production. Producer, William Allyn. Director, George Cukor. Screenplay by Gerald Ayres. Based on a play,* *Old Acquaintance*, by John Van Druten. Director of Photography, Don Peterman. Film Editor, John F. Burnett. Production Designer, Jan Scott. Art Director, Fred Harpman. Set Decorator, Don Remacle. Music, George Delerue. Sound Editor, Paul Hochman. Sound, Darin Knight. Music Editor, William Saracino. First Assistant Director, James Quinn. Running time, 117 minutes. 1981.

CAST

LIZ HAMILTON	Jacqueline Bisset
MERRY NOËL BLAKE	Candice Bergen
DOUG BLAKE	David Selby
CHRIS ADAMS	Hart Bochner
JULES LEVI	Steven Hill
DEBBY AT 18 YEARS	Meg Ryan
THE BOY, JIM	Matt Lattanzi
GINGER TRINIDAD	Daniel Faraldo
DEBBY AT 8 YEARS	Nicole Eggert

---

* Rich and Famous, based on the play *Old Acquaintance* (as was an earlier film adaptation also called *Old Acquaintance*), is an obvious exception to the no-stage-play-adaptations rule for this collection. But I had never seen the two principal characters or their special relationship studied in class until two actresses brought in the last scene from *Rich and Famous*, which is included here.

By the last scene of *Rich and Famous*, Merry Noël Blake and Liz Hamilton have been friends for over twenty years. Across those years they love, resent, honor, fight, admire, outrage, and envy each other, but they never betray each other. With the accumulated exposures of old acquaintance, each can see the other in the context of her larger patterns. This is often uncomfortable. A present dilemma will be attributed by such a friend to some old behavior or attitude that one is positive one has long since outgrown or discarded. The flip side, of course, is that the old friend assumes and respects aspects of one's personality that one may have feared were lost; such expectation is deeply comforting. It sometimes seems the old friend is the one who knows you least of all, right along with knowing you best of all. When Merry's husband Doug says. "I wish I understood you two," Liz answers, "Why should you know the secret? We don't."

During the course of the story both women become professional writers. Liz will have early critical success followed by writer's block. Merry will begin later, but with a landslide commercial success. Although Merry will insist she'd wanted to be a writer since she was eight and started her first diary, Liz thinks otherwise: "Merry, be honest. If I had become a glider pilot, you'd be behind the wheel of a 747 by now." Liz is high-strung, shy, and too good with words and reasons and ironies to just let herself be. Merry is rambunctious, grand-hearted, down-home direct, frosted with Southern belle cunning and charm. She is perfect for television talk shows. Whereas Liz has greeted her ambition with self-conscious resistance, Merry barges straight into celebrity. Media success and money, however, still leave Merry craving what Liz embodies in her low heels and high anxiety—that depressed-witty, draggy-trenchcoated, New York literary cachet. Before she'd ever been published, Merry confessed to Liz that she found Liz's success all the more impressive because Liz was not run-of-the-mill rich and famous, she was only *famous*. "That's harder to do."

Unfortunately, the more rich and famous Merry gets, the more she also seems to require her husband's self-esteem on a platter. In Merry's accelerating performance of herself as a romantic heroine cum blockbuster novelist, her husband and child become exasperating sidelines, except (or especially) when she is in the mood to yank their strings. Merry experiences herself constantly at full epic pitch, clutched at by circumstances too laggardly for the sweep and force of her destiny. On the other hand she is insistent upon having all the middle-class accoutrements of traditional marriage perfectly in place. Eventually, Merry's hyperactive, plot-twisting imagination will warp her two cravings into a single delusion: When Doug leaves her, Merry will actually believe that it is Liz who has been luring him. The reverse is what's true: Doug has offered, and Liz has refused to take him up on it, having very strict rules for herself about what is permissible with friends' husbands. In fact, Liz has told Merry that what Doug and Merry had is the only thing Liz had ever admired: "A marriage. A real child, and you loved each other." If Liz does love Doug, she keeps it to herself. She and Merry's daughter, Debby, however, openly share a very special and loving bond, which is not always to Merry's liking.

Liz's sense of herself as the literary loner, the watcher of Merry the doer, is established at the opening of the story. Merry is sneaking out of their dorm to elope with Doug. They're at Smith in 1959—what else *could* she do? Liz is helping. What else can *she* do? Merry is her roommate, and Doug, a scientist heading out west, had originally been *her* blind date. Liz is left standing on the platform watching the train disappear, and holding Merry's teddy bear, Hamburger. The teddy bear is a kind of mascot for their friendship, and when years later the friendship is being torn apart in a fight (scene two below), the stuffed toy gets shredded.

After the elopement, we jump ahead ten years to 1969. Liz is addressing the UCLA Women's Caucus. Her first novel, *Night Song,* has won the National Writers' Award. Someone in the crowd asks Liz why she doesn't write about women. She answers that she's always loved old men, explaining that her father was old when she was born. She mentions Picasso, Yeats, Brahms, "like walnuts, dark and delicious. Myself, I've always felt green and inelegant." Between doomed affairs, Liz will have erotically eruptive episodes with very attractive strangers—a man in the bathroom on an airplane during landing, a boy off the street. And there is always the mock flirtation with her publisher, Jules Levi, "the Leonard Bernstein of Publicity," but this appears to be understood on both sides as a game of psychological support from a suave older publisher to a favorite and often depressed younger writer. It is directly to Jules Levi that Merry is headed when, after a party she's given in Liz's honor, she pulls out a manuscript.

Well, it seems Merry has written a novel, too . . . By 1969, Merry is a young mother living in a modest house in Malibu, even though the move from Pasadena has involved a major daily commute for Doug to his job at Caltech. She's met her Malibu neighbors, many of whom are famous movie people. She explains to Liz about her novel: "Oh, it doesn't have all the commas in place like yours, but it's something I feel real serious about. These folks around here, they come down here and sit on this beach and it's not any different from down home. They got problems, honey. They tell em to me, cause I like to listen." Merry assures Liz that she has changed all the names.

As Merry begins to read, Liz "watches her with slow concentration, as would, say, a snake its charmer." Liz had been badly blocked, having rewritten the first hundred pages of her second novel five times in the last five years. (Her Freudian therapist has told her that her current celibacy will end only when she starts to write again. Doug has suggested that perhaps it will happen the other way around.) Liz is appalled by the chutzpah of Merry daring to accomplish this writing as if it were just another domestic craft, to be done in the evenings after the dishes are finished. And if Merry's lack of angst weren't enough, Liz begins to sense, through drink after drink, as Merry keeps reading through the night, that what she's hearing may be *golden* trash. Merry is just finishing reading her first novel aloud to her best friend, who is miserable and drunk, in the first scene below.

Liz gives the manuscript to Jules. *A House by the Sea* by Merry Noël Blake is published, launching an astoundingly successful career. Some of Merry's Malibu neighbors are not thrilled with her portraits of them, though, and when someone sets fire to Merry's car, the Blakes move to Beverly Hills.

The story jumps ahead another dozen years. Doug's lab has closed; Merry's had five bestsellers in the last five years. She humiliates Doug with her success, popping out of bed in the middle of lovemaking to plot out story lines. She is at work on a novel about her mother. When *Home Cooking* is published, Merry finally receives the critics' acclaim. The *Times* review says, "...at last she has written from the heart and decided to bypass the obstruction of her brain." In fact, the novel is nominated for the National Writers' Award, and this year Liz is sitting on the panel of judges.

To attend the judges' meetings, Liz comes into New York from the millpond house where she lives in Connecticut, alone. Merry has come to New York to openly campaign for the award.

She trails Liz around town or arrives unannounced at Liz's room at the Algonquin Hotel, unmercifully noodging at her to leak how Merry is doing in the voting. Not only is there nothing yet to tell Merry, but Liz also has something else occupying her mind. A reporter from *Rolling Stone* was sent to interview her. He was young enough that she didn't think twice about being rude to him. It didn't throw him. In fact, his simple, flat acceptance of *her* throws her so far off her defensive balance, that when he eventually proposes marriage, she dares to think it might be possible. It's Merry who finally realizes what is happening to her friend and finally tells Liz what Liz needs to hear—just shut up and do it. But in order to cover the enormity of her own vulnerability, Liz has been too flippant with the young man's proposal. By the time she gets back to him, he has met Debby. Merry's daughter has grown into a lovely young woman, despite her mother's incessant, shrill hectoring. (Mothering caught Merry at her least artful; for example, when Debby was little: "Debby, honey we all have interesting things under our clothes, but we don't stand around and pick at them.")

Liz loses her groom. Merry wins her award, though actually she ties, which she finds more galling than losing. The second and third scenes below are the final scenes of *Rich and Famous*, in which Merry and Liz first fight it all out, and then make it all up as they toast their friendship and the New Year.

SCENE 1

THE SAME—DAWN

The sea and beach out the window have turned grey with dawn. LIZ is in a butterfly chair, facing the beach, an empty glass propped on her belly. Indefatigable at the formica table, is MERRY, turning the last page.

MERRY: "...there was sand at her feet, and as many as the grains of that sand, were the memories of her years...Brad ...Elliot...Gerald, in and out of her life as the tide that came now to wash at her feet...gone seemed to say the lapping of the tide, all gone but her memories and this, her simple house by the sea..."

MERRY lets the sheet come to rest on the table. She's moved by her story. She takes off her harlequin glasses, looks over at LIZ. LIZ does not break her gaze out the window.

MERRY gets up, walks over to LIZ, sits down on an ottoman next to her. She's anxious.

MERRY: Was it okay?

LIZ looks at her, drunk, verging on the maudlin.

LIZ: Why do they always end up alone?

MERRY: Who?

LIZ: Those women, in those stories . . . They always end up alone.

LIZ starts to sniffle, then cry, then reach for something to wipe her nose. She's making a mess of this. MERRY is astonished, trying to figure out whether to be pleased.

MERRY: You liked it?

LIZ: It knocked me out.

MERRY: That's good?

LIZ: The Mona Lisa never knocked me out.

LIZ finishes mopping her nose. MERRY is still uncertain of the reaction she's getting.

MERRY: You want some coffee?

LIZ: (*getting to her feet, unsteady*) You got any more scotch?

MERRY: Haven't you had enough?

LIZ: A night cap. (*looking out window*) A morning cap.

LIZ crosses to the kitchen area. In one cabinet, she finds a bottle with a little gin left. MERRY'S eyes narrow.

MERRY: Liz, I don't want you to tell me any lies.

LIZ: Don't worry. I have to have sleep to tell a believable lie.

MERRY: You liked my book?

LIZ turns to look dead on at MERRY.

LIZ: How long did it take you to write it?

MERRY: Oh... almost a year. Wait a minute, I started just before Debby went to... eight months in the afternoons.

LIZ: Eight months in the afternoons.

This sounds like an accusation. LIZ comes back, bottle and glass in hand, to flop down in the butterfly chair.

LIZ: What're you going to do with it? Get it published?

MERRY: I was going to ask you.

LIZ: Go ahead. Ask.

MERRY: I don't like your tone, Liz.

LIZ: What's wrong with my tone? *The New York Review of Books* said I was a master of irony.

MERRY: Drink your gin and go to sleep.

LIZ: You want me to show the book to Jules Levi.

MERRY: I want you to do anything you think is right.

LIZ: Jules Levi is the wrong guy for you, Merry.

MERRY: Why?

LIZ: All that important tailoring, he looks like an apple the butler polishes every day.

MERRY: He's the most impressive publisher in the business.

LIZ: Let's say *he's* impressed.

MERRY: Oh, Liz, would you, would you show it to Jules Levi and tell him it may not be like some translation from the Russian and I haven't just escaped from the Iron Curtain or something, but I do know about what it *feels* to... to—

LIZ: Have feelings. You know what it feels like to have feelings.

MERRY: I suppose.

LIZ: It's not a supposition. It's fact from the master of irony. Merry Noël Blake knows what it feels like to have feelings. That's worth money in the pocket. But not Jules Levi's pocket. He has no pockets. Too much expensive tailoring.

MERRY: Why not Jules Levi?

LIZ: He's interested in something called serious art. *Serious* art. Ask him, he'll tell you there are only two markets for serious art in this country—homosexuals and Jews.

MERRY: That's an ugly thing to say.

LIZ: What? Homosexual or Jew?

MERRY gets up, stalks over to the kitchen area.

MERRY: I could smack your face and not even feel it.

LIZ: Another gin and I wouldn't either.

MERRY grabs a bag of marshmallow cookies out of the cabinet. She bites into one.

MERRY: What's wrong with me writing a book, it makes you so jealous, huh?

LIZ: Nothing. What's wrong with eight months in the afternoon learning to balance balls on your nose? Nothing. Maybe I should learn to balance balls. Balls, I should. I'm too busy writing and rewriting my first hundred pages for that famous apple-polished Jules Levi, my impressed and impressive publisher. He's been waiting *years* for my—what do they call it—second effort. (*she rises unsteadily to her feet*) Don't you know what it is to be blocked? Can't you develop a few hangups? Don't you want to write major art and knock them out at the local gay hadassah?

[DOUG stumbles in, short terrycloth robe.

DOUG: Did I leave my glasses in here? Why are you all shouting?

MERRY: Liz is] just being a simple bitch, is what we call it down home.

LIZ: You're not down home, you're way out west and quit quoting Atlanta as though it were gospel. Atlanta has fallen, haven't your heard? Sherman has spared us any further wisdom from that quotable capital of the South.

MERRY: Give us a quote from Paris in France, then, Miss Smarty.

LIZ: In Paris in France they had a guy who was, for the record, both homosexual and a Jew, who wrote a seven volume book they continue to refer to as a masterpiece, who was such nitro-glycerin in the head, he had to hide out in a cork-lined room or he'da gone up in shrapnel. Proust, Marcel Proust, from Paris in France. He had the good grace to suffer for his art and he didn't push aside the tuna fish on his formica kitchen table to write it.

[DOUG: Has anybody slept around here?]

MERRY: Liz Hamilton, it is my duty to remind you of a promise you extracted from me early in our careers in college. I promised to tell you if you ever went too far and were in danger of hurting me. You are too far. Right now. Apologize.

LIZ gets up, heads for the bedroom, grim.

LIZ: I apologize. [(*as she passes* DOUG) Tell her] I apologize . . . (*opens a door*) . . . for a basic lack of honesty.

MERRY: You *have* been lying.

Turning at door, LIZ drunkenly struggles to unravel her thoughts.

LIZ: Not yet. I would only be lying—if I let you believe—it is merely scotch and gin—that are making me do—what I'm about to do.

MERRY: (*deadly*) What are you about to do?

LIZ: Vomit.

She goes out. [DOUG finds his glasses, pulls them on, looks at MERRY.] MERRY nods to herself in a knowing way. [Looks at DOUG.]

MERRY: She liked my book.

She believes this.

> (*Note:* Although Doug has been bracketed to allow for studying this scene, if necessary, just with Merry and Liz, his presence of course makes a distinct difference. Merry's emotional and psychological temperature always increases when faced with both Doug and Liz together—it's the life/plot possibility she can't live with or without. And his entrance gives Liz an audience for her exit.)

SCENES 2 AND 3

INTERIOR—ALGONQUIN—LIZ'S SUITE—DAY

LIZ is packing, her suitcases opened on the bed. The door buzzer is heard. She goes to open it, carrying articles of clothing draped over one arm.

LIZ opens the door. MERRY is in an even greater fury than before. She marches directly past LIZ. She spots the packing. She wheels.

MERRY: You're leaving?

LIZ: I'm going to Connecticut.

MERRY: What about my party?

LIZ: I'm sorry. I was going to call. I'm so down, I would only spoil it.

MERRY: I think we have come to a serious juncture in our lives when we should examine the terms of our friendship.

LIZ: Hold this.

She hands MERRY a piece of clothing. She opens a suitcase. She puts her hand on the clothing to take it back.

LIZ: Thank you.

Like a stubborn child, MERRY refuses to let go of it. LIZ is forced to do what she's been trying to avoid, look MERRY in the face. MERRY is furious.

LIZ: Merry, I'm truly sorry about the award. It's not the worst thing that could happen, there'll be lots of publicity—

MERRY lets go of the clothing.

MERRY: That is water long under the bridge.

LIZ: How was Doug?

MERRY: Even longer under the bridge.

LIZ: He still drinking?

MERRY: Dry as the Sahara.

LIZ: (*packing*) How's he look?

MERRY: He's getting married.

LIZ: Not to ah—

MERRY: Joyce. From Houston.

LIZ: Oh, poor Merry, what a day you're having.

LIZ puts out a hand to comfort her. MERRY steps back from it.

MERRY: They've bought a house. With a yard.

LIZ: Sounds wonderful to me.

MERRY: Since when?

LIZ: I'm not immune to the attractions of a man and a yard.

MERRY: Or to Doug, specifically Doug and a yard?

LIZ: I never thought of it.

MERRY: Never thought of Doug as a loving husband?

LIZ: Never.

MERRY: Along with his ability to drink, he has lost his ability to lie. Don't look away from me.

LIZ: I'm closing my suitcase.

MERRY: I began to smell there was something he didn't want to say. I bought him a drink, and the words came tumbling out.

LIZ: You bought him a drink?

MERRY: What a petty, disgusting confession it was. Me, the unsuspecting wife, blaming myself over the years as I sensed my husband slowly but surely slipping away from me, into the arms—

LIZ: Those don't sound like Doug's words.

MERRY: Isn't it true that all the years we were married he was pouring out his love to you?

LIZ: He mentioned it.

MERRY: While married to me!

LIZ: At the last.

MERRY: And he proposed?

LIZ: I said no.

MERRY: Because of your friendship with me?

LIZ: You got *that* right.

MERRY: Except for that strange lapse into morality, you would have taken him, huh?

LIZ: He sure deserved better than he was getting.

MERRY: How did you know what he was getting? Did he describe it?

LIZ: If you have any more petty, disgusting revelations, save them for your girlhood diaries, or your novels, they sound about alike.

MERRY: It's happy time for all. Doug and his Joyce. You and your little cradle snatchings. You can have a double ceremony.

LIZ: If you mean Chris, he's gone.

MERRY: Where?

LIZ: Into the arms of what you'd be corny enough to call the other woman.

MERRY: Who?

LIZ: Debby.

MERRY: My Debby? That's absurd.

LIZ: That's what I thought. They're too close in age.

MERRY: I'll put a stop to this.

LIZ: Hell you will. Chris has given her a job. With my blessings.

MERRY: Doesn't that complete the picture!

LIZ: In a painful way.

MERRY: Everything I've ever had, I share because of you. My award. My daughter. My husband. Isn't there anything that's mine?

LIZ: Your bile.

MERRY: My righteous anger.

LIZ: What a preacher you'd make.

MERRY: Because I don't have the morals of a yellow dog?

LIZ: I have great respect for the morals of yellow dogs.

MERRY: One come in the yard, we'd kick it out.

LIZ: They're refreshingly loyal.

MERRY: They'd hump a snake if it stood still.

LIZ: I've never tried snakes.

MERRY: A miracle.

LIZ: Now I'm a slut?

MERRY: You said it.

LIZ: What're *you* saying?

MERRY: How many men *have* you had?

LIZ: Is that the test?

MERRY: How many?

LIZ: How many before you're a slut?

MERRY: Three.

LIZ: (*giving up*) Kick me out of the yard.

MERRY: How many besides my husband?

LIZ: Three sailors and a jockey, but never your husband. (*she slams a suitcase closed*) Which at this point I dearly regret.

That's it for MERRY. She gets very tall in her indignation.

MERRY: What is astonishing is you have no idea why I truly hate you at this point.

LIZ looks stricken at this word "hate."

MERRY: It's not because of your jealousy over my work—

LIZ: Oh, Jesus, your work—

MERRY: But because you lack the moral sensibility to appreciate what I have lost in Doug.

LIZ: Less than nothing.

MERRY: Liar.

LIZ: A possession. You lost more in that bear.

MERRY: That is one thing of mine you won't keep.

She strides over, grabs Hamburger off the bed.

LIZ: Take him. That's one thing that won't talk back so you can turn conveniently to hate, of all godawful exaggerations.

MERRY: I am not such a woman.

LIZ: You're right. You're part such a woman.

MERRY: Meaning?

LIZ: Cunt.

MERRY swings the bear at LIZ, hitting her across the head. LIZ grabs at the bear, knocking MERRY on the cheek with her elbow in so doing. MERRY is stunned, falls back against a chair.

LIZ scoops up the bear. MERRY grabs its leg. A short tug, and the leg comes off.

MERRY: You see!

LIZ screams at this outrage. She clutches the bear to her.

MERRY, just as furious, grabs at it. Its stomach tears open, and the stuffing pours out. It clings in bits to LIZ's clothes as it snows to the floor.

MERRY looks in astonishment. LIZ is in tears.

LIZ: Filthy filthy filthy filthy...

MERRY backs away from LIZ's rage. She hesitates at the door, wanting now to say something. But it is too late. She goes out.

CUT TO:

[INTERIOR—MERRY'S APARTMENT—NIGHT

The suite is jammed with well-wishers. Noise, New Year's Party favors, hats, streamers, the works. But no MERRY.

A COUPLE comes in. The MAID takes their wraps, heads for the bedroom. WE GO with her.

INTERIOR—BEDROOM—NIGHT

The bedroom is dark except for the light of the party in the next room. The MAID enters, dumps the coats on the bed. She goes out.

WE STAY on bed. We notice the dim outline of MERRY sitting at the head of the bed. WE GO in slowly on her. She is watching the party, her face deeply sad.

INTERIOR—LIVING ROOM—NIGHT

MERRY is suddenly striding out of the bedroom, her coat on. JULES, turns, sees her, smiles.

JULES: Darling, I've been looking for you.

MERRY'S face is set as she strides up to the banquet table.

MERRY: Happy New Year, Jules.

She yanks an opened bottle of champagne from its ice bucket. She wraps it in a towel. She heads for the door.

JULES: Where're you going?

MERRY: A party.

Out she goes, leaving JULES confused, to say the least.

CUT TO:

INTERIOR—CONNECTICUT HOUSE—NIGHT

There are two wing-back calico-covered chairs facing the crackling fireplace. LIZ sits on one, her heels upon the chair. She's in jeans, a brandy in one hand, a cigarette in the other. She watches the fire.

SHE HEARS a car pull up outside. Startled, she looks up.

HER P.O.V.

Shooting through the glass top of a Dutch door, we see a yellow Checker cab outside. MERRY in mink, gets out, is paying the driver. She holds the towel-wrapped bottle of champagne.

ON LIZ

She looks back at the fire, remains rooted.

ON DOOR

Shooting from inside, we see MERRY come up to the glass topped door, rap on it. She's calling LIZ's name.

LIZ: Come in.

MERRY opens the door, hurries in out of the cold. She stomps her feet, maneuvers out of her mink while still holding on to the towel business.

MERRY: Do you know how much it costs to take a cab here from New York? Ninety dollars. Ninety. I tipped him five, was that enough?

LIZ doesn't reply, she looks at the fire. MERRY notes this. She comes over, sits in the unoccupied chair. She lifts her feet to the fire.

MERRY: Doesn't that feel good? (*no reply from* LIZ) Do you have glasses?

She lets the towel fall from the bottle. It is without cork.

LIZ flicks the cigarette into the fire, gets up, goes out of frame. MERRY calls after her.

MERRY: I hated my party.

LIZ comes back almost immediately with two wine glasses. MERRY takes them both, sets one on the floor, pours into the other.

MERRY: Damn, the bubbles are gone.

MERRY hands the glass to LIZ.

LIZ: Thank you.

MERRY is encouraged to hear LIZ speak at last. She picks up the other glass, pours flat champagne into it.

MERRY: I'm not much good at apologizing, I guess I never have, actually, but I am now.

LIZ: You don't need to.

MERRY: I certainly do. I couldn't hate you, and even if sometimes I do, I shouldn't say it. You're my oldest friend. What else we got in life?

LIZ: Our oldest enemies.

MERRY: As the years go on, honey, they begin to look alike.

LIZ sips her champagne, makes a face. MERRY sips hers too.

MERRY: (*indicating glass*) Isn't this awful?

LIZ: I've been thinking about us.

MERRY: Really?

LIZ: We're terrific.

MERRY: You don't say.

LIZ: We've accomplished a hell of a lot for one lifetime. What we deserve is a rest.

MERRY: And we shouldn't always argue.

LIZ: You're right. You know what we should do? Take a year off, sail around the Greek Isles. Only sleep with guys who can't pronounce our names. All Greeks.

MERRY: I couldn't do that.

LIZ: Just the fishermen.

MERRY: I mean I couldn't—how would I do such a thing?

LIZ: Simple. Just go there and let it happen.

MERRY: I wouldn't know how to start—what I would say—

She's obviously thinking it out.

LIZ: All my life I've wanted men to find something mysterious and seductive in my work, some poetry.

MERRY: (*a sigh*) Me too.

LIZ gives her a disbelieving glance, goes back to her thought.

LIZ: Now let them find the poetry in my body and forget my books.

They watch the fire, into their thoughts. The clock above the fire begins to ring the twelfth hour. They both look up at it, see its hands standing straight up.

MERRY lifts her glass, in the way of a silent toast, smiles at LIZ. LIZ just stares at her a while, as if studying her, while the clock chimes on. It ends. At last—

LIZ: Merry, do me a favor.

MERRY: What?

LIZ: Kiss me.

MERRY is trying to figure out whether she should be shocked.

MERRY: After all these years, you're going to tell me there's something strange about you?

LIZ: (*low*) This is New Year's Eve, I want the press of human flesh and you're the only human flesh around . . . kiss me.

MERRY: (*also low*) You're serious.

The two women look at each other. By silent agreement they lean across the space between the two wing-backed chairs. Beyond them, the fire flickers.

Their lips join in one, soft kiss.

They pull back. LIZ lifts her glass, toasts MERRY. MERRY silently returns the toast.

They both drink.

FADE OUT

SOPHIE'S CHOICE

A Universal release of an ITC Films, Inc. Production. Producers, Alan J. Pakula and Keith Barish. Director, Alan J. Pakula. Screenplay by Alan J. Pakula. Based on the novel *Sophie's Choice* by William Styron. Director of Photography, Nestor Almendros. Film Editor, Evan Lottman. Production Designer, George Jenkins. Associate Producer and Production Manager, William C. Gerrity. Executive Producer, Martin Starger. Executive for Production, Howard P. Alston. Music, Marvin Hamlisch. Production Executive, Earl F. Wroten Jr. Art Director, John J. Moore. First Assistant Director, Alex Hapsas. Running time, 157 minutes. 1982.

CAST

SOPHIE	Meryl Streep
NATHAN	Kevin Kline
STINGO	Peter MacNicol
YETTA	Rita Karen
LESLIE LAPIDUS	Greta Turken
MORRIS FINK	Josh Mostel
LIBRARIAN	John Rothman
ENGLISH TEACHER	David Wohl
RUDOLPH HOESS	Gunther Maria Halmer
FRAU HOESS	Ulli Fessl
EMMI HOESS	Melanie Pianka
NARRATOR	Josef Sommer

It is as if Sophie were falling backwards, in the dark, down a broken, winding stair, and any sense of balance would only delay this journey's purpose. No single personality could expect to "integrate" in this mortal life the choice that Sophie has had to make. Any personality, given its memory, must become by turns intolerable or irrelevant if you have been, as Sophie has, the mother who answered the drunken Nazi officer on the death camp selection dock. He asked which of her two children, the boy or the girl, she wanted killed. Only one. *Decide quick or it's both.*

Sophie lives with her lies about what happened to her children and her parents and herself, because to "adjust" herself to the "truth" doesn't make anything more manageable, just more acute. There is no place inside where *then* can't get at *now*—even in a present tense awash with music, health, freedom, even ecstasy. Sophie Zawistowska tries to drown her past in them all after World War II when she comes to America and falls in love with Nathan Landau. They meet when one day he scoops up her collapsed body from the floor of the library, where she has come to find the poems of Emily Dickinson, having just heard them in her English language class. Nathan takes home his new-found, anemic treasure to feed, heal, and love her.

Health floods back into Sophie. She and the relationship bloom. But then their affair violently erupts, tenderly mends, erupts again. Nathan is insane with, among other demons, an excoriating guilt at what was done to the millions of humans enslaved and incinerated by the Nazis during the time when Sophie's life was garbage in their hands. And her survival, right here in front of him, is the spit in Nathan's eye. Pumped by amphetamines and alcohol, Nathan demands to know what it was she did that *she* survived. Why her? What did she *do* for her captors? He demands she do it now, again, for him. They are carrying too much shame and love for any two people to bear, but my God, how these two do love each other.

Sophie is so beautiful and so sensually alive that she is a kind of angel to the story's narrator, Stingo, who moves into the large pink house in Brooklyn where Sophie and Nathan have both taken rooms. Stingo, a virgin, is virtually paralyzed by Sophie's radiance, and by what he overhears of Nathan and Sophie's lovemaking. The opening shot of Sophie's face, faint and hovering, is described in the script as having "an expression of supplication, yearning that might be erotic or religious."

Stingo adores her, longs for her, and finally does get to love and live with Sophie for a few days at the end of her life. But Sophie, having left with Stingo for his home in the South, and finally having told him the truth about her choice in the death camp, must return to Nathan. To death, for both of them, in each other's arms. As she had once explained to Stingo about Nathan's violent threats, "I did not fear death. I feared simply death taking him and him alone, leaving me behind."

The Stingo to whom Sophie finally layers back her whole story is a twenty-two-year-old aspiring writer newly up from the South. He describes himself as hardly more than an "exposed nerve with nothing very much to say. I wanted beyond hope or dreaming to be a writer, but my spirit had remained land-locked, unacquainted with love and a stranger to death." She is touched by his eager solemnity. She lets his open sympathies cordon off a place where she can begin to release the truth of what has happened to her. In the first excerpt below, Sophie begins to talk to Stingo about how she arrived in the death camp, but she is still holding back much of the truth, as much from herself as from Stingo. In the second excerpt, Nathan bursts in upon Stingo and Sophie, exploding in one of his paranoid rages, accusing them of disgusting betrayals they have never committed. In the third excerpt, Sophie finally reveals to Stingo the truth about her father, a virulent anti-Semite whom she had been portraying as a friend to the Jews of Poland. Stingo is too sheltered to know they've never had one.

The triangle binding Sophie and Nathan and Stingo has all the more grip because of the affection between the two men. Stingo asks, "How could I have failed to have the most helpless crush on such a generous, mind- and life-enlarging mentor, pal, savior, sorcerer? Nathan was utterly, fatally glamorous." Despite the occasional psychotic diatribes, Nathan seems truly enthusiastic about Stingo's work. And since this is Stingo's first book, he's parched for just such encouragement, particularly from one obviously so well-read. Nathan's rooms look like the attic of a library, stacked with journals and books and files. What Stingo doesn't at first know is that Nathan's academic credentials and prestigious, high-security research at Pfizer pharmaceuticals are completely made up . . . a lie.

The fourth selection, a scene in Sophie's flashback narrative to Stingo, occurs in the house of Reichsführer Rudolph Hoess, Commandant of Auschwitz-Birkenau. Before marrying her off to his disciple, Sophie's father had ensured her usefulness to his career by perfecting her German and secretarial skills. These now allow her to enter the special elite of prisoners, the house slaves. She sleeps in the basement of the Hoess house, which, in the very middle of a death camp, is an appalling oasis of tidy, middle-class comforts. Frau Hoess is worried about delousing the filth she is forced to use for household help. She's worried about her husband's job security. Hoess is a loving daddy whose children refuse to eat their lunch till he comes home from work and joins them. He suffers from severe tension headaches. Working in an upstairs office as a typist/stenographer, Sophie throws herself on the Reichsführer's mercy and body, begging only that her surviving child, who might still be alive in the children's camp, be spared in the adoption program. Hoess will seem to agree in the scene, but he is being transferred, and he will not keep his promise. When Sophie comes to America, she comes as a sole survivor. When she dies with Nathan, Stingo and we are her only heirs.

SCENE 1 INCLUDING MONOLOGUE 1

(*Note*: Stingo is just coming home from a horribly frustrating episode with a young woman named Leslie, who likes to talk dirty Freud and engage in industrial-size kissing matches, but who is horrified at consummation. It would be disloyal to her therapist.)

[EXTERIOR—STREET IN FRONT OF LESLIE'S HOUSE—NIGHT

STINGO emerges from the door and his lonely figure, shoulders slouched, totally broken, walks away from the camera.

NARRATOR: (*VO*) I had come to a critical extremity in my life. This extremity took the form of the craggy rock of sex, upon which I had obviously though inexplicably foundered. I was left with a sense of aching emptiness and failure and I began to wonder if I was doomed to lead a life of sterile celibacy and isolation.]

EXTERIOR—YETTA'S ROOMING HOUSE—NIGHT
A forlorn and bedraggled STINGO climbs the steps and disappears inside the door.

INTERIOR—ENTRANCE HALL—NIGHT

STINGO enters. The door to SOPHIE's room opens.

SOPHIE: (*VO, happy and relieved*) Nathan, my darling, I'm just so glad you're home.

She appears at the top of the staircase, dressed in NATHAN's robe. She looks down and sees STINGO and her face falls in disappointment.

SOPHIE: (*continued, trying to hide her disappointment*) Stingo!

STINGO: Jes' little ol' Stingo.

SOPHIE: Would you like to come up and have a drink? A nighthat, Nathan calls it.

STINGO: (*smiles*) A night*cap*.

SOPHIE: It is not the same?

STINGO: Not if you plan to swallow one. (*he walks up the stairs to her*) Is Nathan doing one of his all night numbers at the lab?

SOPHIE: I think he must be. You know Nathan, when he's involved, he loses track of time.

INTERIOR—SOPHIE'S ROOM—NIGHT

They enter the room.

STINGO: Hey, you've changed all the furniture around.

SOPHIE: Sometimes when I can't sleep, I move furniture.

She pours him a drink.

STINGO: (*easing himself into a chair*) God I love it here, I'm just so glad you couldn't sleep.

SOPHIE: You are talking funny . . . No? You hurt your mouth?

STINGO: (*embarrassed*) I . . . bit my tongue.

SOPHIE: Do you want me to get you something for it?

STINGO: Really, all it needs is to be left alone. (*changing the* subject) This is about the third or fourth time you've moved this room around . . .

SOPHIE: It is good because while you do it you don't think about nothing else.

STINGO: (*smiles*) I'd better try it.

SOPHIE: (*taking up his palm and looking into it like a mock palmist*) You will not have to move furniture. You will move mountains.

STINGO: (*smiles wryly*) I . . . I can't even move my tongue.

SOPHIE: (*laughs*) Maybe you moved it too much!

STINGO: (*passionately*) Oh, God, Sophie, why isn't the world made up of women like you?

SOPHIE: (*Touched, she takes up his palm again.*) I see many many women in your life. Beautiful women who adore you, who make much love with you.

STINGO: They all look like you, I hope.

SOPHIE: Oh, much more beautiful. Much more good. Much more strong. One stands out. a wonderful, bright, sexy lady who becomes your wife. I see it now . . . I see the two of you making love and sleeping happily together in the same bed for many many years.

STINGO: Some times I think I'm going to be alone forever.

SOPHIE: I am not fair with you. Because you are American and you are young and talented, I think: Stingo, oh, he has no *real* problems!

STINGO: You don't know if I am talented. You haven't read anything I've written. Hell, *I* don't know if I'm *really* talented!

SOPHIE: I never ask you about your book, what it is about, because I know writers often don't like to talk about their work.

STINGO: It's about a boy... A twelve year old boy. It takes place in one year. The year his mother died.

SOPHIE: It is how you say? Autobiographical?

STINGO: Only to some extent.

SOPHIE: I didn't know your mother died.

STINGO: (*half smiling*) When I was twelve.

SOPHIE: It must be terrible to have to deal with a parent's death when you're so young and you need them so much.

STINGO: I never really dealt with it. Maybe that's why I'm writing about it now.

SOPHIE: You loved your mother very much.

STINGO: Not enough.

SOPHIE: Not enough?

STINGO looks away and then he turns to her.

STINGO: The winter of the year she died was one of the coldest winters we ever had. I was supposed to come home first thing after school and put some more wood on the fire for her. She couldn't do it herself. The cancer'd hit her bones. She'd just sit there all alone by the fire, reading these long novels. One afternoon at school a friend invited me to see his new car. I forgot all about going home. We saw his new car and played in the snow and went ice skating. It was one of the happiest afternoons of my life. When I got home that night, she was sitting there, helpless, half frozen from the cold. She had counted on me to help keep her alive. And I... I just forgot about her. That was the only time my father ever beat me. I was glad he did. She died a few months later. And I thought, if I'd only remembered to go home that afternoon, and put wood on the fire, maybe she wouldn't have died.

SOPHIE: It is what is so terrible about outliving the people we love. The guilt.

STINGO: Your father?

SOPHIE: And my mother. And my husband.

STINGO: (*surprised*) You were married.

SOPHIE: When I was very young. To an instructor at the University—a disciple of my father's.

STINGO: (*quietly*) They all died?

SOPHIE: My father and my husband were killed by the Nazis.

STINGO: Were they in the Polish army?

SOPHIE shakes her head.

STINGO: Was it because of your father's anti-Nazi writing?

SOPHIE: I don't *know* why. It makes no sense. At first our lives was not changed very much by the German occupation. My father and my husband still taught at the University. I went to church many times to thank God for having spared my family. But one morning, when I prayed at Mass, I had a premonition. I run from the church to the university. There was a great crowd of people near the main gate in front of the courtyard and there were hundreds of German soldiers with rifles and machine guns. They wouldn't let me pass. And then I saw this older woman whose husband was teaching la chimie, you know, chemistry. She was hysterical and crying and she fell into my arms saying "Oh they are all gone, they have been taken away! All of them." I couldn't believe it. And then I saw these closed vans going down the street, and then I believed it.

STINGO holds her hand more tightly.

SOPHIE: They were taken to the Concentration Camp of Sachsenhausen and were shot to death.

STINGO: (*his voice hardly above a whisper*) And your mother?

SOPHIE: We went to Warsaw, my mother and me. For two years we lived quiet, safe, until she start to die of la consumption. Tuberculosis.

STINGO: (*barely even a whisper now*) And you? How...?
Why...?

SOPHIE: Why did they take me to the concentration camp?

STINGO: (*apologizing for his curiosity*) I'm sorry.

SOPHIE: It's alright. (*pause*) I thought that meat might help
make my mother stronger. So one day I went to the country
and I bought a ham. I hid the meat under my skirt and
pretended I was pregnant. On the train back to Warsaw the
Germans stopped me. I was so frightened. They saw my
fear, reached under my skirt and pulled out the ham.
(*pause*) I was sent to Auschwitz.

STINGO: (*incredulous*) You were sent to Auschwitz because of a
ham?

SOPHIE: I was sent to Auschwitz because they saw I was afraid.

STINGO picks up her arms, and gently touches the scars on her
wrists.

SOPHIE: You have already figured out what they mean.

STINGO: You tried to commit suicide.

SOPHIE nods.

STINGO: In Auschwitz.

SOPHIE: It was *after*. After I was released from Auschwitz.
After we had been liberated.

STINGO: After you were safe?

SOPHIE: It was in the refugee camp in Sweden. I knew that
Christ had turned his face away from me. I knew that only a
Jesus who had no pity and no longer cared for me could
permit the people I loved to be killed and let me live with
shame. I went to the church and knelt and I took a piece of
glass and cut my wrists.

She sees STINGO's bewilderment.

SOPHIE: (*continued*) There is so much you could not understand. So much I can not tell.

STINGO: Have you told Nathan?

She seems frightened by the thought. She looks at him, searching his eyes, as if wondering how much she can trust him.

STINGO bends down and kisses the scars on her wrists.

STINGO: (continued) Trust me, Sophie.

There is the sound of the front door opening.

SOPHIE: (her face suddenly alive with hope) It must be Nathan.

She rushes out of the room.

[INTERIOR—HALLWAY—NIGHT

SOPHIE: Ah, Astrid.

ASTRID WEINSTEIN: (as she climbs the stairs) I'm on Night Duty at Brooklyn Hospital this week. My patient's an old lady who's meaner than my mother. If you can believe. I think she stays alive by keeping angry. Sophie, don't you ever sleep?

INTERIOR—SOPHIE'S ROOM—NIGHT

SOPHIE returns to the room, the hope drained from her face.

SOPHIE: Would you like another drink?

STINGO: Sure.

SOPHIE: I think I have another too.

STINGO: The bottle's empty.

SOPHIE: There is some more in Nathan's room.

INTERIOR—HALLWAY—NIGHT

SOPHIE and STINGO walk across the hallway to NATHAN'S room.

STINGO: Maybe you'd feel better if you just called Nathan at the lab.

SOPHIE: He doesn't like for me to call him at work. (pause, embarrassed by her confession) I tried. An hour ago. There was no answer.

STINGO: The switchboard's probably turned off.

INTERIOR—NATHAN'S ROOM—NIGHT

They turn on the light. The room is still covered with books of
every description. Magazine articles of interest that have been
torn out and are scattered around. Periodicals of all kinds: *The
Bulletin of the Atomic Scientists,* biology and chemistry journals, little literary magazines, magazines and books reflecting
the extraordinary range of NATHAN's mind and curiosity.

Somehow, being in his room, surrounded by all his books and
papers, seems to make SOPHIE more afraid.

SOPHIE: Sometimes when Nathan can't sleep at night he gets up
and walks around the city. He goes into all kinds of
neighborhoods. Once, he came back and his eye was black,
his jaw was swollen. I was afraid it might be broken.
(*abruptly*) Oh, Stingo, I don't know where Nathan is. He
could be hurt. I think we should call the police.

STINGO: Why don't we just wait another couple of hours until
there's someone on the switchboard at the Laboratory. He
probably just worked late, got tired and fell asleep.

SOPHIE: Of course. I'm sure you're right.

STINGO takes their glasses, puts them on NATHAN's desk, pours
their drinks.]

(*Note*: The scene can be played in Sophie's bedroom from
when she runs out to greet Nathan and returns instead with
Stingo, clear through to the next time she runs out of her
bedroom to greet Nathan. But the actors may wish to continue
the dialogue through to where Stingo makes suggestions as to
Nathan's whereabouts in order to soothe Sophie's anxiety. In
that case, Astrid can be played by a third actor offstage, and
the bottle need not be empty, removing the need to move to
Nathan's room. The scene in Nathan's room continues only
briefly before Nathan's entrance.)

MONOLOGUE 2

[NATHAN brings in a bottle of wine and glasses. The pupils of his eyes are the size of dimes. His face has softened somewhat, no longer quite the rancorous mask it had been only moments before. But the fierce straight-jacketed tension remains in the muscles of the cheek and neck and the sweat pours forth; it stands out on his brow in droplets. As he hands them the wine glasses, WE SEE the great crescent of soaked white fabric underneath his arms.

He pours wine into their glasses. SOPHIE'S hand holding the out-stretched glass is quivering. She raises her glass as if out of dumb reflexive obedience.

STINGO reaches forward and lightly, affectionately taps the back of NATHAN'S arm.

STINGO: Now, let's cut all this ugly shit and let's all relax while you tell us, for Christ sake, just tell us exactly what the hell it is we're going to celebrate! Man, tonight we want to make all the toasts to you!

NATHAN withdraws his arm. He raises his glass and downs the wine in a single swallow.]

NATHAN: This toast is in honor of my complete disassociation from you two creeps. (*with a tip of his glass at* SOPHIE) Disassociation from *you*, the Coony Chiropractic Cunt of King's County. (*then to* STINGO) And from you, the Dreary Dregs of Dixie.

NATHAN'S eyes are as lifeless as billiard balls, sweat drains from his face in torrents.

NATHAN: You have not fooled me, young Stingo, since you graciously allowed me to discover your ingrained and unregenerate racism, that night you let me read the first part of your magnum Southern opus.

[STINGO: (*incredulous—stunned*) What?]

NATHAN: (*in a Southern accent imitative of* STINGO'S) You have a pretty snappy talent in the traditional Southern mode. But you also have all the old cliches. I guess I didn't want to bruise your feelings. You may be writing the first Southern comic book.

His voice loses the faint throaty Negroid quality and in moist metamorphosis the Southern accent fades and dies, replaced by thorny Polish diphthongs that are in almost exact mimicry of Sophie's own speech.

NATHAN: (*turning to* SOPHIE) Peut-etre after all dese mawnths, you kin explain de mystewy of why you are here, you of all people, walking dese stweets, dwenched in enticing perfumery, engaged in suweptitious venery wiff not wan but two— count dem, ladies and gentlemen—two chiropractors. In short, making hay while de sun shine, to employ an old bwomide, while at Auschwitz de ghosts off de millions off de dead still seek an answer. (*suddenly dropping the parody*) Tell me why it is, old beauteous Zawistowska, that *you* inhabit the land of the living. Did splendid little tricks and strategems spring from that lovely head of yours to allow you to breathe the clear Polish air while the multitudes at Auschwitz *choked slowly on the gas*? A reply to this would be most welcome.

[A terrible drawn-out groan escapes SOPHIE.

SOPHIE: No! No! Menteur! Lies!]

NATHAN: Did the same anti-semitism for which Poland has gained such worldwide renown—did a similar anti-semitism guide your own destiny, help you along, protect you, in a manner of speaking, so that you became one of the minuscule handful of people who lived while the millions died? (*his voice harsh, cutting, cruel*) Explanation, please!

[SOPHIE: No! No!

STINGO: Nathan, for Christ sake, lay off her!

NATHAN: What fine handiwork of subterfuge did you create in order that *your* skin might be saved while the others went up in smoke? Did you cheat, connive, lay your sweet little ass . . .

SOPHIE: (*a deep groan*) No!

STINGO goes toward NATHAN, his knees quaking.

STINGO: Look, you bastard . . .

SOPHIE throws herself between STINGO and NATHAN.

SOPHIE: For God's sake, Stingo, get out! Get out!

He stumbles out of the room, and down the steps and out the door.]

MONOLOGUE 3

[INTERIOR—SOPHIE'S ROOM—NIGHT

There are no lights on in the room.

SOPHIE, silhouetted by the light of the street lamp, is sitting on the window seat, staring out the window. It is her place of waiting. For NATHAN.

A half empty bottle of whiskey sits on the floor beside her. All of her suitcases are packed. The room is totally stripped.

THE DOORWAY OF SOPHIE'S ROOM

As STINGO enters.

In spite of himself, STINGO's heart is broken by the sight of her, still waiting for NATHAN.

STINGO: Sophie, I want to understand.]

CLOSE SHOT—SOPHIE

She turns toward him.

SOPHIE: (*reacting to his pain*) You think that if you know the truth about me you will understand. And then you will be able to forgive me all my lies.

[STINGO: I promise I won't leave you.

SOPHIE: You must never promise that. No one—*no* one—should ever promise that.

She pours herself a drink. There is no sense of drunkenness. The only thing that betrays that somewhere inside she is struggling for control is the shaking of her hand when she holds the bottle.]

SOPHIE: The truth does not always make it easier to understand.

He walks into the room and sits down in a chair across from her. Quietly, almost stealthily, as if afraid that any sudden noise or motion might frighten her away.

SOPHIE puts the bottle down and finishes her drink.

There is the sound of bells from outside. The sound of an approaching Good Humour ice cream truck heralding its good tidings to the children of the neighborhood.

SOPHIE turns to the window.

EXTERIOR—SOPHIE'S P.O.V. OF THE STREET BELOW—NIGHT

Children outside the Pink Palace surrounding the Good Humour truck, buying ice cream, laughing and yelling in the warm summer night.

INTERIOR—SOPHIE'S ROOM—CLOSE SHOT—SOPHIE—NIGHT

She is looking off into the distance.

SOPHIE: The truth. I'm not sure I know what is the truth after all the lies I've told.

The sounds of the Good Humour truck and the shouting, laughing children in the street fade away.

There is a beat of silence and then we hear the sound of the child's flute playing the simple exercise we heard at the beginning of the film.

WE CUT TO SOPHIE'S P.O.V. outside the window of the street. It is slowly engulfed in darkness.

A thin slit of light cuts through the blackness, slashing across the screen like a tear or rip, from top to bottom. The CAMERA MOVES toward the narrow slit.

EXTERIOR—RAILROAD YARD—NIGHT

WE ARE LOOKING OUT through a crack in the boarded up window of a train. WE SEE a glimpse of a railroad yard at night, a soldier in Nazi uniform is stationed across the tracks in the distance. The soldier and the railroad yard seem to slide behind us as the train begins to move.

The screen now bleaches to the harsh and empty white we saw at the beginning of the film. The flute fades away, leaving us in total silence.

A STILL PHOTOGRAPH GRADUALLY BLEEDS INTO THE WHITE.

INTERIOR—SOPHIE'S FATHER'S STUDY—STILL PHOTOGRAPH—DAY

This and the three still scenes that follow are clearly from a series of photographs taken on the same day. Formally posed, as if her father had paid for some Cracow photographer to come in and take pictures of him with his daughter. They are aged and brown, images that have faded into time in the pages of an album.

The CAMERA STARTS on a bust of Goethe on top of a desk—forbidding, awesome, Godlike.

The CAMERA MOVES DOWN the photograph over the objects on an old desk. It stops for a moment at a picture in an antique frame. A proud, conservative Polish man is holding a baby in what is obviously a post-christening photograph. He stands in front of the great cathedral of Cracow.

SOPHIE: (VO) My father . . . all the bad things in my life begin with him.

The CAMERA PANS past the photograph over the typewriter on the desk and settles on the image of a man in his late thirties, who, like the bust of Goethe, looks awesome and Godlike. It is the father who was holding the baby in the photograph on the desk, a few years older. He has a face of authority that seems never to have been young.

The CAMERA MOVES INTO the face of the father who is turned away from his work and looking down benignly . . . at Sophie as a child. She is standing at his feet, looking up at him.

DISSOLVE TO:

ANOTHER STILL PHOTOGRAPH IN SOPHIE'S FATHER'S STUDY . . .

This time SOPHIE (in the same dress, the father in the same suit, everything on the desk the same) is on her father's lap. The father is holding his great hand over her tiny hand, pressing her finger on one of the keys of the ancient typewriter, as if he is teaching her to type. His great hand controls her tiny one. She looks up at him for approval.

SOPHIE: (*VO*) Oh, how can I explain . . . how much I loved my father!

DISSOLVE TO:

INTERIOR—STILL PHOTOGRAPH—SOPHIE'S LIVING ROOM IN CRA-COW—DAY

SOPHIE (the same age, she and her father dressed as in the other photographs) playing the piano. Her father is sitting beside her, smiling encouragingly at her efforts.

SOPHIE: (*VO*) My father believed that human perfection was a possibility if we only had the strength of will. In everything, he tried to will me perfect. When my mother taught me to play the piano, he was convinced that I would be a concert pianist. A perfect one.

The photograph begins to fade.

SOPHIE: (*VO*) But when it came time for me to play in public, I was so terrified that I would fail his expectations that I could not play at all. After that, when my father was in the house, I was not allowed to play the piano.

INTERIOR—STILL PHOTOGRAPH—SOPHIE'S BEDROOM IN CRA-COW—DAY

(The father is in the same suit as in the other photographs.)
SOPHIE is kneeling on the floor, praying in front of the crucifix over her bed.

SOPHIE: I prayed to God every night to forgive me for being so unworthy. For always disappointing him.

THE CAMERA PANS UP the photograph.

The father is standing beside SOPHIE, listening to her prayers. It is as if she is praying to him as well as to God.

SOPHIE: (VO) I prayed to Him to make me worthy of my father.

INTERIOR—FATHER'S STUDY—CRACOW—DAY

The bust of Goethe on top of the desk as we saw in the photographs before.

The CAMERA PANS DOWN the desk and stops momentarily at a wedding picture where the christening picture had been. It has been taken outside the same cathedral. In the middle is the father. On one side is SOPHIE in a wedding dress, looking up at him. On the other side is the young groom, also looking up at him.

The groom's face is turned a little away from the camera and is a bit in shadow.

SOPHIE: (VO) I was a grown woman, fully come of age, married, before I realized that I loathed my father past all telling.

INTERIOR—FATHER'S STUDY—CRACOW—DAY

The CAMERA PANS DOWN to SOPHIE, a grown woman of nineteen, sitting at her father's desk, typing at the same ancient typewriter we saw before. There are earphones in her ears.

We realize now it is not another photograph, but live action.

We hear the sound of a very tinny voice slowly dictating a speech. It is as removed from the sound of life as those voices we've heard on very early records.

The CAMERA FOLLOWS the earphones to an old European cylinder as it circles under a needle from which her father's voice squawks out.

MEDIUM SHOT—SOPHIE TYPING

SOPHIE: (*VO*) It was the winter of 1938. My father had worked for weeks in private on a speech called POLAND'S JEWISH PROBLEM. I was not surprised. I had known his feelings against the Jews, that they were alien and had no right to compete with honest Poles for jobs.

I was to type the speech that afternoon and deliver it to him at the University where he was to speak that night. Ordinarily I typed without listening to his meaning. But this time I found one word repeated several times. A word I'd never heard him use before. "The only solution for the Jewish problem," he concluded, "was Die Vernichtung." Extermination.

SOPHIE rewinds the cylinder and replays the same section. As if she cannot believe what she has heard. She turns off the machine, takes out the earphones, and sits there, shaken.

CAMERA MOVES IN on the page she is typing to a CLOSE SHOT of the word: DIE VERNICHTUNG—(Extermination.)

SOPHIE: (*VO*) I had had little to do with Jewish people. And until I heard that word, I'd had little curiosity about them. But I couldn't go on typing.

EXTERIOR—GHETTO STREET IN CRACOW—SOPHIE'S P.O.V.—EVENING

Life in the Jewish Quarter.

SOPHIE: (*VO*) I hadn't planned to visit the Ghetto when I left the house that afternoon, but without knowing it, something inside of me must have impelled me there. I watched the Jewish women gossiping with each other, or hurrying home with bags of food. I heard them call their children in from play. For all these people, these women, these men, these children: DIE VERNICHTUNG . . . Extermination.

EXTERIOR—GHETTO STREET—CRACOW—EVENING

SOPHIE standing in the shadows watching the life around her.

INTERIOR—PINK PALACE—SOPHIE'S ROOM—1947

SOPHIE: For hours I stood there in the shadows, watching the people my father had condemned to die. I forgot about the speech, about my father waiting, til it was very late.

I barely had time to finish the typing and in my nervousness and haste I confused thoughts and sentences until they made no sense.

My father had no time to check the copy before he spoke.

Afterwards he came up to me and in front of my husband and his friends he said to me: "Your intelligence is pulp." I could not find the courage to even question him about the Jews. But he did not trust me after that and neither did my husband.
Oh, I lied about my husband too. I had no more love for him than for a stone faced stranger... I had never seen him before in my life. He was my father's assistant at the University. I only married him, I think, to please my father.

(pause)

The last time I saw my father was when the Germans were taking him away.

EXTERIOR—CRACOW STREET—OUTSIDE THE UNIVERSITY COURT-YARD—DAY

SOPHIE held at bay by Nazi soldiers, watches the vans containing her father and her husband and the other University professors.

EXTERIOR—CRACOW STREET—SOPHIE'S P.O.V.—WIDE ANGLE—DAY

Professors being marched into a van. Among them are her father and her husband. Her father turns toward her. He seems to be looking directly at her.

SOPHIE: At the last second before the van doors slammed shut, he turned and seemed to find me in the crowd. The way he

looked at me I couldn't tell if it was terror, if he was
pleading for me to help. Or was it rage? Rage at what? His
fate? Or me? Yes, rage at me. Because I'd wished him
dead.

The scene turns into a still. The CAMERA MOVES into the still
until the father's face fills the screen. But, as in blowing up a
tiny portion of a photograph it loses definition. The eyes become
black holes, the mouth a gash, the face a blur of movement. It is
as if this nightmare face is staring not just at SOPHIE in the past
but SOPHIE in the present.

INTERIOR—SOPHIE'S ROOM—PINK PALACE—1947—NIGHT

CLOSE SHOT—SOPHIE LOOKING AT THE BLOWUP OF HER FA-
THER'S FACE

She stares at it unblinking, mesmerized. There is total silence
over the shot of SOPHIE.

Through the silence we hear the sound of the train we heard at
the beginning of the sequence.

SOPHIE'S face is engulfed in blackness, relieved only by the
narrow slash of light in the middle of the screen. The sound of a
child's flute is heard again.

INTERIOR—TRAIN—BOARDED UP WINDOW—MORNING

CAMERA MOVES THROUGH the narrow slit of light and peers
through the crack again. The movement of the countryside
indicates the train has picked up speed. The virgin fields slide by
in the gradually breaking early morning light.

The SCREEN BLEACHES TO WHITE. The flute fades away, leaving
us again in total silence.

SCENE 2

INTERIOR—HOESS'S OFFICE—DAY

CLOSE SHOT—SOPHIE as she types. Taking HOESS's dictation.
Her face has no expression on it.

HOESS: (*VO*) To Reichsführer Himmler, SS Headquarters, Berlin. I have given careful thought to the possible reason such a large percentage of Greek Jews who were delivered here have been unfit for work. Bad nutrition at the point of origin, the extreme length of the journey and lastly a trait of character. Ratlösikeit, common to people of Southern climes and therefore to those of weak moral fiber, which simply causes them to fail to withstand the shock of being uprooted. (*politely*) Am I speaking too fast for you?

SOPHIE: Nein, mein Kommandant.

There is a timid knock on the door. He goes over to it and opens it. FRAU HOESS is standing at the door. Her eyes are swollen with weeping.

FRAU HOESS: I do not want to bother you, but I thought maybe, maybe if you went to Berlin and explained to Himmler how unfair his order is, maybe he would change his mind.

HOESS goes to the other side of the door and partially shuts it. But SOPHIE can hear his whispering.

HOESS: There is no appealing the orders I received this morning. We are being transferred out of here and that is the end of it.

FRAU HOESS: Then it is final.

She starts to cry. He walks back inside the room and shuts the door. He seems very disturbed. He goes over to his desk and starts to open more of his mail.

HOESS: (*reading a letter, his face flushed with anger*) They know it's compulsory that they write in German, these blasted people. But they consistently break the rules! Damn them to hell these Polish halfwits!

He hands her the letter.

HOESS: What does it say?

At that instant SOPHIE sees a fearful headache attack HOESS with prodigious speed.

HOESS: My pills, for God's sake, where are my pills!

SOPHIE goes swiftly to the chair next to HOESS'S cot upon which he keeps the bottle of ergotamine he uses to alleviate these attacks. She pours out a glass of water from a carafe and hands it and two tablets of ergotamine to the Commandant, who gulps the medicine down. Then with a groan, his hand clasped to his brow, he sinks down on the cot.

SOPHIE: Shall I call the doctor? The last time I remember he said to you . . .

HOESS: Just be quiet, I can't bear anything now.

He rolls over on his flank and lies there rigid and motionless except for the rise and fall of his chest beneath his shirt. She goes to work: she commences typing. When she turns her eyes in his direction she realizes with a curious mixture of hope and apprehension that he must have been eyeing her from his cot. He beckons to her and she rises and goes to his side.

HOESS: (*in a subdued voice*) It's better. That ergotamine is a miracle.

SOPHIE: I'm glad, mein Kommandant.

HOESS: How did you come here? Not many prisoners are so fortunate as to find a stenographic billet. You may sit down.

She notices that he is still sweating desperately. Supine now, eyes half closed, he lies rigid and wet in a pool of sunlight.

SOPHIE: (*seating herself*) I think it must have been a stroke of fate. (*a pause as she makes a decision*) Fate brought me to you, because I knew only *you* would understand.

HOESS: Understand what?

SOPHIE: That a mistake has been made. (*she hesitates, tumultuously agitated*) My family were passionate German partisans for many years in the vanguard of those countless lovers of the Third Reich who admire National Socialism and the principle of the Führer. My father was to the depths of his soul Judenfeindlich . . .

HOESS: (*with a small groan*) Judenfeindlich, Judenfeindlich. (*with a hoarse sigh*) Jews. Jews! Will I ever be done with Jews!

He reaches into the pocket of his jacket, draped over the other chair at the side of the cot, and takes from it a tinfoil-wrapped chocolate bar.

Stripping the foil from the chocolate, he extends the bar toward her. Hesitant at the outset, surprised . . . she nervously breaks off a piece and pops it into her mouth, knowing that she betrays a greedy eagerness in the midst of her effort to be casual.

And then, to her amazement, he reaches up with his free hand and plucks a little something from the edge of her upper lip; it is, she realizes, a crumb of the chocolate she had eaten, now held between his thumb and forefinger, and she watches as he moves his tar stained fingers slowly toward his lips and deposits the tiny chestnut-brown flake into his mouth.

HOESS: What's the matter? You're white.

SOPHIE: Nothing, mein Kommandant.

HOESS rolls himself off the cot, standing abruptly erect and walking the few paces to the window.

HOESS: Those people in Berlin. If they just understood the magnitude, the complexity! These Jews, they come on and on from all the countries in Europe, countless thousands, millions, like the herring in the spring that swarm into Mecklenberg Bay. I never dreamed the earth contained so many of das Erwählte Volk. (The Chosen People.)

SOPHIE rises from her chair and draws near to him. She bends down and fumblingly plucks the worn and faded pamphlet of her father's from the little crevice in her boot.

SOPHIE: (*flourishing it in front of him, spreading out the title page*) This is one of the earliest Polish documents suggesting a "final solution" to the Jewish problem. I collaborated with my father in writing it. I do earnestly beg you at least to consider it. Perhaps you could begin to see the entire injustice of my imprisonment here . . .

He gives her a look of absolute concentrated penetration as he takes the pamphlet from between her fingers.

HOESS: You maintain, then, that you are innocent.

SOPHIE: Sir, I freely admit my guilt of the minor charge which caused me to be sent here... I am only asking that this misdemeanor be weighed against my record not only as a Polish sympathizer with National Socialism but as an active and involved campaigner in the sacred war against Jews and Jewry. That pamphlet in your hand, mein Kommandant, will prove my point. I implore you... you who have the power to give clemency and freedom... to reconsider my imprisonment in the light of my past good works, and to return me to my life in Warsaw.

HOESS gives the pamphlet a flat little tap with his fingertips.

HOESS: You seem to forget that you are a Pole, and therefore an enemy of the Reich who would remain an enemy even if you were not also judged guilty of a criminal act.

SOPHIE bursts into tears. The tears spill forth and she thrusts her face into her hands. All... all... has failed. She is finished.

She hears the attic door closed upon a squeak of hinges, slowly, gradually, as if by some reluctant force. She is conscious of his boots as he returns toward her, then his fingers grasping her shoulder firmly even before she allows herself to draw her hands away from her eyes and to look up. She forces herself to stop crying. The clamor beyond the intervening door is muffled.

HOESS: (in an unsteady voice) You've been flirting shamelessly with me.

HOESS's eyes are distraught; they give her the impression that he is about to strike her. But then with a great visceral heave he seems to regain possession of himself; his gaze becomes normal. His clutch on her shoulder is hurting her. He makes a nervous choking sound.

HOESS: (relaxing his grip) It's hard to believe you're Polish, with your superb German and the way you look... the fair complexion of your skin and the lines of your face, so typically Aryan. And yet you are what you say you are . . . a Pole. I don't like flirts. I have always detested this quality in women, this crude use of sex to try and seek out a few rewards. And yet . . . and yet it can't be all your fault, you're an extremely attractive woman.

We hear the camp's symphonic death sounds: of metal clangor, of the boxcars' remote colliding booms and the faint keening of a locomotive whistle, mournful and shrill.

HOESS: There is something about the pure and radiant beauty of a certain kind of Aryan woman . . . fair of skin and of hair that inspires me to idolize that beauty.

He yanks her body up against his own. She has a sense of elbows, knees and a scratchy cheese-grater of stubble. He is awkward and his arms around her seem multitudinous, like those of a huge mechanical fly. She holds her breath while his hands at her back try out some sort of massage. And his heart . . . his rampaging galloping heart! Trembling like a very sick man, he gives nothing so bold as a kiss, although she senses some protuberance . . . his tongue or nose . . . mooning restlessly around her bekerchiefed ear. An abrupt knock at the door causes him to break apart from her swiftly.

HOESS: (*soft, miserable*) Scheiss!

He opens the door. His adjutant SCHEFFLER stands again in the doorway.

SCHEFFLER: Begging the Commandant's pardon, but Frau Hoess has a question for the Commandant. Since she has just recovered from a week-long case of die Grippe, Madam wishes to find out whether in the Commandant's judgement, Iphegenie is well enough to accompany her to a matinee. Or should she consult Dr. Schmidt?

HOESS: Tell Frau Hoess, that if *she* thinks the child is well enough to accompany her to a matinee then I would expect she's well enough to accompany her to a matinee.

The AIDE retreats down the stairs. HOESS turns back toward Sophie and walks back to her.

HOESS: (*continued*) I would risk a great deal to have relations with you.

He seems about to touch or grab her again, but he doesn't.

HOESS: If I were not leaving here I would take the risk. But they have got rid of me, and I must go. And so you must go too. I am sending you back to Block Three where you came from. You will go tomorrow.

SOPHIE: (*reaching for the right words to say*) Herr Kommandant, I know I can't ask much for myself and you must act according to the rules. But I beg you to do one thing for me before you send me back. I have a young son in Camp D where all the other boys are prisoners. His name is Jan Zawistowski, age ten. I am afraid for his health. I beg of you to consider some way in which he might be released. His health is frail and he is so very young.

HOESS turns toward her and looks straight at her without blinking. She reaches out and touches his shirt, then clutches at it.

SOPHIE: Please if you have been impressed only the slightest bit by my presence, by my being, I beg you to do this for me. Not to release *me*, just to release my little boy. Please do this for me.

He grabs her wrist and pulls her hand away from his shirt.

HOESS: You think you could get me to contravene proper authority because I expressed some little affection? (*pause*) I find this disgusting!

She throws herself against him, throws her arms around his waist.

SOPHIE: (*begging*) Please! Please! Please!

HOESS'S muscles are stiff with trembling. It is obvious he is finished with her.

SOPHIE: It would not mean contravening authority. There is Lebensborn. Lebensborn. He is a perfect candidate for Lebensborn. You could have my child moved away from the

Children's Camp and into your program of Lebensborn. You could have him sent to the Reich, where he would become a good German. Already he is blond and looks German and speaks perfect German like I do. Don't you see how my little boy Jan would be excellent for Lebensborn?

She falls on her knees in front of him . . . and presses her face against his boots, surrounding them with her arms.

HOESS: (*after a moment*) Alright, I will. Have your son brought here tomorrow. We will see him and then I will arrange for him to be removed from the camp.

SOPHIE: How will I know? How will I know for certain that he has been taken away from here?

HOESS: (*after another pause*) I promise that the child will be removed from this camp and you will hear of his where-abouts from time to time.

SOPHIE: Danke, mein Kommandant, for helping me.

[INTERIOR—STAIRCASE—DAY

SOPHIE descending. On the landing below she looks into the bedroom from which the little girl had emerged with the portable radio. She looks in the room and catches sight of the radio through the open door. She stands in the shadows of the hallway, only a few feet from the bottom of the attic stairs.

SOPHIE: (*VO*) I told myself I dare not take the radio now when there was hope that I might save my son. But I also knew this might be the last chance I would have.

She starts to move into room, then hesitates.

SOPHIE: (*VO*) Perhaps the God I worshipped as a child was still alive in me, the God who rewarded noble acts. I tried to make a pact with him; I would steal the radio for the Underground if he would save my son.

INTERIOR—EMMI'S ROOM—DAY

She moves, heart rampaging, not shedding the fear that clings to her like an evil companion as she sidles her way into the room. She has to walk only a few paces, but even as she does so, she senses something wrong, a ghastly error in tactics and timing: she places her hand on the cool plastic surface of the radio.]

.   .   .   .   .

(*Note*: Neither Frau Hoess nor Scheffler physically enter the office further than the doorway, but neither of these beats has been bracketed; they are both conversations Hoess must have and Sophie must overhear. So a third and fourth actor, or at least appropriate voices from outside the doorway, are required for the full playing of the scene.)

TOOTSIE

A Columbia Pictures presentation. Producers, Sydney Pollack and Dick Richards. Director, Sydney Pollack. Screenplay by Larry Gelbart and Murray Schisgal. Story by Don McGuire and Larry Gelbart. Director of Photography, Owen Roizman. Editors, Fredric Steinkamp and William Steinkamp. Production Designer, Peter Larkin. Executive Producer, Charles Evans. Music, Dave Grusin. Sound Mixer, Les Lazarowitz. Assistant Director, David McGiffert. Running time, 110 minutes. 1982.

CAST

MICHAEL DORSEY/	
DOROTHY MICHAELS	Dustin Hoffman
JULIE	Jessica Lange
SANDY	Teri Garr
RON	Dabney Coleman
LES	Charles Durning
JEFF	Bill Murray
GEORGE FIELDS	Sydney Pollack
JOHN VAN HORN	George Gaynes
APRIL	Geena Davis
RITA	Doris Belack
JACQUI	Ellen Foley
RICK	Peter Gatto
JO	Lynne Thigpen
PHIL WEINTRAUB	Ronald L. Schwary
MRS. MALLORY	Debra Mooney

The opening shot of *Tootsie* establishes Michael Dorsey's love and respect for the profession, the craft, and the art of acting. We watch an actor, with skill and high seriousness of purpose, meticulously transform his appearance—the scar, the moustache, the mouth appliance—and all applied by his own hand, and out of his own makeup kit. And this is just *one* of the consummate identities Michael creates out of himself, even for a reading or a commercial audition. From the age of six, straight on through high school, to professional awards for roles performed in off-off-off-*off* Broadway lofts, to Shakespeare's kings, to prancing fruit in television commercials . . . Michael Dorsey is AN ACTOR. He is an actor with a scrapbook of brilliant reviews and a catalogue of impressive auditions.

Great . . . except nobody'll hire him.

Michael's insistence on absolute integrity in his art is sabotaging his career. Even when he's right, he's never *co*-creative; his demands, even when legitimate, are always unilateral. By now, his reputation as a pain-in-the-ass precedes him. Instead of getting the job, he's told he's too this, or too that, or even too perfect for the part. Michael seems to have one real friend, a struggling playwright (male) with whom he splits the mess of their shared apartment. They both work as waiters at the same noisy New York pub. A surprise party is thrown for Michael's fortieth birthday. He's toasted as "the Ralph Nader of Show Business." But by party's end, he's treated his girlfriend so shabbily that he finds himself alone. Well, not completely alone. One of the guests, Sandy, absolutely idolizes him and is hanging around after everyone has left. Michael has already been divorced once, and he treats women as a dog does a lamppost. But when Sandy refers to an audition she has the next day for a soap opera, Michael stays up through the night to coach her. He even goes with her to the audition, repeatedly insulting her en route to stimulate the rage she'll need for her character. But Sandy is sent back in two seconds, without even getting to read, because she's "not right physically." Oh, that phrase . . . it's a lit fuse of despair. Michael is so angry he demands to see an actor whom he can't stand, but who is working on this soap, and who's also represented by Michael's agent. He's told the actor is gone, in rehearsal for a Broadway opening of *The Iceman Cometh*. Is this *possible*? That Michael's agent didn't even set up a reading for him? No interview? No *nothing*?! He bolts past Sandy, sprints through midday, midtown Manhattan, races up to his agent's office, barges past the secretary, and (in the scene below) demands to know what happened to *his* audition?

George Fields, Michael's agent, tells him. The idea that Michael gets at the end of the scene, once he understands no one is going to hire Michael Dorsey, is to put himself into drag and audition for the soap opera part for which he'd coached Sandy. *Of course* he gets it. He's always been magnificently equipped as an actor; it's as a person that he's been so stuck—all yang, no yin. He's so far off balance he can't even honor the feminine quotient in somebody else. He must first locate it within himself. As Dorothy Michaels, he learns to behave with a generosity of spirit, playfulness, and honesty which he has never allowed himself as a guy. Drag peps and lightens him up. One of the terrific twists of *Tootsie* is that donning the guise of the female doesn't make Michael passively "ladylike." Certainly it civilizes him, but at the same time it increases his daring and valor. When he's not clenching for control, he's so much braver. As his character becomes a huge success, and the inevitable boundaries of disguise begin to tighten, Michael really takes off: He's now an actor who needs somebody to *fire* him. When Michael-inside-Dorothy falls in love with a nurse on the soap opera, and the nurse's real-life father falls in love with Dorothy, who is already being pursued by her drunken leading man, the plot swirls up into the fiascoes and unveilings of great farce.

When Michael reemerges out of Dorothy, it looks like it will be as a relatively whole human being . . . for an actor. It is another one of the refreshments of *Tootsie* that the character of the theatrical agent is written as a nice, hardworking, funny, decent, warm, quite human, human being—a man trying to do his job properly for a client who appears to be nuts.

SCENE

[INTERIOR—CORRIDOR

MICHAEL striding down miles of carpeting, into GEORGE's office.

SECRETARY: (*jumping up*) Michael, he's tied up now. I swear. He strides past into:]

INTERIOR—GEORGE GREY'S OFFICE

GEORGE GREY is around 50, impeccably dressed, talking on the phone. As MICHAEL enters:

GEORGE: (*into phone*) Hold on a second. (*pushes hold*) Michael, can you wait outside, please? I'm talking to the Coast.

MICHAEL: This is a coast, too, George. New York is a coast!

GEORGE: Wait a minute. (*releases "hold;" then, into phone*) Sy, listen—(*beat*) Sy? (*into intercom*) Margret, get him back, will you? I cut myself off.

MICHAEL: Terry Bishop is doing "Iceman Cometh." Why didn't you send *me* up for that, George? You're my agent too.

GEORGE: Stuart Pressman wanted a name.

MICHAEL: Terry Bishop is a name?

GEORGE: No. Michael Dorsey is a name. When you want to send a steak back, Michael Dorsey is a name. Excuse me. I didn't mean that. That was a rotten thing to say. Let me start again. People *know* Terry Bishop. He was on a top rated "soap." Millions of people watch him.

MICHAEL: And that qualifies him to ruin "Iceman Cometh"?

GEORGE: Look, I can't have this conversation. You want to do socially significant theatre in Syracuse for $35 a week? That's your affair... Stuart Pressman wants a name, that's his affair. I know this will disgust you, but a lot of people are in this business to make money.

MICHAEL: Don't make me sound like some flake, George, I'd like to make money, too.

GEORGE: Oh, really? The Harlem Theater for The Blind? Strindberg in the park? The People's Workshop in Syracuse?

MICHAEL: Don't knock Syracuse. It was a revolutionary idea. For one dollar you could see great plays. "Wozzeck," "The Lower Depths," Gerhart Hauptman's "The Weavers."

GEORGE: Oh, I didn't know about Gerhart Hauptman's "The Weavers." Very shrewd career move.

MICHAEL: I got great reviews from the New York critics in Syracuse. Not that that's why I did it—

GEORGE: —No, of course not. God forbid you should lose your standing as a cult failure.

MICHAEL: (*gently*) Do *you* think I'm a failure, George?

GEORGE: I will not get sucked into this discussion! Hand me the little bottle that says Bufferin.

MICHAEL: (*handing it*) I sent you a play to read, a play that's got a great part for me in it. Did you read it?

GEORGE: (*flinging bottle*) Where do you come *off* sending me an unproduced play that you want to star in? Hand me that Bufferin again. I'm your agent not your mother. I'm not supposed to produce your roommate's play so you can star in it. I'm supposed to field offers.

MICHAEL: Who told you that? The agent-fairy? I'm talking about a significant piece of work that has something to say that's significant!

GEORGE: Nobody wants to do that play! No one is going to produce a play about a couple who move back to Love Canal!

MICHAEL: But that actually *happened*!

GEORGE: Who gives a damn! No one wants to pay $20 to watch people living next to chemical wastes! They can see that in New Jersey.

MICHAEL: I give a damn! No one will do the play?? *I'll* do the play! *I'll* raise the money! Forget about "Iceman Cometh," I'll do anything! Send me up for a pilot, a TV movie—

GEORGE: I can't.

MICHAEL: Why??

GEORGE: Because no one wants to work with you. There!

MICHAEL: (*slowly*) I don't understand. Why shouldn't they want me. I *kill* myself to get a part right.

GEORGE: Yes, but you kill everyone else, too. A guy's got four weeks to put on a play—he doesn't want to argue about whether Tolstoy can walk if he's dying.

MICHAEL: That was two years ago. The guy was an idiot.

GEORGE: They can't *all* be idiots. You argue with everyone. You're a brilliant actor, Michael, but you've got one of the worst reputations in town. No one will touch you. I've told you to get some therapy.

MICHAEL: Are you saying . . . what are you saying? That no one in New York will work with me?

GEORGE: No. That's too limiting. No one in Hollywood will work with you either. I can't even send you up for a commercial. You played a tomato for 30 seconds and they went a half day over because you didn't agree with the blocking.

MICHAEL: It wasn't logical.

GEORGE: (*screaming*) You were a tomato! A tomato doesn't have logical blocking! A tomato can't move!

MICHAEL: (*eagerly*) That's what *I* said.

GEORGE: (*closing his eyes*) Michael . . . Michael . . . frankly, it's nice for me to have an artist who says "screw you" to everyone. It gives me credibility as an agent. But for you—

MICHAEL: (*quietly determined*)—George, I'm going to raise $8,000 and I'm going to do Jeff's play.

GEORGE: (*shaking his head*) Michael, you haven't been listening. You're not going to raise 25¢. (*slowly*) No one will hire you.

MICHAEL: Oh yeah?

[EXTERIOR—MADISON AVE—LONG LENS—DAY

Teeming with people, coming and going. The focus gradually forces us to notice a woman moving towards us unsteadily on high heels. She is MICHAEL.]

FANNY AND ALEXANDER

An Embassy release of a Cinematograph AB Production for The Swedish Film Institute, The Swedish Television SVT 1, Gaumont, Personafilm, and Tobis Filmkunst, BRD. Director, Ingmar Bergman. Screenplay by Ingmar Bergman. Cinematographer, Sven Nykvist. Executive Producer, Jorn Donner. Editor, Sylvia Ingemarsson. Production Manager, Katinka Farago. Art Director, Anna Asp. Set Decorator, Susanne Lingheim. Special Effects, Bengt Lundgren. Sound and Mixing, Owe Svensson, Bo Persson, Bjorn Gunnarsson, Lars Liljeholm. Assistant Director, Peter Schildt. Running time, 197 minutes. 1983.

CAST

HELENA MANDELBAUM EKDAHL	Gunn Wallgren
EMILIE EKDAHL	Ewa Froling
ALEXANDER EKDAHL	Bertil Guve
FANNY EKDAHL	Pernilla Allwin
OSCAR EKDAHL	Allan Edwall
CARL EKDAHL	Borje Ahlstedt
GUSTAVE ADOLF EKDAHL	Jarl Kulle
ISAK JACOBI	Erland Josephson
ALMA EKDAHL	Mona Malm
BISHOP EDVARD VERGÉRUS	Jan Malmsjo
LYDIA EKDAHL	Christina Schollin
MAJ	Pernilla Wallgren
POLICE SUPERINTENDENT	Carl Billquist

Fanny and Alexander are the two younger children of Oscar Ekdahl, whose own father, also named Oscar, was the founder of the family repertory company in a peaceful Swedish university town. The theater was built in the early 1800's, and the present company was established in the 1860's, when the older Oscar married Helena Mandelbaum, a prominent actress from the capital. During her husband's lifetime, Helena ran the theater. It is now fifty years later, and although she is retired from her profession, she still quite definitely presides over the family. Her eldest son, Carl, is a professor, childless, and married for years to a fat German woman who still can't speak proper Swedish. Her middle son Oscar, an awkward actor but a fine administrator, now manages the theater. His wife Emilie is the company's principal actress and its artistic director. Their three children—Amanda (12), Alexander (10), and Fanny (8)—all beg to be allowed to take part in the productions. Oscar is almost certainly not their actual father, though you'd never know that from the warmth and dedication he evidences to his wife and children. He seems to be a very good, very loving man, with a very deficient sex drive. His wife seems definitely to love him.

Helena's third son, Gustav Adolf, more than makes up for whatever virility Oscar lacks. The father of two daughters by his wife Alma, Gustav Adolf will also father a third daughter by the family nursemaid, Maj, during the course of the story. Everyone accepts this gladly, and in the end Maj will leave on very good terms, set up in a life of her own. When Gustav Adolf isn't procreating, he's hosting and serving in the restaurant he runs adjacent to the theater. Within the bosom of the Ekdahl family, Gustav Adolf is indulged because his generosities of affection only epitomize the warm, uniting physicality which characterizes this entire clan. It's not that there is anything shocking or immoral about the Ekdahls. In fact, they live for the most part according to the styles and habits of any rich, conservative, society family. In their theater, certainly, there is a reliance on the traditional favorites, and on heavy doses of Shakespeare. Their loyal audience has little interest in such "moderns" as Ibsen or Strindberg. The brothers and their families live nearby their mother; one actually lives right next door in what used to be the sunnier half of her huge apartment. She can still accommodate the whole brood, gathered for magnificently elaborate holiday feastings and gift-givings, where the unique "protective incubator of physical affection" that enfolds the Ekdahls is everywhere apparent:

They touch each other, shake each other, slap each other's backs, pat, fondle, and hug one another, give each other wet, smacking kisses, hold each other's hands, gaze into each other's eyes, and ruffle each other's hair. They enjoy dramatic squabbles, they burst into tears and abuse one another and seek allies, but they make it all up just as readily, uttering sacred vows and endearments.

The story is told principally through Alexander's point of view, which allows for two of the film's most powerful aspects. One is that "reality" is reality as Alexander *perceives* it, and he is a boy with a strong, sometimes morbid, imagination. When his father dies, his mother marries the Bishop. Alexander comes into open conflict with his severe stepfather over their differing interpretations of what is truth and what are lies. Certainly Alexander knowingly enjoys the powerful effects he creates when he tells terrifying stories of his stepfather's drowned children, whom he claims have appeared to him, blaming their father for their deaths. Alexander is whipped and locked in the attic, both for telling the tale and for denying that he told it. An old Jewish friend of the Ekdahl family, Isak Jacobi, kidnaps the children from the Bishop's cold and punishing household, presumably at the Ekdahls' wishes. Alexander then sees things in the night in Jacobi's house that are so fantastical, it is hard to know if they are actual or if Alexander is dreaming. Either way, these extraordinary visions are real to Alexander.

The other effect achieved by placing Alexander at the helm of so much of the story telling is that most of the film is drenched in a sensory effulgence that is for most of us the province of childhood. Ingmar Bergman's prologue to the script catalogues the "symphony of smells" in Helena's apartment as they are experienced by "a small person like Alexander, whose nose is so near the floor." Moods and apparitions and events in *Fanny and Alexander* are inextricable from the colors and smells and sounds which surround and accompany them. The prologue describes the sensations of sneaking through the tiny connecting door, early one morning, from Alexander's apartment into his grandmother's:

If you stand under the chandelier in the drawing room with your feet sunk in the endless leaf pattern of the carpet, if you stand quite still and hold your breath, you can hear the silence, which consists of many components: above all the singing of the blood in your eardrums, but also the clocks ticking everywhere...the roar of the fire in the tiled stove and faint rattle of the iron doors...a piano can be heard...the sound is barely audible, yet it gives you a twinge of sadness; there is no telling *why*.

In the first excerpt, which occurs one year after Oscar's death, his widow Emilie addresses the company after a production of *Twelfth Night*. She tries to put into words some of her feelings about leaving her life as an actress and seeking a world beyond the theater. After Emilie's disastrous marriage to the Bishop, neither she nor her children join the Ekdahls' annual summer visit to the seashore. Their absence worries Helena deeply, and she shares her concerns with her dead son Oscar in the second excerpt below. Emilie arrives in the third excerpt. She's had to sneak out of the Bishop's house. He would never allow her to visit any Ekdahl, but Emilie *must* unburden her heart. She and the children suffer the most wretched oppression under the Bishop's hand. Soon afterwards, the children are smuggled out of the Bishop's house by Isak, but Emilie is pregnant with another child and must remain. Trapped with her fanatical husband, his disgustingly fat, blistered, dying aunt, and all the other crones who prowl the Bishop's household, Emilie begins to loathe the child she is carrying. One night, she drugs her husband's broth and escapes back to the Ekdahls. In the final excerpt below, a police superintendent appears at Emilie's door the day after her flight. He informs her that the Bishop has died in a fire, and while being drugged didn't help him escape, he would not have escaped anyway, so Emilie is not being held in any way responsible. At the conclusion of the the film, not only have all the Ekdahls been reunited, but there is even a new baby or two to increase their joy.

MONOLOGUE 1

When the applause has died down the actors gather around EMILIE, sitting down on chairs that the stagehands have brought in or leaning against the balustrade behind ORSINO'S throne. The floats and battens are put out one by one, the rehearsal light is lowered, and shadows take possession of the stage. The gray light sways slowly and the actors' faces turn pallid and hollow-eyed. Some stagehands can be glimpsed in the wings, waiting to clear the stage as soon as possible. The safety curtain is lowered, rattling heavily.

EMILIE: A year ago today my husband died. He wanted us to go on as usual, and we have gone on as usual, although everything has been different. We have had many successes and have played to full houses. We have been able to raise our salaries and to engage three new members of the company. We have kept together. . . .

She breaks off and sits for a while deep in thought. When she begins to speak again it is with a different voice, almost inaudible and uncertain.

EMILIE: We draw the theater over our heads like a mantle of security. We hardly notice that the years are passing. That the sands of time are running out, isn't that what they say? The dressing rooms are bright and warm; the stage encloses us with kindly shadows. The playwrights tell us what to say and think. We laugh and cry and rage. People sit out there in the dark liking us; they are remarkably loyal although we often give them stones instead of bread. In order to justify ourselves to the world round us, we make out that our profession is difficult. It's a lie that the world accepts, since it is much more enjoyable to witness something hard than something easy. Mostly we play. We play because we enjoy it. If we don't enjoy it we sulk and blame the circumstances, never ourselves. So we pass our lives in a wonderful self-deception. We are sharp-sighted in regard to others, while glossing over our own faults. What about self-confidence, self-esteem, self-knowledge?—qualities that hardly exist in our profession. If someone says I'm good, then I *am* good and feel happy. If someone says I'm bad, then I *am* bad and feel miserable. What I really am I don't know, as I never bother to find out *the truth* about myself. All I bother about is myself, which is something quite different. I don't bother about reality either. It is colorless and uninteresting; it doesn't concern me. Wars and revolutions and epidemics and poverty and injustices and volcanic eruptions mean nothing to me unless in one way or another they affect the part I am just playing. There are actors who make out they take an interest in the world around them, but I know that they deceive themselves. I am not complaining or bemoaning my lot or making any accusations. But I am longing to get away from the world of the theater.

The actors stand silent and dejected. No one speaks, protests, or argues. EMILE looks about her; she sees empty pale faces under the wigs and makeup, mournful or inquiring looks—*Is it me she's getting at?* She shakes her head as if the question had been asked aloud.

EMILIE: You look at me as if I were angry with you. Quite the reverse. It's because we like each other that I dare to say what I feel. Perhaps I am really as selfish as I don't want to be. Perhaps I am wrong.

[TOMAS: You have grown tired of the theater?

EMILIE: I think so.

TOMAS: Perhaps you want to leave it?]

EMILIE: I think I want to leave it for good.

[MISS SCHWARTZ: What will happen then?]

EMILIE: Even if I do leave, everything will go on as before.

[JOHAN: And who is to be our new managing director?

EMILIE: You must decide that yourselves when the day comes. *If* it comes. I haven't yet made up my mind. (*Pause, then with a smile*)] And now I suggest that we wish each other good night. It's late and I have talked far too much. I didn't mean to worry you.

[EMILIE nods to her colleagues, calls to the children, and withdraws to the dressing room that was formerly OSCAR EKDAHL'S office. The actors remain standing on the stage, regarding each other shamefacedly and with tired, faint smiles.

MR. SALENIUS: What I need is a drink and a sandwich.

TOMAS: I have had an offer from the Lindberg company so it's all the same to me.

MISS SCHWARTZ: I think there's something behind it.

GRETE: Haven't you heard?

MISS SCHWARTZ: You surely don't mean it's true?]

MONOLOGUE 2

HELENA is seized by an unaccountable melancholy, which is so strong that she contemplates the idea of having a little cry. She sits upright in the chair and tries out a few deep sighs. The tears fill her eyes.

The rain surrounds her body and her mind. It trickles down the windowpanes but also over her thoughts and the mental pictures moving behind her eyes. The ripple of rain in the big trees and on the roof has a safe, soothing sound, but it is the safety of an old habit from childhood, and therefore tinged with sadness. *It shows I'm getting old,* HELENA thinks, satisfied in some way with the thought, as after all she can see through her predicament and is thus mistress of the situation. She wipes her tears away with the back of her hand and when she has blinked a few times she can see much more clearly. Sitting opposite her is her son, OSCAR EKDAHL, in his crumpled linen suit. He has put his shabby old summer cap on the table and is looking at her fondly.

HELENA: Yes, Oscar, that's just how it is. One is old and a child at the same time, and cannot understand what became of all those long years in between that were considered so important. Here I sit growing melancholy and thinking that the time was all too short. Your father used to say I was sentimental. As you know, he was not particularly sensitive and was both angry and indignant when he died. He never thought life was cruel or unfair or beautiful. He just lived and made no comments. He left those to me. And when I thought that life was this, that, and the other he laughed at me and said I was sentimental. But heavens above, I was an actress. And as an actress I *had* to be emotional. Oscar, my dear, I may be distressing myself for no reason. When you have nothing to occupy your thoughts you immediately start worrying. May I take your hand?

OSCAR gives her his hand and she holds it for a long time in hers. With the other hand she encloses his wrist, feeling the even beat of the pulse.

HELENA: I remember your hand when you were a child. It was small and firm and dry, and your wrist was so awfully slender. I enjoyed being a mother. I enjoyed being an actress too, but I preferred being a mother. I liked being pregnant and didn't care tuppence for the theater then. For that matter everything is acting. Some parts are nice, others not so nice. I played a mother. I played Juliet, Ophelia. Suddenly I am playing the part of a widow. Or a grandmother. One part follows the other. The thing is not to scamp. Not to shirk. But what became of it all, can you tell me that, my boy?

HELENA does not really expect an answer. She never has, and all her life this has been generally understood.

HELENA: You're a good boy to listen to your old mother's soliloquies, as Isak calls them. Yes, you're a good boy, Oscar, and I grieved terribly when you died. That was a strange part to play. My feelings came from my body and although I could control them they shattered reality, if you know what I mean. (*Pause*) Reality has been broken ever since, and oddly enough it feels better that way. So I don't bother to mend it. I just don't care if nothing makes sense.

OSCAR is still holding her hand. He has turned his face to the window. His smile has faded; he is serious now and looks tired and worn out, as HELENA remembers him from his last years.

HELENA: Oscar, my boy?

[OSCAR: Yes, Mama?]

HELENA: You look depressed and ill.

[OSCAR: I'm worried.]

HELENA: Are you worried about Emilie and the children?

The veranda door is pushed open. Perhaps HELENA wakens at the sound, perhaps she has not been asleep. OSCAR has gone.

SCENE INCLUDING MONOLOGUE 3

[EMILIE and HELENA are sitting opposite each other, holding one another's hands and talking quietly, almost in a whisper. It is still raining over the bay, over the plain, over the summer veranda. The afternoon light is soft and shadowless, all outlines are indistinct, all contrasts mellow. The clock in the dining room strikes.

HELENA: Must you go already?

EMILIE: I have been away too long.

HELENA: Poor Emilie.

EMILIE: (*shaking her head*) It's worst for the children. They are punished for the slightest misdemeanor. Henrietta locks them in and forces them to go to bed in the middle of the day. A week ago Fanny refused to eat up her porridge. She was made to sit there all evening. She was sick at the table. At last she ate it.

HELENA: Alexander?

EMILIE: He is mad with jealousy but doesn't realize it is mutual.

HELENA: My poor Emilie!

EMILIE: I am tormented by a boundless self-contempt.] How could I be so blind? How could I feel sorry for that man? After all I'm an actress and should have seen through his dissimulation. But he was cleverer than I was. His conviction was greater than mine and he dazzled me. I had been living alone so long, ever since Fanny's birth. I hated my occasional emotional storms. I hated the terrible loneliness of my body. Oscar was my best friend, you know that, Helena. You know how fond of him I was; you know that my grief was sincere when he left us. But you also know that we never touched each other.

[HELENA: I reproach you for nothing.]

EMILIE: I thought that my life was finished, sealed up. Sometimes I grieved, but blamed myself for my ingratitude. What is the time, Helena? I must go soon; I'm so afraid of being late. His rage is terrible. I don't know how a man can live with so much hate. I saw nothing; I was too dense. He spoke to me of another life—a life of demands, of purity, of joy in the performance of duty. I had never heard such words. There seemed to be a light around him when he talked to me. At the same time I saw that he was lonely, that he was unhappy, haunted by fear and bad dreams. He assured me that I would save him. He said that together with the children we would live a life in God's nearness—in the truth. *That* was the most important, I think—what he said about the truth. I was so thirsty—it sounds dramatic and overstrung, Helena, I know, but I can't find any other word—I thirsted for the truth. I felt I had been living a lie. I also knew that the children needed a father, who could support them and guide them with a firm hand. (*Pause*) He would also free me from my physical loneliness. I was so grateful, Helena. And I left my old life without regret. Now I must go. A carriage is waiting up by the gate. I am afraid that something may have happened while I have been here. I go in constant dread that Alexander may say something that displeases him. Alexander is so foolhardy. I have tried to warn him, but he can't see that his stepfather is a dangerous opponent who is merely waiting for the right opportunity to crush him.

[HELENA: You must leave him, Emilie.

EMILIE: (*smiling*) I knew you'd say that.] Every hour I think I ought to leave him, sue for a divorce, go back to the theater and our family.

[HELENA: If you are so sure it ought not to be impossible.]

EMILIE: I am pregnant, Helena!

[HELENA: Nevertheless you should . . .

EMILIE: Forgive me for interrupting you. I shall briefly relate all the facts.] I have asked him for a divorce. He refuses. He says not only that he loves me but that a divorce is unthinkable in his position. I tell him I'll leave him just the same. Then he gets out the statute book and explains in detail what will happen: in a court of law I will lose, on grounds of "desertion," as it is called. The children will be taken from me, to be brought up by him. I have written in

secret to a lawyer who is my friend. He has confirmed what
Edvard says. I am shut in and can no longer breathe. I am
dying, Helena. And I hate that man so violently that I
could—(*Silence*)

[HELENA: (*whispering*) We must find a solution.]

EMILIE: Don't tell anyone I've been here. Not a soul!

MONOLOGUE 4

[EMILIE: What has happened?]

POLICE SUPERINTENDENT: Your husband, His Grace the bishop,
lost his life this morning in terrible circumstances. We think
we can make clear the course of events in detail. Miss Elsa
Bergius, who was gravely ill, lay in bed. On her bedside
table stood a lighted paraffin lamp. By an unlucky chance
the lamp fell on to the bed, igniting not only the bedclothes
but also Miss Bergius's hair and nightgown. Burning like a
torch, the sick woman rushed through the house and chanced
to make her way into His Grace, the bishop's bedchamber.
According to His Grace's sister, Miss Henrietta Vergérus,
His Grace was in a heavy sleep after drinking a soporific,
which you, Mrs. Vergérus, had given him earlier in the
evening. After a violent altercation with your husband, you
left the house at twenty minutes past four in the morning.
Miss Bergius flung herself on the sleeping man, thus igniting his bedclothes and nightshirt. His Grace woke up and
succeeded in freeing himself from the dying woman, who
was still burning, but could not extinguish the flames that
were now engulfing himself. Old Mrs. Vergérus found her
son with the top of his body severely burnt and his face
charred. He showed faint signs of life and kept calling out
that his agony was unendurable. Ten minutes later the
doctor and ambulance arrived on the scene, but by then His
Grace had already been released from his suffering and had
breathed his last. Although I cannot overlook the fact that
the sleeping draft you gave him possibly made the disaster
worse, at the same time I cannot attach any serious importance to it. I must characterize what happened as a dreadful
combination of particularly unfortunate circumstances and
therefore beg to offer my deep and sincere condolences.

THE KING OF COMEDY

A Twentieth Century-Fox release. Producer, Arnon Milchan. Director, Martin Scorsese. Screenplay by Paul D. Zimmerman. Executive Producer, Robert Greenhut. Director of Photography, Fred Schuler. Production Designer, Boris Leven. Production Supervisor & Editor, Thelma Schoonmaker. Music, Robbie Robertson. Associate Producer & Production Manager, Robert F. Colesberry. First Assistant Director, Scott Maitland. Supervising Sound Editor, Frank Warner. Art Directors, Edward Pisoni, Lawrence Miller. Running time, 101 minutes. 1983.

CAST

RUPERT PUPKIN	Robert De Niro
JERRY LANGFORD	Jerry Lewis
RITA	Diahnne Abbott
MASHA	Sandra Bernhard
RECEPTIONIST	Margo Winkler
CATHY LONG	Shelley Hack
MR. GANGEMI	Tony Boschetti
JONNO	Kim Chan
BERT THOMAS	Fred De Cordova
WILSON CROCKETT	Edgar J. Scherick
GERRITY	Thomas M. Tolan
GIARDELLO	Ray Dittrich
CAPTAIN BURKE	Richard Dioguardi

Rupert Pupkin—the man's name is funny. Rupert would be the first to invite you to laugh at it. The tanned, gracious, relaxed invitation to come laugh is the hallmark of the elite main-room stand-up comics, and no star is higher in this firmament to which Rupert aspires than Jerry Langford, the host of the late-night *Jerry Langford Show*. Although Rupert is thirty-four years old, works as a messenger in Manhattan, and lives in the basement of his mother's house, in his *real life* he is on his way to appearing on the *Jerry Langford Show*. Rupert's fantasies revolve around Jerry knowing him, loving him, and pleading with him to guest-host the show. (It's interesting how many of the reviews I read of this film considered this an aspect of Rupert's abnormality, while virtually every actor I know confesses identical fantasies about his or her idol.)

In the moments we see Jerry Langford alone inside his vast and exquisite private rooms, he is irritable and bored with how lonely he needs to keep himself. Walking down the street he has too much dignity to alter his famous stride, but his sunglasses and that air of emphatic preoccupation are designed for anonymity. Jerry is mobbed by autograph hounds one night as he is trying to get into his limousine after the show. The fans are so ravenous for him, so wild to literally grab his attention that he is about to be seriously hurt. Rupert is there, comes to Jerry's rescue and, seizing the opportunity of a lifetime, slides in right next to Jerry as the limousine pulls away.

Rupert's most cherished possession is his extensive celebrity autograph collection. He proudly displays it to Rita, a girl he admired in high school and to whom he now reintroduces himself, all aglow with the confidence that comes from being a very close, very dear friend of Jerry Langford. Rupert tries to behave with the saturated assurance of the accomplished show-biz vet as he pesters Jerry Langford at home and at the office. He is thoroughly convinced from their limousine ride that Jerry wants him on the show. Rupert is aggressively sincere and humbly respectful as he crosses right over the line into harassment. Arriving with Rita, 100% uninvited to Jerry's country house, Rupert finally pushes Jerry into being nasty. Rupert feels so betrayed that he sees no alternative but to kidnap Jerry and hold him for ransom. The price? He wants the opening monologue on the *Jerry Langford Show*.

The spot Rupert is demanding is the cherry atop the American Televised Dream. Does he deserve it . . . is he funny? Well . . . he is such an impeccable homage to the *image* of the successful talk show comic, and so thrilling to *himself*, that it is a moot point.

He looks and acts and enjoys himself just like the pros do, so the audience does their part, too. Rupert Pupkin becomes a media celebrity. His jail sentence enhances his popularity, and the film ends with his triumphant return to late-night talk-show television.

The first excerpt below occurs just after Rupert has taken the limousine ride with Jerry. It's everything he has been waiting for—some voucher of his glorious, imminent success—before re-introducing himself to Rita. The excerpt includes two separate but contiguous scenes, each principally for Rita and Rupert, but each requiring the participation of additional actors.

The second excerpt takes place in Rupert's room, which he has designed to contain an exact replica of the *Jerry Langford Show* set. At this point, Rupert is still firmly convinced that Jerry just can't wait to be the one to get this kid to the top where he belongs. The excerpt contains two monologues. The second is the audition that Rupert is tape-recording for Jerry, right down to the speech he wants Jerry to use to introduce him when he appears on the show. But before he actually begins recording, we see him reading a letter, and we simultaneously hear the letter in a voice-over monologue spoken by its author, a girl named Masha. She has directed Rupert to deliver it to her most adored, but bewilderingly aloof god, Jerry Langford. Masha is a highly intelligent, deeply disturbed young woman who lives at her parents' very expensive upper East Side address. It is here that Jerry is brought when he is kidnapped, so that while Rupert is performing his monologue on the air, Masha can offer herself up to her beloved, who is roped to a chair with his mouth taped. She lives inside an outraged delusion that Jerry is jilting her, and that she is the Great Love of his life. Her fantasies, like Rupert's, have fermented into a warped and dangerous reality.

The third excerpt is Rupert's act, performed on national television, during his desperately garnered guest spot on the *Jerry Langford Show*.

SCENES 1 AND 2

[EXTERIOR—A STREET OFF BROADWAY—DAY

A cab pulls up in front of Gil's Steak and Chops, a restaurant of little distinction that has a few checkered tableclothed tables in the rear and a long bar at the front. PUPKIN stares through the window of the bar.] Then he enters.

INTERIOR—THE BAR-RESTAURANT—DAY

PUPKIN goes to the near end of the empty bar.

PUPKIN: Miss!

RITA, an attractive shopworn blonde in her late twenties, comes over.

PUPKIN: A beer please, Miss. Something imported.

RITA: Heineken's alright?

PUPKIN: Fine.

RITA serves him a Heineken's. She stares at him.

PUPKIN: How have you been, Rita?

She stares again.

RITA: You're not Rupert Pupkin!

PUPKIN smiles broadly.

RITA: How the hell did you find me?

PUPKIN: Sally Gardner. I met her after a matinee. Aren't you glad to see me?

RITA: Sure, sure. How is old Sally?

PUPKIN: The same, I guess. You know, two kids, a nice husband, living in Clifton.

RITA: It figures.

PUPKIN: A lot of kids from our class have moved back.

RITA: What are you doing here?

PUPKIN: I just thought I'd say hello. I brought you a little something.

He presents her with a single long-stemmed rose.

RITA: Ah, yes. Mr. Romance.

PUPKIN: Put an aspirin in the water. It lasts longer.

RITA puts the rose in a beer mug and drops in an Alka-Seltzer.

RITA: Nothing's gonna keep it alive in this place . . . Well, what are you up to these days, Rupert?

PUPKIN: Didn't you know you'd see me again?

RITA: Still going to movies all the time?

PUPKIN: You're looking as beautiful as ever.

RITA: Oh, yeah. I was a real knockout.

PUPKIN: I thought so.

RITA: Well, here I am! Local cheerleader makes good.

PUPKIN: I voted for you for Most Beautiful.

RITA: Yeah?

PUPKIN: I didn't have the nerve to tell you then but, now, I guess . . .

RITA: Well, nothing terrible's gonna happen, if that's what you mean.

PUPKIN: You're really looking wonderful, Rita.

RITA: Well, how are things with you, Rupert?

PUPKIN: Great! Great! Everything's starting to break.

RITA: Is that right?

PUPKIN: Yeah. As a matter of fact, that's why I'm here. I've known about this place for a long time. I just didn't want to make my move until I had something to offer you. Everything's a question of timing.

RITA stares at PUPKIN as he rattles on.

PUPKIN: What's the matter?

RITA shakes her head in disbelief and chuckles.

RITA: Rupert! Jesus Christ. Rupert Pupkin!

PUPKIN: (*smiling*) Yeah. Jesus Christ, Rupert Pupkin. The two of us are often confused. He's the one with the famous father.

PUPKIN awaits a laugh but RITA just shakes her head. PUPKIN looks around.

PUPKIN: You like this place?

RITA: Why, you got something better?

PUPKIN: Maybe . . .

RITA: What?

PUPKIN: What are you doing tonight?

RITA: Tonight?

PUPKIN: What's so funny?

RITA: It only took you fifteen years! To ask me out!

PUPKIN: If I'd asked you then, would you have gone?

RITA: Oh, no.

PUPKIN: Why not?

RITA: I thought you were a jerk!

PUPKIN: See! But that guy isn't me anymore, Rita. I've changed. Everything's changed.

A bull-necked MAN in his forties enters, waves a brief hello to RITA as he passes and takes a seat at the far end of the bar. RITA smiles at him.

RITA: (*to* PUPKIN) Excuse me a minute, honey.

PUPKIN: I'm not honey! I'm Rupert.

RITA grabs a beer and takes it to the MAN. They chat as PUPKIN watches uneasily. Finally, PUPKIN downs his beer and raises his glass.

PUPKIN: Miss!

The MAN lets RITA go. She returns to PUPKIN with another beer.

PUPKIN: I'm in the mood to celebrate. I know this nice place. We can have dinner, talk over old times, get to know each other all over again.

RITA: And then?

PUPKIN: I'm free tomorrow night. We could go someplace else, talk some more, get to know each other even better.

RITA: How much better?

PUPKIN: What?

RITA: How much better do we have to get to know each other?

PUPKIN still doesn't understand. RITA spells it out.

RITA: Before we start talking about that job...

PUPKIN: I'm not talking about any job.

RITA: I thought you said you had something better.

PUPKIN: Oh. You'll see. Right now, I'm asking you out. How about it?

RITA: I'm sorry, Rupert. I'm busy.

PUPKIN: Busy?

RITA: Yeah. Busy. B-U-S-Y.

PUPKIN: But this is the biggest night of my life.

RITA: Sorry. I've already got a date.

The MAN at the end of the bar raises his glass.

MAN: Rita!

RITA goes to the MAN, pours him a beer and resumes their chat. PUPKIN watches uneasily, then downs his beer and raises his glass.

PUPKIN: Miss! Miss!

RITA returns to him.

PUPKIN: Is that your date?

RITA: Maybe.

PUPKIN: What do you want to go out with *him* for?

RITA: He's a friend of mine.

PUPKIN: Tell *him* you're busy.

RITA: What's so important about tonight?

PUPKIN: Everything! You don't understand.

RITA: No, I don't.

RITA leaves PUPKIN and returns to the MAN. They resume chatting. PUPKIN sits for a moment, [then heads slowly for the john.

INTERIOR—THE JOHN—NIGHT

PUPKIN enters and goes to one of two urinals. A beat later, the MAN enters and goes to the other. They both stare straight ahead. PUPKIN steals a glance at the MAN's face, then turns eyes straight as the MAN turns to glance at him. When the MAN resumes staring straight ahead, PUPKIN steals a look at his penis. A beat later, the MAN quickly sizes up PUPKIN's penis.

INTERIOR—THE BAR—NIGHT

PUPKIN and, a moment later, the MAN, return from the john and resume their seats. A THIRD MAN is now seated midway between them.]

PUPKIN: Miss!

RITA walks over reluctantly.

PUPKIN: Listen to me for a second.

RITA: I have work to do, Rupert.

PUPKIN: Just listen. I'm at the start of something really big, I don't want to talk about it here, but it's going to happen soon and it's going to be great—for both of us.

RITA: No kidding?

PUPKIN: So see that guy some other night.

MAN: Rita!

RITA turns to go.

PUPKIN: But I haven't finished!

PUPKIN watches RITA pour the MAN another beer. After a few moments, PUPKIN downs his own beer and again raises his glass.

PUPKIN: Miss! Miss!

The MAN says something to RITA [who hands him a bottle of beer. The MAN slides the bottle down the bar toward PUPKIN. As it reaches the middle, the THIRD MAN raises his glass just as the bottle passes under his hand. The bottle stops just in front of PUPKIN who slides it back with equal force. Only this time the THIRD MAN is putting his glass down. The collision creates a mess. PUPKIN shrugs an apology as RITA starts cleaning it up.

RITA: (to the THIRD MAN) I'll get you another one.

As RITA does so,] the MAN approaches PUPKIN, leans on him and wraps a familiar "paw" around his shoulder.

MAN: Look, friend. I'm trying to have a nice civilized conversation with the young lady. Be a good little lad, huh, and give us a break . . . Nobody likes a wise guy.

PUPKIN: What about Bob Hope?

The MAN restrains himself and returns to his seat where RITA awaits him. PUPKIN downs his beer and raises his glass.

PUPKIN: Miss! Miss!

RITA is about to return but the MAN stays her and approaches PUPKIN instead, a bottle in his hand. He pours half of it into PUPKIN'S pocket and slams the bottle hard on the counter, then marches back to RITA.

PUPKIN again bats down his beer as the MAN and RITA watch him, expecting him to call for another. But PUPKIN just sits there, so RITA and the MAN resume talking, occasionally glancing PUPKIN's way. But PUPKIN just sits there, until RITA and the MAN have forgotten him. Then, he seemingly loses his balance and falls to the floor like a stone. RITA and the MAN wait for him to move but he lies motionless. RITA hurries off toward the kitchen while the MAN walks over to the inert PUPKIN and prods him cruelly with his foot.

MAN: Come on, stupid. Wake up so I can kick your ass outta here.

The MAN looks to the kitchen, expecting RITA. PUPKIN opens one eye, grabs a free chair, rises and bangs the MAN smartly over the head. The MAN falls, out cold. PUPKIN gets to his feet quickly and brushes off his suit, which is dark grey, like the MAN's. PUPKIN stands above him, his back to RITA as she returns from the kitchen [in the company of the beefy OWNER.

RITA: (to the OWNER) He was making trouble one minute. Next minute, he's on the floor.]

PUPKIN turns as RITA approaches. She's too startled by the turnaround to speak. [The OWNER lifts the MAN to his feet and sweettalks him out of the bar.] RITA turns to PUPKIN.

RITA: Okay, Tarzan. I get off at nine.

INTERIOR—A CHINESE RESTAURANT—UPPER WEST SIDE—NIGHT

Formica tables. Painfully plain decor. RITA and PUPKIN face each other in a booth. A WAITER sets dishes down. RITA hands him an empty glass.

RITA: Another one, Chan . . . So all this time you've been thinking of me, huh?

PUPKIN: I guess so.

PUPKIN smiles as he gazes at her, which crowds her.

RITA: What kinds of things were you thinking?

PUPKIN drops his gaze.

RITA: Oh, ho! Those kinds of things!

PUPKIN: Rita, that's not . . .

RITA: Rupert Pupkin is an unclean person!!

PUPKIN: Come on, Rita.

RITA: Oh, come on, yourself. Relax. Have a little fun. I'm off duty.

WAITER arrives with RITA'S drink, chopsticks and a beer for PUPKIN.

PUPKIN: It's only this is a very important night to me, Rita.

RITA: Your nose wriggles.

PUPKIN: Really.

RITA: Yeah. When you talk.

PUPKIN serves RITA.

RITA: It always looks like they put worms in this stuff.

PUPKIN: Just taste.

RITA: Well, I guess it won't kill me.

PUPKIN: This is supposed to be the finest Cantonese cuisine in the city.

RITA: Yeah? Then what happened to the tablecloths. (*pause*) Oh, don't worry about it. This is fine. (*She takes a long drink*)

They eat. PUPKIN uses chopsticks.

PUPKIN: I'd look at you and wonder what it felt like, being that normal and in the right crowd, with good marks and respect and . . .

RITA: Ah, for Chrissakes, Rupert, I woke up every day sick, understand! I threw up all the time, I was so tense . . .

PUPKIN: You never told me that.

They eat.

RITA: So you've been devoted to me?

PUPKIN: I used to go to the Garden.

RITA: Oh, the Follies! I didn't know you liked skating, Rupert! How did you know which chicken was me? (*pause*) I thought it would be "Rita Keane's Ice Follies." And there I was, eighteen months in the chorus of "Henny Penny!"

PUPKIN: You just didn't get the breaks. You didn't hang on long enough.

RITA: Didn't get the breaks . . . no great loss . . .

PUPKIN: It was to me. (*beat*)

RITA: Boy, you really must have been carrying a torch. (*drinks*) What did you think when I got married? You knew I got married?

PUPKIN: I knew it wouldn't last. Peter *Drysdale*! Really, Rita!

RITA: You think I should've married you, right? You do, don't you . . . You have insurance? Life insurance?

PUPKIN: My talent is my insurance.

RITA: If he'd only been hit by a train. He was worth a hell of a lot more dead than alive, I can tell you that.

RITA raises her glass to the WAITER who is standing nearby. As she does, a nice-looking MAN sitting right behind PUPKIN raises his glass to her, as a kind of toast. RITA smiles briefly and her eyes return to PUPKIN. The WAITER takes the glass. Throughout the rest of the scene, a subtle flirtation continues between RITA and the MAN.

PUPKIN: Are you seeing anyone?

RITA: What do you mean?

PUPKIN: I want to know about the competition, that's all.

RITA: Well, tomorrow night, I've got a date with Joe Namath— you know Joe. And Thursday—let's see—

PUPKIN: I'm serious, Rita.

RITA: Yeah, I see people. I go out with who I want, when I want. I'm no nun, Rupert. I see a lot of guys.

PUPKIN: Then there's no one special.

RITA: You mean am I going steady! Look at me, Rupert. I'm thirty-two years old.

RUPERT smiles.

RITA: Okay. I'm thirty-four.

PUPKIN: What about that guy tonight? The guy in the bar. Why him?

RITA: Rudy? Rudy runs the garage around the corner. He likes to show me a good time.

RUPERT waits.

RITA: Look, Rupert, what do you think they pay me in that dump, huh? One-fifteen a week, and they're not the world's greatest tippers. *Somebody* has to take care of me.

PUPKIN: Who's your favorite movie star?

The WAITER arrives with RITA's drink.

RITA: You are, Rupert. Especially your nose.

PUPKIN: Just tell me. Who do you like?

RITA: Is this some kind of a game? Are you going to tell me something about my character? Read my palm or what?

PUPKIN: You'll see.

RITA pauses, thinks.

PUPKIN: Everybody's got a favorite movie star. C'mon.

RITA: Okay. Okay. Let's see. (*pause*) Marilyn Monroe.

PUPKIN pulls out his leather-bound ''Talent Register.''

RITA: Oh, Rupert! Are we going to exchange phone numbers!?

PUPKIN expertly flips to a middle page in the book. His finger pointing under a name, he turns the book to RITA.

RITA: That's her name. Alright. "Marilyn Monroe." I was right. Do I get a prize, Rupert?

PUPKIN: She signed this for me when she was in town doing publicity on her last move, "The Misfits."

RITA starts flipping through the book.

PUPKIN: She wasn't a great actress but she had a real gift for comedy. She died tragically, you know, alone, like so many of the world's most beautiful women. I'm going to see that doesn't happen to you, Rita.

RITA: Who's this one?

PUPKIN: (*checking the book*) Burt Reynolds.

RITA: Oh, yeah. The guy with no clothes. And this?

PUPKIN: Mel Brooks. He's always "on," funny. Not every comedian is.

RITA: And this?

PUPKIN: Carol Burnett...

RITA: No kidding. How about this?

PUN: Sid Caesar. Remarkable guy. That's Woody Allen. He's very nice. And Ernie Kovacs. He's dead. A *great* loss.

RITA: Some of these must be worth money.

PUPKIN: Like this one.

PUPKIN flips to the back pages and shows RITA a name.

RITA: (*squinting*) I can't make it out.

PUPKIN: Try.

RITA: I can't.

PUPKIN: Rooooper...

RITA: (*squinting, focusing*) Redford!

PUPKIN: That's *Robert* Redford.

RITA: It is?

PUPKIN: No! It's... it's Rupert Pupkin.

PUPKIN tears out the page and hands it to her.

PUPKIN: Take care of it. In a few weeks, everyone's going to want one.

RITA looks at him. He's still the same.

PUPKIN: That's what I've been trying to tell you. Things are truly breaking for me. Only a couple of hours ago, I was talking with Jerry Langford. That's right. *The* Jerry Langford. He gave me the go ahead, Rita. Would you believe it? Don't tell anyone yet but you're looking at the new King of Comedy.

RITA looks at the MAN who is mimicking PUPKIN "when already?" She laughs, in spite of herself.

PUPKIN: Why not me, Rita? A guy can always get what he wants if he's willing to pay the price. All it takes is a little talent and a lot of sacrifice and the right break for me. Is that so funny? Crazier things have happened.

RITA: You're right.

As PUPKIN continues speaking, RITA sees the MAN mimicking PUPKIN and exaggerating, pointing to his watch, "c'mon!"

PUPKIN: You don't understand what a shot on Langford means. That's coast to coast, national TV, a bigger audience than the greatest comedians used to play to in a whole lifetime. A shot like that means a free ticket on the comedy circuit... a comedy special of my own... and all that leads in one direction, Rita... Hollywood. That's when we really start living. A beach house in Malibu, right on the ocean. You'll get a beautiful tan. We'd keep a suite at the Sherry—that's the only place to stay when you're big—way up, so we can look down on everybody else and yell (*cupping his mouth*) "Tough luck, suckers!" C'mon, Rita, what do you say?

RITA: It sounds wonderful, Rupert. (*checks watch*) It's getting late, I'm a working girl. You know what I mean?

PUPKIN: I don't get it, Rita. I thought you wanted something better... better than... that. Every King needs a Queen, Rita. I want you to be mine. Say yes.

RITA: You really want to help me out? You see this. (*She points to her lower back molar*) A hundred seventy-five bucks. If you could spare fifty, say, until next Monday, that would keep three people really happy—me, my landlord and my dentist.

WAITER: Telephone for you, Miss.

RITA: Me? Nobody knows I'm here. You didn't tell anybody, did you?

PUPKIN: No.

RITA: What the hell's going on?

RITA goes to adjacent phone booths in back of the restaurant.

INTERIOR—THE PHONE BOOTH—NIGHT

RITA: Hello?

MAN'S VOICE: Hi.

RITA: Who is this?

MAN'S VOICE: Who do you think it is? I've been staring at you all evening.

RITA: Where are you?

The MAN taps on his booth. RITA turns and finds herself staring at the MAN. She smiles.

INTERIOR—THE RESTAURANT—NIGHT]

PUPKIN at the table opens fortune cookies. First one reads: "*WISDOM IS THE PROVINCE OF THE HEART.*" Second one reads: "*SOME DINOSAURS WERE NO BIGGER THAN A CHICKEN.*" He opens a third when RITA arrives.

RITA: You know who that was—the bar. I have to go back to work.

PUPKIN: (*reading, holding fortune*) "Blessed are those who reach the turning in the road."

RITA: My backup's got sick. It happens all the time.

PUPKIN: It's your fortune, Rita. Just what I was telling you. You're the one at the turning in the road.

RITA: I had a real nice dinner, Rupert. (*checks herself in the mirror—lipstick?*)

PUPKIN: That was that Rudy on the phone, wasn't it?

RITA: Oh, c'mon, Rupert. Let's see a smile.

PUPKIN: Why don't we finish off the night at the bar where we started it?

RITA: After the stunt you pulled there?

PUPKIN: Well, I could at least drop you off!

RITA: (*leaving*) No, really, I can manage.

PUPKIN: (*following*) But I insist.

RITA: Look, Rupert, it's been a lot of fun, really—but, I'm in a hurry. I'll see you sometime, huh?

PUPKIN: But, Rita...

She is gone. PUPKIN hurriedly pays CASHIER.

After all three exit, Rupert will follow Rita and the stranger to the stranger's apartment, and Rupert will be there to "rescue" her when the stranger turns out to be dangerous.

(*Note*: The set for each of these two scenes requires two entrances. One leads out to the street, and the other leads off into the kitchen and restroom areas. The action in these areas—the size check in the men's room in the first scene, the telephone conversation in the phone booths in the second scene—would not happen onstage. [Unless, of course, the set for the second scene can accommodate phone booths placed so that Rupert cannot overhear or observe the conversation, in which case this *could* happen onstage.]

In the first scene, the specific business with the beer glasses and the fight will have to be adapted to the particular space of the acting studio. This may involve bracketing the entrance of the owner and perhaps even the presence of the third man. But in both scenes, additional actors beyond Rita and Rupert are required for the scenes to play properly—the waiter in the second scene, perhaps the third customer in the first scene, and certainly in both scenes at least one man other than Rupert with whom Rita is making contact.)

MONOLOGUE 1 AND MONOLOGUE 2

INTERIOR—PUPKIN'S ROOM—DAY

He is reading the letter. EXTREME CLOSE-UP letter. (ZIP TILTS.) MASHA VO.

Dear Tormentor!

I'm not apologizing for last night, not to you, Mr. Shut-Me-Out. I was only trying to get this to you! That's all. You've got no right to be angry! And you know it! (Promises, Promises)

If you could have seen your face when you saw mine! Was my baby scared? Did Jerry suffer. Not like I have. (Promises, Promises.) Two years is a long time between meetings, Jerry. But I've been away, playing the solitary room at Westhaven "rest home." Some Rest!!

Did you know God, dog, fag and gland all have something in common? They come from L-A-N-G-F-O-R-D. Interesting, no? You all over!

This is to announce the End of Phase I of the Great Romance. Start Phase II: The Time Limit. Your obligations are three years overdue, sir. This offers you one final chance before DRASTIC ACTION.

Someone has a fortieth birthday coming up. A certain person is knitting him a sweater, (sample enclosed!) because the world is a cold place (which she will make much warmer if he stops playing Mr. Aloof!) Present yourself Chez Moi, Apt. 4C, 64 East 84th St. for a SLEEVE MEASUREMENT. (Promises, Promises.) Keys enclosed.

I'VE REACHED THE END OF MY ROPE, JERRY. END OF MY ROPE. PROMISES, PROMISES.

> Love n stuff,
> M.

P.S. I woke up this a.m. thinking the pain that lives in my tummy was finally going. Delivered. Like a baby, our baby. But, by breakfast, it was back. Only you can deliver it, Jerry. Help me! For God's sake!

P.P.S. I tell my shrink about us. He thinks I have a very rich fantasy life!!!! Ha! Ha! Ha! Jokes on him and on Mommy and Daddy who pay him to listen, so *they* won't have to.

P.P.P.S. I'm *not* crazy. Only over you, lover boy! (Promises, Promises)

PUPKIN finishes the letter and carefully files it away. He then moves to a table in his neat, plainly furnished room. A small cassette recorder and a large tape recorder sit on the table. He speaks into the mike of the larger recorder.

PUPKIN: Testing. Testing. Testing.

We hear a sound montage: replay of "testing, testing"—scraps of his voice, laughter, applause, a fast-forward squeal, a scrap of music. At the same time, CAMERA explores neatly-made collages on the walls: of comedians like Kovacs, Keaton, Chaplin, Caesar, Woody Allen; celebrity figures like Muhammed Ali, Barbara Walters, Mick Jagger, Jackie Kennedy; a martyr section for the fallen Kennedys, King, James Dean; and a talk-show collage, Snyder, Cavett, Griffin, Douglas and Davidson orbiting about Jerry Langford. Bookshelves are a complete library of comedy. Other shelves hold taped TV monologues, i.e., "LANGFORD MONOLOGUES, 6/13/72 to 9/9/81."

PUPKIN starts the larger recorder and lifts the mike.

PUPKIN: First, Miss Long. Thanks very much for your help at the office and for passing this on to Jerry. I appreciate it more than you know.

PUPKIN stops the tape, reflects, then starts it again.

PUPKIN: Now, Jerry, before I begin, I just want to thank you for listening to this material and for the opportunity you've given me. You know, lots of people think that guys like you, you know, people who have made it, lose their feeling for struggling young talent such as myself. But now I know from experience that those people are just cynics, embittered by their own failure. I know, Jerry, that you're as human as the rest of us, if not more so. (*pause*) Oh well, I guess there's no point going on about it. You know how I feel. So let's get on with the show. The best of Rupert Pupkin! I've sketched out this little introduction in order to save you a little time. So close your eyes and imagine it's exactly six o'clock. You're standing in the wings and we hear Rick Ross and the Orchestra strike up your theme song.

PUPKIN pushes a button on the cassette. We hear the Jerry Langford theme song and the voice of BERT CANTER, the announcer.

BERT CANTER'S VOICE: And now, direct from New York, it's the Jerry Langford Show! Tonight, with Jerry's special guest...

PUPKIN deftly stops the cassette and substitutes his own voice.

PUPKIN: ...the comedy find of the year making his television debut, Rupert Pupkin, the King of Comedy!

PUPKIN rapidly presses fast-forward on the cassette, then the "play" button. We hear thundering applause. PUPKIN lets it run then stops it. The large recorder keeps rolling.

PUPKIN: Now you come on, Jerry, and do your monologue. Then, when the time comes, this is how I see you introducing me. You'll say something like this. "Ladies and Gentlemen, we're going to do something a little bit different tonight. It isn't often that you can call someone a sure thing in the entertainment business. After all, the verdict is always in your hands. But I think that after you've met my next guest, you'll agree with me that he's destined for greatness. So, now, will you please give your warmest welcome to the newest King of Comedy, Rupert Pupkin!!!"

Again, another enormous bust of applause. PUPKIN lets it run. He stands up, faces a wall of his room, holding the microphone. WE SEE that the wall is covered by a huge blow-up of an audience laughing and applauding.

The applause fades away. Then:

PUPKIN stands facing the "audience" still holding the mike.

PUPKIN: That's a possible introduction, Jerry. Now let's move on to my act.

MONOLOGUE 3

INTERIOR—THE BAR-RESTAURANT—NIGHT

PUPKIN marches in flanked by the PLAINCLOTHESMEN. The clock over the bar reads 11:30. RITA looks up from talking with a CUSTOMER and sees PUPKIN. She says nothing. There are five CUSTOMERS at the bar. PUPKIN marches up to the bar.

PUPKIN: Turn on Langford.

MAN: Hey! I'm watching that.

PUPKIN: Just turn it. Come on.

MAN: I was here first, mister. You can't just walk in like this.

PUPKIN vaults onto the bar and turns to the Langford show, just as, on screen, he walks from the wings onto the stage to the applause. Perched atop the bar, standing next to the image of himself, PUPKIN looks down at RITA.]

PUPKIN: (on TV) Good evening, ladies and gentlemen. Let me introduce myself. My name is Rupert Pupkin. I was born in Clifton, New Jersey, which was not, at that time, a federal offense. (laughter) Is there anyone here from Clifton? (silence) Good. We can all relax. Now, I'd like to begin by saying that my parents were too poor to afford me a childhood but the fact is nobody is allowed to be poor in

Clifton. Once you fall below eleven thousand you're exiled to Passaic. My parents did, in fact, put down the first two payments on my childhood. Then they tried to return me to the hospital as a defective. But, like everyone else, I grew up, in large part, thanks to my mother. If she were only here today I'd say, "Hey, mom. What are you doing here!? You've been dead for nine months." (*laughter*) You should have seen my mother. She was wonderful—blonde, beautiful, intelligent, alcoholic. (*laughter*) We used to drink milk together after school. Mine was homogenized. Hers was loaded. (*laughter*) Once she was picked up for speeding. They clocked her doing fifty—in our garage. (*laughter*) When they tested her, they found that her alcohol was two per cent blood. They took away her license and she died shortly afterwards. We used to joke together, Mom and me, until the tears would stream down her face and she'd throw up. (*laughter*) And who would clean it up? Not Dad. He was too busy down at O'Grady's throwing up on his own. In fact, until I was sixteen, I thought throwing up was a sign of maturity. While the other kids were off in the woods sneaking cigarettes, I was hiding behind the house with my fingers down my throat. (*laughter*) I never got anywhere until one day, my father caught me. Just as he was giving me a final kick in the stomach, for luck, I managed to heave all over his new shoes. "That's it," I thought. "I've made it. I'm finally a man!" (*laughter*) As it turned out, that was the only time my father ever paid any real attention to me. He was usually too busy out in the park playing ball with my sister, Rose. And, today, thanks to those many hours of practice, my sister Rose has grown into a fine man. (*laughter*) Me, I wasn't especially interested in athletics. The only exercise I ever got was when the other kids picked on me. They used to beat me up once a week, usually Tuesday. After a while, the school worked it into the curriculum. And, if you knocked me out, you got extra credit. (*laughter*) Except there was this one kid who was afraid of me. I kept telling him, "Hit me! Hit me! What's the matter with you? Don't you want to graduate?" As for me, I was the only kid in the history of the school to graduate in traction. The school nurse tucked my diploma into my sling. But my only real interest, right from the beginning, was show business. Even as a young man, I began at the very top, collecting autographs. (*laughter*) A lot of you are probably wondering why Jerry couldn't make it this evening. Well, he's tied up—and I'm the one who tied him. (*laughter*) You think I'm joking, but that's the only way I could break into show business—by hijacking Jerry Langford. (*laughter*) I'm not kidding. Right now, Jerry Langford is strapped to a bedstead somewhere the middle of this city. (*laughter*) Go ahead. Laugh. But the fact is . . . I'm here. Tomorrow you'll know I wasn't kidding and you'll think I was crazy. But I figured it this way: better to be King for a Night than Schmuck for a Lifetime!!! (*laughter*) Good night ladies and gentlemen. God bless you.

[The television AUDIENCE applauds and some CUSTOMERS applaud in good humor.

PUPKIN, satisfied, glances at RITA. She stares at PUPKIN.

PUPKIN: Come on, Rita. Don't spoil the party. (*to the Customers*) Drinks all around on me.

PUPKIN turns to the PLAINCLOTHESMEN.

PUPKIN: I don't suppose you're allowed anything. (*to* RITA) I guess nobody's in a celebrating mood. How about you? You want something?

FIRST PLAINCLOTHESMAN: It's getting time.

PUPKIN: In a second.

RITA: That was true, wasn't it? . . . about the kidnapping.

PUPKIN looks.

PUPKIN: Now you can say you knew me. That's something, anyway.

FIRST PLAINCLOTHESMAN: Come on. Let's go.

PUPKIN: I guess I've gotta go. Take care of yourself, will you. (*pause*) Okay?

RITA: Okay.

The PLAINCLOTHESMEN lead PUPKIN out of the bar.]

TENDER MERCIES

A Universal release of an EMI Films presentation of an Antron Media Production. Producer, Philip S. Hobel. Director, Bruce Beresford. Screenplay by Horton Foote. Associate Producer, Mary-Ann Hobel. Co-Producers, Horton Foote, Robert Duvall. Director of Photography, Russel Boyd. Film Editor, William Anderson. Art Director, Jeannine Oppewall. Sound Mixer, Chris Newman. Supervising Sound Editor, Maurice Schell. Song, "Wings of a Dove" by Bob Ferguson. First Assistant Director, Richard Luke Rothschild. Running time, 89 minutes. 1983.

CAST

MAC SLEDGE	Robert Duvall
ROSA LEE	Tess Harper
DIXIE	Betty Buckley
HARRY	Wilford Brimley
SUE ANNE	Ellen Barkin
SONNY	Allan Hubbard
ROBERT	Lenny Von Dohlen
REPORTER	Paul Gleason
LEWIS MENEFEE	Michael Crabtree
REVEREND HOTCHKISS	Norman Bennett
LARUE	Andrew Scott Hollon
JAKE	Rick Murray
BERTIE	Steven Funchess
STEVE	Glen Fleming
HENRY	James Aaron

God knows how many times Mac Sledge has awakened after a few days, brutally hung over in some motel room, his wallet gone. For Rosa Lee, the young widow who runs the Mariposa Motel and gas station, it is sufficient that God should know. All that concerns her about Mac's past is that he does not bring the drinking part anywhere near her premises (or her boy Sonny) while he is working off his bill. She expects that Mac will be like all the others—working just until he earns enough to go off and get seriously loaded. Unlike the others, Mac comes back. He periodically leaves for his drinking, but after he's been working there a year, and been completely dry for two months, he asks Rosa Lee to marry him and she accepts.

In describing Rosa Lee, the image of a lake or pond seems inescapable: something so still and clear, but when touched, having a response that moves out through the entirety of her. She was married at 16, a mother at 17, and a Vietnam war widow at 18. The Army didn't know the exact circumstances or date of her husband's death; all they could provide was the body. Mac is cut off from his ex-wife and daughter, both of his parents are dead, and he has one living brother with whom he has lost contact. If either Rosa Lee or Mac ever had any easy sentimentality to them, life has beaten it out. They both seem to be feeling their way in the dark, back out to something lighter, something shared, but both with such grave and scarred respect for human feeling that they dare not fling it about in wasteful display. Each other's presence, if carefully attended to, makes much talk superfluous. Rosa Lee *sings,* however, in the church choir. Nothing could be further from this woman's manner than to proselytize, and yet, through the sheer contagion of her simple spiritual radiance, both Sonny and Mac will choose to be baptized (through full immersion) into her faith.

Mac Sledge was once a famous country singer, married to an emotional storm of a woman, Dixie Scott, herself a musical performer whose star ascended on the songs Mac wrote for her. The marriage became such a war zone that Mac has been barred from seeing their daughter since the divorce. Dixie has never remarried. Their daughter Sue Anne is just turning eighteen. When Dixie comes to sing in nearby Austin, Mac goes to hear her perform. Rosa does not go. The script describes Dixie on stage as "flashily dressed, an assured experienced performer, but there is something over-produced and lifeless about what she is doing." Mac does not like what he sees and leaves in the middle.

At the backstage entrance he bumps into Harry Silver, Dixie's manager/companion. Harry is cordial, if slightly wary, at seeing Mac, and accepts a song that Mac has written and thinks would be right for Dixie. He makes no promise, but he'll pass it along. Mac enters the backstage, hoping he might say hello to Sue Anne. Dixie spots him. It's as if someone hollered "Action!" —she just goes wild, demanding he be removed, screaming that he is a dead man to his daughter. Soon afterwards, Harry stops by the motel to return the song, but also to offer to help Mac see his child. Rosa Lee winces for the sorrow this separation has caused Mac: "When his [Sonny's] Daddy died and people said Oh, it's too bad you're left with this little boy to raise—too bad for who? I said—not for me! I consider it a privilege to have this blessed child to raise. And I did, too. And every night when I say my prayers and I thank the good Lord for all his many blessings and tender mercies to me, Sonny and you head the list." Rosa Lee then asks Mac to sing her the song that Dixie has sent back. At first he refuses, then relents, but after a few chords he stops, saying he has no voice left. He thinks she is feeling sorry for him, and it makes him angry. Mac Sledge has tried with scrupulous care to bury a past self and to inch out into a new one. When a cashier in the market asks if he really used to be Mac Sledge, he answers, "Yes Ma'am, I guess I was." But the renewed proximity of Dixie and Sue Anne, and the request for him to sing, begin to pry open the lid he's placed on himself.

While he's out one day, a local band stops by to ask Rosa Lee if they can leave a poster to advertise an upcoming appearance. The musicians (Jake, Bertie, Henry and Steve) have been by before to meet Mac. The boys showed such polite respect to the man, and such sincere admiration for his music, and are themselves such ingenuous hopefuls, that Mac did not shut down, as he usually does, when questioned about his career. He explained, "I'm not going to start singing again, son. I've lost it. Those days are gone. I can't sing anymore. Not like I want to anyway." Rosa Lee, who cannot read music herself, asks the boys to teach her the song Dixie refused. She thinks it would be wonderful for both Mac and the band if he allowed them to perform it. When Mac returns from town in the first scene below, he has bought alcohol, but he has not drunk it. Having maintained his sobriety, and regained some of his inner balance, he agrees to Rosa Lee's suggestion.

The second scene below is the reunion of Mac and his daughter Sue Anne, whom he has not seen for six years. She has gone to the band's club date, having heard that Mac will be there. When she misses him, she goes out to the motel. Mac is out, but Rosa Lee quietly welcomes her, and invites her to wait till Mac returns. Sue Anne is interested in becoming a singer... sort of. Her mother tells her it is impossible because she has no voice. What Sue Anne is *really* interested in is escaping the habitual hysteria and emotional bullying of her mother. This takes the form of running off with Harris, a thirty-year-old, three-times-married musician in her mother's backup band. Harry Silver has previously told Mac that Dixie has spoiled Sue Anne and that the emotional responsibility of marriage will be good for her. In this scene, Sue Anne tells Mac she'll return with her new husband, but she never does. Dixie has Harry fire Harris from the band, so he and Sue Anne elope. Dixie also cuts off Sue Anne's money, which has come from a fund comprised of royalties from songs Mac wrote which Dixie recorded. En route to Mexico, both Sue Anne and Harris are killed in a car crash when Harris is drunk at the wheel.

At the end of the reunion scene, Sue Anne asks her father about a song he used to sing, something about a white dove, and he doesn't remember. Of course he does, but at the moment the emotions evoked by the memory of the song are too powerful to let loose. The lyrics are, "On the wings of a snow white dove/He sends his pure sweet love/A sign from above/On the wings of a dove." Another song, the one which Dixie has refused, will ultimately release Mac back into singing. A small record company has shown interest in the boys' band, and in the song, but it only wants to record the song if Mac will sing, too. By this time, Harry Silver has offered to "help" Mac move the song, but it is too late: Mac wants the boys to have it, and is willing to join them in recording it.

Scene 1

INTERIOR—BEDROOM—NIGHT

ROSA LEE enters the bedroom. She undresses and gets into bed. She closes her eyes and says quietly to herself:

ROSA LEE: Show me thy way, Oh Lord, teach me thy paths. Lead me in thy truth, and teach me for thou art the God of my salvation, on thee do I wait all the day. Remember, Oh Lord, thy tender mercies and thy loving kindness. For thou has been ever of old.

She lies in bed listening; she hears a car. She gets out of bed and runs to the window. She hears it slow down and turn into the driveway. She hurries back into bed and lies in the dark listening. She hears the car stop. She closes her eyes and pretends to be asleep. She hears the car door open and then shut. She hears the front door open and someone come into the living room. Then there is silence, and she opens her eyes listening. She hears footsteps again and she closes her eyes. The door to the room opens and we see MAC enter the room. He stands inside the door. He comes into the room. He begins to undress. He goes over to his side of the bed and stands looking out the window. Then turns and looks over at her. She opens her eyes and looks up at him.

ROSA LEE: Mac? Is that you?

MAC: Yes.

ROSA LEE: What time is it?

MAC: Late. (*a pause*) I'm not drunk. I bought a bottle but I didn't get drunk. I poured it all out. I didn't have one drink.

ROSA LEE: Did you have anything to eat?

MAC: Nope.

ROSA LEE: Are you hungry?

MAC: I guess so.

ROSA LEE gets out of bed.

ROSA LEE: Come on. I'll get you something to eat.

She puts a robe on and goes out to the kitchen. He follows.

INTERIOR—KITCHEN—ROSA LEE ENTERS FOLLOWED BY MAC

ROSA LEE: How hungry are you?

MAC: I'm not very hungry.

ROSA LEE: Want some eggs?

MAC: No.

ROSA LEE: Some chili?

MAC: No. A little soup will do me.

She opens a can of soup. She heats it at the stove.

ANGLE—MAC

MAC: I rode by here six or seven times. I could see you all
sitting here watching T.V. Did you see me ride by?

ROSA LEE: No.

MAC: I rode all over town tonight. Started twice for San Antonio,
turned around and came back. Started for Austin, started for
Dallas. Then turned around and came back. (*a pause*)

She takes the soup off the stove, puts it in a bowl.

ROSA LEE: You know that song you took over to that man in
Austin.

MAC: Yes.

ROSA LEE: You remember those four boys had a band that came
by to see you the other day?

MAC: Yes.

ANGLE—ROSA LEE

ROSA LEE: Well, two of them came by here after you were
gone and left off a poster. (*She points to it*) I asked them if
they could read music and one of them could and so I asked
if they would teach me that song of yours as I thought I
would try and surprise you by singing it for you when you
got home.

ANGLE—MAC

ROSA LEE: I think it's a pretty song, Mac, and so does he—and

he was wondering if you would let him and his band play it.
(*a pause*) I said I couldn't answer that. He'd have to ask
you. (*a pause*) I said I would ask you. I said it was an old
song and you might not...

MAC: (*interrupting*) It's no old song. I only wrote it last week.
That's why I got so upset when Harry said he didn't like it.
(*He goes into the bedroom. He comes out with a small
trunk*) I been writing them all along. I got even more in
here. (*a pause*) Did you say the boy liked the song?

ROSA LEE: He said he did. I sure like it. What are the names of
the other songs?

MAC: One is called, "God Has Forgiven Me, Why Can't
You?", and one is called, "The Romance Is Over."

He opens the trunk, and we can see sheet music inside. She takes
the music and looks at it.

MAC: Did you learn the song?

ROSA LEE: Not good enough to sing it. (*a pause*) I wish I could
read music. How did you learn to read music?

ANGLE—MAC

MAC: I had an auntie taught me. We had an old half-busted
piano, and she sat me down at that piano all one summer
when I came in from the fields, and she taught me.

He gets his guitar. He plays a little.

MAC: I've been missing my music. I may not be any good
anymore, but that don't keep you from missing it.

He plays a little bit of the song she has learned as if trying to
make up his mind about its value. [SONNY comes out.

SONNY: When did you get home?

ROSA LEE: He got here a little while ago.

SONNY: You said you were going to wake me.

ROSA LEE: I forgot.]

MAC continues playing. We sense now he is enjoying it. [SONNY listens for a beat.

SONNY: Good night.

ROSA LEE: Good night...

SONNY goes on back to bed.] MAC continues playing. He pauses and looks up at ROSA LEE.

MAC: I don't care if you give that song to those kids to play.

ROSA LEE: All right.

He continues picking at his guitar.

MAC: Come on try it with me.

He sings a few chords. She starts to sing. She sings a few phrases. ROSA LEE cries.

ROSA LEE: I'm sorry. I just got nervous tonight.

SCENE 2

[EXTERIOR—FILLING STATION—LATE AFTERNOON

ROSA LEE comes out of the house.

ROSA LEE: Hello. Mac is in town. He should be here in a little. Won't you come inside and wait for him?

ANGLE—SUE ANNE

SUE ANNE: Who are you?

ROSA LEE: I'm his wife. Rosa Lee.

SUE ANNE: Was that his son?

ANGLE—ROSA LEE

ROSA LEE: No, that is my son. I was married before, too.

EXTERIOR—HIGHWAY—LATE AFTERNOON

MAC is in his truck driving home.

INTERIOR—LIVING ROOM—ROSA LEE AND MAC'S HOUSE

[ROSA LEE is there with] SUE ANNE. MAC enters. He and SUE ANNE look at each other.

SUE ANNE: I recognize you. Do you recognize me?

MAC: Yes, I do.

SUE ANNE: How did you recognize me?

MAC: I just did.

[ROSA LEE gets up.

ROSA LEE: You all excuse me. Come on, Sonny.

They leave.]

SUE ANNE: You've changed. You don't look like your pictures any more.

MAC: Don't I? Well, God knows when the last picture of me was taken. (*a pause*) It don't make a whole lot of difference about this, but I did try once in a while to get in touch with you. I wrote a few letters. Did you ever get them?

SUE ANNE: No.

MAC: Well, your Mama didn't have to give them to you. The courts gave her complete jurisdiction. And quite rightly, I guess, considering my state at the time. (*a pause*) Are you still going to school?

ANGLE—SUE ANNE

SUE ANNE: No, I've finished. I've been off at boarding school. Mama says I can travel with her as long as I want to, and I might do that. If we don't kill each other in the meantime. I told Mama I was coming here. She told me she would have me arrested if I did. But Harry reminded her that I was eighteen now and she had no jurisdiction over me any longer. (*a pause*) Mama said you tried to kill her once.

MAC: I did.

SUE ANNE: Why did you try to kill her?

MAC: I don't know. She got me mad some way. I was drunk . . .

ANGLE—SUE ANNE

SUE ANNE: Someone told Mama the other night you were the best country and Western singer they ever heard. Mama threw a glass of whiskey in her face. She said they were just saying that to spite her. Do you think you ever will sing again?

ANGLE—MAC

MAC: I think about it once in awhile. Sometimes I think I'd like to earn a little money again to make things a little easier around here, to help out if you ever needed anything . . .

ANGLE—SUE ANNE

SUE ANNE: I don't need any money, Mama set up a trust fund for me out of all the royalties she ever earned singing the songs you wrote. I can buy myself anything I want. (*a pause*) Anything I've got has come from your music.

ANGLE—MAC

MAC: I'm happy for that. (*a pause*) Anyway it wasn't just my music. It was your Mama singing it, too. You mustn't forget that. (*a pause*) Will you have supper with us?

SUE ANNE: Thank you. No. I have a date tonight. He's playing in Mama's band. We have to sneak around, because Mama don't like him. Do you want to meet him? He wants to meet you.

MAC: Well, I don't think that's such a good idea. I really wouldn't want your Mama to think I was ganging up on her behind her back.

SUE ANNE: I'll tell her I'm bringing him out here.

ANGLE—MAC

MAC: Well, all right then.

SUE ANNE: What about tomorrow afternoon?

MAC: That's fine.

SUE ANNE: What time?

MAC: Anytime. I'll be here.

SUE ANNE: Around two o'clock?

MAC: Sure.

SUE ANNE: You know you've never spoken my name once since I've been here. Don't you know my name?

ANGLE—MAC

MAC: Sure I know your name. I've just been kind of figuring out to myself what I ought to call you. When you were a little girl, I used to call you, Sister. I started to call you that this time when I saw you, but I didn't know if it would mean anything to you or not. Or if you'd remember my doing that. (*a pause*) How long are you going to be in Texas?

SUE ANNE: We leave after Mama plays Houston and Corpus.

MAC: Where do you go from here?

SUE ANNE: Shreveport. (SUE ANNE gets up. *She starts away. A pause*) There was a song you used to sing to me, I think. Something about a dove. Mama said she never heard you sing it to me. I think it went: "The wings of a snow white dove—He sends his something, something love. . . ."

MAC: I don't remember.

He follows her outside.

EXTERIOR—HOUSE—DAY

SUE ANNE comes out, followed by MAC. He follows her to her car. She gets in and she starts the motor.

SUE ANNE: My boyfriend, Harris, thinks I ought to sing.

MAC: Do you want to?

SUE ANNE: I don't know. Maybe, if I'm any good. I might sing for you tomorrow so you can tell me what you think.

She drives on. He watches for a beat as the car goes on down the road.

INTERIOR—HOUSE—DAY

MAC enters and sits down, begins to sing "On the wings of a snow white dove, he sends his pure sweet love, a sign from above, on the wings of a dove."

GARBO TALKS

An MGM-United Artists presentation. Producers, Burtt Harris and Elliott Kastner. Director, Sidney Lumet. Screenplay by Larry Grusin. Director of Photography, Andrzej Bartkowiak. Editor, Andrew Monshein. Production Designer, Philip Rosenberg. Animation and Titles, Michael Sport Animation, Inc. Associate Producer, Jennifer M. Ogden. Assistant Director, Alan Hopkins. Sound, James Sabat. Running time, 103 minutes. 1984.

CAST

ESTELLE ROLFE	Anne Bancroft
GILBERT ROLFE	Ron Silver
LISA ROLFE	Carrie Fisher
JANE MORTIMER	Catherine Hicks
WALTER ROLFE	Steven Hill
ANGELO DUKAKIS	Howard Da Silva
SONIA APOLLINAR	Dorothy Loudon
BERNIE WHITLOCK	Harvey Fierstein
ELIZABETH RENNICK	Hermione Gingold
SHEPARD PLOTKIN	Richard B. Shull
CLAIRE ROLFE	Alice Spivak
THE WOMAN	Nina Zoe

I think everyone must know, admire, and sometimes avoid a woman like Estelle Rolfe. She can be exhausting, and always for good and necessary causes. She won't let an injustice go by without stopping everything and insisting that it be corrected. She's a straight-thinking political yenta, so no matter how irritating her insistences become, you are nevertheless grateful that she is there, as keeper of the flame. She would not attend her own son's wedding reception because there was a picket line around the hotel, and Estelle does not cross a picket line. Her protest over an unadvertised price increase at a supermarket, when ignored by the management, leads her to shoplift the *exact* amount in question in the form of a box of frozen zucchini. When she's caught, bail costs $500. She is a disputatious, activist city-dweller of the old school, whose faith in human confrontation on the outside is lined with deep sentiment on the inside. (The first time we see her, Estelle is alone with a soggy Kleenex, watching the end of Garbo's *Camille* on the television.) She understands that every victory for decency must be personally fought for. Construction workers in skyscrapers, catcalling down obscene invitations to passing young women, suddenly find themselves face-to-face with Estelle, who has leapt onto a rising plank to demand to know if *she* will do. "Stop demeaning yourselves in public! If your head is in the toilet, don't blow bubbles."

Though Estelle Rolfe never shortchanged her child, or left him wanting in any way, she adamantly refuses the self-image of a "housewife" or a "mama." Her most condescending contempt is directed at her ex-husband's second wife, who is basically an okay bore, because Claire bakes cakes. Let others (including her horror of a good-little-princess daughter-in-law) cook and trade recipes, Estelle would rather read, march, argue . . . or dance, which she does with such abandon that it's what caught her ex-husband's eye and heart way back when. He still cares about her, but just couldn't stay on board a married life where everything had to be such an *issue*. Even the decor of Estelle's apartment is that 1950's Danish modern meeting of affluent socialism and psychoanalysis. It's the kind of room where people are always up-in-arms, often in a foreign accent, about something they've just read, or someone they've just visited in jail. It's a clearinghouse for causes. The social and political styles and trends to which Estelle has subscribed in her fifty-plus years are epitomized in the incongruity of her appearance: a professionally styled, elegant head of undyed salt and pepper hair on top, and orthopedic clompers on the bottom . . . with no fear of bright, bright colors in between.

Estelle discovers she has a terminal brain tumor. No debates, arguments, or petitions will make any difference this time. She is indignant that she won't know who'll be the next President. Throughout Estelle's life there has been one constant ribbon of effortless inspiration that, when her own instincts and drives broke down, when she just could not figure out how to live with herself, has always shone as the Star to guide her: Greta Garbo. Through watching Garbo's incandescent performances, Estelle has found her way through everything from adolescent self-horror to the collapse of her marriage. Now, with her life ending, Estelle needs to unify her outer social self and her private inner self. She tells her son Gilbert (named for Garbo's great screen lover John Gilbert) that she wants to meet Greta Garbo.

Gilbert grants his mother her dying wish. His search for Garbo becomes his rite of passage, changing him from a sweet, good-hearted, dutiful schlump into an adult. Persevering against every obstacle, Gilbert succeeds in locating, with just hours left in his mother's life, the world's greatest legend of reclusive privacy and transcendent beauty. (Or at least we *think* he does, because he and his mother believe it's Garbo. The woman never actually *says* she's Garbo, and the script just refers to her as "The Woman." It only adds more mystery. She looks and walks and dresses just like Garbo . . . she's just *got* to be Garbo. But it's only in the last moment of the film, after Estelle has died, that we hear the woman speak. And, thank goodness, she sounds just like Garbo.)

In the first monologue below, Estelle Rolfe meets Greta Garbo, who has been brought to the hospital by Gilbert. In the second monologue, Gilbert quits his job as an accountant in a large firm where he's been stuffed into a little airless cubicle. Gilbert has also finally unlocked himself from his suffocating, pretend-person of a wife. He will now be free to know Jane, a lovely actress whom he's met at work and who helped him in his quest to locate Garbo. Jane is unsure of making any personal commitment to anyone at this point in her burgeoning career, but when she and Gilbert pass Garbo out on a walk, and Garbo greets Gilbert by name, Jane's jaw drops and her arm links through Gilbert's in one dumbfounded movement.

MONOLOGUES 1 AND 2

INTERIOR HOSPITAL ROOM—DAY

It's solemnly quiet. It's starting to get dark outside. ESTELLE lies
still and silent. Her eyes are closed. She doesn't appear to be in pain.

INTERIOR HOSPITAL CORRIDOR—DAY

GILBERT leads the woman to ESTELLE'S room. She goes in, he
closes the door.

GILBERT moves to a corner of the corridor. His shoulders heave
convulsively, and he breaks down crying, bringing his head in
his hands. HOLD for a long beat, as GILBERT just lets all his
emotions come out, unrestrained.

INTERIOR HOSPITAL ROOM—DAY

ESTELLE lies in bed. The woman moves slowly toward the bed.
The woman stands there. She makes no attempt to rouse ESTELLE.

CLOSER ON ESTELLE

The way we sense another's presence, she senses the woman in
her room; and gradually her eyes open.

ESTELLE'S P.O.V.—THE WOMAN

Her vision is quite blurred. We see the woman from the front, but
she is virtually indistinguishable through ESTELLE'S failing sight.

CLOSE ON ESTELLE

With what bit of energy she has left, her eyes gleam in a way
we've never quite seen before. It's as though some kind of
miracle has happened, some incredible God-like circumstance.

ESTELLE: I can't believe it. (*a beat*) It *is* you!

The woman in the cape touches ESTELLE'S hand.

ESTELLE: If I'd known, I would have had a manicure, someone
in to fix my hair. (*smiles*) You met my son.

The woman in the cape nods.

ESTELLE: He's a good boy. He works very hard. (*a beat*) I
don't . . . know what to say. You're here, and I don't
have . . . words. It must be thirty, forty years at least! (*a
beat*) I bet you've heard it from people till you're blue in
the face, I've been in love with you ever since the very first

time I saw you. I can't remember, we were living . . . we were living in Flatbush, that's in Brooklyn, Carroll Street, four rooms, eight people. (*a beat*) My father gave me ten cents so . . . Wanda Sternhagen, my girlfriend, and I could go to the movies. The Loew's Pitkin was two blocks away. (*a beat*) My father didn't have anything, a dime to him was . . . well, a lot of money. He had six mouths to feed. (*a beat*) We saw "Flesh and the Devil." You played Felicitas Van Kletzingk, remember? What a name! It stuck in my mind, I've never forgotten it. Movie names don't usually stay in your mind.

The woman in the cape nods.

ESTELLE: I sat in the balcony of the Loew's Pitkin in Brooklyn with Wanda, and I was "Estelle Garbo". Really! Eating a corned beef sandwich from a brown paper bag, and Wanda kept going "Ssssh!" because the bag was crackling. (*a beat*) Being Estelle Garbo is easy when you're in the balcony of the Loew's Pitkin in the dark, where nobody could see . . . (*she laughs*) . . . my huge bust—not like yours! And I probably shouldn't have been eating a sandwich, anyway. I was a fat kid. I needed to lose weight. But show me anything from a delicatessen . . . especially corned beef . . . (*she laughs*) . . . You had me in the palm of your hand! Every time you moved, I sighed. You'd cross from one side of the room to the other and it was like your feet weren't touching the ground. (*a beat*) Wanda and I saw every movie you made. (*a beat*) Wanda always said I loved you because I had big feet too, size ten, and I was only going on twelve years old. Wanda moved away, her father got a job in Trenton. Before she left I took her to lunch and to the movies. We saw a revival of "Wild Orchids." We sat through it twice because we didn't know how to tell each other goodbye. (*a beat*) I wrote you a letter once. I never wrote to any other movie star but you. I didn't get an answer. That's all right, that's all right, I didn't take it personally. (*a beat*) You're not going to believe this, but it's true. I married my husband in 1953. We had a small wedding. It was at home. My mother cooked for weeks, my aunt cooked for weeks, everybody came. Walter and I took the train to Atlantic City. Our honeymoon. Some honeymoon! Two whole nights! That's all we had money for. I didn't plan things right. Female times, you know, so there we were on our honeymoon, and I couldn't do anything. I was a virgin,

Walter was a virgin, and we had to stay that way a little while longer. (*a beat*) We didn't have anything to do so I got a newspaper. "Anna Christie" was playing. I'd never seen it. It's the only one you did I hadn't seen. (*acting out*) "Garbo talks!" (*a beat*) "Gimme a whiskey, chinger ale on the side. An' don' be stingy, babie." (*a beat*) Walter and I had Gilbert. I named him for John Gilbert. When I came out of delivery and woke up, the TV was on. I was so tired I could hardly move. I could hardly open my eyes. "Camille" was on. I kept looking at your skirt going back and forth, back and forth, that heavy velvet skirt.

The woman holds her hand.

ESTELLE: Walter and I got a divorce. (*a beat*) The world's a crazy place to live, isn't it? (*a beat*) He thought I was eccentric. When I got home from the lawyer, I cried all day. I wandered around the house all day, I couldn't find a place to sit. I took three baths. You love someone, you have a child, then it's over. Why? Who knows? I turned on the TV. They were showing "Queen Christina." That closeup of your face at the end. I thought it would never end! God, how I hated you! (*a beat*) I really hated myself. I thought if I looked like you, if I had that face, if I had those eyes, I wouldn't be so alone! And your arms! Those long, thin arms that keep on going, that never come to an end. (*a beat*) I would have been jealous of anybody pretty that day. It was just your luck they were showing "Queen Christina." (*a beat*) You care anything about basketball?

The woman in the cape shrugs—not yes, not no.

ESTELLE: The Knicks are out of the playoffs. I'm not entirely happy about that. Life's full of little injustices, they either bother you or they don't. Me—they bothered. (*a beat*) I saw a picture of you in a magazine a few years ago. You were in Paris. You were walking in a park in a black hat. You've probably got a million hats. (*a beat*) I've been to Paris. Twice. You've got nothing on me there. (*a beat*) Of course, you were with Aristotle Onassis and I was on a B'nai Brith tour.

The woman in the cape laughs.

[INTERIOR HOSPITAL CORRIDOR—DAY

A little later. GILBERT is sitting quietly and alone on a bench in the hallway, his head buried in his arms.

ANOTHER ANGLE—THE WOMAN IN THE CAPE

exits from ESTELLE'S room. GILBERT looks up and sees her, but makes no attempt to talk to her again. She walks briskly and determinedly ahead, reaches the elevator, signals it. When the doors open, she disappears inside.

INTERIOR HOSPITAL ROOM—DAY

As GILBERT enters. He moves closer to the bed and watches his mother in silence. She reaches out and takes GILBERT'S hand.

ESTELLE: You know what she told me? She said her father was very poor, just like mine. He worked in a factory in Sweden. Made auto parts. (*a beat*) She likes delicatessen, only she likes cold chicken better than corned beef. (*a beat*) She hated biology. God, how I hated biology. She was embarrassed about her size. She said she always felt too tall. (*a beat*) She never made a movie about war. She doesn't like war or violence. And her living room . . . (*with excitement*) . . . is red. (*a beat*) She said that she and I . . . are very much alike.

ANGLE—GILBERT

He's silent, he's tired. He's losing his mother and he loves her very much.

ESTELLE: (o.s.) (cont'd) Except for the feet. (*she starts to run down*) She doesn't have big feet at all. She has a size 7AA. She (*a beat*) She's got it all over me there.

He holds her hand. She stares at him in silence. Her eyes close. She dies.

CLOSE—GILBERT

He holds his mother's hand, warms it with his own.

INTERIOR GILBERT'S OFFICE—DAY

GILBERT is collecting his things from his desk and packing them up into a large brown box.

INTERIOR PLOTKIN'S OFFICE/CORRIDOR—DAY

GILBERT strides down the hall to PLOTKIN's office. Just as he's about to go in, JANE comes out. He's surprised to see her here:

JANE: Hi.

GILBERT: Hi.

JANE: I quit.

GILBERT: You did?

JANE: Yeah.

A beat.

GILBERT: I . . . uh . . . I have to talk to Plotkin. (*a beat*) Wait for me?

JANE: What?

GILBERT: Wait for me.

She nods.

He smiles at her, tentatively, before going into PLOTKIN's office.]

INTERIOR PLOTKIN'S OFFICE—DAY

GILBERT enters, walks to PLOTKIN's desk. PLOTKIN is very engrossed in his work, doesn't look up at GILBERT:

[PLOTKIN: I'm very busy, Gilbert.]

GILBERT: (*with strength*) I have to talk to you, Mr. Plotkin.

[PLOTKIN: Later, Gilbert.]

GILBERT: (*with purpose*) I have to talk to you now. (*a beat*) Shephard.

[PLOTKIN looks up: GILBERT has never, ever addressed him by his given name.]

GILBERT: I'm leaving.

[PLOTKIN looks perplexed: everyone's quitting today.]

GILBERT: I'm not saying this because I'm upset. Well, yes, I'm upset, of course I'm upset. (*a beat*) You took my office away and gave me a depressing little room. It's not your fault, I allowed it to happen. The light fixture buzzes, you know, a dull hum all day long. You wouldn't fix it for me, no matter how many times I asked, but it's okay. You reduced the staff and gave me enough work for three people to do. And if I didn't finish I got that speech about consolidating my time. It's not your fault, don't worry. I sat there and listened, didn't I? You deducted a half day's salary because I was late. No problem. I allowed it to happen. You made me come to work at 6 in the morning. There was nothing to do at 6 in the morning. I thought, Plotkin is enjoying doing this to me, but then I said, "No, rules are rules. He's only doing his job." That's okay. A man has to do his job. (*now slowly getting angrier*) I wish you the best of luck. I hope all your dreams come true. I hope you get everything you want in life, and then some, because you deserve it. I love you, Shephard. I'm not angry, I have no resentment. You've been great. I regret we can't stay together any more. (*a beat*) We are who we are. I'm who I am . . . and you're who you are. (*a beat*) So go fuck yourself, Shephard.

Sources

The following list of sources for the excerpts designates whether a script is published, and if so by whom. If the source script is unpublished, first the draft will be identified, and then the non-circulating filmscript library at which it was read. These include the Margaret Herrick Library of the Academy of Motion Picture Arts and Sciences in Beverly Hills (designated as "the Academy"), the Louis B. Mayer Library of the American Film Institute in Los Angeles (designated as "the AFI"), the Theater Arts Library of the University of California at Los Angeles (designated as "UCLA"), and the Special Collections of the Doheny Library at the University of Southern California (designated as "USC"). These collections contain many other scenes and monologues, some in already published scripts, *perfect* for class and audition, but which could not be included here due to restrictions on space, copyright or other permission.

The excerpts from *Ninotchka* are reprinted from the published script in *Ninotchka,* a Viking Film Book from the MGM Library of Film Scripts series, The Viking Press, 1972.

The excerpts from *Sullivan's Travels* are reprinted from the published script in *Five Screenplays by Preston Sturges,* University of California Press, edited by Brian Henderson, 1985. The alternate ending is reprinted from the unpublished shooting script dated 2/3/41 which is housed, along with the dialogue continuity, at the AFI.

The excerpt from *Laura* is reprinted from the unpublished continuity and dialogue script housed at the AFI.

The excerpts from *Brief Encounter* are reprinted from the published script in *Masterworks of the British Cinema,* Lorrimer Publishing Limited, 1974, in the Icon edition published by Harper & Row, Publishers, Inc.

The excerpts from *Children of Paradise* are reprinted from the published script in *Children of Paradise, a film by Marcel Carne,* in the Classic Film Script series, Simon and Schuster.

The excerpts from *The Big Sleep* are reprinted from the published script in *Film Scripts One*, Appleton Century Crofts, 1971.

The excerpts from *The Ghost and Mrs. Muir* are reprinted from the unpublished screenplay, Final, November 21, 1946 (including revision pages up to 2/19/47), housed at UCLA.

The excerpts from *The Treasure of the Sierra Madre* are reprinted from the published script in *The Treasure of the Sierra Madre* in the Wisconsin/Warner Bros. Screenplay series, University of Wisconsin Press, 1979.

The excerpts from *East of Eden* are reprinted from the unpublished shooting script, Final, May 17, 1954 (including revision pages up to 6/22/54) and from the Dialogue Transcript dated January 25, 1955, both housed at USC.

The excerpt from *The Three Faces of Eve* is reprinted from the unpublished shooting script, Final, August 10, 1956 (including revision pages dated 1/7/57), housed at the AFI.

The excerpts from *Breakfast at Tiffany's* are reprinted from the unpublished screenplay, Final Draft, August 3, 1960, housed at UCLA.

The excerpts from *Judgment at Nuremberg* are reprinted from the published script in *Judgment at Nuremberg, The Script of the Film*, Cassell & Company Ltd., printed in Great Britain by Ebenezer Baylis & Son, Ltd., The Trinity Press.

The excerpt from *Dr. Strangelove, or: How I Learned to Stop Worrying and Love the Bomb* is reprinted from the unpublished release continuity script housed at USC.

The excerpts from *The Loved One* are reprinted from the unpublished screenplay dated July 21, 1964 (including revision pages from 9/17/64 and 9/28/64), housed at UCLA.

The excerpt from *Blow-Up* is reprinted from the published screenplay in *Blow-Up, a film by Michelangelo Antonioni*, in the Modern Scripts series published by Simon and Schuster, 1971.

The excerpts from *Bedazzled* are reprinted from the unpublished screenplay dated April 13, 1967, housed at the AFI.

The excerpts from *Catch-22* are reprinted from the unpublished screenplay, Final Revised, July 29, 1968, housed at the Academy.

The excerpt from *Patton* is reprinted from the unpublished shooting script dated February 1, 1969, housed at the Academy.

The excerpts from *Last Tango in Paris* are reprinted from the published script in *The Last Tango in Paris*, Delacorte Press in association with Quicksilver Books.

The excerpt from *American Graffiti* is reprinted from the published screenplay in *American Graffiti*, Ballantine Books, Inc. by arrangement with Grove Press, 1973.

The excerpts from *Dog Day Afternoon* are reprinted from the unpublished shooting script housed at the Academy.

The excerpts from *Funny Lady* are reprinted from the unpublished screenplay, Fourth Draft, March 7, 1974 (including revisions 3/28/74), housed at the Academy.

The excerpt from *Midnight Express* is reprinted from the unpublished screenplay, Final Script, September 1977, housed at the Academy.

The excerpts from *Fame* are reprinted from the unpublished screenplay, Director's Draft, June 7, 1979, housed at the Academy.

The excerpts from *Resurrection* are reprinted from the unpublished original screenplay, Final Draft, January 10, 1979, housed at the Academy.

The excerpts from *Arthur* are reprinted from the unpublished Revised First Draft housed at the AFI, the Third Draft dated June 3, 1980 from a private collection, and from the Final Draft dated October 17, 1980, housed at the Academy.

The excerpt from *Atlantic City* is reprinted from the unpublished screenplay dated January 6, 1980, housed at the Academy.

The excerpt from *The French Lieutenant's Woman* is reprinted from the published script in *The French Lieutenant's Woman: A Screenplay* by Harold Pinter, Little, Brown and Company, 1981.

The excerpt from *Prince of the City* is reprinted from the unpublished screenplay, Final Draft, housed at the Academy.

The excerpts from *Rich and Famous* are reprinted from the unpublished screenplay, Final Draft, April 9, 1980 (including revisions up to 1/2/81), housed at the Academy.

The excerpts from *Sophie's Choice* are reprinted from the unpublished shooting script housed at the Academy.

The excerpt from *Tootsie* is reprinted from the unpublished screenplay dated March 8, 1982, housed at the Academy.

The excerpts from *Fanny and Alexander* are reprinted from the published script in *Fanny and Alexander* by Ingmar Bergman, Pantheon Books by Random House, 1982.

The excerpts from *The King of Comedy* are reprinted from the unpublished script, Final Draft, housed at the AFI.

The excerpts from *Tender Mercies* are reprinted from the unpublished screenplay housed at the Academy.

The excerpts from *Garbo Talks* are reprinted from the unpublished screenplay, Final Revision, January 25, 1984 (including revision pages up to 3/8/84), made available for this collection through the kindness of Larry Grusin.

Acknowledgments

Ninotchka screenplay by Charles Brackett, Billy Wilder, and Water Reisch. (Based on the original story by Melchior Lengyel.) Copyright 1939 Loew's Incorporated. Copyright © renewed 1966 Metro-Goldwyn-Mayer, Inc. All rights reserved. By permission of MGM/UA Entertainment Co., and by permission of Billy Wilder, Mrs. Walter Reisch, and Matthews Fletcher on behalf of the Lillian F. Brackett Estate.

Sullivan's Travels screenplay by Preston Sturges. Copyright 1941 by Universal Pictures, a Division of Universal City Studios, Inc. All rights reserved. Courtesy of MCA Publishing, a Division of MCA, Inc.

Laura screenplay by Jay Dratler, Samuel Hoffenstein, and Betty Reinhardt. (Adapted from the novel *Laura* by Vera Caspary.) Copyright 1944 Twentieth Century-Fox Film Corporation. All rights reserved. Courtesy of Twentieth Century-Fox Film Corporation.

Brief Encounter screenplay by Noël Coward. (Adapted from Noël Coward's *Still Life* from *Tonight at 8:30*.) Copyright 1945 by the Noël Coward Estate. Published in *Masterworks of the British Cinema*, copyright © 1974 by Lorrimer Publishing Limited. By permission of Lorrimer Publishing Limited.

Children of Paradise screenplay by Jacques Prévert. Original French language edition entitled *Les Enfants du Paradis* copyright © 1967 by l'Avant-Scène du Cinéma. English language translation by Dinah Brooke published as *Children of Paradise, A Film by Marcel Carné* copyright © 1968 by Lorrimer Publishing Limited. By permission of Lorrimer Publishing Limited.

The Big Sleep screenplay by William Faulkner, Leigh Brackett, Jules Furthman. (Based on the novel *The Big Sleep* by Raymond Chandler. Copyright 1939 by Raymond Chandler, renewed Copyright © 1967 by Mrs. Helga Greene, renewed Copyright © 1985 College Trustees Ltd.) Screenplay Copyright 1946 Warner Bros., Inc., renewed Copyright © 1973 United Artists Television, Inc. By permission of MGM/UA Entertainment Co. and by permission of College Trustees Ltd.

The Ghost and Mrs. Muir screenplay by Philip Dunne. (Based on the novel *The Ghost and Mrs. Muir* by R.A. Dick.) Copyright 1947 Twentieth Century-Fox Film Corporation. Courtesy of Twentieth Century-Fox Film Corporation and with the permission of Philip Dunne.

Treasure of the Sierra Madre screenplay by John Huston. (Based on the novel *Treasure of the Sierra Madre* by B. Traven.) Copyright 1948 Warner Bros. Pictures, Inc. Renewed Copyright © 1975 by United Artists Television, Inc. By permission of MGM/UA Entertainment Co., and by permission of John Huston.

Personal Acknowledgments

This volume is filled with excerpts from scripts which were never originally intended for publication and which are protected from any unauthorized copying under copyright law. To assemble and print this collection clearly involves out-of-the-ordinary attention and assistance from a lot of people. Ultimately, it knew no greater friend or facilitator than Charles Bloch, into whose hands it so fully expected to find itself. This book is dedicated to his memory, and to his contribution, without which these volumes would not exist.

In addition:

At the film libraries where the scripts can be found and studied, the warmth and generous cooperation of the following people has been particularly valued: Anne Schlosser, along with Howard Prouty and Sue Ellen Picker at the Louis B. Mayer Library of the American Film Institute; Linda Mehr of the Margaret Herrick Library of the Academy of Motion Picture Arts and Sciences, along with Carol Cullen and the people behind the script desk who have smiled encouragingly as they've schlepped all those scripts back and forth over these years; Audrey Malkin at the Theater Arts Library at UCLA, who along with Jeff Baker, unstintingly shared time and available desk space; and Robert Knutsen of the Special Collections of the Doheny Library at the University of Southern California. Scripts which were made available through the generosity of private collections are acknowledged in The Source Index.

Once the excerpts were chosen, contingent upon the writers' and publishers' permissions, agreements to allow reprinting were arranged with the legal and licensing departments of the studios. Without their participation, there would be no book. Especially necessary were the efforts of Ivy Orta with Diane Lawrence at Columbia Pictures; Nancy Cushing-Jones and Laurie Rodich at MCA Publishing; Herbert S. Nusbaum at MGM/UA; Pam North and Margaret C. Rickman at Twentieth Century-Fox; Judith Singer and Irene Slade at Warner Bros.; and Edith Tolkin, Steven Kotlowitz, and Neil Strum at Paramount Pictures.

At Bantam Books in New York, this book became the work of editors Toni Burbank, LuAnn Walther, Vicky Heredia, and Andrew Zega, assisted by Jill Parsons. Terry Moore and Mierre were responsible for homogenizing all the scripts' varied styles and formats into the one which appears throughout the volume. In Los Angeles, Sue Terry of Entertainment Discoveries, Incorporated, on several occasions moved what to me were mountains. As with Volume I, the participation of Linda Lichter has been pivotal. During the final editings, Laurel Pickering read and reread the entire manuscript to me, *aloud,* until all of the words would lie down flat and all of the meanings stand up straight. In arranging permissions, particular assistance has been provided by Beverly Wallace, Julia Chasman, Barbara and Harvey Markowitz, and Charles and Karen Green Rosin.

Several coworkers have contributed to the successful completion of this work specifically by making class for actors a place where I have experienced enormous adventure and reward. Lura Dolas and Candace Barrett offered a place where it was a joy to be a teacher. Joan Darling welcomed me as a student. Terri Hanauer has created spaces for me to be both. And finally, there has been, not for just this project alone, an astonishingly ceaseless flow of support and refreshment from my colleagues at the Free Association Theatre, Alan Blumenfeld and Katherine James.

—J.K.

ABOUT THE EDITOR

JOSHUA KARTON took honors in literature and drama at the Universities of California and Edinburgh before training as an actor at the American Conservatory Theatre. He returned here to teach, after writing and directing the film and video exhibits of the Bicentennial *Theatrical Evolution* 1776-1976 (which received the 1976 New York Drama Desk Award) and after serving as program consultant for the television show *Forever Fernwood*. He is now the Director of Education of Los Angeles' Free Association Theatre and its Applied Theatre Techniques Program, for which he designs curriculum and conducts workshops/classes not only for the professional and student actor, but also for the non-theatrical professions with specialized performance requirements—such as the educator in the museum or the attorney in the courtroom. He is currently at work on *Television Scenes and Monologues for Actors*.

Dedicated to the memory
of Charles Bloch

THE COMPLETE WORKS IN 29 VOLUMES
Edited, with introductions by David Bevington
•Forewords by Joseph Papp

- ☐ ANTONY AND CLEOPATRA   21289-3 $2.95
- ☐ AS YOU LIKE IT   21290-7 $2.50
- ☐ THE COMEDY OF ERRORS   21291-5 $2.95
- ☐ HAMLET   21292-3 $2.75
- ☐ HENRY IV, PART ONE   21293-1 $2.50
- ☐ HENRY IV, PART TWO   21294-X $2.95
- ☐ HENRY V   21295-8 $3.50
- ☐ JULIUS CAESAR   21296-6 $1.95
- ☐ KING LEAR   21297-4 $2.75
- ☐ MACBETH   21298-2 $2.75
- ☐ THE MERCHANT OF VENICE   21299-0 $2.25
- ☐ A MIDSUMMER NIGHT'S DREAM   21300-8 $2.75
- ☐ MUCH ADO ABOUT NOTHING   21301-6 $2.95
- ☐ OTHELLO   21302-4 $3.50
- ☐ RICHARD II   21303-2 $2.50
- ☐ RICHARD III   21304-0 $2.75
- ☐ ROMEO AND JULIET   21305-9 $2.75
- ☐ THE TAMING OF THE SHREW   21306-7 $2.50
- ☐ THE TEMPEST   21307-5 $2.25

- ☐ TWELFTH NIGHT   21308-3 $2.75
- ☐ FOUR COMEDIES   21281-8 $4.95
  (The Taming of the Shrew, A Midsummer Night's Dream, The Merchant of Venice, and Twelfth Night)
- ☐ THREE EARLY COMEDIES   21282-6 $4.95
  (Love's Labor's Lost, The Two Gentlemen of Verona, and The Merry Wives of Windsor)
- ☐ FOUR TRAGEDIES   21283-4 $4.95
  (Hamlet, Othello, King Lear, and Macbeth)
- ☐ THREE CLASSICAL TRAGEDIES   21284-2 $4.95
  (Titus Andronicus, Timon of Athens, and Coriolanus)
- ☐ HENRY VI, PARTS ONE, TWO, and THREE   21285-0 $4.95
- ☐ KING JOHN and HENRY VIII   21286-9 $4.95
- ☐ MEASURE FOR MEASURE, ALL'S WELL THAT ENDS WELL, and TROILUS AND CRESSIDA   21287-7 $4.95
- ☐ THE LATE ROMANCES   21288-5 $4.95
  (Pericles, Cymbeline, The Winter's Tale, and The Tempest)
- ☐ THE POEMS   21309-1 $4.95

Bantam Books, Dept. SH2, 414 East Golf Road, Des Plaines, IL 60016

Please send me the items I have checked above. I am enclosing $_____ (please add $2.00 to cover postage and handling). Send check or money order, no cash or C.O.D.s please.

Mr/Ms _____

Address _____

City/State _____ Zip _____

SH2–1/90

Please allow four to six weeks for delivery.
Prices and availability subject to change without notice.